Trade Growth in Transition Economies

The International Institute for Applied Systems Analysis

is an interdisciplinary, nongovernmental research institution founded in 1972 by leading scientific organizations in 12 countries. Situated near Vienna, in the center of Europe, IIASA has been for more than two decades producing valuable scientific research on economic, technological, and environmental issues.

IIASA was one of the first international institutes to systematically study global issues of environment, technology, and development. IIASA's Governing Council states that the Institute's goal is: *to conduct international and interdisciplinary scientific studies to provide timely and relevant information and options, addressing critical issues of global environmental, economic, and social change, for the benefit of the public, the scientific community, and national and international institutions.* Research is organized around three central themes:

- Global Environmental Change;
- Global Economic and Technological Change;
- Systems Methods for the Analysis of Global Issues.

The Institute now has national member organizations in the following countries:

Austria
The Austrian Academy of Sciences

Bulgaria
The Bulgarian Committee for IIASA

Canada
The Canadian Committee for IIASA

Czech Republic
The Czech Committee for IIASA

Finland
The Finnish Committee for IIASA

Germany
The Association for the Advancement of IIASA

Hungary
The Hungarian Committee for Applied Systems Analysis

Japan
The Japan Committee for IIASA

Kazakstan
The Ministry of Science – The Academy of Sciences

Netherlands
The Netherlands Organization for Scientific Research (NWO)

Norway
The Research Council of Norway (As of 1 January 1997)

Poland
The Polish Academy of Sciences

Russian Federation
The Russian Academy of Sciences

Slovak Republic
The Slovak Committee for IIASA

Sweden
The Swedish Council for Planning and Coordination of Research (FRN)

Ukraine
The Ukrainian Academy of Sciences

United States of America
The American Academy of Arts and Sciences

Trade Growth in Transition Economies

Export Impediments for Central and Eastern Europe

Edited by

Richard N. Cooper

Boas Professor of International Economics, Harvard University, US

and

János Gács

International Institute for Applied Systems Analysis, Laxenburg, Austria and KOPINT-DATORG Rt. Institute for Economic and Market Research and Informatics, Hungary

Edward Elgar

Cheltenham, UK • Lyme, US

IIASA

International Institute for Applied Systems Analysis

Laxenburg, Austria

Published by
Edward Elgar Publishing Limited
8 Lansdown Place
Cheltenham
Glos GL50 2HU
UK

Edward Elgar Publishing, Inc.
1 Pinnacle Hill Road
Lyme
NH 03768
US

A catalogue record for this book
is available from the British Library

ISBN 1 85898 608 7

Contents

List of Figures

List of Tables

Contributors

Laurentiu Ciocirlan
Arthur Andersen & Co.
Bucharest, Romania

Aleksandra Cīrule
Ministry of Finance
Riga, Latvia

Richard N. Cooper
Harvard University
Cambridge, MA, USA

Ágnes Csermely
National Bank of Hungary
Budapest, Hungary

Rumen Dobrinsky
Centre for Economic and Strategic Research
Sofia, Bulgaria

Vladimir Drebentsov
World Bank
Moscow Office
Moscow, Russia

Ján Fidrmuc
Tilburg University
Tilburg, The Netherlands

Jarko Fidrmuc
Institute for Advanced Studies
Vienna, Austria

János Gács
International Institute for Applied Systems Analysis (IIASA)
Laxenburg, Austria; also
KOPINT-DATORG Rt. Institute for Economic and Market Research and Informatics
Budapest, Hungary

Vasile Pilat
National Institute for Economic Research
Bucharest, Romania

Alari Purju
Tallinn Technical University
Tallinn, Estonia

Inna Shteinbuka
Ministry of Finance
Riga, Latvia

Richard E. Stern
International Monetary Fund
Washington, DC, USA

Franjo Štiblar
School of Law
University of Ljubljana
Ljubljana, Slovenia

Ira Yaneva
Bulgarian-Spanish Chamber of Commerce
Sofia, Bulgaria

Introduction and Summary

Richard N. Cooper and János Gács

The Problem

It is now widely acknowledged that good export performance is necessary for general economic progress, especially for small countries. Exports are of course necessary to pay for imported goods, which small countries need in order to achieve and sustain a high standard of living, particularly as investment goods become more highly specialized. Exports permit small countries to benefit from the economies of scale that may exist in production processes. Foreign markets provide a source of demand that differs from, and is much larger than, domestic demand, permitting fuller and more stable use of productive capacity. Above all, in today's world the need to sell abroad creates a challenge to domestic producers to achieve that combination of price, quality of product, and quality of service which is necessary to compete in the world market – characteristics that are conducive to higher standards of living at home as well. For all these reasons, the export performance of economies in transition is of compelling importance.

In fact, exports have gained importance since secular political and economic changes began in 1989–1991 in the small transition economies of Central and Eastern Europe (STEs).[1] The principal reason for this increase in the importance of exports was the collapse of demand in both domestic and former Council for Mutual Economic Assistance (CMEA) markets. The unexpected and severe output decline has been analyzed in many recent studies and was attributed mostly to domestic and external demand factors.[2] As far as their external markets were concerned, most of these countries had had close ties with the CMEA. CMEA relations in turn were dominated by former Soviet markets, the principal target of sales of manufactured products of STEs, with the potential to use economies

The authors are grateful to Richard Stern for his valuable comments on an earlier version of this chapter.

of scale. Neither the dramatic decline of domestic output nor the shrinkage of politically motivated trade with the Soviet Union (or its successor states) in the early 1990s seems to be a temporary development. The need to utilize existing resources in STEs has pushed enterprises in these countries to search for new export opportunities and to expand their exports to previously neglected markets.

In the past the STEs had been relatively closed economies, both in volume of trade and institutionally. Their recent rejection of the principles of central planning and their acceptance of the rules of the market implied the assumption that they would quickly catch up with similar market economies in terms of reliance on trade. Liberalization of trade in these economies in principle has made exports and all the activities that enhance them (for example, collecting information, importing inputs, and taking credits from abroad) free of unnecessary bureaucratic government control. This liberalization has been instrumental to the promotion of exports. Moreover, the impact of internal liberalization was gradually reinforced by improved access to Western, especially West European, markets.

Exports also gained importance because it was assumed that market standards emerging over the course of transition were best transmitted by the conditions the exporters met in the global marketplace. In the economies of new states (the successor countries of Yugoslavia, Czechoslovakia, and the Soviet Union) former intrastate deliveries became interstate trade.

From the outset of transition, most enterprises in STEs that were interested in foreign trade had to make great efforts to maintain their former levels of exports or to expand them. Under the new conditions, as part of a thorough restructuring of their activities, these enterprises were forced to reorganize exports in terms of target countries, commodity composition, quality, terms of delivery, and related services.

On the aggregate level, calculations based on historical trends and gravity models predicted a radical geographical reorientation of trade away from former CMEA partners, most notably the republics of the former Soviet Union (FSU), and toward the West, especially Western Europe.[3] The geographical reorientation of trade in STEs since 1989 has shown the predicted pattern and, according to some calculations, has even surpassed the pace previously envisioned.[4]

The emancipation of exports from their former suppressed and subordinated role in the economy has not proceeded without difficulties. In countries such as Romania, Bulgaria, and Latvia, this process started only after much delay. In some cases, exports could not keep pace with imports; this situation has recently occurred in Hungary, Romania, and Latvia, leading to a buildup of potentially serious trade imbalances. The development of exports has also been quite volatile, showing a wide variation of growth rates among the individual countries. Analyses of the administrative and tariff barriers to trade in Western Europe showed that, despite the recent opening of Western markets, the expansion of STE exports was greatly constrained in that region. Also, many analysts have pointed out that the commodity composition of the emerging trade does not seem to match the perceived pattern of endowments or comparative advantages in STEs and has no prospect for sustainability.[5] Analyses focusing on microeconomic factors have pointed out that many of the recent STE exports to the West were distress exports, which in the long run weaken the financial condition of the exporting enterprises and therefore cannot be sustained.

Theme of the Book and Method of Research

This book aims at exploring the impediments to exports that small transition economies face once the initial systemic changes and the switch to Western markets have taken place. In this kind of exploration, the main questions that arise are the following: Are the impediments to exports mostly external and demand related, or do they have more to do with supply, i.e., are rooted in the inherited or newly created domestic conditions and national policies? Are the impediments to exports similar or significantly different across the STEs? How have governments enhanced exports after losing much of their freedom to interfere in the activities of enterprises? How do enterprises assess their opportunities to export versus selling on the domestic market? What typical strategies have enterprises developed to overcome existing barriers? To what extent do export impediments shape the evolving geographic structure of trade, and which industrial branches seem to show sustainable export potential in the STEs? What role does Western capital in the form of joint ventures play in the development of competitive export potential in STEs?

Unlike the recovery of domestic sales, the expansion of exports has relatively little to do with domestic macroeconomic factors and much to do with numerous and highly differentiated microeconomic conditions, both in the country concerned and in its foreign markets. For this reason, our investigation places an emphasis on microeconomic empirical evidence.

Country studies based on a common scheme were prepared about seven STEs: Bulgaria, Estonia, Hungary, Latvia, Romania, Slovakia, and Slovenia (see Appendix to Introduction and Summary). Originally, the editors arranged for a country study (and 20 enterprise case studies) about the Czech Republic, as well; however, despite all their efforts, this work was not finished successfully. The project's unbroken interest in the Czech Republic is, however, reflected in both this Introduction and in the three topical studies (Chapters 8 to 10), which cover developments in that country as well.

The analysis of each country was based on 20 enterprise case studies about the exporting conditions and behavior of industrial and trading enterprises. The case studies were prepared by the contributors according to a commonly agreed scheme. (That scheme, as well as the so-called checkup questions for the case study interviews, can be found in the Appendix to this Introduction and Summary.) In addition to the country studies, this book also contains three topical studies. The first of these (Chapter 8) investigates impediments to exports to Russia from the importer's side, making it in fact a kind of mirror study to the STE country studies. The other topical studies deal with the development of government support for exports (Chapter 9) and the role of foreign direct investment (FDI) in the export process (Chapter 10).

This volume was sponsored by the Economic Transition and Integration Project at the International Institute for Applied Systems Analysis (IIASA). The contributors were selected from among the top experts in the field in each country. In some of the new countries, where previously own foreign trade was impossible and thus its analysis was lacking, committed and talented young researchers were found to write what are probably the first studies in these countries about the exporting behavior of national enterprises. The work was financed by IIASA, and early versions of the chapters of this book were discussed at two workshops organized at IIASA in January and June–July 1995. The editors thank IIASA for its support and the discussants at these two workshops for their valuable contributions.

As indicated above, the country studies were based on enterprise case studies. Because the case studies contain valuable empirical material, IIASA has decided to make them available to interested readers. The case studies have been published by IIASA in a collected volume entitled Case Studies on Impediments to Exports in Small Transition Economies (WP-96-145), edited by János Gács. The case study volume can be obtained directly from the Publications Department at IIASA (Schlossplatz 1, A-2361 Austria).

In the following section a short summary of the findings in the chapters of this book and some conclusions are given.

The Sample

Table I.1 provides a summary of selected indicators from the countries dealt with in this book. It was decided that the countries selected for inclusion in this volume should be small and representative of all similar transition economies. Included in the study are countries that have not changed their territory in recent years (Bulgaria, Hungary, and Romania), as well as countries that have emerged as new entities. The latter group includes two FSU republics (Estonia and Latvia), one successor

Table I.1. Selected data for countries covered in the study.

	Territory in 1994 (1,000 km^2)	Population in 1994 (mln. people)	Per capita GDP in 1994 (US$ at PPP exchange rates)	Exports in 1994 (bln. US$)	Export/GDP in 1993 (% at market exchange rates)	Export/GDP in 1994 (% at market exchange rates)	Export growth 1994–1995 (% of US$ values)	Trade balance in 1994 (% of exports)
Bulgaria	111	8.4	3,970	4.156	34	41	32.5	–4
Czech R.	79	10.3	8,093	14.294	42	40	30.6	–3
Estonia	45	1.5	6,320[a]	1.304	47	56	133.5	–27
Hungary	93	10.3	6,609	10.775	23	26	46.0	–36
Latvia	64	2.7	4,609[a]	0.967	72	43	14.7	–9
Romania	238	22.7	3,204	6.151	19	21	53.9	–16
Slovakia	49	5.4	6,957	6.727	49	54	48.2	2
Slovenia	20	2.0	8,509	6.806	48	48	36.2	–6

[a]In 1992.

Sources: WIIW (1995), EBRD (1994), UN ECE *Economic Survey for Europe* (various issues), and country studies included in this volume. Data for 1995 from *OMRI Economic Digest* (various issues); Slovenian Economic Mirror, March 1996; Konjunktúrajelentés 1996/1 (Report on Business Tendencies); KOPINT-DATORG, Budapest; and Külkereskedelmi Termékforgalom 1995 (Foreign trade 1995), Ministry of Trade and Industry, Budapest, Hungary, 1996.

Table I.2. Development of exports and the share of CMEA countries.

	Exports in 1989 (bln. US$)[a]	Exports in 1994 (bln. US$)	Share of CMEA in exports in 1989 (%)[b]	Share of former CMEA in exports in 1994 (%)[c]
Bulgaria	6.650	4.156	62	16
Czech R.	9.052	14.294	47	31
Estonia	0.376	1.304	96	43
Hungary	9.670	10.775	41	22
Latvia	0.831	0.967	95	54
Romania	8.080	6.151	25	14
Slovakia	2.899	6.727	47	47
Slovenia	3.408	6.806	19	9

[a]Czech and Slovak Republics: data for 1990, excluding trade with the other republic, calculated with official exchange rates (WIIW, 1995). Estonia: data for 1992 from balance of payments (World Bank, 1993a). Latvia: data for 1992 from balance of payments (World Bank, 1993b). Slovenia: data excluding trade with other republics of Yugoslavia (Bank of Slovenia, 1995). Other countries: intra-CMEA trade revalued with ruble/US$ cross-rates used in Hungary (UN ECE, 1991).
[b]Czech and Slovak Republics: data for Czechoslovakia (UN ECE, 1991). Estonia: Balance of payments data calculated at domestic ruble prices (World Bank, 1993a). Latvia: Balance of payments data calculated at domestic ruble prices (World Bank, 1993b). Slovenia: data for 1990 excluding trade with other republics of Yugoslavia (WIIW, 1995). Other countries: data based on UN ECE (1991).
[c]IMF Direction of Trade Statistics.

state of Yugoslavia (Slovenia), and the successor states of Czechoslovakia (the Czech Republic and Slovakia).

Each country included in the study began its political and economic transformation between 1989 and 1991. With the exception of Romania (which is a borderline case), each can easily be considered small from the point of view of international trade: the number of inhabitants in each country is under 11 million and the territory is under 120,000 km^2. If less stringent criteria are used, even Romania can be considered a small country, and in no way can it be considered a large country. Romania was selected to include a country that existed prior to transition and that had loose political and trade ties with the CMEA (see *Table I.2*).

Measuring the level of openness in these countries involves both conceptual and statistical problems. Discrepancies occur for the following reasons: different approaches are used for the valuation of the GDP; there are different treatments of "transit trade"; and trade statistics vary across countries and have recently been changed. *Table I.1* presents only one of the ways the index of export per GDP can be estimated (i.e., using the official exchange rates). Even with these qualifications, it can be stated that with the average indicator level at around 40% these countries are fairly open to trade and show a tendency toward increasing openness.[6]

Exports have become extremely important for these countries, especially in recent years (1994 and 1995), when they showed a remarkable expansion (see *Table I.1*). When we look at the average 30–50% growth of STE exports in 1994–1995 and the export expansion in Organisation for Economic Co-operation and Development (OECD) countries (19%) and in developing countries (23%) during this period, all in US dollar values, we see that this growth was impressive in a comparative perspective.

The medium-term pattern of development of exports since the start of transition is ambiguous (see *Table I.2* and *Figure I.1*). In the case of countries that have emerged in recent years, data for the period before and after their independence are not easy to compare (from this point of view, the growth rates shown in *Figure I.1* are more reliable than those that can be calculated from *Table I.2*). Because economic transition and the emergence of these new economies more or less coincided, we cannot make any strong statements about changes in export levels resulting from the transition process in 1989–1994.

Of the three countries that were already in existence before 1990, only Hungary showed an increase in exports (in current US dollar terms) from 1989 to 1994. In 1989 Romania already had an excessive export volume due to the decision made in the second half of the 1980s to repay all its external debt. Therefore, it was no surprise that Romanian exports suffered a serious fall or that their recovery to the 1989 level has required more time than export recovery in other countries. Bulgaria is an entirely different case: in the framework of the CMEA, Bulgaria's economy had closer ties to the economy of the Soviet Union than any other existing STE. Consequently, it was bound to suffer the most from the demise of the CMEA and the Soviet Union. Most recent data show that despite their rapid export growth in 1995, neither Romania nor Bulgaria has reached its 1989 export level.[7]

The export growth pattern shown in *Figure I.1* reveals similarities and differences among the countries included in the study. The recession in world trade in 1993 clearly had an impact on the export performance of several countries (Bulgaria, Hungary, Slovakia, and Slovenia). The trade figures for Estonia and Latvia have been heavily impacted by the consequences of establishing independence and the rapid rearrangement of trade with FSU republics. Slovakia's export decline in 1993 was caused in part by Czechoslovakia's separation into two republics; the Czech data, however, do not reflect a similar shock. Explanations of further differences among the STEs can be found in the country studies.

The distribution of trade by region presented in *Table I.3* also shows some similarities and differences among the STEs.[8] In recent years the European Union (EU) has become the dominant export market for most of the countries in the study.

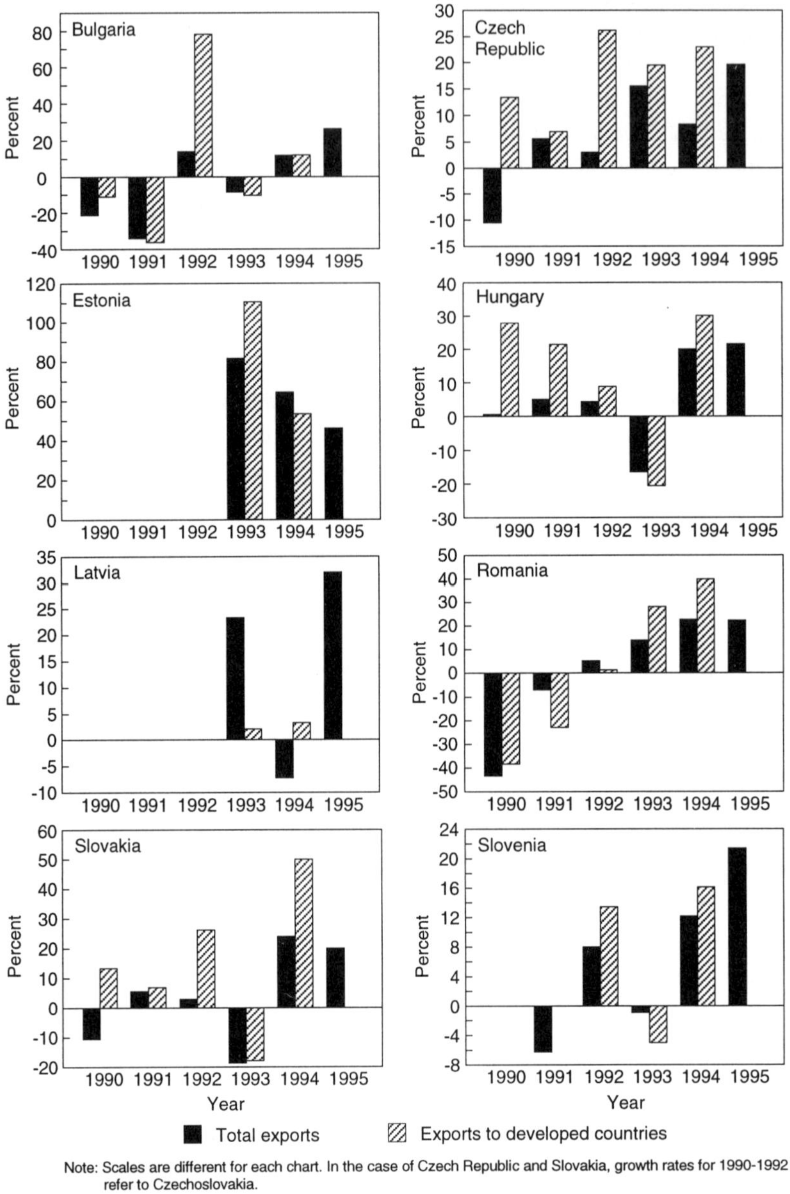

Figure I.1. Growth of value of exports in small transition economies (in US dollars). Sources: Data for years 1990–1994 are from UN ECE *Economic Bulletin for Europe* and *Economic Survey of Europe* (various issues); data for 1995 are from the sources listed for *Table I.1*.

Table I.3. Distribution of exports in 1994 by region (in percent).

	EU	Germany	Former CMEA	Russia	Partners in "new trade"[a]
Bulgaria	45.5	14.0	16.2	10.5	–
Czech Republic	50.9	34.7	30.5[b]	2.8	18.4
Estonia	20.7	7.6	43.0[b]	21.5	41.3
Hungary	48.9	28.0	21.9	6.6	–
Latvia	27.9	10.5	53.7[b]	28.1	51.5
Romania	46.0	16.0	13.5	3.4	–
Slovakia	39.9	25.0	47.1[b]	3.8	42.4
Slovenia	59.2	30.3	9.1	4.3	15.0

[a]Trade with countries that used to belong to the same former large country; that is, the successor states of the USSR, CSFR, and Yugoslavia.
[b]Including "new trade."
Source: IMF Direction of Trade Statistics.

This importance is even greater if we take into account that in 1995 Austria, Finland, and Sweden, countries that traditionally have been important partners for several of the STEs in the study, also became EU members. Within the EU, Germany is the primary trade partner, particularly for those countries that are close to it geographically or culturally (Czech Republic, Hungary, Slovakia, and Slovenia). Despite the formal collapse of the CMEA, trade among its former members remains important. It is remarkable, though, that in 1994 Russia represented only an extremely small share of the exports of the Czech Republic, Romania, Slovakia, and Hungary. The reasons for this loss and the difficulties of regaining FSU markets are addressed in each of the country studies (Chapters 1 to 7) in this volume; they are also addressed in Chapter 8, which analyzes both detailed Russian trade data and the attitudes of Russian enterprises. The most common explanations for this low level of trade are the high risk of exporting to Russia, on the one hand, and the Russian importers' preference for products from the West, on the other. As the last column of *Table I.3* indicates, partners in "new trade" (i.e., trade between countries that were once part of the same country) still have extremely close ties to one another, the only significant exception being Slovenia.

Some Macroeconomic Issues

Our investigation started with the assumption that the first phase of macrostabilization was over by 1994–1995 and thereafter the success of exports from STEs would largely be determined by microeconomic factors. The country studies and the case studies more or less verified our assumption; however, Bulgaria proved to be something of an exception. In 1994–1995 Bulgaria still struggled for minimal consolidation of the economy: the extremely severe austerity measures coupled with unpredictable changes in government regulations, volatile movements of the exchange rate, and the country's continued financial isolation from the world economy have put a burden on enterprises that has seriously blocked export expansion.

The country studies also revealed that some macroeconomic factors, especially the development of exchange rates and the real interest rate, remain among the most important determinants of export performance.

The exchange rate regimes in 1994–1996 showed considerable variation across the STEs. In 1994 the Czech Republic, Estonia, Latvia, and Slovakia had pegged exchange rates (Estonia through a currency board system); Bulgaria, Romania, and Slovenia had free-floating regimes with occasional instances of substantial central bank intervention. Hungary pursued an adjustable peg regime until March 1995, when it moved to a preannounced crawling peg system. In early 1996, in the Czech Republic the bands around the fixed rate were substantially widened (from ± 0.5% to 7.5%), so that in principle rates can fluctuate quite freely.

In the early years of transition (1990–1993), exchange rates, especially directly influenced pegged rates, were used to support the goals of stabilization. By 1994–1995 stabilization efforts seem to have come to fruition: in 1995, in all STEs consumer prices increased less than 35%; moreover, among the STEs, Slovenia approached and the Czech Republic and Slovakia achieved the goal of one-digit inflation. As a side effect of the stable exchange rate policies, the currencies of the STEs invariably went through a process of continuous and substantial real appreciation. *Figure I.2* illustrates this process, which was the most pervasive in countries with strict pegged rates.

There are several views concerning the causes and effects of this real appreciation. Some think that much of the appreciation was a normal reaction, either to the drastic devaluations that were effected in most of the STEs at the outset of transition, or to the existing large discrepancy between the purchasing power parity (PPP) and the exchange rates of these currencies. Others believe that starting from a centrally planned economy with no meaningful single exchange rate means the substantial devaluations cannot be treated in the same way as devaluations in market-based economies (Oblath, 1994). Another view rejects the usefulness of the concept of PPP in the early transition period because of the substantial real disturbances that occur. According to this view, the changes eventually lead to substantial efficiency gains, i.e., an appreciation in the equilibrium real exchange rate. Thus, the real appreciation shown in the statistics would in fact be the combination of an appreciation of the equilibrium real exchange rate and the move of the actual real exchange rate toward this equilibrium (Halpern and Wyplosz, 1995; Rosati, 1996).

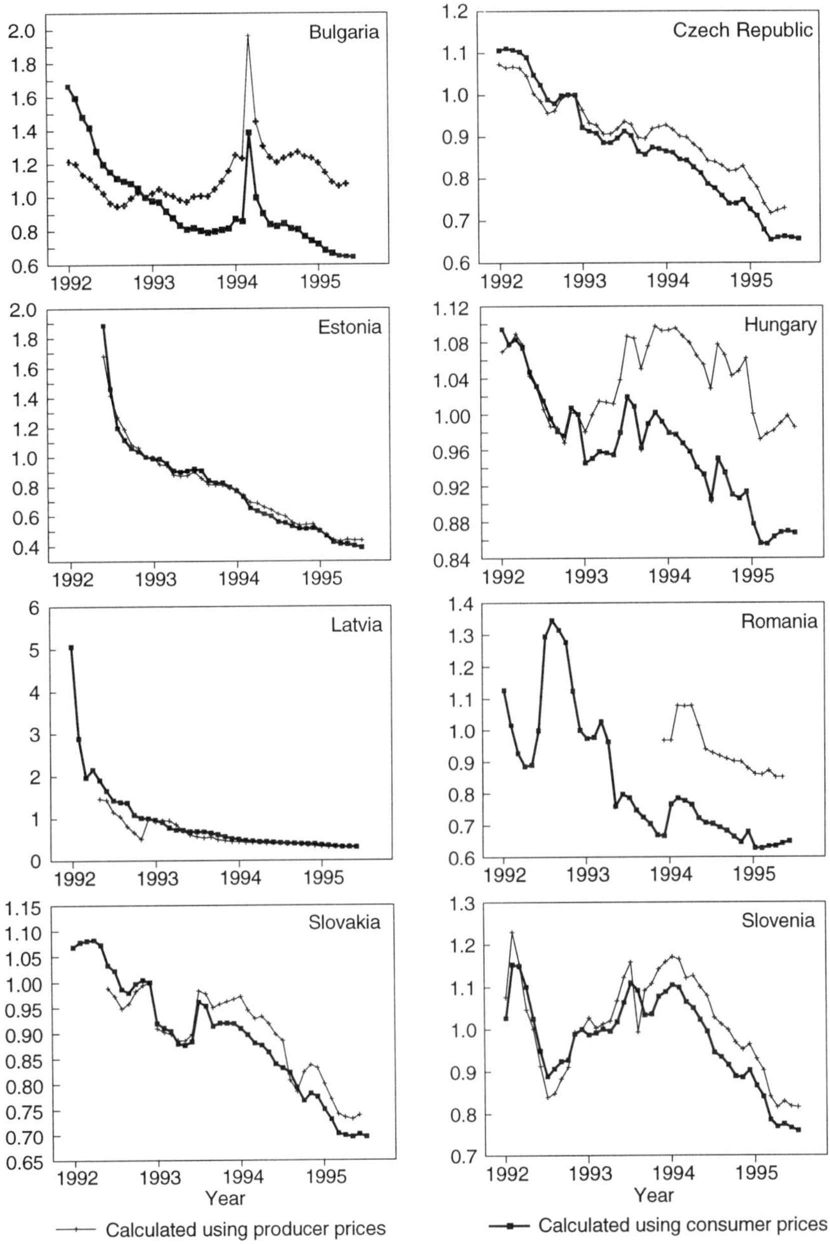

Figure I.2. Changes in real effective exchange rates (December 1992 = 1.00). The decline of the index shows real appreciation. Source: UN ECE database.

As the country studies in this book demonstrate, exporting enterprises feel that the appreciation of the domestic currencies has resulted in a deterioration in export competitiveness. The enterprises most affected were those in countries where the real wage was already high or was allowed to increase (Hungary and Slovenia), or where no substantial devaluation preceded the period of continuous real appreciation (Hungary).[9]

In most STEs stabilization is still a high priority of economic policy, and governments (or central banks) have not made radical changes to reverse the tendency of real appreciation: they either see cost competitiveness for their exports, or hope for the recovery or perpetuation of labor productivity improvements or for structural changes that will diminish the role of exchange rates in export competitiveness.[10]

Everyday transactions connected with exports and restructuring for more competitive future exports both require financing comparable to that available for competitors in the world market. A unanimous finding of the country studies is that STE exporters lack adequate competitive financing. One of the principal reasons is the high real interest rates prevailing in STEs. In 1994 real lending rates were 4% in Slovakia, 7% in the Czech Republic, 13–16% in Hungary, 16–18% in Slovenia, about 20–25% in Romania, 16% in Bulgaria, and 33% in Latvia.[11]

Focusing on stabilization requires tight monetary policies that result in high interest rates and increasing spreads between deposit and lending rates.[12] Similar effects result from financing budget deficits through the issuance of domestic bonds imposed on banks, as was done in Bulgaria, Hungary, and Romania. Other, more institutional, reasons also play an important part in the high lending rates; for example, the weak situation of domestic banks burdened with bad loans and the poor financial situation (and consequently the poor credit rating) of the enterprises.

It appears that the governments in STEs have not considered high real lending rates a binding constraint on exports. This adds to the problems of weak commercial financing infrastructure in these economies and the difficulties STE exporters encounter in establishing credibility in new markets.

High real interest rates coupled with increased stability and the relaxation of capital controls led to increased financial inflow to some STEs in 1994–1995, for example, the Czech Republic, Slovenia, and Hungary. These flows took the form of short-term speculative (hot) money, short- and medium-term credits taken by the business sector, and portfolio investments. Central and East European governments usually only partially sterilized these inflows, which in turn led to further real appreciation of the domestic currency. In countries that applied fixed or strictly managed exchange rates, this appreciation led to revaluation expectations that fueled further short-term capital inflow. Although the inflow of additional foreign currencies can enhance exporting activities (for example, by depressing the real cost of borrowing or creating competition for the domestic banking system), through its upward pressure on the exchange rate it can also contribute to a further deterioration of the cost competitiveness of STE exports.

To a large extent, smooth exporting depends on the characteristic features of the exchange regime, especially access to foreign exchange needed to purchase imports and to market products abroad. From this point of view, the macroeconomic and institutional frameworks in most STEs became favorable quite early in the transition. Multiple exchange rates were abolished and in most countries currencies were made either *de jure* or *de facto* convertible for current account transactions. In some countries, including Hungary, Slovenia, the Czech Republic, and Slovakia, in the early years enterprises had to surrender their foreign currency export earnings shortly after receipt, but were allowed to use the domestic currency without limit to buy foreign currency if they intended to use it to buy imports.

The European Bank for Reconstruction and Development (EBRD, 1994) reports that in 1994, of the countries included in this study, Estonia, Latvia, and Slovenia had full current account convertibility, Hungary had current account convertibility except for tourism, Romania had virtual current account convertibility except for tourism, the Czech Republic and Slovakia had current account convertibility for the enterprises, and Bulgaria maintained few restrictions on current account convertibility. By 1996 all the countries in the study had established so-called International Monetary Fund (IMF) Article VIII convertibility on the current account, except for Bulgaria and Romania, which apply more limited Article XIV convertibility.

Demand-Side Impediments

In the course of their investigations, the authors of the country studies tried to gauge the importance of the different external impediments to exports. No attempt was made to prepare sophisticated quantitative evaluations of the tariff and nontariff barriers that Central and East European exporters meet in their export markets.[13] Rather, the emphasis was on assessing the importance of external hurdles compared with supply-side impediments. This comparison led to unambiguous results: all the studies found external or demand-side impediments to be much weaker than supply-side or internal barriers to exports. No doubt this is partly a reflection of the attitudes of the enterprise managers interviewed, who seem more willing to accept the constraints originating outside their countries than those within their own economies.[14]

However, there is not yet a perception that export markets are easily accessible. Despite the recent acceleration of the abolishment of trade barriers in export markets in EU, European Free Trade Association (EFTA), and Central European

Free Trade Agreement (CEFTA) countries, enterprise managers still find effective barriers to their exports. The high share of "sensitive" products in the exports of STEs has exposed them to a higher incidence of quota and tariff barriers than the general framework of the Association Agreements between Central and East European countries and the EU would have suggested. Moreover, although antidumping cases were more characteristic of 1992 and 1993 than 1994 and 1995, their memory still affects exporting behavior in STEs. The introduction of new licensing requirements in the EU for certain kinds of electric machinery (see the country studies on Bulgaria and Latvia) and the implementation of quotas especially for food products (see the country study on Estonia) are examples of new barriers. The EU's association process has its shadowy side, as well: companies complain about the high limits and restrictive regulations of the rules of origin, which small countries like Slovenia, Estonia, and Latvia can hardly meet. The need to introduce high-level ISO 9000 standards in order to increase or even just maintain market shares in EU markets forces STE firms to make large investments.[15] Many enterprises consider this requirement a weapon used against new suppliers from outside the EU, a purely protectionist measure against goods that otherwise fulfill Western quality requirements. In addition, as the Hungarian country study points out, investments for ISO 9000 standards only serve exports to the West, as neither domestic sales nor exports to Central and Eastern Europe are enhanced by ISO certification.

The country studies suggest that STE exports to the FSU collapsed, not only because of the disintegration of the CMEA (with its decision making and pricing and payments arrangements), but also because trading with most FSU republics poses considerable problems for STE exporters. The lack of financial and trade infrastructure, uncertainties about transport and payments, the lack of exchange risk sharing, the frequently changing regulations, the need to pay bribes and deal with corrupt state representatives, and discrimination against certain countries (Estonia and Latvia) all restrict exports to these potentially large markets. In Central Asian republics, these difficulties are compounded by the remnants of centralized state trading, which means licensing, quotas, and currency exchange regulations.

The high costs of entry into Western markets and the difficulties of establishing a distribution and marketing network and building a reputation are primarily connected with the STE enterprises' lack of experience. With the exception of Slovenia and Hungary, STE producers as a rule did not have any experience in foreign trading, especially trade outside the CMEA. The heritage of centralized trade with a few specialized foreign trade companies is a particularly heavy burden for new countries such as Estonia, Latvia, and Slovakia in our sample, as most of the foreign trade companies were located outside of the country's current boundaries (i.e., in Moscow and Prague, respectively).

The lack of knowledge of foreign languages, foreign regulations and trade practices, and marketing skills has been a serious drawback for the thousands of mostly new producers who embarked on exporting after foreign trade was liberalized in their countries. These impediments will be removed only slowly, with the accumulation of skills and knowledge. Their elimination can be accelerated with the application of certain forms of trade that help to alleviate these difficulties, including establishing joint ventures with more experienced foreign partners; engaging in extensive subcontracting (or outward processing traffic, OPT), where the foreign partner markets the final product; or choosing a step-by-step strategy, first moving back to generic, no-name products and gradually introducing brand names and more sophisticated products to the foreign markets (see the country study on Estonia). Trade strategy in most cases boils down to a simple choice: either use a trade setup that requires little trade experience and capital, but under which potential revenues are limited and STE enterprises are highly dependent on Western partners and are exposed to the trade cycle (subcontracting or production of generic, less sophisticated, no-name products), or embark on setting up a distribution and marketing channel abroad with the aim of introducing more sophisticated, more processed products under one's own name. In the latter case the entry costs may be so high that the products, if they are salable at all, may price themselves out of the market. In certain industries a shift from OPT to outright export may also intensify the importing country's quantitative barriers.

The comparative attractiveness of the domestic market could have diverted potential export products toward domestic sales. The country studies report that enterprises realize substantially higher profits on domestic sales than on exports. Moreover, this difference in profits occurred in a setting in which the products sold at home and abroad were no longer as different as they were before trade liberalization commenced. In fact, with the exception of a few Romanian enterprises, all the enterprise case studies reported that products sold in domestic markets are of the same quality and design as those supplied to export markets. It was not our goal to analyze the reasons for differences in profitability between home sales and exports, but certainly there are many products that enterprises sell only on domestic markets, probably with the advantage of better producer-customer relations. Nonetheless, even if domestic sales are attractive with respect to profits, they are not sufficiently large in volume for the firms of these small economies. Following the initial period of drastic domestic output decline in these countries (on average, a 40% cumulative drop of industrial production), enterprises usually have large underutilized capacities and the only way to employ their resources is through export.[16] From this point of view the attractiveness of domestic sales compared with exports, even if the former are not so demanding and require less investment for entry than the latter, is not very robust.

Supply-Side Impediments

One group of supply-side impediments that the country studies give ample evidence of is connected with institutions of the domestic economies that do not work properly and conditions that restrict enterprise activities in STEs. The widely applied assumption that restrictive domestic conditions would drive enterprise sales to foreign markets has turned out to be an oversimplification, especially because the uncertain and unsettled conditions in the domestic market have failed to provide a secure basis for the enterprises' everyday operations. The enterprises' generally poor financial condition, the uncertainty stemming from the delay of their privatization, the removal of key linkages in the domestic market, the credit squeeze that affected generally undercapitalized enterprises, and poorly functioning financial intermediation are the most common factors impacting enterprise operations.[17]

Another group of impediments is related to the fact that enterprises are unprepared to meet the needs of export markets. Due to the heritage of separation of domestic enterprises from foreign markets, many companies lack information on foreign standards, regulations, and customer requirements. Moreover, many are unable to provide accompanying services and lack a strong reputation, either because they are too new in the market or have not put sufficient effort into building a reputation abroad. Most STE exporters have weak market power in Western markets, which limits the profitability of exports and forces them to accept unfavorable conditions such as long payment periods. Ignorance is still widespread among inexperienced STE companies about what is needed in terms of quality, reaction time, terms of delivery, and marketing in order to gain export contracts and eventually establish a stable position in exports markets.

The third group of impediments is connected with the deficiencies of government efforts to support exporters. Both the country studies and the topical study on this issue (Chapter 9) testify that, for various reasons, the governments of STEs have not paid special attention to exports. Consequently, exports have not been supported by distinct measures in any of these countries. The STE governments' focus on economic diplomacy, especially to ensure access to large markets through free trade agreements (with the EU, EFTA, and CEFTA), was one reason for this limited interest. Past experiences where interventions tended to escalate have also made the administrations cautious with respect to supporting certain export activities. The governments, however, do not perform even those roles that would be expected and acceptable in any market economy: the basic conditions for smooth export operations, especially minimal trade and financial infrastructure, are still missing in most STEs. Institutions offering special credits for exporters (either special credit lines at commercial banks or the services of export-import banks) and those providing export insurance or guarantee schemes are either still in their infancy or are missing entirely in the STEs. The working of the tax and tariff systems also inhibits rather than supports the expansion of exports. For instance, in several STEs exporters were at a disadvantage compared with competitors abroad or producers selling for the domestic market because of delays in or the lack of reimbursement of the value-added tax (VAT) and tariff duties on imports used for exports.

The governments have also shown indecisiveness with respect to permanent trade missions abroad. No doubt the old system of missions was part of the centralized and controlled trade, and needed to be reorganized. However, the STEs tended to effect a simple and sharp reduction in the number of existing trade missions, which seems to show misunderstanding of the needs of inexperienced exporters. A policy that seems more promising was followed by the Latvian and Hungarian governments, which, to promote trade within the rapidly changing environment of the successor states of the Soviet Union, started to establish new permanent representatives there. The creation of a special organization in Estonia that distributes information about Commonwealth of Independent States (CIS) standards is another example of an effective government effort to support exports.

The last group of supply-side impediments, which in fact are related to the previous ones, is the comparatively high level (or growth) of some core costs of producing and exporting: these include wages, energy costs, cost of credit, and costs associated with the risk of trading. Following the application of stabilization policies, which were usually connected with initial large devaluations, STE exports were able to expand relatively quickly in labor-intensive products. However, the comparative advantage of STEs due to their low wages (measured in US dollars) is evaporating as a consequence of real appreciation of STE currencies and recent real wage increases. Because productivity has only recently started to pick up, and only in some of these countries, many leading export products are being squeezed out of their foreign markets. This is especially true for the exports of Slovenia and Hungary, which maintain the highest real wages among STEs; however, the interviews conducted in Estonia and Latvia, countries with much lower real wages, also reflect this difficulty. An indication of this process is the decreasing share of job work in Slovenia's exports, which decreased from 19% in 1993 to 11% in 1995. According to the country studies, in other economies (for example, Romania and Slovakia) high wages do not yet pose a problem to exports. In fact, these are the countries that attract Western outward processing from higher-wage STEs such as Slovenia and Hungary.

In some of the countries, especially Estonia and Slovenia, many recent exports were based on cheap (cheaply imported or domestically subsidized) energy sources. This advantage is bound to decline due to the resistance to "energy dumping" in the EU and the narrowing possibilities of importing energy sources cheaply. Exporters using cheap energy in Estonia in 1992 saw a tripling of the price of this crucial cost element. Similar problems surfaced in Slovenia with respect to the disruption of supplies of cheap raw materials from the republics of former Yugoslavia.

The high cost of credit has already been mentioned above with reference to the interest rate. Additional costs are connected with the risks that exporters must take. These risks generally stem from uncertainties concerning the exchange rate, payment by the buyer, and the disappearance of or damage to goods on the way to the customer. Some of these risks can be either commercial or political in nature. As for recent exports from STEs, especially high risks are associated with exports directed toward FSU republics. As indicated above, specialized institutions that could share the risks with exporters do not yet exist or are operating only at a low level. This prevents STE enterprises from more ambitious export activity in this large market or pushes them toward a large-scale use of Western mediators. The fact that many bills for Slovak exports to the Soviet Union and Slovenian exports to the republics of former Yugoslavia have remained unpaid makes enterprises in these countries especially cautious about making new deals. The discussion of Russian imports from STEs (Chapter 8) does not, however, place so much emphasis on payment and other risks, but sets the difficulties of selling in the Russian market into a different perspective. The study emphasizes that the conditions of selling in Russia have changed because of the structural shifts in Russian import demand (away from military- and heavy-industry-related imports to consumer products), the move of customer tastes toward formerly unaccessible Western products, and the paucity of marketing and distribution efforts by Central and East European exporters in the Russian market.

Typical Aspects of Enterprise Adjustment

As the previous sections (and subsequent chapters of this book) indicate, in recent years STE enterprises have encountered numerous impediments in the course of developing their export activities. From various other sources, however, they have also received strong incentives to expand their exports: the small size of these countries, the fall in domestic demand, and the widening and deepening of the free trade areas with EU, EFTA, and CEFTA countries seem to be lasting encouragements to exports. Among these conflicting factors, the enterprises try to respond to the incentives and circumvent or tackle the barriers to their exports. The country studies give ample evidence of the diverse forms of such enterprise adjustments.

Probably the most obvious effort that enterprises make is reorganizing their production process to improve the efficiency of their operations. Reducing productive capacity was almost unknown for enterprises in centrally planned economies. Now, under the pressure of declining demand, many enterprises have been forced to realize that unnecessary machinery, equipment, and stock can be sold, plants that are not useful can be closed, precious real estate can be sold or leased, and surplus labor can be shed. Moreover, these actions can be taken, not just to keep pace with the drop in demand, but also to improve efficiency. Other downsizing efforts that are frequently used are decreasing batch sizes and closing old product lines.

Some STEs (Hungary, for example) have also reported increases in investments by exporters; as a rule, these investments are focused on quality improvements and technological development, not on capacity expansion. The enterprise studies indicate that the way existing enterprises are privatized has far-reaching consequences for the short- and medium-term prospects of investments and development. A fast turnaround and zealous restructuring can only be expected when foreign strategic investors are involved. Domestic investors tend to exhaust their resources by buying up the enterprise shares: even if they have ideas, foreign contacts, and distributional channels (and they usually do not), financing the reorganization of the enterprise for better export performance is a considerable task. The takeover of a company by insiders (managers and employees) is even less promising from the point of view of radical development aimed at expanding export markets.

It is likely that much of the improvement will be in the marketing process, including conducting market research, improving reactions to the requests of foreign customers, building a reputation, introducing the firm's own brand name, and establishing a network for marketing abroad. Even if they realize the importance of these tasks, most exporting companies are unable to accomplish all the requirements simultaneously. They either attempt to make improvements in one of these fields or rely almost entirely on foreign partners. Foreign partners are made use of in the form of subcontracting, joining an OPT connection, supplying generic products to established distributors, or attracting FDI. The foreign connection can take care of not only marketing, but also other difficulties like quality and standardization barriers, and operating and exporting with limited working capital.

The topical study on FDI (Chapter 10) sheds light on the changing relationship of direct investment into and exports out of STEs. The author uses theoretical arguments and empirical evidence from three countries to show that STEs are approaching or are already in the phase of the "FDI cycle" in which penetration of FDI into STEs leads to positive trade and spillover effects. Exploitation of the re-export advantages from FDI have begun to appear in the *maquiladora* phenomenon, which is becoming more prevalent, especially around the Austrian and German borders.[18] Investments are gradually moving toward tradables, particularly manufacturing sectors that are most promising for exports. However, real growth effects from the export activities of FDI only come when institutional and market conditions make them possible and induce joint ventures to attach the host country sectors more organically to the network of international division of labor.

STEs have also started to establish joint ventures abroad, especially in the successor states of the Soviet Union (but also in other Central and East European countries) as a tool for solving payment problems. Setting up bonded warehouses in Russia and Ukraine is a new way to deal with smaller customers in a large market at a great distance; this approach has been used by Hungarian firms in particular.

There are certain kinds of enterprise adjustments that, although quite widespread, do not seem to provide lasting solutions for the expansion or maintenance of exports. For instance, defaulting on liabilities to overcome financial squeeze in order to finance current enterprise operations (as described in the country study on Bulgaria), or neutralizing unfavorable customs changes by bribing the customs officials (as reported in the country study on Latvia) are arrangements that probably cannot be sustained.

Interenterprise cooperation, such as establishing industry associations for the solution of export-related tasks, is evidence of a new attitude on the part of enterprises, indicating that they no longer expect their governments to provide everything they need. According to the country study on Latvia, associations distribute information about foreign markets, quality management, and marketing abroad; train trade experts; give advice with respect to design; and organize centralized purchasing for their members. Similar associations with some, if not all, of these functions have been formed in other countries as well. Another promising example is the strategic cooperation among Slovenian domestic enterprises in order to enhance exports.

As a conclusion to this brief summary of the book, we must refer to the important role that exports played in the STEs' recent recovery from their transformational recession. Firmly establishing the claim that the recovery of GDP in 1993–1995 was led by exports would require a thorough analysis of national account data, which are not yet available. Nonetheless, *Figure I.3* gives some illustrative evidence of just such a development. In fact, analysts of the output decline of the early 1990s (see, for instance, Holzmann *et al.*, 1995) predicted that the recovery could (and probably should) come from the pull of exports. From the point of view of the sustainability of growth in STEs, the perpetuation of export growth is crucial. Like 1995, 1996 shows a decline in the growth rate of world demand for exports (see IMF, 1995), thus it becomes more difficult for the STEs to maintain their export performance. For this reason impediments to exports, identified and analyzed in this volume, are of crucial importance for the future development of STEs. Policy makers, businesspersons, and managers must further clarify the nature of these impediments. Some of the impediments may just need focus of attention; others may require well-prepared programs, hard work, and accumulation of experience

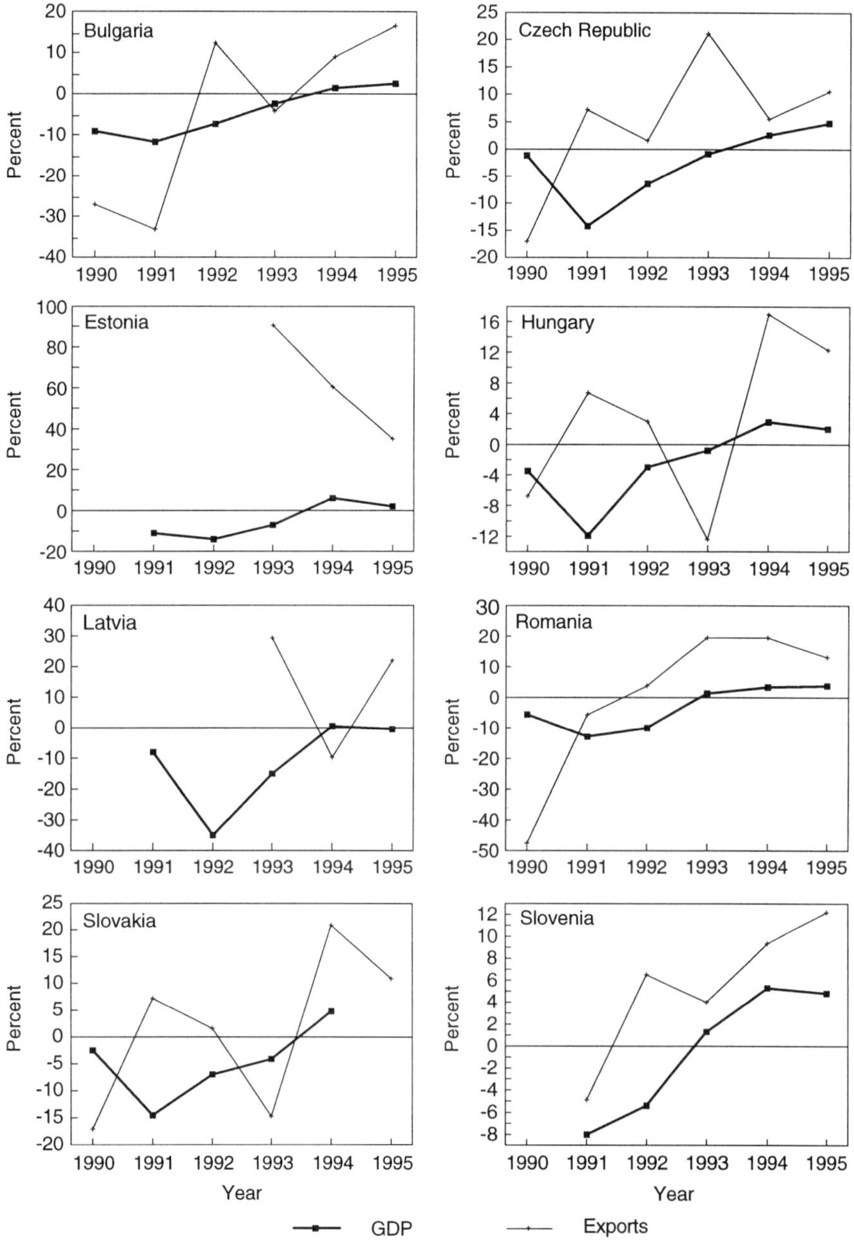

Figure I.3. Real growth of GDP and exports (previous year = 0).

to tackle them. The governments of STEs must find a way of giving more attention to export development while maintaining a basically intervention-free approach to international trade.

Notes

[1] In this context, small transition economies (STEs) simply refer to the countries dealt with in this book in the country studies (Chapters 1 to 7) and in the topical studies (Chapters 8 to 10). The countries discussed are Bulgaria, the Czech Republic, Estonia, Hungary, Latvia, Romania, Slovakia, and Slovenia. General descriptions of the countries are given in the discussion of the sample. Obviously, there are also other countries in Central and Eastern Europe that could qualify as STEs.

[2] See Blejer *et al.* (1993), Kornai (1993), Holzmann *et al.* (1995), and Rosati (1994).

[3] See, for instance, Collins and Rodrik (1991), Hamilton and Winters (1992), Rosati 1992), and Winters and Wang (1994).

[4] In 1988–1993, for instance, the rate at which five Central and East European countries (Bulgaria, Czechoslovakia, Hungary, Poland, and Romania) increased their trade with EU countries was twice that envisaged by the forecasts of Hamilton and Winters (1992) for a 20-year catch-up period (see the Summary to The Economic Interpenetration, 1994).

[5] See, for instance, UN ECE (1994), Graziani (1994), and various chapters in The Economic Interpenetration (1994).

[6] We do not give data for the period preceding transition, because those data have even more distortions than current data.

[7] We should note, however, that it is not evident how the pretransition level of trade was to be calculated, especially due to problems of valuation of CMEA trade. For the valuation used, see note *a* in *Table I.2*.

[8] Here again, data are not completely reliable because of valuation problems and incomplete registration. As an alternative, data from the Vienna Institute for Comparative Economic Studies (WIIW, 1995), which are based on national statistics accounted in national currency, show the following export shares with the EU for 1994: Bulgaria 33.5%, Czech Republic 45.9%, Hungary 51.0%, Romania 46.0%, and Slovakia 29.2%. Although WIIW data were indicated as preliminary, they were not expected to be modified to such an extent as to make up for the sometimes substantial differences with the International Monetary Fund data used in *Table I.3*.

[9] However, through a calculation that entails deflating the nominal exchange rates by unit labor costs, Rosati (1996) finds that exporters in the Czech Republic and Slovakia, in particular, must have been affected by the appreciation of the currency. The country study on Slovakia (and the case studies it was based on) does not seem to support Rosati's prediction.

[10] An exception in this respect is Hungary, where in March 1995 a substantial devaluation was combined with a change in the exchange rate regime.

[11] These figures were calculated based on IMF (1995), WIIW (1995), OECD (1996), UN ECE (1995), the Bank of Slovenia's Monthly Bulletin, and the Romanian and Bulgarian country studies, using producer price index to measure inflation.

Estonia was a peculiar case; according to the Estonian country study there was a 20–22% negative real rate on loans, calculated using the consumer price index (compared with an 8–10% negative rate according to our calculations from the above-mentioned sources). As the Estonian country study testifies, due to limited access to this credit, the high nominal interest rate, and the stability of the nominal exchange rate, exporters did not consider this rate to be favorable. It should also be noted that, contrary to the Romanian country study, our own estimate for the Romanian real lending rate was a 35–50% negative rate.

[12] Spreads in September 1994 varied between 4% (in the Czech Republic) and 42% (in Bulgaria) in the countries included in the study (see UN ECE, 1995). The relevant data from Slovakia were not available.

[13] This was done earlier in other studies, including Rollo and Smith (1993) and The Economic Interpenetration (1994).

[14] Another bias of the case studies is that successful enterprises and exporters are over-represented among the enterprises covered: as a rule, managers of unsuccessful firms and firms that had completely lost their export markets were unwilling to cooperate in preparing a case study about their enterprise.

[15] Published in 1987, the ISO 9000 is a set of international standards for both quality management and quality assurance that has been adopted by over 90 countries worldwide. These standards apply to all kinds of organizations and many industries. The essence of the ISO 9000 standards is documentation. Compliance with a certain ISO 9000 standard can be certified by a third-party registration agency. Certificates typically expire after three years, but even within this period the registration agency usually requires surveillance audits at six-month intervals to check the currency of the certificate.

Even Western experts find ISO 9000 certification costly, particularly for the small companies that really need it. German chemical companies, for instance have to make serious calculations before they decide to spend the DM 20,000–30,000 needed for ISO 9000 certification of a single chemical process. See Chynoweth and Roberts (1992).

[16] The Bulgarian country study mentions that a large number of firms have under 50% capacity utilization; the Romanian study cites statistics according to which average industrial capacity utilization varied between 51% and 57% in Romania in 1991–1993.

[17] For more on the importance of the disruption of former domestic supply connections, see the country studies on Bulgaria and Hungary.

[18] This phenomenon was first experienced in the 1970s and 1980s in the regions of Mexico bordering the USA, where US firms set up their plants (known as *maquiladora*) and, with the support of special exemptions from US import tariffs and Mexican trade restrictions, managed to utilize cheap labor and low transport costs for production that basically served US markets.

References

Bank of Slovenia, 1995, Monthly Bulletin, March, Bank of Slovenia, Ljubljana, Slovenia.

Blejer, M. *et al.*, eds., 1993, Eastern Europe in Transition: From Recession to Growth?, World Bank Discussion Paper No. 196, Washington, DC, USA.

Chynoweth, E., and Roberts, M., 1992, Quality in the European Community: A market test for unification, *Chemical Week*, **150**(17):36–41.

Collins, M.S., and Rodrik, D., 1991, Eastern Europe and the Soviet Union in the World Economy, Institute for International Economics, Washington, DC, USA.

EBRD, 1994, Transition Report – Economic Transition in Eastern Europe and the Former Soviet Union, European Bank for Reconstruction and Development, London, UK.

Graziani, G., 1994, Trade patterns and comparative advantages of Central Eastern Europe with EC countries, in J. Gács and G. Winckler, eds., *International Trade and Restructuring in Eastern Europe*, Physica Verlag, Heidelberg, Germany.

Halpern, L., and Wyplosz, C., 1995, Equilibrium Exchange Rates in Transition, CEPR Working Paper No. 1145, Centre for Economic and Policy Research, London, UK.

Hamilton, C.B., and Winters, A.L., 1992, Opening up international trade with Eastern Europe, *Economic Policy*, No. 14, April, pp. 77–104.

Holzmann, R., Gács, J., and Winckler, G., eds., 1995, *Output Decline in Eastern Europe – Unavoidable, External Influence or Homemade?*, Kluwer Academic Publishers, Dordrecht, Netherlands.

IMF (International Monetary Fund), 1995, World Economic Outlook October 1995, IMF, Washington, DC, USA.

Kornai, J., 1993, Transformational Recession: A General Phenomenon Examined Through the Example of Hungary's Development, *Economie–Appliquee*, **46**(2).

Oblath, G., 1994, Exchange rate policy and real exchange rate changes in economic transition, in J. Gács and G. Winckler, eds., 1994, *International Trade and Restructuring in Eastern Europe*, Physica Verlag, Heidelberg, Germany.

OECD (Organisation for Economic Co-operation and Development), 1996, Short-term Economic Indicators – Transition Economies, 1996, No. 1, OECD, Paris, France.

Rollo, J., and Smith, A., 1993, The political economy of Eastern European trade with the European Community: Why so sensitive?, *Economic Policy*, **16**(April):139–181.

Rosati,, D., 1992, Problems of post-CMEA trade and payments, in: *the Economic Consequences of the East*, Centre for Economic Policy Research, London, UK.

Rosati, D., 1994, Output Decline during Transition from Plan to Market: A Reconsideration, *The Economics of Transition*, Vol. 2, No. 4.

Rosati, D., 1996, Exchange rate policies during transition from plan to market, *The Economics of Transition*, **4**(1), May, pp. 159–183.

The Economic Interpenetration between the EC and Eastern Europe, 1994, *European Economy* 1994, No. 6.

UN ECE, 1991, *Economic Bulletin for Europe*, Vol. 43, 1991, United Nations Economic Commission for Europe, New York, NY, USA.

UN ECE, 1994, *Economic Bulletin for Europe*, Vol. 45, 1993, United Nations Economic Commission for Europe, New York, NY, USA.

UN ECE, 1995, *Economic Survey of Europe in 1994–1995*, United Nations Economic Commission for Europe, New York, NY, USA.
Winters, A.L., and Wang, Z.K., 1994, *Eastern Europe's International Trade*, Manchester University Press, Manchester, UK.
WIIW (The Vienna Institute for Comparative Economic Studies), 1995, Countries in Transition 1995, *Handbook of Statistics*, WIIW, Vienna, Austria.
World Bank, 1993a, Estonia: The Transition to a Market Economy, World Bank, Washington, DC, USA.
World Bank, 1993b, Latvia: The Transition to a Market Economy, World Bank, Washington, DC, USA.

Appendix to Introduction and Summary: Common Schemes for Research

The following schemes were used by the contributors to prepare their country studies and the underlying enterprise case studies.

1 The Structure of the Country Studies

1.1 Short overview and evaluation of export performance of the country in 1994 compared to 1988 (overall development of exports, geographical reorientation and commodity composition, evaluation of commodity composition); (the starting year may be different for countries where 1988 would not be reasonable for comparison).

1.2 Impediments to exports – Demand

(a) Orientation to low demand regions and commodity groups
(b) Foreign protection: tariffs, non-tariff barriers (quotas, antidumping regulations, quality, health, environmental, and other inspections, voluntary export restraints)
(c) Lack of credit abroad and smooth payments arrangements
(d) High entry costs (information needed by potential buyers, learning the market, marketing and services costs, reputation building, etc.)
(e) comparative attractiveness of domestic market

1.3 Impediments to export – Supply

(a) costs (inputs, wages, credits), exchange rates, risks
(b) lack of information about potential customers and about trading practices
(c) low quality, quality control, reliability
(d) underdeveloped public infrastructure: transport, freight, communications, financial arrangements
(e) difficulty in getting critical inputs
(f) deterring domestic trade policies (export licencing, quotas, export taxes, necessity to use monopsonic state trading organizations, foreign exchange surrender of export revenues)

(g) general poor condition of enterprises (indebtedness; pre-privatization uncertainty, absorption of assets, permanent crisis management, etc.)

1.4 Temporary or artificial incentives to exports (distress exports, reexport of smuggled materials, exports related to tax evasion, etc.)

1.5 Typical enterprise efforts to tackle impediments to exports

1.6 Government policies contributing to impediments to exports; policies to remove impediments (macro-policy, economic diplomacy, legal regulation, institution building, subsidies in different forms)

2 The Setup of the Enterprise Case Studies

2.1 Selection of enterprises

When selecting the enterprises the following criteria is to be used (of course, even these do not ensure that the sample will be representative).

- Enterprises should be selected that are currently (or were in 1990) non-marginal exporters (at least 5% of output exported, some of the enterprises more than 20%).
- They are exporters of manufacturing products or services. Some of them should export their own products or services, some of them are exporters for others.
- Both exporters to Western and former CMEA (USSR) markets should be selected.
- Some new exporters should be selected.
- Both state owned and private firms should be investigated; small, medium and large firms.
- At least one firm should be selected which operates outside the capital.
- At least two joint ventures or fully foreign owned companies should be selected.

2.2 Commodity orientation

Given their importance in exports, it is advised that producers/exporters of at least five of the following commodity groups should be selected where possible:[1]

Manufacture of chemicals obtained from petroleum (petrochemicals) and from coal (NACE 252)
Iron and steel industry, excluding integrated coke ovens (NACE 221)
Manufacture and assembly of motor vehicles and manufacture of motor vehicle engines (NACE 351)
Manufacture of tools and finished metal goods except electrical equipment (NACE 316)
Manufacture of electrical machinery (comprising electric motors, electricity generators, transformers, switches, switch gear and other basic electrical plant) (NACE 342)
Manufacture of ready made clothing and accessories (NACE 453)
Knitting industry (NACE 436)

[1]Products here are given in NACE classification. Corresponding commodity groups could be chosen from SITC, ISIC, or any national trade or industry classification.

Manufacture of mass produced footwear (NACE 451)
Manufacture of wooden furniture (NACE 467)
Slaughtering, preparing and preserving of meat (excluding butchers's trade) (NACE 412)
Processing and preserving of fruit and vegetables (NACE 414)

The above 11 commodity groups made up 48% of the CEEC manufacturing exports to EC in 1993, and 46% of the growth of CEEC manufacturing exports to EC from 1988 to 1993.[2]

2.3 Standard information to collect about the enterprises (See also check list below for details)

2.3.1 Characteristics of the enterprise in 1990-1994: Size, date of birth and consecutive steps of transformation, ownership and organization, main products, main markets, performance (output, employment, profit, indebtedness).

2.3.2 Export orientation: traditional or new; is exporting important for the overall production and profits of the firm; East or/and West, target countries, direct exporting or through mediators, own product or production for contract (subcontracting), products how much developed for foreign markets, characteristics of export strategy in 1990-2000 (competition in price, quality, terms of delivery, finance; own brand, acquired brand, or generic product; structure of markets and mediators), assessment of competitive characteristics of products and the enterprise.

2.3.3 Domestic environment and exports: relation of domestic sales and export sales (similarity or complementarity of products; comparative resource intensity, costs and profitability), export financing and insurance (production pre-financing, export revenue pre-financing, insurance against default or political risk), access to necessary inputs, the impact of government regulations, the relation to state administration.

2.3.4 Foreign environment and exports: relation to foreign customers, banks, competitors and other partners (subcontractors, license owners), nature of mediators (exclusive or competing agents at home or abroad, joint ventures abroad, assembly shop abroad), the system of collecting information on products and markets; foreign regulations impeding exports; market structure (of the foreign market), assessment of risks and prospects in the different markets.

3 Suggested Checklist of Questions for the Enterprise Case Studies

3.1 Background Information

(a) Date of establishment
(b) Output capacity, delineated according to main products
(c) Size of labor force
(d) Estimated size of the capital stock
(e) Traditional markets
(f) Total sales since 1990
(g) Size of profit since 1990

[2]CEECs: Bulgaria, Czech and Slovak Republics, Hungary, Poland, and Romania.

(h) Level of indebtedness

3.2 Structure of ownership

(a) Steps of transformation from 1988–1995
(b) Current structure of ownership

3.3 Export Orientation Now and in Retrospect (1988–1995)

(a) How much of total sales are for export markets (in percentages)?
(b) To whom are you exporting (what kind of firms or organizations)?
(c) Where are exports going (by country and region)?
(d) Is exporting done through direct contact or through mediators?
(e) Do you export your own products or product on contract by your foreign partner (subcontracting, outward processing, job work)?

3.4 Production for Export

(a) Is production oriented toward export markets? If so how, and to which markets?
(b) Is there a company strategy which is pushing for exports? If so then to which markets?
(c) What is the current competitive strength of your products/your enterprise in foreign markets and how do you expect these advantages to change in the next five years?
(d) Are products produced for export different in terms of input usage (or factor intensity) than those produced for the domestic market?
(e) What is the difference between the profitability of goods produced for the domestic market versus those produced for the foreign market?
(f) Does production for the domestic market support exporting activities (through differences in quality, complementary relations, cross-financing)?

3.5 Domestic Environment for Exports

(a) Characterize the domestic environment for exports in terms of export licencing, the tax system, incentives for exports, availability of credit for exports, and availability of insurance.
(b) Are there impediments to get the necessary inputs? Is there preferential treatment when purchasing inputs for exports?
(c) What is the impact of government regulation on the choice whether to export or not, or for the choice of product?
(d) Do good relations with state administration help much when arranging export deals?

3.6 The Foreign Environment for Exports

(a) What is the relationship between your foreign customers, mediators, and your firm?
(b) Who are your competitors abroad?
(c) How do you collect information about your foreign markets?

(d) Are foreign regulations impeding exports? If so how (directly through tariffs and quotas or indirectly through quality standards, dumping regulations, or health standards)?
(e) How much do conditions of payment by foreign partners affect your decision to export?
(f) Have the Europe (Association) Agreements of your country (if applicable) affected your choice of imports or your choice of targeted markets?
(g) How is the market structure of foreign markets affecting your export performance?
(h) Is your firm a joint venture or a fully foreign-owned company? If so, how does your foreign partner's presence affect:
    a. Your financial situation?
    b. Your access to foreign markets?
    c. Your access to inputs, especially high technology inputs?
    d. Retraining firm workers with more efficient techniques?

Part I

Country Studies

Chapter 1

Bulgaria

Rumen Dobrinsky and Ira Yaneva

Competitive export performance and export expansion are correctly considered vital for successful economic transformation in the countries of Central and Eastern Europe. These developments are particularly important for small transition economies whose domestic markets have limited capacity and are not sufficient to support domestic producers aiming at competitive advantages based on economies of scale and economies of scope. Thus, successful adjustment of Central and East European producers to the highly competitive international economic environment is crucial for economic recovery and overcoming the transitional shocks.

Bulgaria belongs to those small transition economies that experienced the strongest shocks of transition and the deepest transitional depression. The high dependence on former Council for Mutual Economic Assistance (CMEA) markets made its large producers extremely vulnerable to the external shock associated with the loss of these markets. Thus, unlike the Central European countries that have managed to reorient considerable portions of their trade flows to new markets and have almost recovered the levels of their pre-transition export flows, Bulgaria's exports are still at about half the level they were in the late 1980s.

This indicates the existence of serious impediments to Bulgarian exports during the transition period. These barriers stem from different sources such as the inherited trade specialization of the country, its geographical location and natural endowments, its macroeconomic situation and the economic policies pursued in the transition period, as well as the process of enterprise reform and microeconomic adjustment.

This chapter addresses issues related to Bulgarian export performance during the transition period and the effective obstacles to export expansion on macro and micro levels. Part of the study concentrates on impediments to exports faced by Bulgarian exporters as they are viewed by the companies themselves. This part of the study is based on a sample survey of some 18 Bulgarian enterprises.

The results confirm that Bulgarian producers still face significant export barriers, many of which are of domestic origin. This creates serious challenges for Bulgarian economic policy in the next phase of the transformation process.

1.1 Economic Transition and Restructuring of Bulgarian Exports

Since the economic transformation began, the Bulgarian economy has gone through a period of severe turmoil. The transitional depression was combined with high macroeconomic instability (see *Table 1.1*). Although this was a common feature for all countries in transition, it is worth noting that the magnitude of the decline (especially in the manufacturing branches and in trade) and the level of inflation in Bulgaria were much higher than, say, in the transition countries of Central Europe. Systemic transformation also proceeded more slowly: some major reforms such as privatization suffered substantial delays. The inherited economic structure and macroeconomic imbalances contributed to Bulgaria's transitional difficulties, which were exacerbated by inconsistent economic policies, political instability, and low credibility of policy making in general.

The domestic difficulties in Bulgaria were combined with a foreign debt crisis. Sluggish economic performance in the late 1980s, incompetence, and mismanagement of foreign borrowing brought about the accumulation of large foreign debt with an unfavorable maturity structure. In March 1990, the Bulgarian authorities abruptly and unilaterally suspended the servicing of the foreign debt. This decision undermined international confidence in Bulgaria and limited the potential sources of external financing to support economic reform and exports.

In the first phase of the transition, Bulgarian trade underwent substantial restructuring. The most dramatic changes took place in the geographical orientation of trade flows (*Table 1.2*). In the 1980s, Bulgarian trade was heavily concentrated in CMEA markets, which accounted for some 80–85% of Bulgarian exports and some 75% of imports. By this measure, Bulgaria was much more dependent on CMEA trade than any other former CMEA member country and thus more vulnerable to external shocks. The disintegration of the CMEA was a severe blow to the country's economy. When the countries of the region turned to trade in convertible currencies at world market prices, Bulgarian exporters were no longer competitive

Table 1.1. Selected macroeconomic indicators in Bulgaria (average annual rate of change, in percent unless otherwise indicated).

Indicator	1990	1991	1992	1993	1994	1995[a]
Gross domestic product (GDP)	–9.1	–11.7	–7.3	–1.5	1.8	2.6
Gross industrial output	–16.7	–22.2	–15.9	–10.9	8.5	5.4
Total employment	–6.2	–13.0	–8.1	–1.6	0.6	2.1
Employment in industry	–9.0	–25.3	–13.3	–8.3	–4.7	–1.1
Unemployment rate (percent of labor force, end of period)	1.7	11.1	15.2	16.4	12.8	11.1
Consumer prices (annual average)	23.8	338.5	91.3	72.9	96.2	62.2
Industrial producer prices	14.7	296.5	55.9	26.9	75.0	52.7
Average wages and salaries[b]						
Nominal	31.8	167.7	102.3	53.6	49.2	51.7
Real	6.5	–39.0	5.8	–11.2	–24.0	–6.5
Money supply (M1)	24.0	24.2	40.7	27.3	55.5	43.6
Money supply (broad money)	16.1	118.0	52.5	53.1	78.6	39.6
Budget deficit ("-" surplus) (percent of GDP)	4.9	3.6	5.7	11.0	6.2	6.7
Central interest rate (annual compound rate, percent)	4.5	56.5	58.2	58.1	81.8	59.8
Average short-term lending interest rate of commercial banks (annual compound rate, percent)	n.a.	67.8	74.0	78.3	102.6	79.8
Merchandise exports (mln. US$)	5266	3279	3499	3721	3985	5112
Merchandise imports (mln. US$)	5482	2647	3453	4757	4185	5053
Trade balance (mln. US$)	–216	632	46	–1036	–199	59
Exchange rate (leva/US$, period average)	n.a.	16.7	23.3	27.6	54.2	67.1

[a]Preliminary.
[b]Excluding private sector.
Note: n.a. = Not available.
Sources: Bulgarian National Statistical Institute; Bulgarian National Bank; authors' calculations.

in these markets and started to lose many of their positions. In 1991, the year that marked the steepest drop in the country's trade, total Bulgarian exports plunged to 46% of their 1988 level and total imports contracted to 34% of their 1988 level (calculated in current US dollars). In subsequent years trade recovered slightly, but still remained far below previous levels (see *Table 1.1*).

Since 1990, trade with former CMEA countries has been declining systematically in both absolute and relative terms (with the most dramatic drops occurring in 1991 and 1992); in 1995 it made up just 20.5% of exports and 37.5% of imports. The still relatively high import share is exclusively due to energy imports from

Table 1.2. Geographical orientation of Bulgarian trade (distribution in percent).[a]

Destination/origin	1988	1989	1990	1991	1992	1993	1994	1995
Exports								
Former CMEA	82.6	84.0	80.5	55.1	27.5	23.7	22.5	20.5
EU	4.6	5.5	5.0	15.7	29.4	28.2	35.6	37.2
EFTA	1.3	1.5	1.5	3.4	3.7	3.0	2.7	1.6
Others	11.5	8.7	13.0	25.8	39.4	45.1	39.2	40.6
Total[b]	100.0	100.0	100.0	100.0	100.0	100.0	100.0	100.0
Imports								
Former CMEA	75.3	73.7	76.4	46.8	33.9	38.5	37.0	37.5
EU	9.7	10.3	9.6	20.7	31.1	29.8	32.8	38.1
EFTA	3.6	3.9	3.2	7.8	6.0	8.2	6.2	1.8
Others	11.4	12.1	10.8	24.7	29.0	23.6	24.1	22.7
Total[b]	100.0	100.0	100.0	100.0	100.0	100.0	100.0	100.0

[a]Based on official exchange rates before 1991.
[b]Discrepancies due to rounding may exist.
Source: Bulgarian National Statistical Institute.

Russia. At the same time, the relative importance of other trading partners – most notably the member countries of the Organisation for Economic Co-operation and Development (OECD) and neighboring Balkan countries – increased substantially. However, it must be noted that this growth was mainly in relative terms: the absolute levels of the trade flows to and from these groups of countries did not change dramatically. Thus, for example, Bulgarian exports to European Union (EU) countries increased from US$853.8 million in 1988 to US$1,903.6 million in 1995; however, this increment was much smaller than the drop in exports to Eastern markets.[1] Indeed, Bulgaria managed to reorient only a small portion of its former CMEA exports to new markets; the bulk of these sales were simply lost to Bulgarian producers, and this was one of the worst shocks to the Bulgarian economy.

The changes in the geographical orientation of Bulgarian exports are most visible when looking at the changes in the list of the country's 10 largest export markets (*Table 1.3*). With the exception of Russia, which is still the largest Bulgarian export market (although its share has plunged substantially), the 1995 ranking is completely different from the ranking in 1988. Perhaps the most striking feature is the emergence of small Macedonia as the third largest market for Bulgaria. This fact has to be assessed vis-à-vis the war in former Yugoslavia and the United Nations sanctions imposed on rump Yugoslavia (Serbia and Montenegro). Obviously, the final destination of these exports was the other republics of former Yugoslavia.

Table 1.3. The 10 largest Bulgarian export markets, 1988 and 1995 (export shares in percent of total Bulgarian exports).

1988		1995	
Country	Export share	Country	Export share
1. USSR	62.5	1. Russia	10.1
2. GDR	5.2	2. Germany	8.5
3. Czechoslovakia	4.6	3. Macedonia	8.3
4. Poland	4.1	4. Italy	8.2
5. Iraq	2.7	5. Turkey	7.3
6. Libya	2.3	6. Greece	6.9
7. Hungary	2.0	7. Ukraine	3.6
8. Romania	2.0	8. USA	3.0
9. Cuba	1.8	9. France	2.9
10. FRG	1.0	10. Spain	2.5
Total top 10	88.2	Total top 10	61.3

Source: Bulgarian National Statistical Institute.

Table 1.4. Commodity composition of Bulgarian trade (in percent).

Commodity group	1988	1989	1990	1991	1992	1993	1994	1995
Exports								
Foods	14.3	14.7	15.0	21.0	21.0	17.4	18.6	18.1
Raw materials	5.5	6.1	7.5	7.0	5.7	8.1	8.1	7.5
Energy	4.4	4.6	2.4	0.7	4.3	8.7	6.8	6.1
Manufactures	75.8	74.7	75.1	71.2	69.0	65.8	66.6	68.3
All goods	100.0	100.0	100.0	100.0	100.0	100.0	100.0	100.0
Imports								
Foods	6.4	8.1	5.1	7.5	6.6	8.2	9.0	7.1
Raw materials	13.8	12.4	10.9	10.9	4.6	5.1	7.1	7.2
Energy	23.0	23.7	25.2	49.7	36.7	38.3	29.6	28.9
Manufactures	56.8	55.8	58.8	31.9	52.1	48.5	54.3	56.9
All goods	100.0	100.0	100.0	100.0	100.0	100.0	100.0	100.0

Sources: Bulgarian National Statistical Institute; authors' calculations.

It can be expected that, after the lifting of the sanctions following the Dayton Peace Agreement, Macedonia will lose this position.

At the aggregate level, the commodity composition of Bulgarian trade did not change dramatically over this period (*Table 1.4*).[2] However, the aggregate figures tend to disguise important restructuring that took place in the trade flows to and from different markets. In past decades there was little (if any) opportunity to substitute Bulgarian manufacturing exports produced for Eastern markets for those produced for Western markets. The technical and quality standards of products going to Western countries were completely different from those of products going to CMEA markets. This discrepancy and the lack of managerial and marketing skills were major obstacles to reorienting former CMEA trade flows to other markets. Basically, overcoming these obstacles requires a complete restructuring of the whole production process, starting from the technologies and the fixed assets and ending with the retraining of the work force. In view of the investments required, this turned out to be an insurmountable problem, at least on a large scale.

Large flows of exports of manufactures in mechanical and electrical engineering, electronics, industrial chemicals, processed foods, and other sectors that had been directed to former CMEA markets simply vanished, and these industries will probably never recover. Agriculture was badly damaged by the clumsy and inconsistent agrarian reform in the country; the exports of agricultural products declined also in absolute terms. Only a small number of industries, such as clothing, footwear, and some industrial chemicals, were able to reorient their sales to other (mainly Western) markets.

The available data are still too scarce to permit thorough analysis of the scale of trade restructuring and the changes in the composition of Bulgarian export flows that have taken place since the start of the transition. Such analysis is possible, though, where consistent mirror statistics exist, such as the statistics collected by the EU (*Table 1.5*). Among the important changes in the composition of Bulgarian exports to the EU, one should note the dramatic increase of the export shares of clothing and leather products whereas other sectors, such as food and agricultural products, chemicals, and iron and steel, experienced substantial declines. Furthermore, the growth of footwear and clothing exports in recent years is mostly driven by the unprecedented growth of outward processing traffic (OPT) from Western Europe in these sectors, with Western manufacturers taking advantage of liberalized access to cheap labor in these labor-intensive branches. Moreover, exports of OPT products do not fall under the quantitative restrictions imposed by the EU in these "sensitive" sectors.

Despite the restructuring of all trade flows that has taken place since the start of the transition process, notable differences remain in the composition of Bulgarian exports going to developed market economies, to former CMEA countries, and to other markets (*Table 1.6*). Food exports still occupy significant shares in Bulgarian exports to former CMEA countries (mainly, Russia), whereas food items are not major components of the exports to other markets. The situation is similar for exports of chemicals [Standard International Trade Classification (SITC) 5]. On the other hand, the exports to OECD countries and especially to other markets are dominated by manufactures classified by material (SITC 6), in this case metals

Table 1.5. Commodity composition of Bulgarian exports to the EU, excluding fuels (in percent).

Commodity group	1988	1992	1993
Agricultural products	13.1	11.4	9.5
Raw materials	0.8	0.9	1.1
Manufactured products	84.5	87.2	88.7
Processed food	12.4	9.2	9.8
Chemicals	20.0	11.2	12.3
Leather products	1.5	6.9	8.1
Textile products	3.6	3.3	3.5
Clothing	8.7	18.9	20.0
Wood and paper	4.2	4.0	3.4
Building materials	0.7	1.3	1.7
Glass and ceramics	0.9	0.9	1.1
Iron and steel	8.4	7.7	3.5
Nonferrous metals	4.7	7.2	7.3
Mechanical engineering	8.4	6.9	7.0
Electrical engineering	3.3	3.9	4.5
Transport equipment	0.4	0.9	0.6
Other manufactures	7.4	5.1	5.9
Other	1.6	0.5	0.7
Total	100.0	100.0	100.0

Source: Lemoine, 1994.

Table 1.6. Commodity composition of Bulgarian exports by SITC commodity group (in percent).

	Total exports				Exports to major regions in 1993		
SITC commodity group	1992	1993	1994	1995	OECD	Former CMEA	Other
0 Food, live animals	12.1	9.2	9.5	8.7	7.2	12.2	8.0
1 Beverages, tobacco	10.5	9.9	9.0	9.4	7.1	17.3	2.4
2 Crude materials except fuels	6.8	6.5	7.5	6.6	7.7	5.4	5.8
3 Mineral fuels, energy	6.7	7.6	6.8	6.1	7.7	4.5	13.3
4 Animal and vegetable oils	0.4	0.7	0.5	0.9	0.5	1.0	0.2
5 Chemicals	13.0	14.8	14.8	17.1	13.3	20.8	8.2
6 Manufactures (by material)	23.0	25.6	28.2	28.8	27.2	12.3	45.5
7 Machinery, transport equip.	18.7	15.8	14.4	13.7	10.1	20.9	14.2
8 Miscellaneous manufactures	7.8	8.8	7.9	7.6	18.1	4.3	1.4
9 Other	1.0	1.1	1.3	1.2	1.0	1.1	1.1
Total	100.0	100.0	100.0	100.0	100.0	100.0	100.0

Sources: Bulgarian National Statistical Institute; authors' calculations.

Table 1.7. The top 10 items in the commodity composition of Bulgarian exports for 1994 and their shares in 1992 and 1993: ranking by commodity group (export shares in percent of total Bulgarian exports).

Commodity group	1992	1993	1994
1. Food and agricultural products	20.8	20.9	20.3
2. Metals and metal articles	15.0	18.4	18.9
3. Chemicals	14.5	16.9	12.9
4. Mineral products	8.2	9.5	10.5
5. Machinery	13.5	12.5	10.4
6. Textiles and clothing	8.0	8.6	8.0
7. Wood, pulp, and wood products	2.9	3.8	3.0
8. Footwear	2.0	2.1	2.2
9. Transport equipment	4.0	2.7	1.9
10. Articles of stone, plaster, and cement	1.7	1.4	1.5
Total 1994 top 10	90.6	96.8	89.6

Source: *Bulgarski biznes*, No. 6, 10–17 February 1995.

and metal articles, which occupy a much smaller share in exports to former CMEA countries. Exports of miscellaneous manufactures (SITC 8) also play a leading role in Bulgarian exports to OECD countries (footwear and clothing are reported in this commodity group) but have a negligible share in exports to other regions. Exports of fuels and energy (SITC 3) hold an important position in Bulgarian exports to other countries (mainly fuels exported to neighboring countries), which cannot be observed in the structure of Bulgarian exports to other regions.

In the composition of total exports, food and agricultural products are the most important commodity group in recent years (*Table 1.7*). The leading commodity group in the export structure of the 1980s – machinery (mechanical and electrical engineering and electronics) – has lost ground since the disbanding of the CMEA, and its share in the composition of exports has been declining steadily. In fact, not one commodity from this group is represented in the list of the leading Bulgarian export commodities (*Table 1.8*).

The relative importance of exports of ferrous and nonferrous metals and metal articles has been growing recently: three items from this group are among the top 10 export commodities (*Table 1.8*). Exports of chemicals (fuels and industrial chemicals) also occupy important positions on this list.

In general, after the disintegration of the CMEA, Bulgaria lost substantial amounts of exports that were highly processed and had relatively high technological content (and hence high value-added content), such as computers, electronics, and machine tools. With OECD countries becoming a leading export market, Bulgarian exports have been increasingly dominated by goods with a relatively high resource

Table 1.8. The top 10 items in the commodity composition of Bulgarian exports for 1994 and their shares in 1992 and 1993: ranking by commodity (export shares in percent of total Bulgarian exports).

Commodity	1992	1993	1994
1. Cigarettes	5.25	4.84	4.87
2. Gas oil	3.97	4.11	3.89
3. Copper anodes	1.84	1.69	2.44
4. Urea	1.94	1.43	2.01
5. Gasoline	1.77	1.92	1.92
6. Bottled wine	1.18	1.43	1.57
7. Steel rods	0.23	0.96	1.41
8. Pharmaceuticals	0.43	2.95	1.22
9. Refined-copper articles	0.40	0.53	1.18
10. Tobacco	1.96	1.42	1.10
Total 1994 top 10	18.97	21.28	21.61

Source: *Bulgarski biznes*, No. 6, 10–17 February 1995.

content and by low-skill, labor-intensive goods, which are less processed and have relatively low potential value-added content. The loss of export markets was devastating for the affected industries, which practically collapsed. The damage that was incurred by a number of large producers in the mechanical and electrical engineering branches and in electronics is of such magnitude that these companies will find it difficult to recover and survive.

1.2 Liberalization of Trade and Its Impact on Export Performance

One of the first steps in the transition was the opening up of the Central and East European economies and the liberalization of trade. In contrast to the past, when these economies were quite closed and protected, the opening up placed domestic producers in a completely different environment, exposing them thoroughly to foreign competition. Despite the market distortions that existed, the pressure of international competition became one of the strongest driving forces of enterprise reform, pushing firms to adjust their costs and prices toward competitive levels.

This process, typical for all transition economies, took place in Bulgaria as well. The liberalization of foreign trade in the country started in 1990 and 1991 when most administrative restrictions on exports were lifted and all economic agents were granted the right to perform export and import operations. The exchange rate was liberalized and internal convertibility of the lev was introduced in 1991 (based on a floating exchange rate regime). Exporters were granted the right to dispose of foreign exchange earned from export operations in accordance with their will. They could either retain the foreign exchange on convertible currency accounts or could sell it in the foreign exchange market.

Since 1990 the foreign trade regulations have undergone two major phases of change. The first reform, in 1991, amounted to a sweeping liberalization of foreign trade. However, a relatively small number of transactions at that stage were kept under state control or were closely monitored, which created certain distortions. With respect to exports, the following regulations can be considered to have had distorting and hampering effects:

- Price controls (lower limits of export prices) on certain commodities and commodity groups; in 1991 these included meat and meat products, dairy products, sawlogs, and some wood products.
- Export bans on certain commodities; these were of different duration and included crude oil, raw skins, wool and vegetable textile fibers, some cereals, vegetable oils, scrap metal, some milk products, sugar, some chemicals, and roundwood.
- Export taxes that were applied to a wide range of commodities.
- Registration requirements on exports of some commodities.

A second important change in export regulations was introduced in June 1992. A major innovation of the new system was that it eliminated the most perverse form of export restriction – the export ban – and replaced it with more lax forms of control. Also, the range of direct price controls over exports was limited to specific commodities. As a general rule, the system treats all goods as freely tradable, with the exception of certain goods that are subject to regulation. Among the instruments applied to perform this regulation are the following:

- A subset of commodities is subject to mandatory registration (in principle it cannot be an obstacle to exporting but the procedure is rather bureaucratic and time consuming); included in this subset are live animals, dairy products, vegetable oils, wine and alcoholic beverages, fuels and electricity, and ferrous and nonferrous metals.
- A subset of commodities is subject to export licensing; this subset includes tobacco and tobacco products, precious metals, roundwood, scrap ferrous and nonferrous metals, antique pieces of art, pharmaceuticals, radioactive materials, and explosives.
- A further subset comprising mainly agricultural commodities is subject to domestically set export quotas; included in this subset are live animals for breeding, wine grapes, wheat and wheat flour, sunflower and sunflower oil, and raw hides and skins.

- A number of commodities are subject to export price controls through set lower limits on export prices: this group includes live animals, meat, cheese, sunflower seeds, wool, and fuelwood.
- In 1992 the export quotas were replaced by export taxes on the same commodities.

The basic philosophy of the 1992 reform is still valid, but some changes were introduced in 1993, 1994, and 1995. These changes affect the scope of the application of the different controls (effectively including or excluding certain commodities from regulation). In reality, it has been the practice of every government in office during this period to announce before the start of each calendar year which goods would be subject to regulation in that year and what type of regulations would apply. Moreover, ad hoc modifications of these regulations have often been instituted in the course of the year.

Generally, subsequent changes in export regulations have tightened controls, not loosened them. Thus the authorities have practiced so-called temporary bans on exports of some commodities (e.g., wheat). The number of goods subject to registration and licensing has increased to include the following additional commodities: grains, tobacco and tobacco products, and textiles in 1994; and meat, sunflower seeds, and sunflower oil in 1995.

In 1994 and 1995 the lists of goods subject to export taxes were also expanded to include a wider range of grains and flour, wood and wood products, and copper products. However, the 1995 regulation removed wines and other alcoholic beverages from the list.

What appear to be most problematic for exporters (and this is confirmed by the survey results reported in the following sections) are the lack of long-term, stable export regulations and the government's substantial *de facto* discretionary power to impose ad hoc changes in the regulations. This situation creates great uncertainties and risks for exporters as negotiated deals may fail or become unprofitable if a sudden change in the rules is introduced in the course of their implementation. In turn, these risks impede the establishment of longer-term business relations and contacts between companies and drive producers and exporters to make mainly short-term contracts.

Instability also features in import regulations. As imports are vital for many producers in a small economy (who in turn export their products), this reinforces the trade uncertainties and risks and places producers in a rather unfavorable situation. In the final run, it reduces their competitive position vis-à-vis their competitors on foreign markets.

1.3 Supply Constraints and Domestic Impediments to Exports

1.3.1 An overview

Enterprises' incentives or disincentives to export are instituted either by the macroeconomic and microeconomic environment or by economic policy measures. In general both these groups of factors have had a negative impact on the export performance of Bulgarian enterprises in recent years.

The country's continuing macroeconomic instability (see *Table 1.1*) is a factor that adversely affects all aspects of economic activity, including exports. The most painful implication of the persistent high inflation for enterprises is the monetary austerity that has dominated monetary policy in Bulgaria recently. The monetary restrictions, continuously pursued by the Bulgarian National Bank, result in a scarcity of credit resources and in excessively high interest rates, which effectively depress all types of business activity.

One negative feature of the Bulgarian macroeconomic stance is the relatively large gap between consumer and producer prices (*Table 1.1*). Although this phenomenon is common for many transition economies, its magnitude in Bulgaria is probably higher than in the other countries, with further serious negative implications.[3] The problem is that the central bank tunes the central interest rate to the dynamics of consumer prices; subsequently, the gap between producer and consumer prices translates into highly positive interest rates, which create an effective barrier to enterprise borrowing. Thus, in 1993 the average *ex post* real interest rate for short-term credit extended to industrial producers (deflated by the average official industrial producer prices) was 40.5% (see *Table 1.1*); of course, this rate depended on whether the reported producer price index had correctly measured producer price dynamics. In 1994 and 1995 it dropped substantially to 15.8% and 17.7%, respectively, but these levels still create serious financial burdens for producers.

The situation was also aggravated by the large budget deficit (see *Table 1.1*). Intensive government borrowing has pushed interest rates up further and has crowded out potential corporate sector borrowers.

The floating exchange rate regime in effect since 1991 also seems to have adversely affected export performance. Due to macroeconomic instability, the exchange rate in the country in this period has been excessively volatile. Because of low foreign exchange reserves, the central bank has not been in a position to set specific exchange rate targets or to maintain certain bands of fluctuation of the currency. Thus, the dynamics of the exchange rate have been practically unpredictable for the economic agents, even for fundamental movements. Under these circumstances, all exporters (as well as importers) take on serious exchange rate risks, especially when undertaking transactions that require essentially longer payment periods. This high risk (which was confirmed in practice by several currency crises) has effectively reduced the scope and intensity of a number of trade transactions.[4]

Economic policy in this period has been practically neutral toward exporters. Since the start of the transition no policy measure has been initiated or implemented that aims at stimulating export performance.[5] In principle this can be considered a "healthy" policy approach, aiming at increasing the international competitiveness of local producers. However, for these local producers it was coupled with the sudden loss of traditional markets, lack of experience and skills for operating in competitive international markets, and severe depression in domestic markets. Moreover, the institutional market infrastructure in the country was and still is underdeveloped. No specialized export crediting institutions exist to provide conventional export credit, and there are no institutions for export insurance, let alone export guarantees by the state. Of course, as has already been mentioned, the Bulgarian budget has also experienced serious problems and the amount of public finance that could potentially be allocated for such purposes has been rather limited.

Nevertheless, Bulgarian exporters have been trying to gain access to new markets, competing with producers who are much better positioned in terms of institutional support and, in some cases, in terms of export stimuli, providing them with certain competitive advantages.

The lack of a system for settling bilateral payments between entities in the former socialist countries has created serious barriers to trade between them. This was especially detrimental to Bulgarian exporters because of the former large share of the CMEA market. In 1991 and 1992, Bulgarian and Russian authorities attempted to find a partial solution to the payments problem by signing a clearing agreement that covered the mutual exchange of listed commodities. But Bulgaria has had painful experiences with the implementation of this agreement. At first it was decided to apply the current US dollar market rate to settle the payments with the local entities. This decision motivated many Bulgarian companies to start exporting. However, the clearing imports were irregular and sometimes long delayed. Within several months, Bulgaria had accumulated a substantial positive trade balance, which started to exert strong pressure on the budget. Faced with the impossibility of finding a more reasonable solution, the Bulgarian authorities cut the clearing dollar exchange rate drastically. This measure led to losses for most of the Bulgarian exporters and discouraged further expansion of exports to Russia.

In addition, Bulgarian exporters had to face the adverse consequences of the unilateral suspension of the servicing of the country's foreign debt. As a result Bulgaria, and all Bulgarian entities, fell into almost complete financial isolation, losing access to all sources of international finance including access to short-term export-crediting facilities.

On the whole the Bulgarian economy was not well prepared for the rapid liberalization of trade. Although liberalization was more or less symmetric in exports and imports (or perhaps more restrictive in imports), supply adjusted more slowly than demand. A number of systemic factors limited the possible speed of adjustment of enterprises to the competitive pressures introduced through the opening up of the economy. Some of the factors that impeded the process of market-oriented restructuring are the loss of former CMEA markets, disturbances in the supply of some inputs, the lack of marketing and managerial skills, the malfunctioning of the imperfect domestic markets, distortions in managerial motivation, and general resistance to change. Moreover, the sudden influx of foreign competitors on the domestic market drove out some producers and thus also adversely affected overall export performance.

The introduction of the value-added tax (VAT) in 1994 and, more specifically, the mechanics of its collection created another shock for specialized export companies. The newly introduced regulation requires exporters acting as intermediaries (not the producers themselves) to prepay the VAT due on the exported goods. After the successful completion of the export transaction, such exporters are entitled to reclaim the sum of the prepaid VAT. However, the actual procedure for reclaiming the VAT on exported goods is rather cumbersome and slow and is subject to bureaucratic obstacles. In practical terms, it may be several months before the exporters get back the tax advance (if at all). In fact, this is equivalent to the enforcement of an involuntary credit to the budget by the exporting firms at zero interest rate. At the current level of interest rates in the country, these companies incur huge losses. This regulation has effectively driven many, mainly small exporters out of business.

The macroeconomic and microeconomic conditions in Bulgaria at the moment appear rather hostile toward exporters. For example, recent studies (Dobrinsky, 1994b, 1995) have shown that some 50–55% of Bulgarian manufacturing exports going to EU countries are affected by "discouraging" domestic market distortions, stemming from regulations, institutional rigidities, underdeveloped markets, and the like. In turn, the daunting situation of exporters has a serious negative impact on overall economic performance.

1.3.2 Evidence from case studies

The domestic factors affecting and impeding export performance have been analyzed on the basis of a survey of 18 Bulgarian exporting firms. Although limited in size, the sample has been selected to represent different categories of firms by several criteria such as sector of economic activity, ownership, legal status, and size (see *Table 1.9*). In selecting the companies for the survey, the goal was to find a representative cross section of the overall structure of the population of Bulgarian exporting firms.

The firms selected were surveyed on the basis of a uniform interview. Not all firms approached agreed to take part in the survey, so the survey covers only companies that responded positively to this request. It is normal to expect that companies with serious problems in their performance are more likely to refuse to take part in such a survey; therefore, there is some danger that the survey may be biased toward firms that are relatively better off.

Also, it must be emphasized that the survey covers only companies that are currently actively involved in export activities. By definition, this excludes enterprises that may have been active exporters in the past (to CMEA markets) but have stopped due to the loss of traditional markets. While it is not feasible to analyze the current export performance of such enterprises (although some of them may still be considered as potential exporters), it should be borne in mind that it is exactly firms in this category that face the greatest obstacles and impediments to exports at present.

We now turn to the survey results related to the domestic impediments to exports (a summary of the responses is presented in *Table 1.10*). The companies surveyed identified 10 groups of domestic obstacles to their export performance. The four most commonly listed domestic impediments are financial squeeze generated by monetary austerity (indicated by 61% of the respondents); the uncertainties and risks inherent in the Bulgarian business environment (39%); the lack of institutional support for exporters such as export insurance or export guarantees (33%); and bureaucratic hindrances related to the implementation of regulation procedures (28%).

The financial squeeze appears as the single most important domestic impediment to Bulgarian exporters. Its negative effect takes a variety of forms. The most commonly listed negative impact of the monetary austerity is the high cost of credit, which raises total business costs and distorts the cost structure of the firms (as reported by companies B7, B10, B11, B13, B15, and B16). This financial burden reduces the firms' competitiveness vis-à-vis their competitors in foreign markets.

Apart from being costly, bank credit in Bulgaria is difficult to access for Bulgarian companies because of the banks' selective and restrictive credit policies (at least, this appears to be the perception of the enterprises surveyed). The difficult access to credit for working capital blocks the day-to-day business activities of the enterprises, and they are not able to operate at full capacity even if they have markets for their output (reported by companies B1, B3, B5, B7, and B16). Some

Table 1.9. Profiles of the companies covered in the survey.

Company	Sector	Ownership[a]	Legal status[b]	Size[c]	Export/ sales ratio (%)	Main markets
B1	Trade	S	SOE	M	40–45	UK, USA, Japan, Canada, Australia
B2	Mechanical eng.	S	LLC	M	65–70	Germany, Italy, Greece, Turkey, Algeria, Chile
B3	Clothing	S	JSC	L	95	Netherlands, UK, France, other EU
B4	Clothing	S	LLC	M	65	Germany
B5	Electrical eng.	P	P	M	20	Russia, Poland, Macedonia
B6	Trade	S	LLC	S	60–75	Russia, Turkey, Germany, Czech Republic, Netherlands
B7	Trade	P	LLC	S	95	Russia, Italy, Macedonia, Albania
B8	Trade	P(JV)	LLC	S	100	Balkan countries
B9	Trade	P	LLC	S	100	Poland, Czech Republic, Balkan countries, Ukraine, Slovakia, Hungary
B10	Chemical ind.	M(P,S)	LLC	S	10	India, Ukraine, Jordan, Syria, Morocco, Italy
B11	Timber ind.	S	LLC	M	80	Germany, other EU
B12	Mechanical eng.	S	JSC	M	70	Russia, Ukraine, Albania, Macedonia, Kazakhstan
B13	Textile ind.	S	JSC	L	35–40	Germany, Italy, Greece, Syria, Hungary
B14	Metal products	S	JSC	L	25–30	Western Europe
B15	Textile ind.	S	LLC	M	95	Germany, Italy
B16	Footwear ind.	S	JSC	M	80	UK, Canada, USA, Russia, Germany, Arab countries
B17	Chemical ind.	S	JSC	L	90	China, India, Romania, Brazil, Greece, Turkey, Macedonia
B18	Tourism	S	JSC	M	70	Germany, Italy, UK, USA

[a]S = State owned; P = Private; M = Mixed ownership; JV = Joint venture with foreign participation.
[b]JSC = Joint-stock company; LLC = Limited liability company; SOE = Unincorporated state-owned enterprise; P = Partnership.
[c]L = Large (>1000 employees); M = Medium-size (50–1000 employees); S = Small (<50 employees).

Table 1.10. Survey results on domestic impediments to exports. An X denotes a major impediment indicated by the responding company.

Company	1	2	3	4	5	6	7	8	9	10
B1	X	X	X	X		X				
B2		X	X					X		
B3	X									
B4									X	
B5	X	X								
B6				X		X				
B7	X		X		X	X				
B8		X	X		X					
B9			X			X				X
B10	X						X		X	
B11	X						X			
B12		X								
B13	X									
B14		X					X			
B15	X								X	
B16	X						X			
B17	X		X			X		X		
B18	X		X							

1 = Financial squeeze; 2 = Lack of export insurance/guarantees; 3 = Uncertain local environment; 4 = Heavy VAT regulations; 5 = Restrictive export regulations; 6 = Bureaucratic practices; 7 = Difficult access to inputs; 8 = Transportation problems; 9 = Lack of marketing skills; 10 = Slow payments.

enterprises report hampered access to new credit because of the accumulation of bad loans (B3, B7, B15, and B17).

The credit crunch negatively affects the future competitive positioning of Bulgarian companies as well. Many enterprises are equipped with obsolete fixed assets and use outdated technologies, which reduces their competitiveness in international markets. However, under the current situation, they are not able to raise and/or service the long-term financing necessary for modernizing their productive capacities (reported by companies B5, B13, B17, and B18).

It is necessary to mention here one additional deterrent to investment. High inflation and the high level of nominal interest rates imply a penalizing repayment scheme for the borrowers, because relatively large shares of *de facto* real repayment of the principal have to be carried out at early stages of the repayment period. This would put a very heavy cash burden on the borrowers, which most Bulgarian companies are not able to bear.

The economic and political uncertainties and the business risks associated with them also encourage short-term thinking. Moreover, some enterprise managers are quite uncertain about their future positions in the firm, which further shortens their planning horizons (reported by companies B1, B2, and B18). Short-term thinking erodes the competitive position and the export potential of the companies.

The lack of stable export regulations is particularly detrimental to specialized trading companies, and this is reflected in the survey results (reported by companies B7, B8, and B9). Trading companies build their profiles by specializing in certain commodity groups. Any ad hoc decision concerning the export regulation of such commodities changes the operating conditions of the exporters and creates additional risks for them. The normal business response to alleviate this risk is to avoid long-term commitments. However, the practical result for the exporters is that they lose market shares in the markets of long-term contracts.

The lack of a proper system of export risk-sharing bodies (such as export credit agencies and institutions for export insurance or export guarantees) has a similar negative impact on exporters (reported by companies B1, B2, B5, B8, B12, and B14), who are left to take all the risks. In this situation a strategy to reduce risk inevitably leads to missed opportunities and a loss of market shares. However, the alternative strategy of taking all the export risks increases the chances of failures and bankruptcies.

It is interesting to note that only a relatively small number of companies complained of the actual restrictive character of the export regulations. The Bulgarian firms appear to be more dissatisfied with the frequent changes in these regulations, as well as with the bureaucratic obstacles emerging in their practical implementation (reported by companies B1, B6, B7, B9, and B17). It is a well-known phenomenon that in an institutionally weak environment the enforcement of regulations provokes corrupt behavior. Although one cannot possibly expect to reveal from this type of survey the extent of corruption in the administration of export regulation, it would not be unreasonable to guess that at least some of the complaints of bureaucratic obstacles are related to the existence of corruption.

Two other domestic impediments to exports highlighted in the survey seem to be Bulgarian specialities: difficult access to inputs (reported by companies B10, B11, B14, and B16) and local transportation problems (reported by companies B2 and B17). Difficult access to inputs is reported mostly where inputs traditionally supplied locally have been affected by transitional changes. In some cases the output of these products has dropped substantially, as has happened with many agricultural products. In other cases local suppliers have switched to other markets and in particular to exports driven not so much by higher prices (sometimes even lower prices are accepted) as by the higher reliability of the payments. The transitional depression drained the enterprises' resources; the firms went into arrears in their payments to many suppliers and so the response of the suppliers was to stop deliveries.

The transportation problems reported by the enterprises are related to the poor infrastructure in the country and the unreliability of some freighters. The latter refers especially to the state railways, which enjoy a monopolistic position and do not provide high-quality service. Some exporters complain of substantial delays in local transportation that erode their competitive positions and cause losses.

The survey confirms that OPT is an important factor determining export performance in recent years. The two clothing companies surveyed (companies B3 and B4) export almost exclusively OPT products; OPT is also present in the exports of the textile and footwear companies (companies B13, B15, and B16). Although the positive impact of OPT for such companies is clear, it should be kept in mind that it also has a displacement effect on other local industries, because OPT imposes on the companies inputs that they might otherwise have demanded from local suppliers.

1.4 Demand Constraints and Foreign Impediments to Exports

1.4.1 An overview

The opening up of the economy provided Bulgarian producers and exporters with a number of new opportunities for marketing their output. At the same time they had to face some serious challenges, such as the extremely high competition in international markets and the rapid changes of market conditions. They also soon realized that even in mature market economies markets are far from perfect. Protective regulation, barriers to entry, deficiencies, and the high cost of relevant information are some of the distorting market imperfections that still feature in international trade, even in developed market economies.

After the collapse of the CMEA, Bulgarian exporters turned to obvious alternative markets – Western Europe and neighboring countries. Due to its capacity, the EU rightfully had high priority in the trade reorientation that was taking place. However, Bulgaria had to overcome a number of obstacles on the way to liberalizing trade relations with the EU.

The process of liberalization of the existing restrictions by the EU toward Bulgaria started with the Trade and Cooperation Agreement signed in January 1991, which granted general system of preferences treatment to a range of Bulgarian commodities. A further, more significant step was the Association Agreement with the EU, which was finalized in December 1992 after six rounds of negotiations and signed officially in Brussels on 8 March 1993.[6] Similar to agreements with other Central and East European countries, this agreement provides for a period of gradual abolishment of most of the existing EU barriers to Bulgarian exports to the EU till 1997–1998. Later, at the Copenhagen summit in June 1993, the EU decided to accelerate this process and granted further concessions to the associated countries (see UN ECE, 1994, p. 152).

Despite the generally liberal spirit of the trade part of the Association Agreement, the few remaining restrictions create serious impediments for some Bulgarian exporters. Agricultural producers and exporters find themselves in a disadvantageous situation as agricultural products are not envisaged for free trade under the Association Agreement.[7] Since the EU expansion in 1995 the situation has deteriorated further, as Austria used to be a major export market of Bulgarian agricultural products.

In trade of manufactured goods, the remaining restrictions are few in number but cover some very important Bulgarian export items (such as steel, textiles, and clothing), which are regarded as "sensitive" in the EU. For example, it has been estimated that in 1991 about 40% of Bulgarian manufacturing exports (in value terms) to EU countries were negatively affected by EU protection measures, most of which were related to "sensitive" goods (Dobrinsky, 1994b). Although the trade barriers were eased somewhat with the Association Agreement, they still negatively affect a significant portion of Bulgarian exports to EU countries, as the "sensitive" sectors remain protected.

Moreover, the Association Agreements allow for a wide range of contingent protection measures and the past couple of years have seen a rise in such actions against Central and East European countries. Two such measures have been taken by the EU against Bulgarian exports in recent years: the antidumping procedure for imports of fertilizers in 1993 and the general suspension of imports of livestock from Eastern Europe in the spring of 1993. The most recent case of this type is the decision in December 1994 to suspend the imports of fresh poultry meat and goose liver from Bulgaria.[8] The formal reasons are the supposedly inadequate sanitary and veterinary controls in the country, but the underlying factor was probably that Bulgarian exports of goose meat and liver in 1994 exceeded the EU quota by several times.[9] In 1994–1995, Bulgaria barely escaped the initiation of an antidumping procedure for the export of steel to EU countries. But the price for this escape was a form of voluntary export restraint, resulting in the introduction in 1995 of double licensing of Bulgarian steel exports to EU countries: both by the EU and by authorized Bulgarian institutions.

An obvious reason for the drastic drop of Bulgarian exports to former CMEA countries is the lack of suitable payment mechanisms. However, there are other obstacles as well. In December 1992, the Visegrád countries signed the Central European Free Trade Agreement (CEFTA) and started to liberalize trade relations among themselves almost on par with the liberalization vis-à-vis the EU. Since

January 1996 Slovenia has also been a member of CEFTA, but Bulgaria is still detached from this process. The problem for Bulgaria is not solely a matter of political will, there are other implications as well.

Finally, it is necessary to mention another specific international impediment to Bulgarian exports: the war in the Balkans and the consequent United Nations (UN) sanctions against rump Yugoslavia. Following the escalation of the war in former Yugoslavia, the United Nations Security Council imposed a comprehensive set of sanctions against the Federal Republic of Yugoslavia (FRY; Serbia and Montenegro). Among the sanctions was an effective ban against all commercial transactions with and through the FRY that lasted until the Dayton Peace Agreement of November 1995.

The sanctions had a twofold negative effect on Bulgarian exports. First, Bulgaria lost an important neighboring market. Second, and probably more damaging, the country's transportation links to Europe were disrupted, as the main transportation routes pass through the FRY. Long delays and high costs (added to transportation costs from Bulgaria that are high in general) further reduced the competitiveness of Bulgarian products in European markets. In the case of perishable goods, the transportation risks increased to such an extent that they directly affected the level of exports.

1.4.2 Evidence from case studies

A summary of the results of the survey concerning foreign impediments to exports is presented in *Table 1.11.*

One general observation is that Bulgarian enterprises have been relatively less critical of foreign impediments than domestic obstacles to exports. Enterprises seem more inclined to accept the former as something given and difficult to change, whereas the domestic environment may be more prone to remodeling.

A number of the companies surveyed indicated high competition on foreign markets as an obstacle to their exports (companies B1, B2, B3, B4, and B16). Although this perception may truly reflect the attitude of enterprise managers and the fact that Bulgarian exporters have a relatively weak competitive position in foreign markets, it cannot be seriously accepted as a barrier to exports, because competition is the essence of trade and markets in general. Such a result is more an indication of the lack of experience and marketing skills and perhaps of some misunderstanding or misperception of the fundamentals of the market economy.

The most commonly listed foreign impediment to exports is the deficiency and high cost of relevant marketing information (indicated by 39% of the respondents). This is a market imperfection equivalent to effective barriers to entry to foreign markets. It is not surprising that this problem is the most frequently cited in the

Table 1.11. Survey results on foreign impediments to exports. An X denotes a major impediment indicated by the responding company.

Company	1	2	3	4	5	6
B1				X		
B2	X		X	X		
B3	X	X		X		
B4	X		X	X		
B5						
B6	X					
B7					X	
B8						
B9	X					
B10			X			
B11			X			
B12					X	X
B13		X	X			
B14						
B15						
B16			X	X		
B17						
B18			X			

1 = Restrictive foreign regulations; 2 = UN sanctions against FRY; 3 = High cost of and difficult access to marketing information; 4 = High competition on foreign markets; 5 = Inefficient payments from former CMEA countries; 6 = Political risk (former Soviet Union).

survey. In the past, most companies were not direct exporters; trade was performed by specialized trade companies. So foreign trade as a business activity in general is a new experience for Bulgarian firms; moreover, in the transition a large number of firms had to switch to new and unfamiliar markets. Under these circumstances information and expertise in general are scarce resources.

The second most frequently quoted foreign impediment to exports is the restriction stemming from foreign regulations (28% of the respondents). Most of these respondents are referring to barriers to exports either to the EU or to the USA and Canada; in only one case is Central Europe mentioned (company B9, referring to exports of agricultural products). This may be indicative of the rather small sample, which does not cover other cases of export restrictions resulting from protectionist measures. Nevertheless, this result clearly demonstrates the burden that remaining EU trade protection places on Bulgarian exporters because it is directed at important Bulgarian export items.

One company (B2) points out the peculiar character of a new type of EU regulation due to enter into force in June 1995 that requires the licensing of the export of certain types of machinery set in motion by electrical power. As the licenses are expected to be quite expensive (and valid for three months, after which they must be renewed), this regulation will effectively cut the access of smaller producers to EU markets.

Some of the companies trading with Central and East European countries and with countries from the former USSR report difficulties in payments from these countries and uncertainties due to political factors (companies B7 and B12). The UN sanctions against the FRY were also indicated as obstacles to exports by some of the firms (companies B3 and B13) for the reasons outlined above.

The very fact that the Bulgarian enterprises continue to export to markets where they face export barriers indicates that they have probably found ways to circumvent these difficulties or to reduce their negative impact. Besides, they have the options of selecting their markets and trying to switch to other markets if they find the obstacles too great. This is not the case with most of the domestic impediments to exports, which stem from the specific macroeconomic and microeconomic conditions and environment. These problems are often beyond the enterprises' control and the companies are helpless to change the situation.

1.5 Enterprise Response to Export Barriers

The fact that enterprises report numerous impediments to their exports does not imply that export activity is totally blocked. On the contrary, Bulgarian firms currently have to search for ways to overcome existing difficulties as exports are vital for their survival. In fact, the active response of enterprises to these export barriers is an element of microeconomic restructuring and adjustment in the process of economic transformation. The macro data confirm that in the aggregate such a process of adjustment and more aggressive export behavior of enterprises has been underway in Bulgaria in recent years: the value of total Bulgarian exports has grown every year since 1991 (see *Table 1.1*).

In analyzing the enterprise responses to export barriers we must clearly distinguish impediments that are within the reach of enterprise decision making ("weaknesses") from those that are beyond their control ("threats"), as these two categories imply different types of response.[10]

When the obstacle is related to a diagnosed internal weakness of the company, the company can cope with it by taking appropriate action, which usually requires internal reorganization or restructuring. A number of Bulgarian companies have made some progress in this direction, and the results of our survey confirm this.

The most commonly listed internal weakness of the companies surveyed with respect to their export performance was poor marketing information and the lack of marketing skills. These companies are undertaking a variety of measures to overcome this weakness, such as expanding their marketing departments (reported by companies B3, B12, and B16), improving their information systems (companies B4, B6, B16, B17, and B18), promoting aggressive marketing (company B11), and training the staff (companies B4 and B18). Obviously, these activities require investment and only the large and medium-size companies can afford to follow such policies; none of the small firms reported measures of this type. Company B2, a medium-size firm, reported that it has identified the problem of poor marketing information but has not had the resources to undertake the measures it considers necessary to correct the situation.

Also, most of the enterprises surveyed reported that their export strategies are based on the establishment of long-term, stable business relations with reliable foreign clients. Some of the firms consider that they have been successful in implementing this strategy.

Unfortunately, because of the poor quality of some of the accounting data that were made available for the survey, it is not possible to analyze in detail the enterprises' measures related to internal restructuring, reduction of costs, and raising production efficiency. The fact that many of the enterprises surveyed have reported losses in the first years of the transition does not necessarily mean a lack of adjustment. Internal restructuring is usually a medium-term process that is not automatically reflected in current performance indicators.

However, it is possible to trace that on the aggregate level Bulgarian enterprises have responded actively to the changing conditions and have taken measures for internal restructuring. For example, while the cumulative decline of total industrial output in Bulgaria in the period from 1989 to 1995 amounts to 44.5%, employment in industry during the same period dropped by 48.5% (see *Table 1.1*). This shows that enterprises have been shedding excess labor on par with the output decline and even more intensively in the most recent years. At least one of the surveyed enterprises (company B18) reported, however, that it has not been able to restructure its labor force because of the insecurity of the managers' positions.

The survey results cast some light on the way Bulgarian enterprises view their competitive advantages in exports. Almost every enterprise surveyed regards its relatively low prices (resulting mainly from low labor costs) and the implied price/quality ratio as its main competitive advantage in international markets. Some firms believe that their brand names and their image as reliable partners also add to their competitive edge.

Also, one striking result of the survey is the disappearance of the gap between domestic and foreign markets in terms of the nature and quality of the products sold on these markets. In the past these markets were two clearly distinct segments and the products supplied on those segments were, as a rule, also distinctly different.

Presumably, the opening up of the economy and the liberalization of trade have made both markets almost equally competitive and have eroded the differences in consumers' demands: local customers have a variety of alternatives and are becoming almost as demanding as foreign clients. Domestic producers have been forced to adjust to this change by supplying equally competitive products to local markets.

The enterprises' responses to problems that are beyond their direct control (the "threats" to exports) are more difficult to analyze. In only two cases did the enterprises report the measures they have taken to overcome such threats. Company B2, which has been experiencing chronic local transportation problems with the railways, has redesigned the traditional packaging of its products so that it can use standard containers and alternative transportation. Company B14, which has experienced serious problems with local suppliers, recently reported that it is trying to negotiate long-term contractual agreements with some of these partners.

Several firms reported that they have advised the government and other state authorities of their export problems stemming from domestic regulation and have suggested modifications to these regulations. However, none reported a positive outcome from such moves.

Obviously the enterprises were not very cooperative in sharing some of the approaches they presumably use in trying to cope with their threats, but in principle these are known from other studies and from anecdotal evidence. A common response to the financial squeeze has been a shift to alternative sources of finance such as defaulting on some liabilities; most often this defaulting has forced banks to accumulate bad loans (see Dobrinsky, 1994a). The informal approaches to dealing with bureaucratic obstacles to exports are well known; the new private firms in Bulgaria have been especially ingenious in coping with such difficulties.

Our enterprise survey provides only a sample of the different responses of companies to export barriers. In spite of the considerable evidence of enterprise adjustment, the active measures undertaken by the enterprises should not be overstated. In the overview above we have featured those companies that have diagnosed their weaknesses and have taken some active measures to overcome them. The fact that some of the enterprises did not report weaknesses does not necessarily mean that they have no weaknesses; it may well be that the weaknesses have not been identified by the firms' managers and, accordingly, no actions have been taken. The outcome of such a passive attitude to export behavior is a reduction of the actual exports versus the potential exports, or complete discontinuation of export activities. Also, the fact that an enterprise undertakes active measures to overcome its export difficulties does not guarantee that it will be successful. Indeed, many of the companies (including the active firms) reported that their potential exports are much higher than what they actually export (or produce and export). It would not be unreasonable to suggest that this is a widespread phenomenon and that the current impediments to exports do depress the overall export performance (and thus the level of economic activity) of the country.

Also, it must be taken into account that most medium-size and large enterprises surveyed in the study (in fact all with the exception of one medium-size private firm) are still 100% state owned. Although this fairly well depicts the current structure of ownership in Bulgarian industry (where there is almost no privatization of larger enterprises), it may also reflect a certain type of enterprise behavior characteristic of state-owned enterprises. The lack of responsible owners and the weak corporate governance of the state-owned firms do not encourage entrepreneurship, and in state-owned enterprises a passive attitude to market adjustment is more likely to be tolerated than in privately owned firms.

Finally, we would like to reiterate the possibility of a bias in the sample of enterprises surveyed as the most troubled enterprises were probably less willing to be interviewed and were thus not represented in our sample.

1.6 Conclusions

Direct exposure to international competition is one of the challenges of economic transformation in Central and Eastern Europe. The Bulgarian experience with trade liberalization thus far shows mixed results. Some firms have been able to adjust and reorient a large part of their output to new markets or have found new market niches given the new opportunities of liberalized trade. Others have been able to market only relatively small shares of their output. Some enterprises have completely lost their foreign markets and seem unlikely to recover from the current depression. In general, the adjustment of the supply side in Bulgaria has been slower than was observed in other Central and East European countries. The inherited high level of dependence on CMEA markets has had a negative effect on this process.

The process of market adaptation in Bulgaria was impeded by the severe transitional depression, prolonged macroeconomic instability, and general uncertainty in the business environment in the country. Most Bulgarian enterprises operate below capacity; apart from the loss of markets this is due to protracted macroeconomic austerity. Moreover, a number of systemic risk factors exist that effectively depress export activity. In general, the results of this study suggest that the difficulties stemming from domestic macroeconomic and microeconomic problems and institutional rigidities are more serious impediments to exports of Bulgarian enterprises than the obstacles that characterize their foreign markets. Obviously, such a conclusion implies that a properly designed economic policy and further reforms can potentially bring about substantial improvements in this situation.

There is evidence that in some cases companies have adopted an active stance in trying to cope with the impediments to their export activity. Internal restructuring and adjustment could increase these firms' export capacity and flexibility. However, many difficulties are beyond the enterprises' control. In these cases, the firms must learn to live with such problems.

Notes

[1] It is not possible to present the precise dynamics of all flows in this period because pre-transition CMEA trade was denominated in transferable rubles and the Bulgarian statistical authorities have not performed a consistent revaluation of these flows.

[2] The only exception is 1991 when the drastically reduced trade volumes distorted the commodity composition.

[3] While the discrepancy has been observed statistically in a number of transition economies, there are no clear-cut and consistent explanations for it. Different interpretations have been suggested, though, which may provide partial clues to the problem. One possible factor may be the faster growth of the prices for services [included in the consumer price index (CPI) and not included in the producer price index (PPI)] compared with the dynamics of prices of industrial and agricultural goods. It has been often speculated that such a differentiation may be due to the siphoning of profits from state-owned industrial enterprises to private trading firms (through price differentials mirrored in the PPI and CPI statistics). However, although this hypothesis seems highly plausible, because of the semi-legal character of such activities there are no systematic hard facts to support it, only anecdotal evidence. Other explanations suggest that the gaps between the CPI and PPI dynamics are due to deficiencies in statistical practices and especially to the lack of experience in monitoring producer prices. The existence of a sizable shadow economy (mostly engaged in the service sector) undoubtedly contributes further to price distortions.

[4] The main policy goal of the Bulgarian National Bank has been to avoid abrupt changes in the exchange rate. However, even this policy goal has turned out to be difficult to implement, and the country has experienced several exchange rate crises. The most severe was in 1994 when the lev depreciated vis-à-vis the US dollar by about 70% in the course of two weeks.

[5] The only exception is the availability of preferential credits for agricultural producers for a limited number of seasonal activities related to the treatment of agricultural land.

[6] The actual ratification of the Association Agreement by the parliaments of all EU member states took almost two additional years; it formally entered into force 1 January 1995. However, the most important trade part was effectuated in 1994 under the Interim Trade Agreement.

[7] The only concessions on the part of the EU regarding agricultural products are certain increases in the quotas and reductions of the import tariffs.

[8] Reported in *Trud*, 27 March 1995.

[9] See *Duma*, 8 May 1995.

[10] We use here the terms adopted in strategic planning and management.

References

Dobrinsky, R., 1994a, The problem of bad loans and enterprise indebtedness in Bulgaria, *MOCT-MOST*, **4**(3):37–58.

Dobrinsky, R., 1994b, The economic interpenetration between the EC and Eastern Europe: Bulgaria, in, The Economic Interpenetration between the European Union and Eastern Europe, *European Economy*, No. 6.

Dobrinsky, R., 1995, Trade liberalization and market distortions: An assessment of Bulgarian manufacturing trade, in M. Jackson and W. Biesbrouck, eds., *Marketization, Restructuring and Competition in Transition Industries of Central and Eastern Europe*, LICOS Studies on Transitions in Central and Eastern Europe, Vol. III, Avebury, Aldershot, UK.

Lemoine, F., 1994, CEEC Exports to the EC (1988–1993): Country Differentiation and Commodity Diversification, CEPII Document de Travail No. 94-15, Centre D'études Prospectives et D'informations Internationales, Paris, France.

UN ECE (United Nations Economic Commission for Europe), 1994, *Economic Survey of Europe in 1993–1994*, UN ECE, Geneva, Switzerland.

Chapter 2

Estonia

Alari Purju

Estonia, which has a small economy and is located between West European and Scandinavian countries on one side and Russia on the other, has always offered challenges for economic development and cooperation. During its transition from a centrally planned to a market economy, Estonia's one-sided link to Eastern markets was replaced by more complex economic relationships. The inherited production capacities and general economic structure have also influenced the development of foreign economic relations. Estonia's monetary framework, a modernized currency board arrangement, has had an important impact on new international trade and exchange relations as well. The changes in geographical orientation and commodity composition of foreign trade are a result of the adjustment of the enterprises to these preconditions of development.

2.1 A Small, Open Economy

During Soviet rule, Estonia's economy was part of the all-Union production complex. Estonian enterprises typically imported raw materials from, and exported a majority of their production to, other regions of the Soviet Union. Light industry, food industry, and power engineering were developed as Estonia's specializations in the Soviet economy. Machine building and electronics were also important within the Estonian economy, but Estonian output of these commodities was of only marginal importance for the Soviet Union. Because Estonia was a border region, military industry was not concentrated there. In the 1970s Estonia started producing import substitutes for the Soviet market. Consequently, a number of enterprises were allowed, even encouraged, to purchase Western technologies. In the 1980s major investments were made to meet the transportation needs of Soviet foreign trade. The largest project was Muuga port near Tallinn. Estonian agriculture specialized in milk and meat products: a large share of its production (30–40%) was exported to the other Soviet republics.

The features of the Estonian economy were typical of an industrialized country. However, unlike developed countries, Estonia had only modest levels of infrastructure, services, and trade. The economy was relatively open. Exports formed 51% of the gross domestic product (GDP) in 1989. However, these foreign trade indicators and the apparent openness of the economy were arbitrary; production and trading partners were determined by the state plan and by distribution schedules. The producer was obliged to sell products at a fixed price and the buyer was obliged to purchase the products offered. Trading under these rules was mainly oriented toward other regions of the Soviet Union; in 1990 trade with Soviet republics accounted for 94% of Estonian exports and 82% of imports.

Economic reform in Estonia progressed simultaneously with the restoration of political independence. A detailed plan for integrated economic reform was formulated in 1989. Reform began in 1990, its first stage characterized by rapid development of business and the emergence of a number of private firms and farms. The first steps of reform were the gradual liberalization of prices in 1990 and 1991 and a significant cut in subsidies. In foreign trade, quotas and licenses were abolished in 1991 and, in principle, trade became open to every registered and licensed enterprise. These developments were also influenced by other political and economic events, especially the restoration of Estonia's independence in August 1991.

A sharp rise in the prices of raw materials took place in the Soviet Union at the beginning of 1991; this price increase significantly contributed to inflation in Estonia. At the same time, the supply of Russian natural resources to Estonia was cut for political and economic reasons. Estonia was forced to start importing fuel from Western Europe as early as 1991. The need to buy fuel at world prices and the impact of inflation in the ruble zone prevented the Estonian government from employing effective anti-inflationary measures. Adaptation to the new economic conditions was mainly confined to a rapid price increase. Annual inflation in 1991 was 303%; in 1992 it was 952%. A major price increase took place in early 1992 as prices of raw materials were liberalized in Russia.

Almost complete deregulation was accomplished in 1992. The state retained control of only the prices of energy, oil shale (the main input for producing electricity in Estonia), transport, telecommunication services, and rents.

The monetary reform that began in June 1992 was a major turning point in economic reform. The currency board arrangement and convertibility of the

Estonian kroon were introduced. The kroon's exchange rate was fixed to the Deutsche mark (1 Deutsche mark is equal to 8 kroons); this exchange rate has remained at the same level since 1992. Private individuals and enterprises can convert the kroon into foreign currencies without restriction. All transactions within Estonia must be conducted in kroons.

To establish the kroon's initial exchange rate, past rates from foreign exchange auctions were used. As a result the kroon's official rate was undervalued by a factor of seven to eight vis-à-vis the purchasing power parity (PPP) rate, which made Estonia's imports expensive, favored the export of goods and services, and provided the exchange rate of the kroon with a reserve against inflation in the domestic market.

Estonia's balance of payments has been calculated since 1992. The current and capital accounts were positive until the end of 1993; however, by 1994 the current account was negative. The positive balance of the capital account was the result of foreign direct investment [2,804 million kroons (US$230 million) during 1994 and 2,321 million kroons (US$195 million) during 1995, according to the Bank of Estonia] and foreign loans (totaling US$444.8 million, of which US$268.6 million was paid out by the end of 1995) (Ministry of Economy, 1995).

The currency board arrangement leaves few economic policy options. Flows of goods and services, money, and capital were liberalized from the start of the reform. A fundamental reason for adopting a policy based on an open economy is the small size of the domestic market (Estonia's population is only 1.5 million). Also, economic decline and the population's low purchasing power forced Estonian enterprises to export a large share of their production. Another reason for increasing exports was the kroon's undervalued (in comparison with the PPP rate) foreign exchange rate, which made Estonian labor cheap (the average monthly wage was DM 100 at the end of 1992 and DM 337 at the end of 1995), thus promoting both exports and foreign direct investments into the country.

Estonia's economic reform has not favored any one branch of the economy; the single determining factor for successful restructuring has been an enterprise's ability to adapt to economic conditions and orient itself to Western markets. This approach emerged as a consequence of the indeterminate economic situation, the sharply changing relative prices, and the rapid contraction of the Eastern market. But it was also caused by the strict monetary policy used by subsequent governments and the market-oriented economic environment this policy supported.

The most evident change in the economic environment has been the sharp decline of production in all branches of the economy, a consequence of liberalized prices and foreign economic shock. The GDP fell 3.6% in 1990, 13.6% in 1991, 14.2% in 1992, 8.6% in 1993, and 3.2% in 1994. The cumulative decline of the GDP during the period from 1990 to 1994 was 36%. The decline of industrial

Table 2.1. Selected economic indicators in Estonia.[a]

Indicator	1989	1990	1991	1992	1993	1994	1995
GDP (mln. kroons)	614	798	1,832	14,255	22,845	30,103	41,503
GDP (% real growth)	–	–3.6	–13.6	–14.2	–8.6	–3.2	2.9
Industrial output growth (%)	–	0.0	–10.0	–38.9	–27.0	–6.7	3.7
Inflation (%)[b]	4	60	303	952	35.6	41.7	28.9
Unemployment (%)[c]	0.0	0.0	0.1	1.9	2.6	2.2	1.8
Average wage (kroons)[d]	–	–	115	802	1,165	2,096	2,697
Exchange rate (kroon/DM)	–	–	–	8	8	8	8
Exports (mln. kroons)	312	262	510	5,425	10,632	16,947	21,177
Imports (mln. kroons)	381	342	445	5,069	11,891	21,535	29,109
Foreign trade balance (mln. kroons)	–69	–80	66	356	–1,259	–4,588	–7,932
Foreign trade balance GDP (%)	–11.2	–10.0	3.6	2.5	–5.5	–15.2	–19.1
Exports/GDP (%)	50.8	42.9	29.8	38.0	46.5	56.1	51.0
Current account balance (mln. kroons)	–	–	–	430.2	300.5	–2,195.6	–2,123.7
Capital account balance (mln. kroons)	–	–	–	628.1	2,952.9	2,274.1	2,992.8
Foreign currency reserves (mln. kroons)	–	–	–	2,370.4	4,488.9	5,341.1	6,541.5

[a]Recalculation of indicators from the pre-kroon period (for the period from 1989 to 1991) is based on the following exchange rate: 1 kroon is equal to 10 rubles.
[b]Retail price index for 1989; consumer price index for other years.
[c]The number of persons receiving unemployment benefits in comparison with the total number of employed and unemployed persons at the end of the year.
[d]Average monthly wage in the fourth quarter of the year.
Sources: Statistical Office of Estonia, 1992, p. 15; Statistical Office of Estonia, 1994a, p. 11; Statistical Office of Estonia, 1994b, pp. 31–32; Statistical Office of Estonia, 1995, p. 10; Statistical Office of Estonia, 1996, pp. 10–11; Bank of Estonia, 1995a, pp. 6–22; Bank of Estonia, 1995b, pp. 22–35; Rajasalu, 1992; p. 19.

production began in 1991 and was much steeper than that of the GDP. The economy appears to have stabilized during the second half of 1994; in 1995 already a 2.9% growth in the GDP and a 3.7% growth in industrial production were recorded. However, the figures published by the Statistical Office of Estonia have been strongly criticized. The Bank of Estonia, for instance, estimated some economic growth in 1994. One reason statistics underestimate real economic changes is that the number of small enterprises is increasing, and these companies can and do hide their incomes from statistical recording. Also, the Statistical Office has changed its method of calculating several indicators, which complicates a comparison of figures for different years (see figures for 1989 to 1994 in *Table 2.1*).

Estonia is overcoming the economic crisis with a notably changed economic structure. The shares of the trade, transportation, and service sectors in the production of GDP have increased rapidly. In 1989, the share of manufacturing was 35.1% of the GDP; that of agriculture (together with hunting and forestry) was 21.5%. In 1995 the shares of these branches were 14.9% and 6.7%, respectively. Trade's share of the GDP increased from 7.0% in 1989 to 16.4% in 1995; the share of financial institutions and insurance increased from 0.9% to 3.1% over the same time period. The structure of Estonia's GDP is now quite similar to the GDP structure of developed countries. However, because these structural shifts occurred during a deep economic decline, some restoration of the role of manufacturing and perhaps agriculture should be expected in the next few years.

2.2 Changing Geographical and Commodity Patterns of Foreign Trade

Dramatic changes in the development of Estonian exports started in 1992. It came as a shock when Russia introduced import duties and quotas for imports. These regulations did not substantially restrict Estonian exports to Russia, but together with difficulties with payments and transportation of goods, they caused serious problems for Estonian firms interested in trading in the Eastern market. While rapid inflation continued in Russia and most of the other Commonwealth of Independent States (CIS) countries, after monetary reform Estonia managed to stabilize its monetary system (1 kroon was equal to 10 rubles in June 1992, whereas 1 kroon was equal to 430 rubles in December 1995). Thus many Estonian goods quickly became too expensive for the Eastern market.

Geographical reorientation of exports also caused a radical change in the commodity structure of these exports. Estonia used to deliver mainly foodstuffs, consumer goods, machinery, and chemical products to the Soviet market. Because these goods were not accepted by Western consumers, exports of manufactured goods were replaced by exports of timber and wood, and base (ferrous and nonferrous) waste metals. Re-exports of metals from the East to the West and transport vehicles from the West to the East acquired remarkable positions in the export structure. Many Estonian enterprises started to work on the basis of subcontracts, mainly with Scandinavian firms, or used the product licenses of these firms. Sometimes Scandinavian traders served as intermediaries and resold Estonian products to consumers in third countries.

The structure of Estonian imports has been determined by the need to purchase from abroad fuel and other raw materials (cotton, for example, is an important input for Estonia's large textile industry). Machinery, mechanical appliances, and electrical equipment have also been important imports. In recent years fuel prices have increased rapidly in Russia and reorientation in import markets has started; however, up to now some resources have been cheaper in Russia, which keeps Estonian producers interested in Russian commodities. The trade-off between quality and price is also an important factor in this market.

Estonian foreign trade started to grow very rapidly after the 1992 monetary reform. In comparison with the previous year, the value of exports grew by a factor of 1.96 and the value of imports by a factor of 2.35 in 1993. This strong growth continued through 1994 and 1995, albeit at a slower rate. Because Estonia has had the same fixed exchange rate since 1992, this increase in foreign trade also occurred in convertible currency terms. A negative development is the increasing foreign trade deficit, which made up 19.1% of the GDP in 1995. However, until the end of 1995 the foreign trade deficit and the current account deficit were covered by foreign capital inflow (see *Table 2.1*).

The *geographical pattern of Estonian foreign trade* changed substantially in 1992. Reorientation to Western markets was not easy, and most producers were not ready for it. *Finland*, encouraged by knowledge about these markets and linguistic similarities with Estonia, played an important role. In 1991 Finland's share of Estonian exports was 2.3%, with a 2.0% share of imports; in 1992 its shares increased to 21.2% and 22.6%, respectively, a remarkable shift. By 1995 Finland accounted for 21.4% of Estonian exports and 32.6% of imports. Finland has also acted as an intermediary for Estonian entrepreneurs. Several products imported from Finland are only packed or processed there (vegetables, for example), but are registered in Estonia as Finnish imports. Part of Estonia's exports are transferred from Finland to other countries. Another reason Finland's share of Estonian foreign trade is high is Finland's large number of direct investments in Estonia; nevertheless, Finland comes in second to Sweden when the value and not the number of foreign direct investment projects in Estonia is considered. Frequently, Estonian producers and traders who began looking for foreign contacts in Finland have later moved to other Scandinavian and West European countries. The leading items of Estonian exports to Finland are machinery and mechanical appliances (30.6% of Estonian exports to Finland in 1995) and textiles and textile products (25.4%). In both commodity groups, exports rely on subcontracting, where Estonian producers manufacture intermediate products for Finnish enterprises. The share in exports of base metals (mainly scrap metal) was relatively high in 1992 and 1993; however, base metals made up only 9.0% of the 1995 exports. Wood and wooden articles accounted for 15.6% of Estonian exports to Finland in 1995.

The structure of Estonian exports to *Sweden*, the third largest Estonian foreign trade partner, is similar to the structure of exports to Finland. The leading exports are machinery and mechanical appliances (30.6% of Estonian exports to Sweden in 1995) and textiles and textile products (26.2%). However, exports of wood and wood products (27.9%) have been relatively more important than in the case of Finland.

Russia's share of Estonian foreign trade declined dramatically in 1992 but has since been relatively stable. Russia accounted for 16.1% of Estonian imports and 17.5% of Estonian exports in 1995. Trade flows between Russia and Estonia are highly concentrated in certain product groups. In 1995 food products formed 33.6% and transport vehicles (mainly as re-exports) made up 18.7% of the exports to Russia. The dominant item of Estonian imports in 1995 was mineral products (mainly oil), which accounted for 48.4% of Estonian imports from Russia.

Trade with *Latvia* and *Lithuania* has been rather modest. In 1995 Latvia's share in Estonian exports was 7.6%; its share in imports was 2.0%. Electricity was Estonia's largest single export to Latvia in 1992 and 1993. In 1995 the share of electricity was smaller and the leading Estonian exports to Latvia were food products and chemicals. The share of food products exported to Latvia increased in 1994–1995 because Estonia had problems exporting food products to Russia, which has been its traditional market for foodstuffs, and because Latvia's higher prices gave an advantage to Estonian food producers and traders.

Germany has been a target for textile, wood, and metal exports; these items make up 19.3%, 16.8%, and 14.7% of exports to Germany, respectively. In 1995 Estonia mainly imported machinery and mechanical appliances and transport vehicles from Germany. Between the two World Wars, Germany was Estonia's main trading partner. Figures for different countries' shares of Estonian foreign trade are presented in *Tables 2.2* and *2.3*.

From among regional country groups and integrations, European Free Trade Association (EFTA) countries dominated Estonian foreign trade until 1994, with 30.9% of exports and 40.6% of imports in 1994 (see *Tables 2.4* and *2.5*). European Union (EU) countries accounted for 19.0% of exports and 23.8% of imports in 1994. Estonia's main trading partners, Finland and Sweden, joined the EU in January 1995; consequently, EU members' shares were as high as 53.8% of Estonian exports and 66.0% of imports in 1995.

The shares of CIS countries were 25.0% in Estonian exports and 18.8% in imports in 1995. In 1995 Estonia negotiated conditions for closer contacts with Ukraine and Belarus. On 24 May 1995 a free trade agreement between Ukraine and Estonia was signed. To some extent foreign trade relations with the other CIS countries have been a substitute for trade relations with Russia; these countries have been able to supply several natural resources and they are a good market for Estonian products. Figures for different regions' shares of foreign trade are presented in *Tables 2.4* and *2.5*.

Table 2.2. Distribution of Estonian exports by main trading partners (in percent).[a]

Trading partner	1991	1992	1993	1994	1995
Russia	56.5	20.8	22.6	23.1	17.5
Finland	2.3	21.2	20.7	17.8	21.4
Sweden	0.5	7.7	9.5	10.8	10.8
Latvia	7.7	10.6	8.6	8.2	7.6
Germany	0.2	3.9	8.0	6.8	7.2
Lithuania	3.8	1.5	3.7	5.4	4.7
Denmark	0.1	2.4	2.4	3.4	3.3
Netherlands	0.3	5.1	4.1	3.1	4.6
Ukraine	12.9	6.9	3.6	3.1	3.7
United Kingdom	0.1	0.8	1.4	2.8	3.2
Belarus	4.1	1.4	1.1	2.0	2.5
USA	0.1	1.9	1.9	1.8	2.4
Other countries	11.4	15.8	12.4	11.7	11.1
Total	100.0	100.0	100.0	100.0	100.0

[a]Based on values at current prices.
Sources: Statistical Office of Estonia, 1994a, p. 13; Statistical Office of Estonia, 1995, pp. 12–13.

Table 2.3. Distribution of Estonian imports by main trading partners (in percent).[a]

Trading partner	1991	1992	1993	1994	1995
Finland	2.0	22.6	27.9	29.9	32.6
Russia	45.9	28.4	17.2	16.8	16.1
Germany	0.8	8.3	10.7	10.0	9.6
Sweden	0.8	5.9	8.9	8.9	8.5
Netherlands	0.1	1.8	3.6	3.1	3.1
Japan	0.2	2.7	4.2	2.9	1.9
Lithuania	6.3	3.6	3.3	2.6	1.6
Denmark	0.1	1.7	2.6	2.6	2.8
USA	3.5	2.4	2.7	2.5	2.4
Italy	0.3	0.5	2.1	2.4	2.6
United Kingdom	0.1	1.2	1.5	2.1	2.2
Latvia	5.1	1.7	2.3	1.5	2.0
Other countries	34.8	19.2	13.0	14.7	14.6
Total	100.0	100.0	100.0	100.0	100.0

[a]Based on values at current prices.
Sources: Statistical Office of Estonia, 1994a, p. 13; Statistical Office of Estonia, 1995, pp. 12–13.

Table 2.4. Estonian exports by region (at current prices, in percent).

Region	1990	1991	1992	1993	1994	1995
Total distribution (mln. kroons)	262	510	5,425	10,632	16,947	21,177
Total	100.0	100.0	100.0	100.0	100.0	100.0
CIS	94.0	82.7	34.3	30.3	30.4	25.0
EFTA	–	3.0	31.2	31.4	30.9	2.6
EU	–	0.7	13.4	17.8	19.0	53.8
CEE[a]	–	11.9	16.4	14.9	15.3	13.9
Other	6.0	1.7	4.7	5.6	4.4	4.7

[a]CEE consists of Albania, Bulgaria, Poland, Romania, Hungary, the Czech Republic, Slovakia, Latvia, and Lithuania.
Sources: Statistical Office of Estonia, 1994b, pp. 220–228; Statistical Office of Estonia, 1995, p. 10; Rajasalu, 1992, p. 22.

Table 2.5. Estonian imports by region (at current prices, in percent).

Region	1990	1991	1992	1993	1994	1995
Total distribution (mln. kroons)	342	445	5,069	11,891	21,535	29,109
Total	100.0	100.0	100.0	100.0	100.0	100.0
CIS	82.0	73.3	42.5	21.6	20.4	18.8
EFTA	–	3.1	31.3	38.1	40.6	1.7
EU	–	3.1	14.4	23.2	23.8	66.0
CEE[a]	–	13.2	5.9	7.1	5.9	5.5
Other	18.0	7.3	5.9	10.0	9.3	8.0

[a]CEE consists of Albania, Bulgaria, Poland, Romania, Hungary, the Czech Republic, Slovakia, Latvia, and Lithuania.
Sources: Statistical Office of Estonia, 1994b, pp. 220–228; Statistical Office of Estonia, 1995, p. 10; Rajasalu, 1992, p. 22.

The structure of Estonia's exports by *commodity group* is presented in *Table 2.6*. Estonian exports have been led by textiles and textile products (13.5% of total exports in 1995). The single most important item was clothing (5.5% of total exports), which was exported to Finland (46% of clothing exports), Sweden, Germany, Norway, and Lithuania. A large share of these exports was made up of intermediate products subcontracted to Estonian enterprises by Finnish and Swedish firms, which subsequently processed them further.

Foodstuffs were the next largest commodity group. Canned fish was the main item in this group (5% of total exports); other important items were chocolate and other goods containing cocoa, confectioneries, and beverages and spirits.

From the machinery, mechanical appliances, and electrical equipment group (13.0% of Estonian exports in 1995), exports of electronic equipment (radios and televisions, radio and television parts, and communication equipment) were more

Table 2.6. Commodity composition of Estonian exports (in percent).[a]

HS	Commodity group	1991	1992	1993	1994	1995
I	Live animals, animal products	10.1	11.5	11.0	7.7	7.7
IV	Foodstuffs, beverages, spirits, tobacco	4.1	5.5	10.7	12.3	6.9
V	Mineral products	5.2	11.1	7.6	8.2	8.1
VI	Chemicals	11.0	7.0	4.8	6.8	7.5
IX	Wood and wood products	2.2	8.1	7.5	10.2	12.2
XI	Textiles and textile products	26.5	14.3	12.3	13.7	13.5
XV	Base metals and base-metal products	2.1	11.6	10.5	8.0	6.8
XVI	Machinery and mechanical appliances, electrical equipment	11.6	6.9	7.7	9.3	13.0
XVII	Transport vehicles	1.0	7.0	10.7	7.6	6.9
XX	Miscellaneous manufactured goods	7.5	5.8	5.1	5.4	5.7
	Other	18.7	11.2	12.1	10.8	11.7
Total		100.0	100.0	100.0	100.0	100.0

[a]The commodity classification is based on the Harmonized Commodity Description and Coding System (HS).
Sources: Statistical Office of Estonia, 1994a, pp. 15–24; Statistical Office of Estonia, 1994b, pp. 220–228; Statistical Office of Estonia, 1995, pp. 14–23.

important than exports of machinery and mechanical appliances. The principal export markets for electronic equipment were Finland, Russia, and Sweden. Computers and computer parts were also important in Estonian exports.

Wood and wood products made up 12.2% of Estonian exports in 1995. The Ministry of Economy estimated that approximately 85% of the output of this commodity group was exported. In 1994 the export of wood and wood products more than doubled compared with 1993 export levels, and this rapid growth continued in 1995 with a 49% increase. The share of processed wood increased at the expense of firewood and unprocessed wood (mainly for paper mills). Unprocessed wood made up only 37% of the exports in 1994. The export of furniture has been rather important (4.7% of total exports in 1995). In 1994 the value of furniture exports grew 66% over the 1993 level, and this growth continued with a 30% increase in 1995.

Mineral products and energy sources accounted for 8.1% of the exports. The most important items were fuels such as distilled oil products, electricity, and peat. Cement was also exported, mainly to Russia, Latvia, Denmark, Netherlands, and Ukraine.

The share of base metals diminished in Estonian exports, from 11.6% in 1992 to 6.8% in 1995. The largest component was ferrous metal, half of which was scrap iron exported mainly to Germany and Finland. One-third of the ferrous metal consisted of rolled metal leaf exported mainly to Finland and Belgium.

Transport vehicles made up 6.9% of the exports. Most of these vehicles were cars re-exported to Russia and Belarus.

In the *structure of Estonian imports*, the leading commodity group, comprising machinery and mechanical appliances and electronic equipment, accounted for 21.6% of the total imports in 1995. The most important Estonian import item was electronic equipment (radios and televisions, radio and television parts, and communication equipment). Telecommunication equipment ranked second among the goods of this commodity group. These items have high shares in both exports and imports because of the flows of materials and parts between foreign enterprises and their Estonian subcontractors. Finland was the source of 49% of the imports in this group; however, part of these imports were products from other countries resold to Estonia.

The second largest commodity group in Estonian imports was mineral products, which made up 11.5% of the imports in 1995. Part of the imported oil was re-exported to third parties. Textiles and textile products made up 10.4% of the imports in 1995. Cotton and cotton articles were the largest component, with 2.9% of the total 1995 imports. Also in 1995, transport vehicles accounted for 8.0% of Estonia's imports, and base metals and base-metal products made up another 7.1%. A large share of products in each commodity group were re-exported.

2.3 Impediments to Exports

The analyses in Sections 2.3 to 2.6 are partly based on 20 enterprise case studies that were carried out in the first half of 1995 in Estonia. Firms were selected to give a sufficient representation of Estonian exporters in terms of size, ownership, sector, and export markets. The main characteristics of the enterprises that were investigated are presented in *Table 2.7*.

2.3.1 Demand

Estonian foreign trade was more closely linked to the low-quality goods markets of the Soviet Union then the trade of other East European countries. In the 1980s, Estonia's role was to produce substitutes for Western consumer goods for the other Soviet republics. Several enterprises were supplied with relatively modern technologies. These investments were financed mainly by the central budget; the contribution of enterprises themselves was quite modest.

When economic agents gained some independence at the end of the 1980s and the first joint ventures emerged, the dominant expectation was that adjusting to the requirements of Western markets would be relatively easy, especially for

Table 2.7. Profiles of the companies covered by the case studies.

Company	Sector	Ownership[a]	Number of employees	Exports/ sales ratio (%)	Main markets
Lembitu	Clothing	State JSC	610	44	Finland, Sweden, Germany
Tondi Elektroonika	Electrical machinery	Private JSC	1,100	90	Russia, Germany, China
Emor	Market research	Private JSC Est. 60%	52	40–50	Finland, Sweden, Latvia, Lithuania
Baltic Tours	Tourism	Private JSC	30	23	Finland
Nagu	Trade	Private JSC	6	90	Germany
Saku Brewery	Food	Private JSC Est. 30%	194	10	Finland, USA, Latvia
ELCOTEQ Baltic	Electronic equipment	Private JSC Est. 40%	400	100	Finland, Sweden, Germany
Tarkon	Electronic equipment	State JSC	600	80	Russia, Ukraine, Belarus, Kazakhstan, Denmark
Eesti Talleks	Mechanical engineering	Private JSC	1,020	80	Russia, Finland, Sweden, Germany
ARS–Juveel	Jewelry	Private JSC	85	10	Finland, Sweden, Denmark
Paide Piima-kombinaat	Food	Private JSC	250	50	Russia, Germany, Switzerland
Cibus	Food	Private JSC	176	5	Latvia, Lithuania, Russia
Pioneer	Metal processing	Private JSC Est. 34%	245	90	USA, Germany
Tööstusaparaat	Mechanical engineering	Private JSC	600	90	Russia, Latvia, Lithuania
Estel	Electrical machinery	State JSC	500	80	Russia, Ukraine, China
Ilmarine	Mechanical engineering	Private JSC	300	70	Russia, Germany, Finland
Klementi	Clothing	JSC, pr. 80%, state 20%	809	90	Finland, Sweden, Germany
Tallinna Far-maatsiatehas	Pharma-ceuticals	JSC, pr. 67%, state 33%	210	90	Russia, Latvia, Lithuania, Poland, Hungary
Viisnurk	Furniture	Private JSC	830	85	Finland, Sweden, Norway, Russia, Canada, USA
Smarten	Trade	Private JSC	100	15	Latvia, Russia

[a]Private JSC = Joint-stock company; State JSC = Estonian state holds 100% of shares in the company; Est. = Estonian owners; Pr. = Estonian private owners.

light industry. Most managers did not expect that the gradual marketization would lead to the dismantling of barter transactions between former centrally planned economies. The barter system had created an economic environment quite different from market competition based on accounting for costs, innovation of new products, and marketing products. Economic agents did not realize how different the structure of relative prices in socialist economies was from the structure of prices in developed market economies. Many Western wholesalers and retailers do not accept the products of unknown Eastern companies. A number of Estonian enterprises have been supported by their foreign partners, whose investments and contacts have helped to bring their products up to the standards of developed countries and to find outlets for the products. In many cases, however, the price of this support has been a change from manufacturing final products to producing semi-manufactured products or components for Western companies.

The situation of heavy industry enterprises (mechanical engineering, electrical machinery, and chemical industries), which used to be closely connected with the Eastern market, is especially critical. Enterprises like Tondi Elektroonika, Tarkon, Tööstusaparaat, Ilmarine, and Estel in our sample have seen output and employment decline two- to threefold during the last five years. They are in principle interested in cooperating with Western partners, but they overestimate their current levels of technology and are not ready to accept the organizational methods, attitudes, and values of Western entrepreneurship. The situation is further complicated by managers and engineers who lack necessary language skills. Yet some of these enterprises have managed to find a market niche and to sell their products. Several big enterprises (Eesti Talleks, for instance) were reorganized into dozens of small firms that are active in metal processing, or in other activities like wholesale and retail trade or office space rentals. Most engineers have resigned from such enterprises and the technical level of production at these small firms has declined.

Payment problems with other CIS countries have been one reason for the decline of output in those enterprises that continue to export to CIS markets. However, this payment situation has also induced enterprises to attack Western markets, thus leading to a successful change of trade partners.

Several enterprises have found market niches for their old-fashioned products, which because of their low price are in demand among special groups of Western consumers. Hearing aids produced by Tondi Elektroonika are an example of how a 15- to 20-year-old model that meets international quality standards (ISO 9002) can be sold in Germany with considerable success. The main problems with such production are related to product design and finishing.

The entry costs have been very high for new firms trying to break into new markets using their own names. Large and medium-size enterprises have had to switch to subcontracting (for example, in the clothing industry, electrical machinery, and metal goods). Many enterprises have adopted a step-by-step strategy aimed at improving technology and product design and moving toward a bigger share of finished goods. However, representatives of several of the firms we surveyed (for example, the clothing industry firms Klementi and Lembitu) mentioned that subcontracting was not good business for them and that it left few resources to invest in new technologies.

Another way for Estonian enterprises to facilitate selling in the West is to create a joint venture with a Western firm. Several Western enterprises were rather eager to start joint-venture businesses when Estonia was part of the Soviet Union because this approach guaranteed them automatic access to the huge Eastern market. Now foreign firms prefer to participate in privatization and in cooperation schemes where they play the predominate role and control the share capital. In our sample, Pioneer, Saku Brewery, and ELCOTEQ Baltic are firms where foreign ownership is dominant.

For small enterprises a foreign partner (in many cases just one person) who has information and links to production or trading firms is a solution to marketing problems. In this situation, the foreign partner takes care of only the market in the country in which it is located. The importance of such a partner was mentioned by two companies in our survey, Nagu, a trading company, and ARS-Juveel, which deals in jewelry.

Enterprises that had negotiated contracts with foreign partners specifying a product's design and model were in relatively favorable situations. High price has been a major obstacle to the use of foreign information about technologies, licenses, and other technical requirements. The main sources of information about foreign market requirements have been personal experience, advice from foreign partners, exhibitions and fairs, catalogues of foreign firms, scientific research projects, and contacts with other producers. Exhibitions and fairs are highly valued, but the costs of participation have been considered too high. Representatives of several enterprises noted that these contacts have been not used intensively enough. Lack of information has caused losses for enterprises; products have frequently been sold too cheaply or intermediators have been granted too high a percentage of revenue. This problem was listed by companies in the clothing industry (Lembitu and Klementi) and by mechanical engineering firms (Eesti Talleks and Ilmarine).

Among the important impediments to exports mentioned by the surveyed enterprises were technical barriers connected with ISO 9000 standards, Good Manufacturing Practice requirements, and the need for certificates testifying that certain technical operations were done by workers having the required classification. The companies often did not know how to initiate these kinds of certifications, especially when they did not have foreign partners. The situation in the pharmaceuticals industry seems to be the most complicated, because compatibility with standards is only a precondition to the long process of registering medicines before these items can be traded in other markets.

Foreign regulations on origin of goods turned out to be important for Estonian exporters and influenced their exporting strategies. For example, the export of clothing has been realized mainly through subcontracting. One reason for this subcontracting has been that Estonian trademarks are not well known in other countries; another reason has been import barriers. Though Estonia has a free trade agreement with Finland and Sweden, it has not been profitable to sell finished goods there. Under the prescribed rules of origin, only clothing produced from material manufactured in Estonia or in a partner country (Finland and Sweden, but also Latvia and Lithuania) is exempt from custom tariffs (which can be as high as 35%). However, Estonia and the other states mentioned do not produce materials of sufficient quality, the necessary materials cannot be purchased from these sources, and therefore these preferential conditions cannot actually be used. This was a problem for the companies Klementi and Lembitu when they tried to sell their final products in Scandinavia.

The quotas introduced in trade with EU countries are effective limits for some products, for example, preserved fish and milk powder, which is an important export item for the company Paide Piimakombinaat. For several items, however, Estonia's total exports were below the quotas for 1995.

High inflation in the countries of the ruble zone created additional problems. Russian rubles earned through export and collected with delay lost value because the kroon was relatively stable and high inflation in Estonia was practically overcome in the second half of 1992. Because frequently there was no agreement on sharing foreign currency exchange risk, the payments received after delays in transportation and money transfer caused significant losses for the exporters. Estonian goods face another problem in Russia recently: they have to face increasingly fierce competition since their quality is comparable with that of the Western imports that have recently flooded the Russian market.

Since the dissolution of the Soviet Union, Russia has applied double customs tariffs to countries without most favored nation status, including Estonia. This policy blocks the export of foodstuffs in particular. In addition, the Russian government's decree of 6 May 1995 introduced high customs tariffs for a number of goods and services. Several groups of products affected by this decree have an important share in Estonian exports. The situation worsened for the Estonian food-processing industry, especially for confectioneries and beverages, starting in July 1995 (*Table 2.8*). For furniture exported to Russia, the "Made in Estonia" label costs an additional 60% of the product's value. This problem was mentioned by two of the companies surveyed, Viisnurk (furniture) and ARS-Juveel (jewelry).

Trade with Russia has been obstructed by unstable trading conditions. In 1994 the Estonian Chamber of Commerce investigated problems that enterprises trading with Russia were having. Responses to the Chamber's questionnaire showed that of 78 firms with close contacts with Russia in the past, 42% had interrupted or were considering interrupting those relationships. Increased customs tariffs was

Table 2.8. New Russian import tariffs (in percent).[a]

Commodity	Old tariff	New tariff	Tariff applicable for imports from Estonia
Fish	5	10	20
Milk powder	2	10	20
Butter	15	20	40
Confectioneries	15	20	40
Chocolate products	–	10	20
Beverages	–	25	50
Mineral fuels	1	5	10
Furniture	20	30	60

[a]For most commodities the new tariffs were introduced 1 July 1995.
Source: Ministry of Economy of the Republic of Estonia.

the reason cited most often. Several firms reintroduced contacts through third countries (Ukraine, Finland) (Ranne, 1994). Russian and Estonian membership in the World Trade Organization (WTO), which according to optimistic forecasts could be achieved in 1996, could end this kind of trade discrimination.

Several Estonian enterprises have tried to use former contacts to sell products to customers in Asian and African countries that were targeted for exports in the 1980s. For example, excavators for land reclamation had frequently been sold to these countries, but recent attempts to sell them failed completely. These countries prefer barter transactions and the payment conditions that used to be provided by the central foreign trade organization of the former Soviet Union; Estonian companies, however, cannot offer these features of trade and financing.

2.3.2 Supply

Estonian monetary policy created relatively favorable economic conditions for exporters who used mainly domestic inputs and did not need considerable improvements in technology relying on imported equipment and materials. Low wages and the low price of electricity have helped keep costs low for firms in the metal industry, where electricity makes up a high share of the costs, and other industries where the work is labor intensive. Nevertheless, the price of electricity has increased continuously, from 10 cents per kilowatt hour in June 1992 to more than three times that by 1995. Respondents from several firms (Tondi Elektroonika, Estel, Tööstusaparaat, and Ilmarine) asserted that the price of electricity should not increase more because it has achieved a critical level in their production costs. However, the price of electricity covers only operational costs for the power engineering stations; to carry out investments in electricity generation without the use of state subsidies the price of electricity must increase even more.

Relatively low wages were one precondition for keeping production costs low. The average monthly wage was US$170 (2,096 kroons) at the end of 1994 and US$240 at the end of 1995. However, recent wage increases have turned out to be excessive for labor-intensive industries that base their business strategies on low wages and that have to compete with companies from other low-wage areas of the world. If relative wages continue to grow at the pace of recent years, their cost advantage will disappear soon.

Negative real interest rates for loans offered by commercial banks are a peculiar phenomenon of the Estonian money and capital market. Annual consumer price inflation was 41.7% in 1994, but the average interest rate in 1994 was 20–22%. In 1995 inflation was 28.9% and the average interest rate was 16–18%. However, such interest rates are acceptable only for firms with a short turnover period (primarily the trade and service sectors); they are too high for manufacturing enterprises. Estonian interest rates are especially high for exporters to Western markets because the export price level and the exchange rate are relatively stable, and it is impossible to compensate for the high price of loans with an increase in sales prices. The high interest rates and the lack of working capital due to difficulties getting loans were cited by firms with a longer technological cycle, especially those in the mechanical engineering and electrical machinery industries.

A serious problem for enterprises has been the lack of credits to advance costs or export payments. A system of export credits and support is not yet in place. The Estonian Export Credit Fund (the institution that is bound to be developed into the Estonian Exim bank) has limited resources for extending credits. This problem was cited by most of the companies in our sample. Only one manager from the Klementi company reported good cooperation with an Estonian commercial bank for the provision of export credits.

There were serious problems with receiving payments on time, especially in the period immediately after the monetary reform. This situation has improved during the past two years. The payment schedule of foreign partners is all the more important because support by commercial banks and by the Estonian Export Credit Fund is limited for exporters. Producers of finished metal goods (Ilmarine and Eesti Talleks), for example, receive from regular customers 30% of the payment in advance, an additional 40% after the product is received, and 30% after installation. This scheme is quite common, especially with German firms. However, a very different payment scheme is applied with Finnish firms; because of geographical proximity, they often pay only after the order has been filled.

The kroon has been stable since June 1992, but the fluctuation of the Finnish markka and the Swedish krona has damaged those Estonian firms that have had especially close contacts with these countries. However, many enterprises envisage payments in Deutsche marks or kroons to reduce the foreign exchange rate risk.

The value-added tax (VAT), which must be paid when goods are imported, has been a rather serious problem for enterprises that use imported inputs. In the case of domestic inputs the producer must pay only the price of the input and the VAT on the difference between the input price and the selling price. In the case of imported inputs, in addition to the tax on value added to the input, the producer must pay the tax on the full value of the imported input. The deadline for such a payment was decreased from 45 days to 15 days in Estonia in April 1995. For several enterprises this is too short a time for manufacturing a product with imported inputs, exporting it, and reclaiming the VAT. Enterprises assert that this setup freezes their liquid assets. Opportunities to cover these costs with short-term credit were limited until 1994; however, since mid-1994 commercial banks have been more eager to give credit to enterprises with better economic results.

Estonian customs policy has not been a source of major problems. Of course, several enterprises have been dissatisfied with some of the requirements, but this is related mostly to the enterprises' individual circumstances. Estonia's procedure taxes for exported and imported goods were changed on 1 April 1995 from a 0.5% tax to a lump sum tax of 200 kroons per entry or exit. This innovation was favorable for enterprises that trade larger quantities, but it did not satisfy small enterprises that trade small quantities of products (especially in the electronics branch). At the same time, some enterprises (for example, Klementi) complained about the limited organizational capabilities custom offices had for treating the volumes of goods traded.

Public infrastructure has not been a major obstacle for international contacts in Estonia. International communication has improved remarkably during the past two years; however, there can be problems with local telephone calls. These problems were mentioned by firms from the cities of Pärnu (Cibus and Viisnurk), Tartu (Tarkon and Nagu), and Paide (Paide Piimakombinaat).

At times, quality problems have emerged with the subcontracts and the solution required particularly smooth cooperation between the partners. The representatives of companies that produce under subcontract several operations for Western firms (Lembitu and Klementi) estimated their positions positively, especially when a representative of the foreign partner participated in the introduction of a new product. Although all the technical information was given to the Estonian company to start a new product, differences in technical conditions often made it necessary to make changes in the initial scheme. The representative of the foreign partner then estimated the consequences of these changes on technical standards and production quality. In order to maintain the envisaged quality, several such contracts guarantee the partner open access to the Estonian subcontractor's production process.

Estonian enterprises usually were not satisfied with the normative time limits suggested by foreign partners for individual operations in the technological process. In some cases the normative time limits for operations were determined by Estonian firms, but in these cases the price of a time unit was open to bargaining. The lower limit of this price already exists for some enterprises for different operations, but these are enterprises that have had more opportunities to choose between different contracts and thus had more bargaining power. The Estonian companies often were inexperienced at bargaining; frequently the foreign partner was ready to pay a much higher price for subcontracted operations than it initially offered. Enterprises that have technological capacity for more complicated operations are in a relatively good position. Enterprises located in Tallinn on average charge higher prices for the same operations than firms located elsewhere. These issues were also analyzed in a recent research project carried out by Estonian and Finnish economists (Lavikka *et al.*, 1994).

A combination of Russian inputs and units imported from Western countries has been the basis for cost competitiveness for several enterprises, especially in metal processing industries. The managers of the firms Eesti Talleks and Ilmarine underlined this as a potential source of international competitiveness. For these enterprises an end to low-cost inputs would create a serious problem. However, the transition to higher-quality production and selling products on more advanced markets also requires high-quality inputs. Several enterprises had to stop buying cheap Russian metal for some products because they were forced by the Russian supplier to buy in large quantities (a minimum of 60 tons), and due to past unfavorable experiences they had to carefully check the quality of each and every shipment. By switching to metals imported from Finland, for example, these enterprises would probably pay higher prices but they could receive benefits such as better timing of shipments, better product quality, and the opportunity to buy in smaller quantities.

During the first year of Estonian independence it was common for foreign economic agents to order free samples of products from a number of enterprises, many of which never received an order. Later, Estonian embassies abroad and representatives from different industry associations started to collect information about the economic backgrounds of foreign partners; this knowledge radically improved reliability and payment situations.

Problems due to quality standards have affected different firms to different degrees. For production with stringent safety regulations and conditions, such as high-pressure pumps and lifting mechanisms like cranes produced by Ilmarine, special relationships and consultations with foreign state administrations and private follow-up inspections have been necessary. Estonia has relatively good relations with the relevant German organization of welding. This organization first trained two Estonian specialists in Germany and later financed a project that introduced a special center into the Lilleküla School of Mechanics. Now some enterprises like Ilmarine have a special certificate from this German organization certifying that welding has been done by workers with the required skill classification; that the technical conditions in the enterprise satisfy German requirements; and that the materials, control system, and supervision meet German quality standards. This certificate has been crucial for orders from German enterprises. Unfortunately, there are several other fields where such cooperation is missing, and consequently Estonian companies do not have access to Western markets.

Machinery and equipment for work that does not have such stringent safety requirements are not controlled so strictly. An example is welding for mechanisms that do not need any special inspection; it is enough if a representative of the contractor observes the quality of production and accepts it. Several mechanisms produced by the company Eesti Talleks were accepted by foreign partners based only on this type of general observation.

Standardization problems might be resolved if Western partners who have certificates in their own countries were to introduce their own quality-control models into Estonian firms and provide their own guarantees for Estonian products. Guarantees of satisfactory product quality given by foreign partners in their own countries and the refusal to recognize certification given by Estonian officials are reasons subcontracting has become so widespread. Several metal processing and electrical machinery firms, such as Ilmarine, Tondi Elektroonika, and Estel, have complained about this problem.

Quality requirements and certification for products exported to CIS countries are unified through a special organization called Mikrosert, which works under the supervision of the Board of Standards of the Republic of Estonia. Enterprises that continue to produce for the Eastern market often maintain contacts with former trade partners, and the technical standards in these cases should correspond to the former Soviet standard GOST and other technical requirements from the Soviet era. Differences in standards are one reason it is complicated for enterprises to move from Eastern markets to Western markets. In contrast to the experiences with Western markets, there have been few problems with Russian state administration on standardization issues.

2.4 Influence of Privatization

The operation of industrial enterprises has been seriously impeded by delays in the sale of firms listed for privatization. Such enterprises find it practically impossible to receive bank loans and have major problems with contracts for purchasing raw materials or selling their products. Altogether 373 large and medium-size enterprises have been included in the list of privatization in 10 waves of tenders. From 1993 to 1995, 347 contracts were signed. From 1991 to 1994 almost all the small businesses owned by the state (approximately 1,500 companies), including mainly service, trade, and catering establishments, were sold at auctions. Privatization of small businesses was nearly completed by the end of 1994 (Estonian Privatization Agency, 1995).

The method of privatization seems to have had an important influence on the financial situations and subsequent performance of the enterprises. If an enterprise or some part of it was sold to a foreign partner, its restructuring started sooner and the necessary investments were carried out more smoothly than if the firm was sold to a domestic investor. In addition to the sale price, the amount of future investments and the maintenance of employment at a certain level were crucial conditions in tenders with preliminary negotiations, the main way medium- and large-scale enterprises were privatized by the Estonian Privatization Agency. These commitments also seem to have had some influence on the decision to privatize and on subsequent performance. There also exist cases where a foreign investor's main reason for participating in the privatization was to protect its own market from cheaper Estonian products. By contrast, in several cases privatization was the starting point for connecting the Estonian enterprise to the production chain of a foreign partner. For enterprises in this situation, a number of the problems hindering the exports of other firms disappeared. ELCOTEQ Baltic is one such example. To make this adjustment, however, the company was required to change from producing final products to producing parts and intermediate products. In other cases, a foreign partner who appropriated shares of an enterprise during privatization was interested in helping that enterprise adjust to the requirements of foreign markets.

In our sample, the case of Pioneer exemplifies how cooperation between a prospective Estonian enterprise and a foreign partner has sometimes been hampered by ownership problems and the terms of the privatization contract. An American investor achieved majority ownership in the company in the course of its privatization and also made commitments for future investments. The Estonian partner, however, did not accept the leading role of the foreign partner because it suspected that the majority share was bought much under value. While the Estonian partner was negotiating with an alternative, German investor, the American owner stopped paying the installments of the original privatization deal, which drove the highly indebted Pioneer to financial crisis and bankruptcy.

Many enterprises, particularly those in the engineering, metal, and electronics industries, became joint-stock companies formed by the workers or managers. Such enterprises in our sample are Tondi Elektroonika, Eesti Talleks, Paide Piimakombinaat, Cibus, Tööstusaparaat, Klementi, Tallinna Farmaatsiatehas, and Viisnurk.

Because Estonian new owners took advantage of the opportunity to pay in installments, many of these enterprises have had no funds for necessary investments and product innovation. This has become an obstacle to expanding export markets.

The time schedule of privatization, which starts when an enterprise is placed on the list of offered enterprises and concludes when a contract of sale is signed, has also been a source of problems. On average this time frame has been one year, which is not long in comparison with the time schedules of other former socialist countries. However, Estonian privatization has not been organized in one or two large waves of offers, as was done in the Czech Republic. In Estonia, the sale of enterprises has been arranged in smaller groups and the entire process has lasted much longer than in other countries. During this time enterprises have suffered greatly. One reason this time schedule is so long is related to the liabilities the enterprises accrued following the monetary reform. These liabilities must be dealt with in some way during the tender process, yet no special loan fund has been organized by Estonian officials, although the creation of one was discussed in 1993. Most loans have been added to the price of the enterprise (in several cases a sum of liabilities was subtracted from the initial price of shares or assets); in a few cases arrears of taxes were simply canceled. As more than half of the enterprises were privatized by the summer of 1995, the clarification of ownership relations should be one factor that promotes future economic growth.

2.5 Artificial Incentives to Exports and Enterprise Efforts to Tackle Impediments

Estonia's population is 1.5 million; therefore, its market is too small for many of the products produced in the country. The purchasing power of this market also suffers due to the considerable undervaluation of the kroon. This creates a strong stimulus for producers to export and gives an advantage from the cost side until inflation and increasing wages under the fixed exchange rate regime diminish it. The combination of low wages as a cost-side factor and the domestic market's low purchasing power on the domestic demand side forces the enterprises to export their products. These incentives were mentioned by the firms that could sell more products in the domestic market if the demand were higher (Paide Piimakombinaat, Viisnurk, Lembitu, Klementi, and Smarten).

Estonia's liberal foreign trade regime and the virtual absence of export tariffs promote exports. The undervalued foreign exchange rate (in comparison with the PPP) has reduced the costs of domestic inputs versus those of foreign inputs, and thus supports exporters. Moreover, Estonia is among the few countries that do not protect their domestic agricultural product markets. This is another reason Estonian food processing companies must export their products. Several supporters of the Estonian currency board system and the undervalued fixed exchange rate argued that this regime protects Estonian agricultural producers through low input costs that could not be achieved with customs tariffs in a more stable economic environment. However, these producers in fact need a lot of imported technical equipment to produce exports acceptable for other markets. If they do not manage to export their products, the low revenues from the domestic market will not cover investment requirements; yet to export they need resources for investments and for expensive imported equipment.

There exist some artificial incentives to exports and especially to re-exports. Transport vehicles and base metals, especially scrap metal, have important shares in the trade flows passing through Estonia. Official figures on Estonian foreign trade suggest that the value of imports has been artificially low. In 1994 the imports of ferrous metals were valued at 340 million kroons and exports at 425 million kroons; the imports of copper and copper products were valued at 33.7 million kroons and exports, 99.9 million kroons; the imports of nickel and nickel products were valued at 1.4 million kroons and exports, 173.5 million kroons. One reason for the comparatively low levels of registered imports was that Estonian regulations did not require a confirmed declaration of the value of imported goods when imports were reported at the border. To avoid taxes (especially the VAT) it was possible to declare an unrealistically low value of imported goods. A value closer to the real one had to be declared when these goods were exported from Estonia. Also, it is possible that a large share of these items were smuggled into Estonia. In January 1996 a new Customs Valuation Law was put into force to tackle these valuation issues. The customs office, however, has not been able to implement the new law, and since August 1996 an amendment to the Turnover Tax Law has addressed the problem with the application of minimum prices for the valuation of imports.

One result of the high customs tariffs introduced by Russia recently is that several Estonian firms have created joint ventures in Russia because no customs tariffs are imposed on imported inputs for such enterprises. One of the companies surveyed, Eesti Talleks, has a subsidiary in Russia; ARS-Juveel and Ilmarine are also considering taking a similar approach. Several Estonian companies have increased their exports to Latvia and Lithuania, which do not have such customs-related obstacles with Russia, and a part of these products have then been re-exported to Russia by intermediators in these countries.

The manager of the wholesale company Smarten mentioned that the company is interested in trading with Russian companies; however, the high customs tariffs are a significant, but not insurmountable, obstacle. Latvia has most favored nation status in trade with Russia and customs tariffs that are half those of Estonia; this promotes exports of Estonian goods to Latvia with the aim of re-exporting them to Russia.

2.6 The Government's Foreign Trade Policy

2.6.1 Regulations

Estonia's foreign trade regulation has been extremely liberal since 1991. In 1991 the export of over 200 goods was still limited by quotas and licenses. Continuing liberalization of prices during the autumn of 1991 and the price increase shock early in 1992 made continued protection of domestic markets unreasonable. In 1992 the number of quotas was down to 38 and by 1993 only 5 were in force: those for oil shale, shale oil S-1, gravel, fire clay, and quartz sand. At the beginning of 1995 even these restrictions were phased out. Free trade agreements with the EU made the introduction of some new quotas necessary. Export license is issued by the Ministry of Economic Affairs to exporters of goods limited by EU quotas. In addition, a special certificate of origin is granted for knitted products and clothing that according to EU classification belong to groups I and II of sensitive goods but which do not meet the EU's requirements of origin. These certificates are issued on the condition that the two final stages of manufacturing take place in Estonia.

Only licensed exporters and importers can trade in metals, alcohol, tobacco and tobacco products, pharmaceuticals, weapons, ammunition, explosives, lottery tickets, and private passenger vehicles. Licenses are given to any firm that applies and meets the application requirements, irrespective of its ownership.

Goods carried over the Estonian customs border are liable for customs duties, excise taxes, the VAT, and procedure taxes. The weighted average of Estonian custom duties was 1.4% in 1994 (Ratso 1995). Nearly all imports, as well as domestic production, are subject to the VAT. Exports of goods and services cleared by customs declaration are exempt from the VAT.

Time-consuming customs procedures at Estonia's borders have been a major problem. Recently, substantial improvements have been introduced, including computerized electronic registration of exported and imported goods.

In accordance with agreements between Estonia and the EFTA and the EU, technical materials on the application of the unified customs procedures of transit trade have been prepared and are scheduled to be introduced in 1996.

2.6.2 Trade and economic agreements

The reorientation of Estonian exports to the West has been supported by bilateral agreements with several countries. The Protocol on Temporary Measures on

Economic and Trade Cooperation, in essence a free trade agreement, was signed by Estonia and Finland in February 1992. The agreement was exceptionally beneficial and strongly promoted Estonian foreign trade activities. Estonia signed free trade agreements with Sweden and Switzerland in 1992 and with Norway in 1993. Also in 1993, the prime ministers of Estonia, Latvia, and Lithuania signed a free trade agreement. In 1995 a free trade agreement between Ukraine and Estonia was signed. Most favored nation trade agreements have been signed with Georgia, Armenia, Moldavia, and Kyrgystan.

On 18 July 1994 a free trade agreement between Estonia and the EU was signed, which established free trade from 1 January 1995 between the EU and Estonia.

2.6.3 Promotion of exports

A significant problem mentioned by several enterprises is the weak system of export guarantees and credits. The Estonian Export Credit Fund was established to promote domestic exports. Loans are provided to companies that introduce new, internationally competitive products or manufacturing processes that promise rapid increases in production for exports. However, the fund's financial resources are small. Allocations from the state budget were 10 million kroons in 1993, 5 million kroons in 1994, and 4 million kroons in 1995, always below one-thousandth of the annual export value.

Recent confusion about the Export Credit Funds financing is the result of the simultaneous introduction of several government projects. In November 1994, a memorandum on the creation of the legal system of export guarantees was signed by Estonian government institutions, the Export Credit Fund, and representatives of the Ministry of Foreign Affairs, the export credit institution, and the State Center of Export Guarantees of Finland. It was planned that the Export Credit Fund of Estonia would develop into an export–import bank. At the same time, the government discussed another project to combine all state funds (including the Export Credit Fund) into one fund for the development of entrepreneurship and the enhancement of regional policy. This discussion also stopped work on the project developing export guarantees, and the solution to this problem was still unclear in the summer of 1996.

The Estonian Agency of Foreign Investments was established in 1994. One of the Agency's goals is to introduce different projects aimed at promoting investment opportunities in Estonia. These foreign investments are considered a long-run precondition for developing exports.

Several industry federations and associations have been actively pursuing international contacts and organizing visits to industrial exhibitions and fairs. The associations also organize the distribution of orders and cooperation between several enterprises. For example, the Federation of Estonian Engineering Industries has been actively organizing contacts with similar associations abroad. The companies surveyed also mentioned beneficial support by the Association of Food Manufacturing Industries, the Association of Dairy Industries, and the Association of Electrotechnical Industries. These contacts have been very important for transferring know-how and information about regulations and technical standards in other countries.

References

Bank of Estonia, 1995a, Overview of Estonian economy in 1994, *Bulletin of the Bank of Estonia*, no. 2:6–22 [in Estonian].

Bank of Estonia, 1995b, Estonian balance of payments in 1994, *Bulletin of the Bank of Estonia*, no. 3:22–35 [in Estonian].

Estonian Privatization Agency, 1995, *Privatization in Estonia 1994/1995*, Estonian Privatization Agency, Tallinn, Estonia.

Lavikka, R., Teder, J., and Varendi, M., 1994, Estonian Manufacture of Clothing at the Crossroads, Working Paper of Tampere University, no. 49, Tampere, Finland [in Estonian and Finnish].

Ministry of Economy, 1995, *Overview of Estonian Economy in 1994–1995*, Ministry of Economy, Tallinn, Estonia [in Estonian].

Rajasalu, T., 1992, *Estonian Economy at the Dawn of Independence*, Institute of Economics, Estonian Academy of Sciences, Tallinn, Estonia.

Ranne, T., 1994, Problems with Russian Trade, *Business Newspaper*, 15 November [in Estonian].

Ratso, S., 1995, Trade policy is restricting export, *Business Newspaper*, February 20 [in Estonian].

Statistical Office of Estonia, 1992, National accounts in Estonia 1991, *Statistical Yearbook*, Statistical Office of Estonia, Tallinn, Estonia.

Statistical Office of Estonia, 1994a, *Foreign Trade 1993*, Statistical Office of Estonia, Tallinn, Estonia.

Statistical Office of Estonia, 1994b, *Statistical Yearbook 1994*, Statistical Office of Estonia, Tallinn, Estonia.

Statistical Office of Estonia, 1995, *Foreign Trade 4/94*, Statistical Office of Estonia, Tallinn, Estonia.

Statistical Office of Estonia, 1996, *Foreign Trade 4/95*, Statistical Office of Estonia, Tallinn, Estonia.

Chapter 3

Hungary

Ágnes Csermely

In this chapter a study of the factors determining the performance of Hungarian enterprises in external markets is summarized. Forces affecting demand for Hungarian exports, production bottlenecks, and other supply-side constraints, as well as enterprise efforts to tackle these impediments are also identified.

Some 20 structured case studies were undertaken in the first quarter of 1995. Firms were selected according to a common scheme elaborated at the International Institute for Applied Systems Analysis (IIASA), and interviews were designed in the following way. First, we selected prominent export sectors of Hungarian manufacturing. Firms within sectors were selected according to their market orientation, size, and ownership structure to create a diverse sample. Firms whose exports were facilitated by export-promotion policies were also included. The firms chosen are listed in *Table 3.1* according to selection criteria. A questionnaire served as the basis for the in-depth interviews; however, we also left enough space for description of specific enterprise features.

Evaluation of government policies was prominent in survey responses because a stabilization package, the so-called Bokros package, had been announced a few days before the interviews took place. This package included a 9% devaluation of the domestic currency, the implementation of an 8% surcharge on imports, and the introduction of a preannounced crawling peg system for determining exchange rates. The shock produced by the package was reflected in the enterprises' responses.

Section 3.1 contains a short overview of recent export performance in Hungary with a description of the changes in the geographical and commodity patterns of

Table 3.1. Profiles of the companies covered in the survey.

Industry/ company	Ownership[a]	Export/sales ratio (%)	Number of employees	Other characteristics[b]
Food processing				
Ringa	100% state owned	50	1,600	Debt consolidation
Gallicoop	DP	50	120+300[c]	–
Komáromi	100% state owned	8	817	Eastern exports
Győri Keksz	JV	7	1,100	Eastern exports
Clothing				
ZAKO	JV	90	1,800	OPT
Hunostyl	DP + MBO	66	250	OPT
Sal-kon	DP	85	550	OPT
Glovita	JV	45	300	No OPT
Elegant	JV	90	311	OPT
Elit	JV	75	1,400	OPT
Agora	100% state owned		370	Disabled workers
Engineering				
Lehel-Elektrolux	100% foreign owned	50	3,284	Tax rebates
Ganz-Ansaldo	JV	60	1,600	Loss maker + OPT
Chemicals				
Borsodchem	100% state owned	–	4,074	Debt consolidation
Taurus	100% state owned	58	1,043	Debt consolidation
Richter	63% state owned	66	4,623	Eastern exports,
	+ stock exchange	–	–	tax rebates
Glass				
Hunguard Float	JV	73	327	–
Metallurgy				
Csepel Metal	100% state owned	50	1,300	Debt consolidation
Textile				
Gardenia	JV	70	650	–
Footwear				
Bonsa	JV	100	–	OPT + tax rebates
Wood processing				
Kecskeméti	MRP	80	–	–
Other light ind.				
Graboplast	Stock exchange	50	1,000	Eastern exports
Rico	DP	7	510	Eastern exports

[a]DP = Dominant private ownership; JV = Joint venture; MBO = Management buy-out; MRP = Employee share buy-out program.
[b]OPT = Outward processing traffic.
[c]Permanent staff plus leased blue collar staff.

foreign trade. Sectors driving the recent export growth, as well as sectors that lost ground in international competition, are identified. In Section 3.2 the pattern of foreign direct investment (FDI) inflow and investments into fixed assets is presented to give insight into ongoing industrial restructuring. The main findings from the case studies are summarized in Section 3.3, and some conclusions are presented in Section 3.4. It should be emphasized that, because of the relatively small number of case studies, generalizations about the findings should be limited. The findings expressed here are, to a large extent, impressions from case studies and should be the subject of further analysis.

3.1 Changing Patterns of Foreign Trade

Since the early 1980s a series of changes in legislation and regulation have been adopted in Hungary in an effort to establish a solid basis for economic development. Reform measures have included both the emancipation of microeconomic decision making and the liberalization of foreign economic relations. This shift away from central regulations of economic activity has led to radical changes in corporate structure. The private sector's contribution to the gross domestic product (GDP) rose from 15–20% in 1989 to 40–45% in 1993 (NBH, 1993). The proliferation of small enterprises conducting foreign trade has destroyed the state organizations' monopoly of exports. Most of the firms that traditionally produced for export have started foreign trade activity on their own accounts. The trade liberalization program increased the share of license-free imports from 40% of hard currency imports in 1989 to 90% in 1991. The protection structure became more transparent and nominal tariff rates were reduced for most commodities. Free trade agreements with Hungary's main trading partners led to a further reduction of protective measures. *De facto* convertibility was established in current account transactions in 1990–1991, and *de jure* convertibility was achieved at the beginning of 1996.

These measures to establish a liberal institutional framework for foreign trade induced only a moderate change in the volume of exports between 1988 and 1994, but the volume of imports increased significantly (35%). The exports-to-GDP ratio declined between 1988 and 1994, whereas the imports-to-GDP ratio increased considerably. The decline in domestic absorption brought about an improvement in the trade balance until 1992. In 1993 the trade balance deteriorated dramatically, and the deficit amounted to 9% of the GDP in both 1993 and 1994. Deterioration in net exports in 1993 was an outcome of the combination of export contraction and import surge boosted by recovering domestic demand. Although the drop in exports was reversed in 1994 and, as a result of the stabilization package of March

Table 3.2. Trend of main aggregates, 1988–1995 (volume change from previous year, in percent).

	1988	1989	1990	1991	1992	1993	1994	1995
GDP	–0.1	0.7	–3.5	–11.9	–3.1	–0.6	2.9	1.5
Domestic demand	–2.9	0.9	–3.1	–9.1	–3.6	9.9	2.2	–3 to –4
Private consumption	–4.2	2.3	–3.6	–5.6	0.0	1.9	–0.2	–5 to –6
Public consumption	5.5	–6.3	2.6	–2.7	–4.9	27.5	–12.7	–6
Gross investment	–9.1	7.0	–7.6	–10.0	–20.4	32.3	19.8	3 to 4
Exports of goods and services	6.5	1.2	–5.3	–3.1	2.1	–10.1	13.7	15 to 16
Imports of goods and services	0.5	1.8	–4.3	5.4	0.2	20.2	8.8	–1 to 0

Notes: Data before and after 1991 are not fully comparable; 1993 data include Russian arms received in lieu of debt repayment.
Sources: HCSO, *Statistical Yearbook of Hungary*, 1991; NBH, 1996.

Table 3.3. Distribution of the use of GDP, 1988–1995 (in percent of GDP).

	1988	1989	1990	1991	1992	1993	1994	1995
Private consumption	60.3	59.8	61.4	69.9	72.8	74.4	72.2	68.3
Public consumption	11.7	10.3	10.6	10.6	12.5	13.8	12.1	11.5
Gross investment	21.6	21.6	19.3	20.5	16.1	20.0	22.2	22.4
Exports of goods and services	36.8	36.0	31.1	32.8	31.4	26.4	28.9	34.9
Imports of goods and services	34.1	32.7	28.5	33.7	31.7	34.6	35.4	37.0

Notes: Data before and after 1991 are not fully comparable; 1993 data include Russian arms received in lieu of debt repayment.
Sources: HCSO, *Statistical Yearbook of Hungary*, 1991; NBH, 1996.

1995, the growth rate of imports declined, the gap between exports and imports still persists (*Tables 3.2* and *3.3*).

3.1.1 Geographical reorientation

The geographical pattern of Hungarian foreign trade has undergone a large-scale shift. In 1988, 46% of Hungary's total exports went to Council for Mutual Economic Assistance (CMEA) countries and 40% went to developed market economies. CMEA countries and developed market economies each accounted for 44% of total imports. As a consequence of gradual liberalization, reorientation of foreign trade started earlier and was smoother in Hungary than in other countries of the region. In 1990 the volume of CMEA exports was 25% lower than in 1988 and exports to the West increased 22.2%; imports from CMEA countries declined 20% and imports from developed market economies increased 7%.

The dissolution of the CMEA brought about a large reduction in mutual trade. This drop amounted to a 44% decrease in volume for both exports and imports.

Since 1991 countries in transition (a group of countries comprising almost all the former CMEA countries) have accounted for a stable 19% share of Hungary's exports and 22% of imports. Despite persistent liquidity crises and high levels of uncertainty related to trade deals in the former Soviet Union, the level of trade with this region has not diminished further. Although domestic institutions providing insurance against various types of trade risk were eventually set up, problems associated with high risk of nonpayment could only be partially mitigated by them and by other arrangements like barter trade and the use of Western intermediaries. For other countries in the region, most notably Central European Free Trade Agreement (CEFTA) countries, the 1991 drop in trade was followed by a moderate expansion of deliveries. Restoration of trade relations was more marked on the import side. In addition to the demand shock caused by the demise of the CMEA and by the collapse of the Soviet Union, the Hungarian economy suffered a tremendous terms-of-trade shock, comparable to the oil-price shock in the 1970s. Hungary's terms of trade declined almost 30% in trade with former CMEA countries.

The adverse effect of the collapse of the CMEA on foreign trade was partially mitigated by trade reorientation toward developed countries, which was supported by better market access to these economies. The early 1990s brought about a large increase in Hungarian trade with developed countries. Between 1990 and 1992 the US dollar value of exports to developed market economies increased 47% while imports rose 68%; this represents a 28.4% and 24% increase in volume, respectively. Trade with European Union (EU) member countries expanded more than trade with non-EU countries. These favorable export developments ended in 1993, when exports to developed market economies dropped 21%. The following year exports recovered, returning to the 1992 level. Imports from developed market economies have been growing continuously since 1992.

3.1.2 The commodity pattern of foreign trade

During the CMEA era, Hungarian foreign trade was dichotomous: highly processed manufacturing products were exported to CMEA countries; less processed or labor-intensive products, to Western markets (*Table 3.4*). A comparison of the commodity structure of exports in 1988, 1992, and 1995 shows that until 1992 export expansion to developed market economies had more or less an across-the-board character. Producers that had specialized their exports for CMEA markets could not significantly increase their shares of exports to developed market economies. This early export boom was basically a reorientation of minimally processed goods or products utilizing simple labor from domestic and Eastern markets to Western markets. The bulk of the increment in exports came from heavy loss-maker companies that financed their activities by accumulating debt and by depleting their

Table 3.4. Commodity composition of Hungarian exports by SITC commodity group, 1988–1995 (in percent).

	Former CMEA markets			Developed market economies		
SITC commodity group	1988	1992	1995	1988	1992	1995
Exports						
0 Food, live animals	17	35	31	20	16	13
1 Beverages, tobacco	2	4	8	1	1	1
2 Crude materials except fuels	2	3	3	8	6	6
3 Mineral fuels, energy	1	2	4	5	3	3
4 Animal and vegetable oils	0	2	2	2	1	0
5 Chemicals	10	12	16	13	10	10
6 Manufactures (by material)	8	10	12	24	19	20
7 Machinery, transport equip.	48	23	18	13	20	28
8 Miscellaneous manufactures	11	5	6	12	24	20
9 Others	1	0	0	2	0	0
Total[a]	100	100	100	100	100	100
Imports						
0 Food, live animals	2	2	2	5	4	3
1 Beverages, tobacco	1	0	0	1	1	1
2 Crude materials except fuels	7	7	9	6	3	2
3 Mineral fuels, energy	27	55	43	1	0	2
4 Animal and vegetable oils	0	0	0	0	1	0
5 Chemicals	10	8	11	25	15	16
6 Manufactures (by material)	15	16	22	20	23	24
7 Machinery, transport equip.	31	9	9	34	37	38
8 Miscellaneous manufactures	6	3	4	8	15	13
9 Others	1	0	0	0	0	0
Total[a]	100	100	100	100	100	100

[a]Discrepancies due to rounding may exist.
Sources: HCSO, various publications; KOPINT–DATORG database.

capital stock. The collapse of exports in 1993 was triggered by the credit crunch and the 1992 bankruptcy law that eliminated financing for loss-making companies (Valentinyi, 1995). In addition, protectionist trade measures were introduced by the EU to limit the outflow of some representative export products such as certain kinds of meat, steel, and chemicals.

The renewed export growth from 1994 reflected subtle structural changes. In the period from 1992 to 1995, changes in the commodity composition of exports to developed market economies favored machinery and transport equipment

Table 3.5. Unit values of EU trade with Poland, Czechoslovakia,[a] and Hungary, 1988–1993 (in ECU/kg).

	1988	1989	1990	1991	1992	1993
Poland						
Imports to EU	0.53	0.56	0.48	0.38	0.34	0.35
Exports to EU	2.03	2.33	2.83	2.14	2.07	2.09
Exp.–imp. ratio	3.85	4.18	5.92	5.58	6.02	5.94
Czechoslovakia						
Imports to EU	0.54	0.59	0.57	0.42	0.35	0.43
Imports to EU	3.16	2.89	3.56	1.76	2.16	2.81
Exp.–imp. ratio	5.83	4.90	6.30	4.20	6.16	6.59
Hungary						
Imports to EU	0.88	0.97	1.01	1.10	1.30	1.45
Exports to EU	3.04	3.32	3.49	3.20	3.30	3.04
Exp.–imp. ratio	3.46	3.44	3.47	2.91	2.53	2.09

[a]Figures for 1993 are for the Czech Republic and Slovakia combined.
Source: Drabek and Smith, 1995.

[Standard International Trade Classification (SITC) 7], while exports of manufactures (by material) and miscellaneous manufactures (SITCs 6 and 8) maintained their traditional importance. According to Oblath (1995), this swing toward machinery and transportation equipment can be characterized as a unique feature of Hungarian exports among Central and East European countries (CEECs). Other countries, particularly the Czech Republic, also increased exports of engineering products, but these increases did not overtake the expansion of traditional export products. An analysis of unit values of trade by Drabek and Smith (1995) concerning CEEC–EU trade also supports this view (*Table 3.5*). Another approach led the authors of a report published by the United Nations Economic Commission for Europe (UN ECE, 1994) to similar conclusions. Regarding CEEC exports to Germany, high-quality exports exhibited a declining trend in all countries in the region except Hungary. The report concludes that Hungary is the only transition country that has been able to establish a relatively strong position in exports of more sophisticated products.

The commodity composition of Hungarian exports to former CMEA countries shifted toward natural resource–based industries. Sophisticated products (SITCs 7 and 8) have been losing ground to food, tobacco, and beverages (SITCs 0 and 1). The share of chemicals and other manufactured products has also increased (SITCs 5 and 6).

Imports showed a more stable commodity composition, but there was a shift in the geographical pattern. Former socialist countries lost their importance as exporters of machinery (SITC 7) to Hungary but reinforced their importance in fuel imports (SITC 3). Developed market economies increasingly specialized in machinery and miscellaneous manufactured articles, mainly consumer goods (SITCs 7 and 8).

An analysis of export specialization indices based on highly detailed data can reveal changes in the product composition of exports. This method has been applied by several analysts (Rodrik, 1992; Gács, 1994; Bucher *et al.*, 1994; Halpern, 1995a; Lemoine, 1994; Kovács, 1995). Although these studies used different classifications of trade and different base periods, and thus the results are not completely comparable, two clusters of results can be detected. None of the studies that covered trade developments up to 1992 found significant evidence of change in export specialization; the authors concluded that "distress exports" triggered by the collapse of CMEA markets did not dominate the expansion of exports to EU countries. However, studies that incorporated 1993 and 1994 trade data point to a marked tendency toward changes in the product composition (Lemoine, 1994; Kovács, 1995).

According to Gács (1994), Hungary's leading export sectors to the EU were mostly natural resource–based or labor-intensive branches. The first period of trade reorientation (1988–1992) was characterized by an increase in export shares of those commodity groups that were already prominent in exports before the transition; labor-intensive industries, however, gained shares in Western markets, while resource-based industries lost export shares.

Lemoine (1994) was able to show marked structural changes in exports for the period from 1988 to 1993. She computed two kinds of relative specialization indices, one measuring specialization relative to CEECs' average specialization in exports to EU countries, the other indicating specialization relative to world exports to EU countries (*Table 3.6*). According to the specialization indices based on CEEC exports to the EU, Hungary continues to specialize in agricultural products and chemicals, although specialization in agricultural products in comparison to world exports is declining due to domestic conditions and trade barriers. Hungary's traditional specialization in labor-intensive industries (clothing, leather, and shoes) is declining, but the country has reinforced its specialization in mechanical and electromechanical machinery industries. Lemoine found evidence of diverging export specialization among CEECs. In the countries of Central Europe, diversification of industrial exports is taking place, whereas in the Balkan countries exports still rely heavily on labor-intensive sectors.

An analysis of present patterns of inter- and intra-industry trade also supports the hypothesis of ongoing restructuring in exports. Studies by Dobrinsky (1994), Lemoine (1994), Drabek and Smith (1995), and Kovács (1995) conclude that intra-industry trade has gained increasing importance in trade between Hungary and

Table 3.6. Relative specialization indices for Hungarian exports to EU countries (excluding fuels, in percent).

	Relative to CEEC average[a]		Relative to world average[b]	
Commodity group	1988	1993	1988	1993
Agricultural products	167.1	183.4	312.0	219.8
Food	146.2	149.4	130.9	11.4
Raw materials	23.2	4.4	22.1	6.3
Chemicals	110.4	120.5	129.3	106.7
Leather products	134.7	128.3	186.0	230.4
Textile products	103.4	74.7	85.1	59.7
Clothing	107.8	95.9	286.1	240.2
Wood and paper	54.1	58.1	50.4	49.1
Building materials	85.8	67.7	196.1	196.4
Glass	57.6	82.1	350.1	358.3
Iron and steel	80.9	63.2	251.4	204.0
Nonferrous metals	68.5	87.8	104.1	126.6
Engineering products	125.4	147.4	40.1	57.5
Transport equipment	20.5	41.9	13.4	35.5
Electrical machinery	144.6	172.8	48.4	91.7
Other	60.2	59.2	55.4	48.5
Manufactured products	91.6	95.8	87.9	93.0
Total	100.0	100.0	100.0	100.0

[a]Share of the products in the country exports to the EU divided by share of the products in the CEEC exports to the EU, in percent.
[b]Share of the products in the country exports to the EU divided by share of the products in the world exports to the EU, in percent.
Source: Lemoine, 1994.

EU countries. According to Lemoine, the Czech Republic and Hungary recorded the most rapid increases in intra-industry trade from among CEECs, and in 1992 these two countries exhibited a level of intra-industry trade similar to that of Asian countries such as South Korea, Taiwan, Indonesia, Philippines, and Malaysia.

An analysis of marginal intra-industry trade indices in the EU–Hungary relationship by Kovács (1995) provides valuable additional information about Hungary's pattern of industrial adjustment. In the case of intra-industry adjustment, the basic adaptation is a switch to a more sophisticated product line within an industry, while inter-industry adjustment involves a change from one industry to another. Obviously, the former generally has lower adjustment costs in terms of investment needs and worker dismissals. Kovács, however, concludes that the increment of EU–Hungary trade between 1991 and 1994 was more the inter-industry type than the intra-industry type.

Certainly in the short run, changes in the commodity pattern of trade are limited by the existing production capacity. The present pattern of exports also reflects special characteristics of the transition period, where the low level of wages moves the production structure toward more labor-intensive products. Nevertheless, the results cited above give evidence of enhanced restructuring of the commodity composition of Hungarian exports since 1993 in favor of exports of more sophisticated products. The development of mutual trade with EU countries is likely to follow the pattern of intra-industry trade, based on product differentiation rather than reliance on low labor costs alone.

According to several analysts (CEPR, 1990; Hamilton and Winters, 1992; Graziani, 1994; Halpern, 1995a), this process corresponds to Hungary's underlying pattern of comparative advantage. They argue that Hungary is relatively well endowed with human capital, which implies a relatively higher growth in the output of more sophisticated, skill-intensive products.

3.2 Accumulation of Fixed Capital

The depletion of existing capital stock and the ongoing changes in trade specialization indicate that Hungary needs enormous investments in fixed capital to more effectively utilize its underlying comparative advantage. Adaptation in trade specialization is a long-term process, but we can assess its direction by analyzing the flow of capital. The sectoral distribution of actual investment spending and FDI may reveal the future pattern of trade specialization.

Investment into fixed capital declined considerably in 1988. It showed an upturn only in late 1993, followed by a 12% increase in volume in 1994 and a 1% growth in 1995. Increasing investment spending favored infrastructure and service sectors; only a quarter of the investments were directed at manufacturing. Data in *Table 3.7* show that investment projects in manufacturing industries were concentrated in the food processing and chemical branches. Although in 1992 engineering industries as a group accounted for 30% of total investment spending due to large greenfield investment in the car industry, the group's share dropped to 12% after 1992.

Of all CEECs, Hungary has been the most prominent FDI target. Several studies surveying the main motives of investors in CEECs (Collins and Rodrik, 1991; Wang, 1993; Berényi, 1995) reported that the chief motivation for investing in Hungary was establishing a market share. Better access to Hungary and other East European countries was another important motive. These survey results also imply that Western firms did not consider the skill of the labor force to be a major attraction for investments in Hungary or in other former CMEA countries.

Table 3.7. Pattern of FDI and investments in manufacturing, 1992–1994 (in percent).

	FDI (1994)		Investments[a]		
Industry branch	Total inflow[b]	Equity[c]	1992	1993	1994
Food products	30.7	46.2	13.6	20.6	26.5
Tobacco	2.4	96.3	1.4	3.7	2.1
Textiles	2.3	30.9	1.5	1.3	1.5
Clothing	1.3	30.7	1.3	1.2	1.0
Leather and footwear	0.4	19.5	0.6	0.4	0.3
Wood	1.2	25.7	1.1	9.2	1.0
Paper	3.2	41.4	3.7	2.3	1.7
Publishing and printing	2.5	28.5	2.5	3.0	2.3
Petroleum products	0.4	1.6	17.4	23.4	21.9
Chemical products	8.1	27.0	8.3	9.7	11.9
Rubber and plastics	4.8	47.5	1.8	2.4	2.6
Nonmetallic minerals	8.2	59.6	3.0	51.0	3.5
Base metals	1.3	17.0	2.0	1.3	1.8
Metal products	4.9	35.4	10.6	4.2	6.2
Machinery and equipment	4.5	31.1	3.5	3.0	3.4
Office machinery	0.7	42.8	4.5	1.5	3.4
Electrical machinery	11.4	80.8	0.0	0.1	0.0
Telecom. equipment	1.6	25.7	1.4	2.2	1.8
Precision instruments	1.1	15.0	0.7	0.7	1.2
Motor vehicles	7.2	43.5	19.6	4.3	2.5
Other transport equipment	0.5	36.5	0.0	0.0	0.0
Furniture	1.3	27.3	0.9	1.0	0.9
Total manufacturing	100.0	37.1	100.0	100.0	100.0

[a]Investments = Share of branch in total investment spending in manufacturing.
[b]Total inflow = Share in total FDI inflow to manufacturing.
[c]Equity = Foreign investors' share in aggregated equity capital of the branch.
Sources: HCSO, various publications; KOPINT–DATORG database.

Although the most important motivation for foreign investment in Hungary was penetrating domestic and East European markets, these joint ventures (JVs) have also taken an active role in Hungarian foreign trade, most notably in trade with developed market economies. In 1994 firms with more than 20% foreign stake in equity contributed 50% to total exports. Their share of imports was as high as 53.5% (KOPINT–DATORG database).

In terms of the number of companies, the majority of newly founded JVs were in service industries. JVs in manufacturing industries accounted for only 19.6% of total JVs at the end of 1994. Nevertheless, the influence of foreign partners was much more pronounced and by the end of 1993, 37.1% of the total equity capital

Table 3.8. Share of state-owned companies and joint ventures under foreign control in total turnover and in export revenues by industry branch, 1994 (in percent).

	State owned[a]		Joint ventures[b]	
Industry branch	Total turnover	Exports	Total turnover	Exports
Food products	18.1	15.9	48.9	58.8
Tobacco	0.0	0.0	99.5	92.7
Textiles	18.6	15.6	41.3	53.1
Clothing	4.6	4.4	41.6	49.6
Leather and footwear	21.8	19.3	33.3	52.1
Wood	20.4	30.2	29.5	44.3
Paper	27.3	47.3	74.8	91.0
Publishing and printing	15.7	48.0	41.4	30.4
Petroleum products	97.9	95.8	1.6	4.2
Chemical products	47.3	61.9	47.9	47.5
Rubber and plastics	15.2	25.4	55.4	60.0
Nonmetallic minerals	7.0	7.9	63.1	70.2
Base metals	29.3	32.7	20.3	26.4
Metal products	12.7	12.0	48.7	70.7
Machinery and equipment	8.9	8.8	41.1	63.5
Office machinery	3.6	10.4	33.7	74.5
Electrical machinery	1.3	1.1	77.3	93.2
Telecom. equipment	10.9	5.4	62.7	69.5
Precision instruments	15.8	17.9	38.5	52.6
Motor vehicles	14.7	15.9	72.0	77.3
Other transport equipment	6.0	0.7	57.8	74.3
Furniture	12.4	11.2	27.7	48.3
Total manufacturing	26.7	26.7	44.8	57.2

[a] State owned = State owns more than 50% in equity.
[b] Joint ventures = More than 20% of equity in foreign ownership.
Source: KOPINT–DATORG database.

accumulated in the manufacturing sector was owned by foreign investors, while state ownership was registered at 34% (based on information from the KOPINT–DATORG database).

The distribution of FDI among industries can be investigated on the basis of 1994 year-end financial statements of individual Hungarian enterprises taken from the KOPINT–DATORG database. This database incorporates the balance sheets of all enterprises that paid corporate taxes at the end of the year. From *Tables 3.7* and *3.8* we can see that of the manufacturing industry branches food processing had the highest gains in FDI inflow. More than one-fourth of the foreign capital benefited the engineering branches. Only a minor part of the capital inflow went to the textiles, clothing, and leather and footwear industries. In tobacco, electrical machinery, and nonmetallic minerals, industries with foreign ownership became dominant. With respect to sectoral distribution, in 1992–1994 investments and FDI show many similarities. Processing of petrochemicals and basic chemicals are exceptions; here the largest firms are still state owned.

Joint ventures under foreign control exported more of their total production than domestic firms did (see *Table 3.8*). With the exception of publishing and printing and tobacco and chemical manufacturing, in every industry branch JVs contributed more to the branch's total exports than to its domestic sales. In most of the engineering industries (manufacturing of electrical machinery, office machinery, motor vehicles, and other transport equipment) the JVs' contributions to total exports were outstanding. Investment and FDI patterns point to the same tendency with respect to restructuring as was identified by the analysis of actual trade flows above. This indicates that restructuring in the export structure will gain momentum in the future.

In the case studies we sought information on how these changes in market positions and competitiveness are reflected in enterprise performance and adjustment efforts.

3.3 Main Findings from the Case Studies

Before turning to the conclusions of our case studies, let us look at the main findings of a series of business surveys carried out by the KOPINT–DATORG Institute, Budapest, for the manufacturing industry in the period from 1987 to 1995. Although these surveys cover both exporting and non-exporting companies and focus on total production, they may provide a representative picture of manufacturing companies. The results also reflect changes in export conditions over time, from the beginning of 1987 to the present.

The questionnaires were sent to selected companies four times a year. The companies were asked about factors impeding production, including demand constraints and supply-side factors. According to the responses, in 1987 demand factors hindered the expansion of production for 25% of the surveyed firms. From 1988 until 1991, insufficient demand was cited more and more frequently; in 1991 already 70% of the surveyed companies faced demand constraints. Since then, insufficient demand seems to have played a decreasing role as a production impediment, although at the beginning of 1995, more than half of the companies still mentioned it as a restricting factor.

Major production impediments on the supply side varied from 1987 to 1995. The most frequently mentioned factor was lack of capital and money. Instability of macroeconomic conditions and frequent changes in regulation were also troublesome during this period. In 1987 and 1988 the lack of imported materials and parts was a significant production impediment, but since 1989 it has only minimally affected the companies surveyed. The lack of domestic materials was not initially listed among the impediments. However, since 1990 the surveyed companies have mentioned it more frequently than the lack of foreign materials; since 1992 this frequency has only increased. Also cited, but to a lesser degree, was the lack of production capacities and the lack of labor force.

3.3.1 Demand constraints

In our survey, which focused on factors constraining exports, the company managers listed impediments more frequently on the supply side than on the demand side. The majority of the companies involved in this project recovered from the shock of the collapse of Eastern and domestic markets which had hit them in 1991. Almost every company faced a steep decline in production in 1991–1992, but by 1994 they had stabilized their respective market positions. Most were able to direct their sales to Western countries, while the enterprises that remained interested in Eastern markets reported an increase in demand. Only one of the firms interviewed (the Ringa Meat Processing Company) planned to reduce exports; the rest envisaged a further expansion of sales in foreign markets. Some companies considered production capacity to be the primary obstacle to expanding exports, because they had already reached full utilization of their capacities or were facing production bottlenecks. At the same time, domestic demand for the products of most of the companies surveyed remained modest. By early 1995 this reduced domestic demand became one of the most significant limits to production. Companies active on the domestic market were hit harder by intensified import competition than by the reduction in the overall level of demand.

Neither the extent of capacity utilization nor the nature of capacity reserves indicated that the companies faced grave restrictions in demand. Favorable capacity utilization figures in many cases were due to previous cuts in the companies' production capacities. Among the reasons for keeping capacity reserves, managers most frequently mentioned the inherent fluctuation of production (seasonal, fashion) and market maneuvering possibilities. At four firms (Csepel Metalworks, Ganz-Ansaldo, Taurus, and Rico) poor capacity utilization was mainly due to the lack of domestic demand. In other cases the lower level of output was justified by supply factors.

With respect to external trade barriers, it seems the liberalization of foreign trade in Hungary and the scheduled free trade agreements (FTAs) with main trading partners [EU, CEFTA, and European Free Trade Association (EFTA) countries] have established a liberal environment for exports. The FTAs have significantly improved market access for Hungarian exports; however, the country's main exports still belong to the EU's group of sensitive products and still face substantial tariff and nontariff barriers. This EU regulation imposes binding constraints on exports of food products, metallurgical products, and chemicals. Safeguard provisions may also hinder exports of these sensitive products. The barriers have taken the form of a series of antidumping procedures that were initiated against metallurgical exports and other products of heavy industries. Meat exports were also hit by an EU embargo initiated for sanitary and veterinary reasons. Although companies in the meat industry were adversely affected by high agricultural levies, they were more interested in increased domestic protection than in the removal of external restrictions. The regulations of the Multi-Fibre Agreement exhibit a latent restriction on textile and clothing exports. Most of these deliveries are conducted under outward processing traffic (OPT) contracts and enjoy preferential status. If, however, clothing companies were to surpass the job-work status, the existing quotas would also become binding.

According to their responses, the surveyed firms were more concerned about the impact of FTAs on imports than about changes in their access to markets. The majority of the companies considered Hungary's recent abolition of quota and tariff protection granted in the FTAs too rapid, because sweeping import competition has undermined their positions in the domestic market. They frequently indicated the extensive black economy and smuggled goods as the most important factors constraining sales. They urged strengthening customs controls and severely punishing tax evaders. Concerning competition operating within the legal framework, they complained mostly about the highly subsidized exports arriving from CEFTA countries and from the former Soviet Union.

3.3.2 Supply constraints and the transformation of companies

A key component of establishing a solid market position is setting up the necessary infrastructure. This requires the establishment of a distributional and promotional network as well as the gathering of relevant marketing information, which is extremely costly and requires special skills. Improvements in the companies' export performance indicate partial success in overcoming trade barriers. However, without the establishment of accepted brand names and without distribution channels in the West, the export performance of these firms might remain fragile and dependent on Western business cycles (the recession in 1993 led to a large drop in Hungarian exports, particularly in exports related to OPT).

None of the surveyed companies was able to start exporting using only its own resources. Of the companies exporting to the West, Taurus is the only company that possesses a completely independent distributional network and sells its products directly to customers using its own brand name. Two companies retaining Eastern markets have also been pursuing an active marketing strategy (Richter and Graboplast). Richter, a pharmaceutical firm, has created an independent consignment storehouse network; Graboplast, an artificial-leather company, has endeavored to strengthen its market positions using direct investments. Other companies have sold their products via various intermediaries, such as exporting under OPT contracts or, in the case of JVs, using the facilities of the foreign partner. In the case of exports through intermediaries, the interviewed managers perceived demand constraint to be less effective than in the case of companies selling their products themselves. In several cases the Hungarian producers were not aware of relevant regulations on their markets (for example, the Multi-Fibre Agreement in the case of clothing companies).

The responses indicated that a common form of adjustment has been switching to exporting under an OPT contract. This adjustment has been particularly widespread among light industry companies (one shoe and six clothing companies) and among engineering firms (Ganz-Ansaldo). The OPT arrangement enables companies to survive without independent marketing and distribution networks. However, this arrangement does not imply any investment. OPT is the most precarious form of cooperation with Western partners because it requires a low level of sunk costs from the Western partners but a highly dependent sales pattern may be created for Hungarian companies. This dependency restricts the range of products a company can manufacture and limits market expansion.

In the clothing industry, most companies have experienced long-term cooperation with Western firms. In 1988, 35% of the industry's total production was conducted under job-work contracts. Based on these contacts, most companies have been able to reorient their production to Western markets. Consequently, these firms were less affected by the collapse of the CMEA and domestic demand. In some cases the cooperation was enhanced through the establishment of JVs (companies like Zako, Glovita, Elegant, and Elite, and Bonsa, which makes shoes). The Western partners' participation in these companies, however, has been relatively small compared with participation in the other branches of the industry, which indicates the vulnerability of these cooperations.

OPT has emerged in a different way in the engineering industry. Hungary used to be a large net exporter of engineering products to CMEA countries. In 1986, 40% of the total turnover was in Eastern markets. The collapse of the CMEA and shrinking domestic investment demand contributed to the decline in engineering production. Only a few companies were able to overcome the sales crisis resulting from the dissolution of the CMEA. Efforts to sell engineering companies to foreign investors in the framework of privatization were not very successful.

A few financially sound firms with sales patterns oriented toward Western and domestic markets were picked up by foreign investors when privatization began (GE-Tungsram and Lehel-Elektrolux). A number of companies were shut down, and survivors in the traditional household electronic appliances industry turned to job work, as did electrical engineering firms and companies that processed precision instruments. (At the same time the vast majority of FDI inflow into Hungary was aimed at precisely the engineering sectors, but in the form of greenfield investments.)

Privatization using FDI has led to mixed results in the market positions of these firms. On the one hand, investment in a Hungarian company is a sunk cost that may ensure longer-term cooperation. Moreover, the Hungarian partner can use the marketing and distribution network of the parent company and benefit from brand-name reputation established by the foreign partner. In those cases where a Hungarian firm became a member of a large multinational company, the parent company has assisted its Hungarian affiliate in order to reinforce marketing in domestic markets and to expand its exports to external markets. In several cases, the parent company has integrated the Hungarian affiliate into its worldwide distribution network (Lehel-Elektrolux). More often, the Hungarian affiliate was allowed to sell products only on Eastern markets or in a limited number of countries (Győri Keksz-United Biscuits). For other JVs, the cooperation facilitated exports but neglected domestic sales. On the other hand, buy-outs by foreign investors have also led to significant restrictions in product range and the end of production under traditional brand names (Lehel-Elektrolux and Ganz-Ansaldo). In the press there were also reports of hostile takeovers, where foreign investors did not use the production capacity acquired in Hungary; instead they used their Hungarian subsidiaries to enter the Hungarian market. The subsidiaries were used thereafter as simple distributors.

The firms gave little indication of efforts to restore their domestic market positions. As a consequence of the collapse of the traditional wholesale sector, they have lost their traditional home distributors (Kecskemét Parquet and clothing companies, for example). Besides a lack of knowledge, scarcity of financial resources also prevented most of them from applying active marketing strategies to counteract the stagnation in the internal market (two multinationals in our sample are exceptions: GE-Tungsram and Lehel-Elektrolux). Several companies reported that domestic sales were more profitable than exports and therefore they would be rather willing to deliver goods to domestic markets if they were in demand. In spite of this, most of the companies have been waiting idly for an increase in domestic demand. The companies continue to export because it is relatively cheap to do so, especially in an OPT setting. In terms of working capital requirements producing for the domestic market is more expensive than exporting because of the less advantageous payment conditions on both the input and output sides. However, the lack of a domestic trading network or the financial weakness of the existing one necessitate large investments for the restoration of domestic distribution channels.

3.3.3 Adaptation efforts

In the case studies we surveyed how firms responded to the changing market environment. We asked about adaptation efforts concerning the product line, production technology, and management of the firm's liabilities. Generally, recent expansion of production enhanced the efficiency and improved the profitability of the firms. In former years, almost every firm reported losses, but by 1994 the share of firms with losses declined to 20%.

Where technology permitted, companies usually reacted to the reduction in demand by cutting their production capacities. They sold obsolete or excess machinery and closed plants. Extensive layoffs and economizing on costs led to a significant improvement in X-efficiency.

Changes in product lines were twofold. Firms originally designed for bulk production decreased batch sizes and became more flexible in the face of changing demand (clothing companies, Graboplast, Gardenia). Most firms involved in OPT and firms owned by multinational companies (Lehel-Elektrolux and Ganz-Ansaldo) reported closing some product lines or activities (like research and development, and design), as these functions became unnecessary or could no longer be financed from operating revenues.

Almost every firm has improved the quality of its products; many firms reported implementing international quality standards. As of 1996 International Organization for Standardization (ISO) 9000 standards are required for EU exports. In several cases, considerable investment spending on the part of the company is required to meet these standards. Moreover, extra costs needed for more sophisticated production technology are not necessarily rewarded by the domestic market. Whereas a manager of a clothing company reported that the firm faced the most vigorous domestic demand in the high-price/high-quality category of products, other companies have had the opposite experience. In general, domestic and Eastern markets prefer lower-quality products at reasonable prices. Two of the five firms that reported an interest in Eastern exports explained their market orientation by pointing out that their products do not meet the quality requirements of Western markets.

The responses suggest that the lack of, or limited access to, production inputs plays a more important role in determining the fluctuation of production than was implied by the results of the business survey by KOPINT–DATORG Institute reported above. A lack of inputs was encountered only in the meat processing industry, where the strongest impediment to exports was a reduction in livestock. Imports of meat are restricted; therefore, the two companies concerned have been unable to deliver to rejuvenated Eastern markets. The companies are in poor financial condition and therefore cannot subsidize their suppliers that have found themselves in trouble. They consider it a task of the government, although the Gallicoop Company has taken an active role in establishing a network of suppliers.

For the majority of the companies, the lack of inputs does not constitute a direct impediment to production, as products that are not available domestically can be easily replaced by imported goods. However, when asked whether imported inputs can be replaced by domestic resources, the majority of the firms answered negatively. This situation is obvious in the chemical industry and in metallurgy, since a substantial part of their inputs are raw materials that are not available in Hungary. Other firms, particularly those engaged in commission work, tried to incorporate cheaper domestic inputs into their products, but usually they could not find suppliers who could provide consistent quality and who could work on a flexible schedule. The unsuccessful attempts by car manufacturers to establish a network of domestic suppliers were widely published in the press (c.f., Figyelő, Feb. 16, 1995, pp. 14–27). Of the four principal car factories, GM-Opel, Ford, Audi, and Suzuki, only Suzuki employs enough Hungarian subcontractors to provide a significant share of the installed domestic parts. In this case the EU's "rules of origin" provisions compelled the company to increase the share of domestic suppliers; this policy required a substantial financial sacrifice from Suzuki. Although the Hungarian government has made efforts to encourage the other car manufacturers to employ Hungarian suppliers, the companies have not been interested in doing so.

In the case of those companies where the proportion of commission work was substantial, we asked whether they thought it was possible to appear on the market with their own products as independent exporters. The responses were negative in almost all cases. Respondents listed a number of reasons why it was impossible, including the lack of a distribution network and the market power of the partner company in import procurements. Moreover, the lack of financial assets was indicated in each case. The scarcity of working capital and the high interest rates on available loans compel companies to maintain the commission work arrangement: they are simply unable to buy the necessary inputs on their own account and pay customs duties on the imports.

Most firms covered in our survey face a contradictory situation on the labor market. In recent years 30–50% of the employees have been dismissed. Although originally overstaffing was higher among administrative workers, the number of manual workers has also been reduced. Actual staffing problems were reported by three companies, two of which employ qualified foreign workers. In addition to the extensive lay-offs, several companies complained about the lack of a labor force.

Observing the revival of demand they had intended to launch an additional shift of work. However, they were unable to gather sufficient staff for the second shift. The reason generally was not a lack of qualified workers, but the fact that potential employees refused to accept the work for the wages offered by the company. Company managers blamed their refusal on higher incomes attainable on the black market and criticized the system of unemployment benefits. The interviewed managers said that if they were to pay a higher level of wages their production would become unprofitable. A particularly rigid constraint on wage increases prevails for companies conducting commission work. All of them expressed fear that their consignor would transfer production to a site farther East because of the increase in wages. This has actually occurred in one of the companies (Hunostyl).

A few companies in the sample have neglected to replace obsolete machinery; other companies have started new investment projects. Since the beginning of 1994, investment activity has been booming. According to the responses, the investments primarily serve to ensure that quality requirements are fulfilled and that new technology is developed. These investments are necessary for maintaining the current level of production; only a few firms reported investments for increasing capacity. Investment projects rely primarily on companies' internal financial resources. When these resources are lacking, companies would rather suspend investments than finance them with a loan. Large companies in the chemical industry had launched investments based on what the demand of Eastern markets was just before the CMEA collapse. These companies had to go through years of increasing indebtedness and never ending liquidity problems and later were involved in the government's central crisis-management program of 1993, wherein their debts were canceled or rescheduled.

The evidence suggests that loans provided by foreign banks directly to Hungarian enterprises are an important way of financing investments. In the first three months of 1995, the influx of foreign credit to Hungarian enterprises and commercial banks amounted to US$1.5 billion, whereas the FDI inflow was only US$200 million. Companies drawing credits directly from foreign banks are not represented in our sample. Two of the companies in the sample took foreign loans from parent companies (Ganz-Ansaldo and Hunguard); another received credit from the company that provided its inputs (Rico). Two companies obtained loans disbursed in foreign exchange from Hungarian banks (Rico and Elite). Other managers attributed their aversion to taking foreign credit to the high risk resulting from unpredictable exchange rate changes (the switch to the crawling peg had been announced only a few days before the interviews took place).

The method of privatization and the ownership structure of a company are closely related to its development possibilities. In companies owned by Hungarian individuals, the purchase of the company has often exhausted the owner's financial resources, leaving no additional sources for necessary investment. However, in companies where privatization has involved foreign capital, the availability of additional resources ensures a financial basis for investments: all the JVs but one reported completed or ongoing investments and modernization of technology. Two of the firms were privatized by selling shares on the stock exchange. One of them (Graboplast) obtained sufficient resources through this method of privatization; the other (Richter) suffered from a lack of funds and has not been able to implement indispensable technological renewal.

No development funds are available for companies that are under state governance; however, the financial positions of these companies have improved, because four of them (Ringa, Taurus, Borsodchem, and Csepel Metalworks) have been released from their debt.

3.3.4 The role of the government

We reviewed the surveyed firms' opinions of several government policy measures. We were interested in the impact of macrostabilization policy on the companies' performance and how the company managers perceived these policies. The effects of some trade policy and industrial policy measures were also surveyed.

It is no wonder that restrictive monetary policy and high interest rates were condemned by most of the surveyed companies. In 1991–1992 reduced liquidity contributed to the demand shock and forced many companies into bankruptcy.[1] The debt service of firms that carried out large investments in the late 1980s was severely affected by high nominal interest rates. Debt consolidation was the only way they could recover from permanent liquidity crisis. Tight credit policy was listed as a main factor in restraining investment plans, because firms were forced to carry out investments exclusively from internal resources. Unfortunately, the interviews provide little information about the firms' actual efforts to find the funds for implementing viable investment projects. Consequently, we cannot really evaluate whether the tight credit policy was a barrier to investments.

The entire period can be characterized as having a high level of real interest rates on enterprise credits [deflated by the producer price index (PPI)]. Among other factors, the persistent difference between the consumer price index (CPI) and the PPI has contributed to the high interest rates. Consequently, the financial burden of credits has increased disproportionately compared with other costs. However, the wedge between the CPI and the PPI declined in 1994 and disappeared in early 1995, and there is hope that this cost distortion will also disappear.

The enthusiasm individual managers showed concerning recent changes in the exchange rate regime and increased tariff protection (import surcharges) depended on the import intensity of their firm's production. Because firms rely on imported inputs to a large extent, only a few of them expected that these measures would improve their profitability. Firms exporting food products or commission work appreciated the changes, albeit the latter group must share profits with their contractors. Most of the managers expressed an aversion to the uncertainty that they had previously experienced with nominal exchange rate changes. The new crawling peg rule significantly diminished the exchange rate risk of estimating future export revenues or burdens of credits disbursed in foreign exchange.

All companies considered tax rates and social security contributions to be too high. They believed that high rates induced widespread noncompliance and promoted the black market.

Turning to trade policy, most companies found the existing system of export promotion and the protection of the domestic market ineffective and insufficient. Hungary's export promotion policy consists of two basic elements: subsidized credits for export-oriented investments and tax rebates and exemptions for companies making export-oriented investments. In 1994 new institutions were founded to provide special financial services and insurance for exporters. These services currently cover only a minor part of the export deals, but they will grow in importance in the coming years. Subsidies do not play a great role except in meat processing. Meat processing companies found the current system of production subsidies biased toward exports of low-quality products. Most of the companies called for subsidized export financing. In particular, companies trading with East European countries complained that their competitors, backed by state subsidies, were able to offer more favorable payment conditions, and they called for government support in the marketing and financing of Eastern deals.

Most firms considered the available credits for export-oriented investments too expensive, even with subsidized interest rates. Two companies (Gardenia and Ringa) have carried out investment projects with the financial help of the Export Promotion Fund. Both companies were disappointed by the endless administrative requirements compared with the small benefit in the interest rate they received. Three of the surveyed companies were enrolled in a program that offered tax rebates to promote exports: a foreign-owned firm (Bonsa), a JV (Lehel-Elektrolux), and a state-owned company (Richter). State promotion in the form of canceling old debts turned out to be more effective than allocating new credits for promising exporters. The government's debt consolidation program focused on large exporting companies. Freed from debt service, these companies have expanded their exports, and some of them have even become profitable.

Most companies felt that Hungarian trade barriers to foreign companies had been removed too quickly. Enhanced import competition spoiled the market power of the companies on the domestic market. Several companies expressed a preference for a higher level of domestic protection over better conditions for exports.

Taurus considered import competition to be a constraint on exports, because in the period preceding liberalization the company's profits were secured by sales in domestic markets and, therefore, they could maintain unprofitable exporting. It is interesting that the implementation of import quotas against chemical and metallurgical products originating from several East European countries coincided with a tremendous export drive in these sectors. This might suggest that this type of cross subsidization persists in other companies, as well; however, other explanations referring to international price movements or debt consolidation seem more convincing.

3.4 Concluding Remarks

Most of the firms in our enterprise survey have successfully adapted to changes in their trading environment. After a period of shrinking production and persistent liquidity problems, most companies have exhibited considerable progress in enterprise performance measured by increasing profitability and increases in total sales revenues, particularly in exports. The majority of the companies are aware of the requirements of Western markets (e.g., quality and flexibility in supply), and they devote significant efforts and resources to meet these requirements.

Several weaknesses in this adjustment process can be surmised on the basis of the case studies. The most serious problems are related to the vulnerability of newly established trade relations and to the lack of an independent distribution and promotion network that could help establish good reputations for the products. These facilities are insufficient in both domestic and foreign markets. What is extraordinary is that entry costs to domestic markets seem to be as high as those to external markets as a result of the collapse of the old wholesale network and the infant stage of new intermediary trade.

Successful adjustment at the firm level was accompanied by significant external macro-imbalances and deterioration of the current account. One possible explanation for the divergence of macro and micro level tendencies is the fact that the sample used in this analysis was not representative of Hungarian exporting companies as a whole. Moreover, the study involved only companies that currently are exporters; companies that could not survive the collapse of CMEA trade or that could not enter the market were not included. A study by Halpern (1995b) showed significant mobility among exporting companies. He found that in the period from 1991 to 1993, only two-thirds of the large exporting companies (export turnover exceeding US$1 million) qualified as large exporting companies for all three years.

Several manifestations of growing macro-imbalances were detected in the case studies. Survey responses indicated that the companies' procurement policies have relied on the substitution of upgraded imported inputs for domestic inputs that were unavailable or were of low quality, or whose delivery was inflexible. According to Tóth (1995), replacement by imports is a common adaptation strategy for many Hungarian manufacturing enterprises. This has resulted in a significant increase in the import intensity of the Hungarian economy, which imposes a balance-of-payment constraint on growth.

Several companies complained about increasing input prices, especially increasing wage costs. Managers indicated that they could not pay competitive salaries to attract workers, because the enterprises would not have been profitable had higher wages been paid. Firms conducting OPT exports worried that their consignor would transfer production to a site farther East because of Hungary's high dollar wages. Hungarian exports are extremely vulnerable to OPT exit, because a quarter of the total turnover results from this activity. In the first years of adjustment, products based on low labor costs were the driving force behind export growth. However, differences in wage levels among CEECs reduced the competitiveness of such activities in Hungary. Hungary's specialization is changing to activities where wage differentials can be compensated by productivity differentials (for example, the pharmaceutical industry and engineering).

The wage problems experienced by the managers interviewed in our survey became widespread in the export sector. According to Halpern (1995b), the wage-to-output ratio increased throughout the exporting sector in the early 1990s. Among companies with export turnover exceeding US$1 million, the average unit wage cost increased from 9.5% to 19.9% between 1991 and 1993. No firms engaged in OPT were free from the pressure to increase wages. According to data from the tax authority covering all companies carrying out OPT, in the manufacturing of products made under OPT contracts the wage-to-output ratio was 27% in 1993 and 37% in the first quarter of 1995 (KOPINT–DATORG, 1995). A part of the wage increase is offset by increasing productivity, since unit labor costs lagged behind wage growth. However, wage increases coupled with persistent external imbalances are indicative of problems with competitiveness and the real exchange rate.

Another issue related to trade incentives was raised by the companies' changing sales patterns. The companies surveyed have been quite successful at expanding their exports. At the same time, their products have been crowded out of domestic markets to a greater extent than is justified by the decline in demand. The managers interviewed in our survey pointed to the collapse of the domestic trading sector to explain this. In the early 1990s Hungary's traditional domestic distribution network disintegrated, partly due to a series of bankruptcies and partly due to inadequate privatization. By contrast, on Western markets an effective network of intermediaries has provided marketing services for Hungarian companies.

The undersized and undercapitalized domestic service sector has not been able to provide payment conditions that are as advantageous as those of their foreign competitors in Hungary. As a rule, foreign distributors selling foreign products in Hungary offer better payment conditions than domestic distributors or producers specializing in Hungarian products. Furthermore, the scarcity of working capital has compelled companies to enter into production arrangements with low financing needs, like OPT contracts. These developments suggest that the reason for the low competitiveness of Hungarian production in competition with imports is not simply high costs. Policy measures to improve domestic intermediation could also be an effective tool in fighting against the trade deficit.

The rapid deterioration of the current account prompted the Hungarian government to introduce corrective measures to improve the competitiveness of domestic products both at home and abroad. In addition to the change in the exchange rate regime and the devaluation of the currency, the government introduced a uniform import surcharge (exempting only energy, investment goods, and inputs for OPT). It is alarming that pressures for selective protection have also gained momentum in the past few years. Intensified claims for market protection have frequently been accepted since the second half of 1992. According to Borszéki (1994) the protective measures have been directed mainly against raw materials and energy-intensive products coming from East European countries. The list of protected goods reveals that these measures have supported two groups of interest. For cement, paper, and bicycles, domestic production is completely dominated by foreign investors. Protective measures have also supported enterprises taking part in the government's crisis management program: quotas have been imposed on imports competing with the products of the four largest firms of domestic heavy industry.

Notes

[1] On the macro level, the so-called credit-crunch hypothesis investigates the effect of a tight credit policy on output decline through supply factors. According to Valentinyi (1995), the importance of the credit crunch in the output decline was not really supported by the Hungarian data. The credit crunch seems to have played a role only in 1992, when real credits declined faster than production.

References

Berényi, J., ed., 1995, Foreign Direct Investments in Hungary, Survey Results, KOPINT–DATORG, Budapest, Hungary [in Hungarian].

Borszéki, Zs., 1994, Market Protection: Snapshot, Prospects and Propositions, KOPINT–DATORG, Budapest, Hungary [in Hungarian].

Bucher, A., Hazden, M., and Toledano, L.E., 1994, Economic evaluation of EC-CEEC trade, in The Economic Interpenetration between the European Union and Eastern Europe, *European Economy*, 6:77–128.

CEPR (Centre for Economic Policy Research), 1990, *Monitoring European Integration, The Impact of Eastern Europe*, CEPR, London, UK.

Collins, S., and Rodrik, D., 1991, Eastern Europe and the Soviet Union in the World Economy, Institute for International Economics, Washington, DC, USA.

Dobrinsky, R., 1994, Trade Restructuring in Central and Eastern Europe: A Comparison of Eastern and Western Trade Structures, New York, NY, USA [mimeo].

Drabek, Z., and Smith, A., 1995, Trade Performance and Trade Policy in Central and Eastern Europe, CEPR discussion paper No. 1182, Centre for Economic Policy Research, London, UK.

Gács, J., 1994, The Economic Interpenetration between EC and Eastern Europe: Hungary, *European Economy*, 6:191–224.

Graziani, G., 1994, Trade patterns and comparative advantages of Central Eastern Europe with the EC countries, in J. Gács and G. Winckler, eds., *International Trade and Restructuring in Eastern Europe*, Physica Verlag, Heidelberg, Germany.

Halpern, L., 1995a, Comparative advantage and likely trade pattern of the CEECs, in R. Faini and R. Portes, eds., *European Union Trade with Eastern Europe*, Centre for Economic Policy Research, London, UK.

Halpern, L., 1995b, Export growth and profitability in the exporting companies, 1991–1993, Budapest, Hungary [mimeo, in Hungarian].

Hamilton, C., and Winters, A., 1992, Opening up international trade with Eastern Europe, *Economic Policy*, 14:78–104.

Havlik, P., 1995, Exchange Rates, Wages and Competitiveness of Central and Eastern Europe, WIIW (Vienna Institute for Comparative Economic Studies), Vienna, Austria.

HCSO (Hungarian Central Statistical Office), 1992, Foreign Trade in Hungary 1991, HCSO, Budapest, Hungary.

HCSO (Hungarian Central Statistical Office), *Statistical Yearbook of Hungary*, various volumes, HCSO, Budapest, Hungary.

KOPINT–DATORG, 1995, Survey of Business Tendencies 1995/2, KOPINT–DATORG, Budapest, Hungary.

KOPINT–DATORG, *Business Survey*, various issues, KOPINT–DATORG, Budapest, Hungary.

Kovács, Z.A., 1995, Changing Pattern of Trade Between Hungary and the European Community: A Retrospective Analysis, 1989–1994, KOPINT–DATORG, Budapest, Hungary.

Lemoine, F., 1994, CEEC exports to the EC (1988–1993): Country Differentiation and Commodity Diversification, CEPII Document de Travail No. 94-15, Centre D'études Prospectives et D'informations Internationales, Paris, France.

NBH (National Bank of Hungary), *Annual Report*, various issues, NBH, Budapest, Hungary.

Oblath, G., 1995, Eastern Europe's Trade Performance on Western Markets and Eastern Europe as a Market for Western Exports: A Review of Developments between 1990 and 1993, KOPINT–DATORG discussion papers, Budapest, Hungary.

Rodrik, D., 1992, Foreign Trade in Eastern Europe's Transition: Early Results, CEPR discussion paper No. 676, Centre for Economic Policy Research, London, UK.

Tóth, I.J., 1995, Methodological Study for the Estimation of Import Intensity of Manufacturing, KOPINT–DATORG, Budapest, Hungary [in Hungarian].

UN ECE (United Nations Economic Commission for Europe), 1994, *Economic Bulletin for Europe*, Vol. 46, UN ECE, New York, NY, USA.

Valentinyi, Á., 1995, Macroeconomic Adjustment in Transition: Hungary 1988–1994, Badia Fiesole, Italy [mimeo].

Wang, Y.Q., 1993, Foreign investment in Hungary: A survey experience and prospects, *Communist Economies and Economic Transformation*, **5**(2):245–254.

Chapter 4

Latvia

Inna Shteinbuka and Aleksandra Cīrule

Latvia, a country about the size of the Republic of Ireland with a population of 2.7 million and a resource-poor economy, has a centuries-old tradition in trade as a gateway between East and West. Its ice-free ports on the Baltic Sea and its location at the mouth of an inland river system enabled it to become a central trading post in the Middle Ages, when Riga, the capital, was an important Hansa city. During its brief period of independence between the two World Wars, much of Latvia's economic activity depended on trade. This pattern continued during its five decades as part of the Soviet Union, albeit with a highly distorted allocation of resources.

Since it regained its independence in August 1991, Latvia's macroeconomic record has exhibited contrasting features. On the positive side are the successful introduction of a stable national currency (the lats), early and successful price liberalization, a dramatic reduction in inflation, and the achievement (at least until 1995) of nearly balanced budgets despite a severe decline in tax revenues. On the negative side are the catastrophic declines in output and living standards, especially in 1992. Other negative features include persistently high interest rates, restrictive lending practices of commercial banks, and the negligible pace of large-scale privatization. All these factors have probably contributed to the lack of significant industrial restructuring.

The priorities of macroeconomic policy in 1995–1996 are inflation suppression, exchange rate stability, and fiscal balance. It is also aimed at creating preconditions for sustainable economic growth. The government does not consider industrial policy to be a priority or an engine of economic performance. Only the development of infrastructure is bolstered by limited budgetary disbursements and state guaranteed credits.

One of the Latvian government's most important achievements during the first years of transformation from a centrally planned system has been early and rapid economic liberalization.

4.1 The Liberalization Process

When it was part of the USSR, Latvia's economy was completely removed from international markets. Because the currency was not convertible and internal prices were not suitable for external trade arrangements, all transactions were dependent on the decisions of the authorities. For political reasons trade with Western countries was especially limited: even in 1991 non-Soviet countries' shares of total Latvian exports amounted to less than 3%. Merchandise exchange between the Soviet republics was artificially promoted and frequently had no economic grounds. Taking into account the bureaucratic allocation of exports and imports in the USSR, the degree of transparency was extremely low.

The liberalization process began with the liberalization of prices, which was accomplished in 1991 and early 1992. Deregulation of prices was accompanied by a sharp reduction of subsidies to enterprises, especially agricultural firms. In 1990 subsidies constituted 41% of the state budget; in 1992, only 1.6%. Currently, there are price restrictions only for public transport, utilities, telecommunications, and state medical services.

The second stage of liberalization concerned liberalization of the currency exchange market, which in turn was accompanied by currency reform. A free market exchange rate and a foreign currency market were established in November 1990. Driven at first by necessity (a shortage of notes) and then by design, Latvia gradually extricated itself from the ruble zone after May 1992. Following the extraordinary appreciation of the lats against all currencies in March 1993, the Bank of Latvia instituted a policy of exchange rate management to prevent sudden fluctuations. The implicit reference point for this policy was special drawing rights (SDR), the exchange unit created by the International Monetary Fund (IMF).

In March 1993 the Bank of Latvia began to introduce the lats as the permanent replacement for the Latvian ruble at a fixed exchange rate of 200 Latvian rubles per lat. By October 1993 the new currency had completely supplanted the Latvian ruble in circulation.

After a volatile period in March 1993, the lats gained 17% against the US dollar over the subsequent year. Although it was not explicitly announced at the time, the crawling peg against the SDR was abandoned in mid-February 1994 in favor of a straightforward peg to the SDR with a central rate of 0.7997 lats.

In contrast to Estonia and Lithuania, Latvia achieved exchange rate stability without introducing the currency board system.

At present, Latvia has one of the most liberal foreign exchange regimes in the world, having full current and capital account convertibility. The liberalization of the foreign trade regime, the third stage in the liberalization process, was initiated in June 1992, when all export quotas and licensing requirements (except those for pyrotechnics, arms and ammunition, fighting vehicles, prepared explosives, and metals purchased in Latvia) were abolished and replaced with a system of export taxes, most of which were abolished in September 1992. The taxes were intended to compensate for the undervaluation of the real exchange rate. The export tax rates were highly dispersed and were higher on exports to nonconvertible currency areas and on barter trade in order to encourage exports to the West. At the end of 1993 the remaining export tax rates were lowered, which substantially reduced their dispersion and restrictiveness. Duties were eliminated for many final goods. The bias against exports to areas with nonconvertible currencies was reduced and then totally abandoned. According to Sorsa (1994) most remaining export taxes have an industrial policy tilt. They are levied on raw materials (for example, unprocessed wood), which reduces the price of inputs for domestic industries processing these raw materials. Stimulating higher value-added goods in such a way does not seem to be a bad system. However, it should be mentioned that all export tariffs will be abolished by 1999, except those for antiques.

Since mid-1992 imports have also been largely free from licensing requirements (except for arms and ammunition, pyrotechnics, fighting vehicles, prepared explosives, alcohol, grain and sugar, and tobacco products). Latvian authorities continue to favor an open trade system with a low uniform tariff regime as a medium-term objective. The use of tariffs for revenue purposes is contrary to government policy. The impact of customs revenues on the fiscal balance is decreasing; currently, the share of customs tariffs in general government revenues is approximately 2%. The tariff law that came into force 1 December 1994 fits this tendency. A 20% basic tariff rate is levied on most goods for final consumption. Minimal tariffs (0.5–1%) are imposed on some raw materials, spare parts, capital goods and some goods for final consumption not produced in Latvia. Specific tariff rates are levied on seed and animal feed, certain grains, flour, bread, sugar, certain confectionery products including chocolate, alcohol, cigarettes, and cars. Due to a powerful agricultural lobby, tariff rates for certain agricultural goods and food products were increased under the new tariff law, in extreme cases reaching 55%. According to IMF estimates, the average production-weighted agricultural tariff under the new law is around 53%. Because of difficulties in monitoring border trade (problems with smuggling), the effective tariff burden on agricultural imports may in fact be significantly lower. Latvia's weighted average tariff decreased significantly during 1995. As a result, the weighted average customs tariff decreased from 3.4% in 1994 to 2.0% in 1995.

In April 1995 the Cabinet of Ministers adopted provisions "On the temporary import of goods into Latvia for processing." According to these provisions, those who import goods into Latvia for processing and re-export can be exempted from customs duties or can be reimbursed for any duties paid once the processed goods have left Latvia. When importing goods for processing, an importer must pay a value-added tax (VAT) guarantee payment amounting to 2% of the goods' customs value. However, in the face of the 1995 governmental budget crisis many enterprises have reported difficulties collecting the guarantee-payment reimbursements due following the exports.

4.2 Economic Diplomacy

For a country as small as Latvia, it is important to be part of multilateral trade organizations and treaties that give access to large markets and so provide new opportunities for export development. Moreover, a stable trade environment, which is guaranteed by the legal framework of international treaties, is an important precondition for the inflow of foreign investments to Latvia because it has a positive impact on development of export potential. With this in mind, the Latvian government has done much to stimulate export development. Latvia officially requested membership in the General Agreement on Tariffs and Trade (GATT) in December 1993. Multilateral accession negotiations for the World Trade Organization (WTO) were initiated at the end of March 1995. The greatest problems in Latvia's relations with the WTO seem to be connected with the customs valuation procedure applied with respect to agricultural goods (use of reference prices); quantitative restrictions applied to sugar and grain imports; and excessively high import tariffs for certain agricultural products. These problems will soon be resolved and, hopefully, Latvia will be admitted to the WTO by the end of 1996.

Latvia is becoming increasingly integrated with the other Baltic states and the European Union (EU). A free trade agreement between Latvia and the EU covering industrial goods came into force 1 January 1995. The agreement provides for establishing a free trade area within a period of four years. Certain textile products of Latvian origin, in particular, benefit from zero customs duties on imports to EU countries as long as these imports do not exceed the quantities specified in the agreement. The benefits for agricultural products are not yet obvious. For each product from the agricultural sector, the EU and Latvia will discuss the possibility of increasing the existing export limits. In June 1995 Latvia also signed an Association Agreement with the EU, which still has to be ratified in some EU member states. This agreement will stimulate Latvia–EU integration in both the social and economic (labor force movement, capital movement) spheres.

Integration within the Baltic region has been important as well. The Baltic states' free trade agreement covering industrial goods has been operating successfully since April 1994. In June 1996 an agreement on free trade in agricultural goods between three Baltic republics was also signed; it will come into force after ratification by the Parliaments of the Baltic states. Furthermore, a declaration on establishing a customs union between the three Baltic states by January 1998 has been accepted. In reality, however, the primary focus of Baltic integration efforts is the EU.

Latvia has also signed free trade agreements with European Free Trade Association (EFTA) states (which entered into force in July 1996), and with the Czech Republic, Slovakia, Slovenia, and Ukraine (all of which will come into force during 1996). Moreover, the government plans to sign free trade agreements with other associated EU member states by the end of 1998.

Trade with other states has chiefly been promoted through most favored nation trade agreements, of which Latvia currently has 18. This trade status was the most difficult to achieve with Russia (an agreement has been in force since June 1994). Most favored nation status is very important from both an economic and a political point of view; however, Russia has granted this status to Latvia only on a temporary basis. The impermanent nature of the agreement has caused uncertainty for producers. Considering the unstable political relations between the two republics, Latvia's most favored nation status could be canceled any time, which would mean a doubling of import duties for Latvian exports to Russia.

Regarding trade with Russia, an important achievement was the agreement between the Latvian Ministry of Economy and Russia's Committee of Mechanical Engineering on cooperation in the sphere of mechanical engineering. This agreement is revised and renewed annually and contains an indicative list of goods to be delivered by each side. Russia exports raw materials (fuel, metals, metal products, plastics, and acids). Latvia, in turn, exports electric parts for automobiles, microchips, pumps, electronic instruments, and diesel and electric trains. For Latvian producers in the relevant sectors, both raw materials and final products can cross Russia's border duty free. Quantities specified in the agreement are not mandatory and the enterprises concerned are free to change them. Of the 20 enterprises that we prepared case studies about for this chapter, 4 benefit from this agreement.

4.3 Export Promotion Organizations

Four strong export promotion organizations have been founded since Latvia regained its independence: the Latvian Chamber of Trade and Commerce (LCTC), the Latvian Development Agency, the World Trade Center (WTC) Riga, and the Latvian Export Crediting Company. All these organizations were founded with government support but are now largely independent formations from both the financial and the political points of view.

The LCTC was organized in 1991 and has steadily expanded its activities. After liberalization of foreign trade, the LCTC began to issue non-preferential certificates of origin and approvals of compliance with rules of origin to receive EUR 1 and FORM A certificates. Under the auspices of the LCTC, a Latvian bureau of the International Article Numbering Association (EAN) was organized. Currently, approximately 50 Latvian enterprises have EAN codes; of the enterprises included in our survey, two had such codes, Laima (candies) and Vermerk (electric lamps). The court of arbitration also operates under the guidance of the LCTC.

The LCTC is supported by foreign chambers of commerce. It has also prepared and now maintains several databases and organizes participation in international exhibitions for Latvian enterprises.

The second organization is the Latvian Development Agency whose main task is promoting exports and foreign investments. It has approximately 5,000 clients who regularly receive its booklets. Every year the Agency prepares the *Latvian Export Directory*, with detailed information on all exporters classified by commodity group. It also organizes participation of Latvian enterprises in exhibitions abroad.

The third organization, WTC Riga, is the first WTC established in the Baltics. It is a regular member of the World Trade Centers Association (WTCA), one of whose goals is fostering increased participation in world trade by developing nations. WTC Riga has the largest trade-related database in Latvia. It has access to the WTCA Bulletin Board, where it is possible to post offers and to read offers posted by other network subscribers around the globe. It is active in organizing Latvian exhibitions abroad and foreign trade missions in Latvia. It currently has a project with the US World Trade Institute aimed at promoting Latvian exports in the USA. Thirty-five enterprises from different industries have expressed their intention to participate in the project; an individual marketing plan will be developed for each participant.

The Latvian Export Crediting Company was established in January 1995 as a state company with the following tasks: to provide guarantees for trade operations; to insure export–import operations; and to credit export–import operations. The greatest obstacle to the expansion of the Company's activities has been the lack of financial resources. Currently, the Company's fixed capital amounts to 220,000 lats (approximately US$420,000). Possibilities for attracting private capital are limited by government provisions. As a result, the soonest the Company will be able to start export–import insurance and crediting is 1996. For the near future, the company's priority is providing guarantees for Latvian exporters for the purchase of inputs abroad and in Latvia.

Unfortunately, it seems that Latvian enterprises do not take full advantage of even the limited range of services offered by these organizations.

4.4 Export Performance During Transition

To evaluate export performance during the past few years, it is necessary to refer to the changes in the composition of the GDP. In 1990 services accounted for 32% of the GDP and manufacturing and agriculture for 55% (agriculture and forestry, 21%; manufacturing, 34%); by 1995 these percentages had almost reversed. Because of severe supply and demand shocks, GDP fell some 50% during transition, with the sharpest decreases in agriculture and manufacturing. Manufacturing currently constitutes only 20% of the GDP and agriculture and forestry make up 10%. As a result of the high proportion of services in output, the private sector now accounts for over 50% of the GDP. These developments in the national economy are also reflected in Latvia's foreign economic relations.

4.4.1 Balance of payments

The balance of payments for 1995 shows a current account deficit of US$171 million, or 3.6% of the GDP (see *Table 4.1*). The 1995 trade balance had a deficit of US$445 million, or 9.4% of the GDP; this deficit was partly offset by the net export of services, mainly in the transport sector which showed a surplus of US$274 million. The worsening of the trade balance was connected with the decline in Russian oil re-exports, currency appreciation, and high export duties for unprocessed wood. Latvia's trade balance with Commonwealth of Independent States (CIS) countries was positive, but there was a trade deficit with the other countries. A prospective factor was the increased share of mechanical and electrical equipment and machinery in imports, which in 1995 amounted to 17.4%. Because increases in this sector have a positive influence on enterprise modernization, export performance could improve in future.

The 1995 capital account surplus was estimated at US$79 million. Foreign direct investment (net) was estimated at US$165 million. The largest investment was in the telecommunications sector.

Table 4.1. Latvia's balance of payments, 1992–1995 (in millions of US dollars).

	1992	1993	1994	1995 (estimated)
Current account balance	21	151	–86	–171
Trade balance	–215	–160	–378	–445
Exports	831	998	997	1,306
CIS and Baltic	396	504	503	499
Other countries	435	494	494	807
Imports	–1,046	–1,158	–1,375	–1,751
Energy	–503	–525	–407	–492
Non-energy	–543	–633	–968	–1,259
CIS and Baltic countries	–626	–237	–245	–239
Other countries	–420	–396	–723	–1,020
Services, income, and transfers balance	236	311	292	274
Capital account balance	–21	151	274	79
Foreign direct investment, net	43	51	155	165
Other medium- and long-term capital	33	98	87	64
Net errors and omissions	36	–15	–49	–7
Net foreign assets of deposit money banks ("–" increase)	–79	–38	–87	76
Bank of Latvia reserves ("–" increase)	–108	–282	–63	40
Overall balance	133	322	139	–98
Memorandum item				
Exchange rate (lats/US$, end-year)	0.843	0.595	0.548	0.530

Source: International Monetary Fund and European Bank for Reconstruction and Development data.

4.4.2 Changes in the geographical pattern of exports

Latvia has begun to diversify its exports and move away from excessive dependence on the former Soviet Union (FSU), but much still has to be done. The most significant changes in geographical patterns of trade came about in 1992. One contributing factor was liberalization of trade. A second was the large depreciation of the domestic currency in late 1991 and early 1992, which led to a jump in the unit values of trade (accounted in domestic currency) with countries outside the ruble zone and made export to Western countries especially lucrative. As a result, the share of exports to non-FSU countries increased dramatically, from less than 3% in 1991 to 50% in 1992. Since then Latvian exports have remained almost equally divided between FSU and non-FSU countries despite the remarkable recent changes in currency markets. The year 1995 strengthened the earlier observed trends: trade with countries of Western Europe continued to gain in importance, while the share of CIS countries continued to decrease. In 1995 Western Europe's share of Latvian

Table 4.2. Distribution of Latvian exports by country, 1994 and 1995 (in percent).

Country	1994	1995
Russia	28.1	25.3
Germany	10.5	13.6
United Kingdom	9.7	9.0
Sweden	6.9	9.3
Ukraine	5.9	5.5
Lithuania	5.6	5.5
Belarus	4.3	4.3
Others	29.0	27.5
Total	100.0	100.0

Source: Latvian State Committee for Statistics.

exports increased five percentage points, which reflects a strengthening of business contacts with Western countries.

The distribution of Latvian exports within the FSU has remained more or less the same as in previous years, although the share of the other Baltic states in Latvia's exports is growing. This increase is mainly the result of weakened trade ties with other FSU republics and the establishment of a free trade area between the three Baltic republics. Trade between Latvia and distant Asian republics, which was established during the central planning era, has been losing importance because in many cases it has proved economically unprofitable.

According to official statistics, distribution of trade with non-FSU states fluctuates remarkably from year to year. This fluctuation could be explained by the low reliability of statistics, the ongoing process of establishing business contacts (often, existing relations are not stable), and changes in the price structure over the course of transition. However, countries such as Germany, UK, Sweden, and Finland have been among Latvia's main partners, with Germany in first place. In general, geographical proximity is a leading factor in relations with non-FSU states. For a summary of the geographical distribution of Latvian exports, see *Table 4.2*.

4.4.3 Changes in the commodity pattern of exports

When Latvia was part of the Soviet Union it had monopolies in the production of many important items such as passenger cars for electric and diesel trains (100% of total Soviet production), telephones (53%), motorcycles (57%), and various kinds of building equipment, electric components for cars and tractors, agricultural machines, and medicines. Latvia was a primary producer of textiles, perfume, and jewelry for the USSR as well. Moreover, 98% of the minibuses, 89% of the

Table 4.3. Distribution of Latvian exports by commodity group, 1990, 1994, and 1995 (in percent of total exports).[a]

Commodity group	1990	Commodity group	1994	1995
Engineering and metalworking machinery	27.4	Wood and wooden articles	20.3	26.4
Foodstuffs	23.2	Textiles	13.2	14.0
Light industrial products	17.6	Foodstuffs	12.8	11.1
Chemicals	12.9	Base metals and base-metal products	10.1	7.9
Wood and wooden articles	2.3	Vehicles	10.0	6.4
Base metals	2.2	Mechanical and electrical equipment	9.2	8.7
Building materials	1.4	Chemicals	7.4	6.4
Others	13.0	Others	17.0	19.1
Total	100.0		100.0	100.0

[a] A new classification system for commodities went into use in 1992; accordingly, data for 1990 and 1994 are not directly comparable.
Source: Latvian State Committee for Statistics.

washing machines, 79% of the radios, and 71% of the diesel engines and diesel generators manufactured in Latvia in 1990 were exported to other Soviet republics. Of Latvia's 400 industrial enterprises, 140 were All-Union (that is, they were the Soviet Union's sole producer of a product) and others were near monopolies. The overall commodity structure of Latvian exports for 1990 is shown in *Table 4.3*.

With the collapse of the Soviet Union, Latvia's export situation changed drastically. Some Latvian producers maintained semi-monopolistic positions in FSU markets because their prices for some items were still much lower than those of comparable Western products: for example, electric trains produced by RVR-Riga Carriage Plant (a company selected for our case studies) are about one-third the cost of trains built by Asea Brown Boveri, a leading Western producer. Nonetheless, these enterprises have only been able to reap negligible benefits because of the sharp decline of economic activity in the FSU. They have often experienced almost insurmountable problems in recent years (output in most cases fell 80%), because of their complete dependence on imports of cheap raw materials from other FSU republics and because their production was suitable only for Eastern markets. Many of these enterprises had production that was highly energy intensive and vulnerable to the energy price adjustments that accompanied the collapse of old trading arrangements when the Soviet Union dissolved.

Since it liberalized foreign trade, Latvia has been an important trader of goods from East to West and vice versa. Latvia's role as a re-exporter is reflected in the number of products that have significant shares in both imports and exports, notably mineral products (including fuels) and base metals, but also machinery and equipment. However, official statistics do not adequately show the extent of re-exports: officially, the shares of re-exports and re-imports are slightly above 3% of total exports and imports. This is probably a significant underestimation of real flows, in which case we can suppose that the real export structure also differs from the official version. These discrepancies refer to the abnormally large exports of base metals and base-metal articles: even with no ore deposits, Latvia exports about twice the amount of base metals and base-metal articles that it imports. According to official statistics (see *Table 4.3*), in 1995 wood and wooden articles led exports (26.4%), while textiles and textile products took second place (14.0%), and foodstuffs (including tobacco products and alcohol) came in third (11.1%). Exports of mechanical and electrical machinery and equipment also remained important (8.7%). It should be noted, however, that both the commodity and geographical patterns of exports are still changing and it is not likely that they will become even relatively stable in the near future.

Despite the problem of data incompatibility and the changing pattern of export distribution, it is possible to make some general conclusions. It is evident that the focus of Latvian industry has shifted from relatively high technology production to production on a lower technological level. Whereas previously production of communications equipment, consumer electronics, electrical machinery, and pharmaceuticals were important, the current top exports are unprocessed wood, sawn timber, plywood, and furniture. The explanation is simple: in the woodworking sector good results were achievable in a short period of time with minimal capital investment and research and development. Furthermore, there was access to cheap local raw materials. The problem of compatibility with certain standards also was not as acute as in the electrical engineering and electronics or pharmaceuticals sectors. As a result, a large number of small viable enterprises have recently been established in the woodworking and furniture sector. In principle it is not bad to develop this sector, provided that the emphasis is on highly processed products. Actually, increasing the role of the woodworking industry might be characterized as a return to historical origins.

The second group, textiles and clothing, also has considerable potential for the near future. Latvian knitted garments, for example, have always been popular in the USSR and now are proving equally successful in the West. This sector has strong traditions and a skilled labor force. At the same time, the high labor intensity of production and the steady increases in labor costs have meant that something must be done to increase efficiency; the lack of productivity improvements may especially disturb current subcontracting relations. The other problem is that this sector is practically completely reliant on imported raw materials, and this condition increases its vulnerability. The only subsector that has not faced this constraint and that has rapidly regained its former positions is hosiery production, because Latvia has a strong producer of polyamide filament yarns called Dautex.

Only manufactures in the woodworking and textile sectors have had any real success in the West. Reorientation of trade is easier in raw material production, because these products are more homogeneous. In labor-intensive industries, the high skill levels of Latvian workers make retraining easier and facilitate reorientation to Western quality standards.

The third largest sector, the food industry, has always been important to the Latvian economy. However, it is difficult to say how successful it will be in the future because of low efficiency and the low level of automation in the agricultural sector, where the fall in output still has not been stopped. A powerful farm lobby has led to excessively high agricultural tariffs that do not stimulate efficiency or modernization in the sector. The tariff scheme needs to be changed now, before production adjusts to distorted incentive structures. However, production of canned fish, chocolate products, tobacco, and alcohol has a stable footing and good export prospects. On the whole, the food industry continues to develop and restructure faster than the agricultural sector.

The situation is more difficult in the transport equipment sector. This sector needs a massive injection of capital to preserve its current position and to overcome current stagnation. Despite the fact that electric and diesel trains and minibuses are currently among the main exports to CIS countries, everything in this sector must be changed, including business ideology. There are many indications that the situation at RAF, a company that produces minibuses, is a bit better than those at other enterprises; but even here injections of capital and fresh ideas are needed. The main opportunities for Latvian manufacturers of vehicles are in the FSU and developing countries.

A comparatively low position now belongs to other (theoretically) medium- to high-technology articles: communications equipment, electrical appliances, microelectronics, mechanical devices, chemicals, and pharmaceuticals. It appears that production of articles such as radios and tape recorders, for which Latvia was one of the USSR's main producers, will never recover, because of the disruption of relations with scientific centers, the need for huge investments, and problems of restructuring. In this sector, only producers of telephones, electric lamps, and power tools (for both professional and consumer use) have been relatively successful.

The present commodity distribution of exports clearly indicates that neither Latvia's scientific potential nor its skilled labor force is used sufficiently. The expected pattern of buying cheap Eastern goods to process and sell in high-income Western markets has not materialized. Practically all the products of the machinery sector are sent to the rest of the FSU following patterns established during the period of central planning.

4.5 Impediments to Exports: Demand

The following sections are based mainly on the findings of 20 case studies of Latvian manufacturing enterprises active in exports. A summary of the characteristic features of the enterprises is presented in *Table 4.4*.

Undoubtedly, orientation of trade to low-demand regions is one of the greatest obstacles to export growth. This is particularly true for industries such as electric engineering, electronics, and auto and pharmaceutical manufacturing, which export up to 90% of their total production to the East. The problem is that most representatives of these sectors simply have no choice at present but to serve the FSU, because usually they do not have the money or skills to reorient toward Western markets. Also, foreign investors have not been active in these sectors, because of the massive injections of capital that are needed. A few companies that have found foreign partners have been more or less successful in the West; however, the primary market is still the CIS countries. Another issue is that many companies in these sectors had highly specialized production (for example, instrument panels for Russian cars), the demand for which is falling steadily.

Exports to Russia have often been impeded by high import duties: 20% for furniture, clothing, footwear, and telephones; about 15% for dairy products; 30% for cigarettes; and ECU 0.6 per liter for beer. These duties increased the problems generated by the lats' stability against hard currencies and the depreciation of the ruble until 1995. Another problem in 1995 was the excessively high VAT rate (28%) applied in Russia (in some cases a VAT of only 15–18% was levied if the entrepreneur could prove that imports were for the so-called social sphere).

Another problem is disorder in customs procedures in all CIS states. Regulations are changing so frequently that Latvian exporters often must pay for storage of goods in customs warehouses while obtaining additional documentation. Therefore, exporting perishable goods is simply impossible. Significant problems are caused for Latvian pharmaceutical producers because each delivery requires a permit from Russia's health protection committee. Moreover, some of the CIS republics have requested re-registration of medicines that had already been registered in the Soviet era, which is a very costly procedure.

Economic relations with the republics of Central Asia and other southern republics of the FSU are especially difficult because centralized state trading, with such features as export/import licensing, quotas, and currency exchange restrictions, still prevails. For instance, when Latvia's largest perfume producer,

Table 4.4. Profiles of the companies covered in the survey.

Company	Sector	Ownership[a]	Main markets (percent of sales)[b]
Latvijas Finieris	Woodworking (plywood)	JSC	WE (90)
Mêbeļu serviss	Furniture production	JSC, lease with redemption	CIS (40), WE (30)
Vidzeme	Furniture production	State company	WE (≈40)
Juglas Manufaktūra	Textiles (cotton spinning)	JSC, lease with redemption	WE (68), Lithuania (15)
8 March	Textiles (fabrics)	State company	WE (58.6), CIS (2.3)
Aurora	Clothing (hosiery)	JSC	WE (68), CIS (10)
Latvija	Clothing	JSC (S 29%)	WE (90)
Venezia	Footwear	JV, LLC (S 67%)	Former CIS
Meteors	Footwear/chemicals	State company	CIS (40), Baltics (14)
Laima	Food (candies)	JSC (S 30%)	FSU (≈25)
Kaija	Food (canned fish)	JSC	FSU (71.8), CEE (11.3)
RVR	Transport vehicles (railcars)	State company	CIS (100)
Rīgas Motorūpnīca	Transport vehicles (mopeds)	State company	CIS (48.4), Baltics (11.7), WE (28.2)
Rīki	Mechanical appliances	LLC, lease with redemption	WE (15)
RINAR	Mechanical appliances	State company	CIS (84.2); Baltics, devel. countries (15.8)
RAR	Electric components for automobiles	State company	CIS (90)
Vermerk	Electric lamps	JV, LLC (S 14%)	WE (71.8), FSU (19)
VEF KT	Telecommunications	State company	FSU (90)
Ausma	Chemicals (plastics)	JSC	Total exports (10)
Olaine Pharmaceutical Plant	Medicines	State company	FSU (64.8); WE, Poland (19.2)

[a]JSC = Joint-stock company (private); LLC = Limited liability company; JV = Joint venture; S+% = Latvian state share of fixed assets.
[b]CEE = Central and Eastern Europe; CIS = Commonwealth of Independent States; FSU = CIS + Baltics (Lithuania, Estonia); WE = Western Europe.

Dzintars, exports to Uzbekistan, it receives payment in the national currency, which can be converted only at the central bank under unfavorable conditions. The present foreign trade regimes in the Asian republics of the FSU also have a negative impact on imports of raw materials, mainly cotton. For example, in Tajikistan all export contracts must be approved by the Ministry of Foreign Relations, and in Uzbekistan only the president can distribute cotton export quotas.

Many industries face serious competition from regions with low labor costs (such as China and India) in CIS markets and in some Western markets. Often the only factor in favor of Latvian goods is the slightly higher quality of products such as clothing, footwear, pharmaceuticals (active ingredients), chemicals, and consumer electronics. Latvian cotton processors are likely to find it increasingly difficult to remain competitive in cotton spinning and weaving, because cotton-producing countries, including those in the Asian part of the FSU, have begun to develop their own industries.

Problems obtaining payments for exports substantially increase transaction costs. Initially, the largest payment obstacles were related to difficulties clearing the correspondence accounts between central banks of FSU republics, payment delays in the banking system, the difficulty and expense of obtaining trade financing, and nonpayment by trading partners. Bank-related payment difficulties are gradually being resolved through improved links between commercial banks abroad. However, the instability of many of the new currencies in the FSU continues to impose high costs for trade in these currencies. Because of the high risk of holding some of these currencies, banks charge higher commissions for these transactions. As a result, there is an increasing shift to convertible currencies in trade with CIS countries, which rarely has a positive effect on demand for Latvian goods. Taking into account difficulties with export crediting, a significant problem with exporting to the West is the period of payment settlement. Western importers usually settle their liabilities within 30 to 60 days. For CIS states, Latvian producers usually do not provide the customers with such credits, sometimes even requesting payment in advance because of high instability in the importing country. Such unpopular measures, of course, reduce demand.

Access to Western markets is precluded by technical barriers. One problem is incompatibility with ISO 9000 (EN 29000) quality standards; to date, no Latvian enterprise is certified as meeting ISO requirements. However, the biggest problem is with mandatory regulations. For the pharmaceuticals industry, the problem is incompatibility with Good Manufacturing Practice (GMP) requirements, which impedes exports of finished products to the West and lowers the price for intermediate products. Most Latvian pharmaceutical enterprises regard this regulation as a purely protective measure allowing developed countries to shield their own producers, because the chemical parameters of Latvian medicines do not deviate from those accepted in the West. The cumbersome procedure of registering new medicines, which also implies an unbearable financial burden, is another significant obstacle to exports. However, even greater problems are faced by producers in the electrical engineering industry, as they are subject to mandatory EU regulations. The biggest difficulty will occur by 1996, when regulation on electromagnetic compatibility (EMC) will come into force, which will have serious implications for electronic consumer goods, power tools, and other electrical engineering products. Actually, in many cases incompatibility with some standards is the only formal obstacle to exports to Western markets.

During our enterprise interviews no mention was made of tariffs, tariff quotas, or antidumping regulations as problems for exports to the EU. Even producers in the textile industry, who deal with products regarded as "sensitive" in the EU, have not had to pay import duties because the tariff quotas granted by the EU to Latvia have been well above present textile exports to the EU. With respect to the use of dumping, which might be an effective way to conquer new markets, it is very difficult to imagine Latvian producers being able to finance it considering how gloomy the financial state of these companies is.

It is difficult to discuss the economic positions of producers of dairy or meat products because no such enterprises were included in our case studies (according to official statistics, Latvia does not export food to the West). However, we can say with confidence that the inflow of highly subsidized food from the EU, a dubious merit of the Common Agricultural Policy, will definitely have a negative impact on domestic producers.

For most product groups, starting with food and ending with transport vehicles, the domestic market is much more attractive than either Eastern or Western markets. When exporting to the East, Latvian manufacturers must keep prices as low as possible because of the customers' economic circumstances, including weak currencies in CIS countries (particularly in previously important partner states like Ukraine and Belarus), the continuous fall in GDP, and the resulting decrease in the population's purchasing power. It is practically impossible to trade with Ukraine, where, for example, the average pension was US$4 per month in the spring of 1995.

In the West the problem is a bit different. Latvian companies have been offering low prices to undercut competing products, which often have superior performance. Another problem has been difficulties entering these overcrowded markets because of inexperience in Western marketing and the lack of money for product promotion. Creating brand-name recognition is a long, cumbersome, extremely costly procedure. Therefore, even firms that can and do produce goods that meet the highest Western standards are forced to distribute these products through mediators, who resell them under their own, better-known brand names. Such export operations are used by practically all sectors exporting products to the West. These mediators often produce identical goods and subcontract with Latvian producers only under conditions that are especially advantageous to the foreign company. In the best case for the Latvian firm, the foreign enterprise makes only a 15% profit on such transactions; however, this figure is usually closer to 50% and in extreme cases it can reach 200%. Latvian companies often receive ready packing from abroad (as in the case of Vermerk in our sample). A large portion of exports (mainly textiles and clothing) are sold through well-known trade intermediaries such as Otto and Quelle, again under foreign brand names. It is not a bad starting point: none of these famous companies would risk selling low-quality goods under its own name. However, such mediation is extremely expensive for the producer. Only manufacturers of completely standardized products (e.g., Latvijas Finieris, which produces sheets of plywood, or Juglas Manufaktūra, which spins cotton) can contract with foreign partners under less discriminatory conditions, because a company's name is not as important here and the products are often sold directly to the final users.

Of course, it should be mentioned that despite the comparative attractiveness of domestic markets, Latvian enterprises, especially medium-size and large companies, cannot survive without exports because the local markets are too small.

The last export impediment that must be mentioned in this section is the lack of foreign direct investment (FDI). In Latvia FDI is much lower than in many other transition countries; it is lower than in Estonia, to take a comparable example. Moreover, the main motive for foreign companies to establish joint ventures is to acquire dominant positions in local markets, rather than to enhance exports using relatively low labor costs or other export potential. This tendency can be seen in the developments in the telecommunications, food, and chemical industries. The most famous joint ventures – the tobacco producer House of Prince and the brewery Aldaris – have acquired dominant positions in the domestic market and for the most part do not export. In two chemical enterprises that we visited, Ausma and Latvijas Krâsas (not described in the case studies), the situation is the same: the primary target market is domestic. Latvijas Krâsas, however, has also been used as a platform for expanding into other Baltic states. At the same time, some investments have been made in the woodworking sector by producers in Scandinavian countries that are the main importers of woodwork in their own countries. The recently increasing foreign interest in cooperating with Latvian engineering enterprises is due to their continued strong positions in FSU markets.

4.6 Impediments to Exports: Supply

4.6.1 Common problems

Problems with Restructuring of Medium- and Large-scale Enterprises

One of the largest obstacles to recovery of exports is the intolerably slow pace of restructuring in most enterprises. To a large extent, this pace is a result of prolonged privatization. Although 55% of the GDP is generated by the private sector, industry is still dominated by state enterprises. If we compare privatization at the central and local government levels, we find that local government property (small-scale enterprises, rural land) has been privatized much more rapidly and successfully. Some reasons for this difference are the large interenterprise payments arrears of state enterprises and the much higher levels of capital needed for privatization of these state enterprises. Until April 1994 privatization had been in the hands of slow-moving government ministries and had been completed in only 85 cases, 61 of which involved a lease with the option to buy. The veto power of branch ministries slowed sales, and discrimination in favor of managers and workers and the wide use of leasing led to poor corporate governance. The new stage of privatization began in May 1994, when the privatization agency became fully operational and announced a list of 23 enterprises that had been selected for privatization. As in Estonia, core investors were sought in each case, with a minimum of 25% of the shares to be sold through the Riga Stock Exchange for vouchers.

Latvia has faced serious problems during economic transformation, because more of the huge Soviet industries were headquartered there than in any other Baltic state. Latvia has been left with a large number of inflexible dinosaurs in practically all sectors of the national economy. One example is the pharmaceutical giant Olaine, described in one of the case studies. Many companies, especially state-owned enterprises, have sites that are far too large for any conceivable future requirements. The costs of heating and ventilating large, unused spaces can be considerable, sometimes leading to heavy financial losses; energy costs currently constitute 11–16% of the total expenses for most manufacturing companies. However, rationalization and disposal of these sites have often been hindered by legal restrictions imposed by privatization agreements or by a lack of money to spend on moving machinery and refurbishing a more suitable accommodation. As a consequence, market mechanisms that would allow companies with spare capacity to sell surplus assets have not functioned effectively. Also, there has been little demand for spare equipment and capacity at present, and many companies have merely eliminated large parts of their capacity.

Some enterprises face extensive problems due to continuing obligations to provide heat, water, and other services to local housing units, schools, and other centers. This was the case for enterprises such as Aurora and Olaine in our case studies. Moreover, some companies inherited social centers such as kindergartens, hospitals, and health resorts.

Lack of Reliable Supply Systems

The high level of industrial concentration that evolved during the Soviet era must be transformed through a process of disintegration to separate related and supporting industries. The emergence of a new structure is a long-term process. Currently, most enterprises cannot concentrate production where they have the greatest competitive advantage, because they must also produce intermediate goods that in a rational setup could be bought from suppliers at more reasonable prices. However, supply systems are still weak and unreliable.

Quality Problems and Incompatibility with Western Standards

Other crucial impediments to exports are insufficient quality of goods and incompatibility with Western regulations and standards. Recently, however, many efforts have been made to cope with the quality problem. The National Program of Quality Assurance, which was started in 1994, is one of the most important national programs for further developing industry. During 1994 the National Accreditation System was developed and accepted by the Cabinet of Ministers; this system complies with EN 45000 standards, which were adopted nationally. Gradually, the main mandatory regulations of the EU are being incorporated into national legislation; ISO standards are expected to eventually be integrated, as well.

Latvia is one of 11 participants in the regional quality assurance program PHARE PRAQ 92. According to experts in the European Commission, who visited Latvia in 1995, of all the participants Latvia has been the most successful at developing a quality assurance infrastructure that corresponds closely to the infrastructure existing in the EU. Because of its positive evaluation, Latvia will receive additional funds for further development of this structure and for the purchase of necessary testing equipment. During 1995, two Latvian enterprises, the perfumery factory Dzintars and the Aldaris brewery, were prepared for certification in accordance with ISO 9000 standards, with the assistance of EU experts.

Another problem is that most state and former state enterprises, including joint-stock companies where most of the shares are held by employees, keep far too many workers in their factories. Considering the relatively low wages paid, there is little motivation to reduce the work force. Social factors also discourage cutting jobs. As a result, over-employing on such a scale negates the competitive advantages of having low-cost labor.

Lack of Strategic Planning

In general, the companies surveyed appeared to have a fairly realistic understanding of their situations, their needs, and the problems still facing them. Few examples of overambitious or poorly conceived strategies were encountered. The opposite was more common; most companies were too preoccupied with their immediate situation to think strategically at all. Although it was not referred to as such, it was evident that in some instances there was a conflict in marketing and sales priorities between the pressing need to find customers for the current product range and the less-pressing, but in the long run equally important, need to research the market to determine customers' requirements for the future.

Developing new products is especially important considering the relatively narrow product range that has been a common problem for most Latvian enterprises. Typically, companies produce a small number of products in large quantities and sell to a small customer base that dictates both price and product specification. This is particularly true of state and joint-stock companies, but it applies to private companies as well. As a result, companies are forced to accept low prices in order to achieve the volume of sales needed and are unable to establish themselves in the final marketplace because their products pass through several channels of distribution. The need for several intermediaries (typically agents and distributors) to handle the large volumes offered for sale results in severely squeezed profits. Typically, prices are on the order of half of what could have been attained had the company sold smaller volumes directly to retailers. Many companies claimed to have their own designers, although this sometimes turned out to be a purely technical or experimental function rather than a creative one. Where there were genuine designers, their experience was almost entirely in Eastern markets, where colors and designs demanded are completely different from those demanded in the West. Well-designed packaging and brochures for attracting potential customers have been the exception rather than the rule. Thus, customer requirements for products, services, and support have not been adequately addressed, which has almost certainly led to missed business opportunities both at home and in export markets.

The lack of sales activities has also been obvious in many Latvian enterprises, particularly in state-owned and former state-owned companies. Many large firms have no employee responsible for actively seeking new sales avenues. These companies have typically relied on existing outlets and sometimes on private agencies to achieve sales.

On the whole, because of inherited managerial and production problems, many companies seem to be locked in a vicious circle of low prices, inadequate profits, low investment in products and processes, low quality and productivity, and an ability to compete only at low prices.

Problems with Working Capital

For most enterprises working capital has been so desperately short that few opportunities have arisen for optimizing the purchase of raw materials and spares in order to obtain better prices and terms of supply. Required inputs are purchased on an almost day-to-day basis from wherever they happen to be available, with a consequent loss of bargaining power with suppliers and frequent stoppages due to delays in delivery or the inability to refuse substandard goods. There are a number of causes for the shortage of working capital, most of which are common to all sectors. Initially the problem of working capital arose due to huge losses sustained by many enterprises during the currency reform in 1992, when the parity between Latvian and Russian rubles was, retroactively, abandoned by decision of the Latvian National Bank. Furthermore, substantial inflation of the ruble in 1992 encouraged Russian importers of Latvian products to accumulate payment arrears. As long as Latvian exports to Russia were denominated in rubles at fixed contract prices, delaying payments to Latvian enterprises provided substantial gains for Russian importers and losses for Latvian producers. Of particular concern to newly privatized joint-stock companies was the practice of not providing the new enterprise with any working capital and, what was worse, requiring the company to take over debts generated when it was a state enterprise. In effect, the newly formed companies have had no funds to finance new stock, and any marginal profits they have made have been greatly reduced by the need to repay inherited debts.

Newly formed private companies face working capital problems because they begin without sufficient reserves. Because these companies tend to grow at a fast rate, they do not have sufficient levels of retained earnings, i.e., profits, to pay for wages or for the increasing amount of raw materials, whose purchase often has to be financed in advance.

The high cost of borrowing added to the lack of any factoring facilities (whereby companies would be advanced 80–90% of an invoice's value) has meant that companies have been unable to afford to seek outside financing from traditional sources. Difficult access to credit, especially until mid-1994, slowed the supply response to reforms and affected trade financing. The main lending activity was the financing of transit trade from Russia through the Baltic region, based on the gap between controlled Russian commodity prices and world market prices. Since this activity was immensely profitable it could carry per annum lending interest rates above 140% against a deposit rate of 70–90%. Because of these opportunities, for a long time two-thirds of lending was offshore; involvement in domestic activity was limited.

Many companies carrying out exports (as opposed to re-exports) were and often even now are forced to offer even lower prices in return for their customers' providing cash advances against future supplies. A price realignment has occurred and lending rates are gradually coming down, although they are still high (27% annual rate for short-term credits). A further decrease in interest rates has been hampered by a severe banking crisis in 1995. The problems of guarantees and collateral still remain.

Unfortunately, the Latvian Export Crediting Company, which might be able to improve the situation, still has not started real activities. The development of an export guarantee mechanism by the state is still in the discussion phase.

The tax system has also attracted criticism from industrial enterprises, who consider it a barrier to exports. Delays in refunding the 18% VAT on inputs for exporters were evaluated especially negatively. Taking into account that many Latvian industries rely on imports of raw materials, this delay has meant that large sums of money have been frozen at a time when the shortage of working capital was already acute. In effect, Latvian producers have been providing their government with interest-free credits.

On the financial side, the most negative survey responses concerned the exchange rate policy of the Bank of Latvia. Because of the strict exchange rate regime (a straightforward peg of the lats against SDR) and the still relatively high level of inflation (26.3% for 1994 and 23.1% for 1995), exports have become less and less profitable for Latvian producers.

Another problem connected with financial issues is the lack of any representation in overseas markets by either full-time sales staff or agents. As a result, companies have only a vague insight into foreign markets and must rely on foreign partners. Customers frequently must locate and visit Latvian companies themselves, although they often find their partners through the LCTC, through manufacturers associations, or through the Latvian Development Agency or WTC Riga. Most companies are aware of specialized Western trade fairs and some have been involved as visitors, but very few have been exhibitors. Pressure on companies' financial resources is a constraint here. This is an area where collaboration between complementary companies could be of value. The Latvian government, in turn, could help by providing free use of buildings for exhibitions. Language is also a serious barrier for many companies trying to establish contacts with the West. However, German and English language skills can rarely be a substitute for the use of experienced professional local staff or agents in each major export market.

Capital Investments

It is difficult to generalize about the state of existing machinery and the need for investments in fixed capital. Although many companies date back to well before the Soviet era, the foundations of current Latvian industry were laid in the postwar period. A number of large enterprises were equipped using central funds provided by All-Union Ministries. Virtually no investment has taken place in the past four or five years, and so companies are entirely dependent on what they were left with from the Soviet system. Of course, Latvia has some striking examples of restructured Soviet enterprises thanks to foreign investments or credits from abroad, but their impact on the country's overall situation has been negligible.

Unfortunately, present interest rates do not allow companies to finance the reconstruction of plants through commercial bank loans. The Latvian Investment Bank, established in 1992, also is not active enough despite its access to cheap credits from abroad [its shareholders are the Latvian government (35%), the European Bank for Reconstruction and Development (35%), and Swedfund, Finnfund, and DEG (Germany) (each 10%)]. According to the bank's managers, the reason for this inactivity is a lack of experience on the side of Latvian entrepreneurs when preparing long-term projects. It seems strange that this bank, which is proud of its highly skilled staff, cannot help entrepreneurs solve this problem. Of course, some companies simply did not understand the need to generate sufficient surplus funds to repay the costs of capital investments. When investment credits were discussed in our survey, it was apparent that many company managers did not realize that their planned projects could not possibly cover even the interest costs, let alone the principal of the loans they were seeking.

Inflow of investments from abroad has been negatively affected by the crisis of the Latvian banking system in 1995. As a result, there is now a real threat of capital flight from the republic.

The new Law On Foreign Investment (March 2, 1995) eliminated corporate income tax exemptions that had been available to enterprises with foreign investment. Depending on the size of the investment, it had been possible to be exempted from corporate tax payments for up to three years and to receive a 50% reduction in corporate income tax for another five years. These kinds of changes in legislation can have a negative, albeit probably marginal, impact on foreign investments.

The capital market, which is still at an early stage of development, could be effectively used as an alternative way to attract investments, especially in view of the large gap between credit and deposit rates prevailing in the market. There are few enterprises issuing shares for the secondary market, largely because of the slow pace of privatization. A successfully functioning securities market, however, would be crucial precisely because the full benefits of privatization cannot be realized without it.

Many of the problems encountered by industry are connected with government policies or inactivity; however, much must be done on the enterprise level. Perhaps the greatest problem is that companies base their activities on questionable assumptions.

The first of these assumptions is that the company will be able to compete abroad because it has low costs and prices. It is true that in most cases current Latvian prices are well below international market levels. However, low prices are based on costs that do not include the need to amortize recent fixed capital as most Latvian plant and machinery is relatively old. Moreover, rapidly developing Asian countries have low prices and are improving their quality levels. In most cases, prices for Latvian goods are low only because the companies have been forced to market their products in the least attractive markets.

The second assumption these enterprises make is that they know the Eastern market well and have contacts there, whereas Western markets are difficult to enter. This assumption is especially common in the engineering sector and in the majority of the huge state-owned enterprises in all sectors. It is true that Latvian companies have a competitive advantage in traditional markets, but competition is growing in the FSU from both other foreign and new Russian companies. Competition from Asian states and imports of second-hand products from the West cannot be neglected either. The costs of marketing in Russia are growing because of border controls and the costs of transport and distribution. Western markets frequently require high-quality products, but there are also market opportunities for low-cost, simple products.

The third assumption is that the enterprises would be able to compete if they could invest in plants and machinery. Although good plants and machinery are essential for high quality and productivity, it is also important to know what products to make with the new equipment and how to buy appropriate machinery. It is pointless to buy modern equipment to manufacture an obsolete product more efficiently.

The last of these assumptions is that the enterprises would be able to compete if they had sufficient working capital. It is true that many firms have reached a difficult position regarding cash flow and would be technically bankrupt in a market economy. However, loans should not be seen as a panacea, because many firms have extensive stocks of raw materials, work in progress, and finished goods, and there is often a need to address fundamental issues before new loans with competitive conditions are granted.

4.6.2 Industry-specific problems

Woodworking and Furniture Industry

The biggest problem in this sector has been land reform, which has slowed progress and hindered the use of forest resources in Latvia. Additionally, logging companies, which were mainly state owned, have insufficient technical equipment and low organizational standards.

Producers of sawn timber sections, joinery (doors and window frames, for example), lathed details, and fences, who in most cases are located in rural areas, have been more or less successful. The largest plywood producer in Latvia, Latvijas Finieris, has also had success.

Although there are differences in the situations of individual woodworking and furniture enterprises, there are some common problems. Typically, a large Latvian company may produce only 6 to 12 items; a company in the UK of comparable size usually offers between 150 and 250 items. A major reason for this is historical: under the planned economy, companies were set up to produce narrow ranges of products in large quantities.

Moreover, designs were provided by other government departments and were extremely simple and uniform. For example, practically all furniture was produced from rectangular parts; curved components were seldom used. In addition, the manufacture of furniture from chipboard (which is unhealthy, as 10% of the inputs are binding substances) has been widespread.

In order to gain markets most former state companies must reorient themselves toward production of solid furniture, which is what is demanded most in the West. Until now, few companies in the furniture sector have managed to achieve stable positions in the West. Some exceptions are new, dynamic, small-scale enterprises that produce solid furniture. Among traditional furniture producers, Mêbeļu serviss, one of the companies surveyed, has made excellent reorganization efforts, although temporary difficulties have spoiled their financial performance.

Even the largest of the state-owned furniture companies do not possess sufficient in-house capability to produce new designs. Because of the lack of market knowledge, they are incapable of deciding which trends to follow. As a result, companies continue to produce the same products and rely on customers to provide their own designs. Private companies tend to be more up to date because they copy the designs that sell in the marketplace.

There is a further negative aspect of this reliance on old or customer designs. Because these companies do not offer their own, distinguishable products, they are forced to compete only on price versus offering a quality/price/product mix.

Textile and Clothing Industry

Inappropriate equipment. Most of the equipment in the textile and clothing industry was manufactured in the Soviet Union or elsewhere in Eastern Europe, although some was based on leading Western designs produced under license. Late in the Soviet era, selected companies received additional modern Western machinery, but the pattern of this investment was uneven and incomplete. For example, the main Riga factory of the large clothing company Latvija received massive investment in state-of-the-art design, cutting, sewing, pressing, and conveyer machinery just before the collapse of the Soviet system, whereas other plants in the same company received almost nothing. In the textile sector, the availability, capability, and appropriateness of dyeing and finishing services are generally poor and constitute an important obstacle to recovery. Even where fairly modern machinery is available, its capacity tends to be too high to be suited to economical production of the short runs of fabrics required by the local market or by most export customers.

Linkages within the supply chain. A serious consequence of the pattern of enterprise closures in 1992 and 1993 was the disruption of key linkages within the local supply chain. For instance, the closing of Rigas Tekstils took away the only wool-washing facility in the entire Baltic area. The main victims in this case are Astotais marts, a producer of wool fabrics (reported in our case study), and Ogre, an important producer of knitted clothing. As a result, the companies have had to rely on expensive imports of scoured wool, usually from the EU. Another example is Rigas Manufactūra's suspension of its bleaching, dyeing, and finishing activities, which has deprived the principal flax and linen producer, Larelini, of its only local source of bleaching. Currently, the latter company is unable to obtain any credits toward the purchase of a bleaching plant, which it considers crucial.

Raw materials and working capital. The shortage of working capital is very often a major obstacle to exports. One example is Ogre, whose inability to raise some US$3 million worth of credits to purchase Australian merino wool has prevented it from filling potential orders amounting to US$10 to 20 million.

On the whole, problems with working capital in the clothing industry have not been too severe in the short term, because most of the raw materials (fabric, threads, and accessories) are provided by the customers. However, total reliance on such labor-only subcontracting work has its limitations: while it is highly competitive, it pays poorly and generates few additional resources for investment in new equipment, product development, and marketing.

Labor costs. Latvian labor costs will inevitably start to rise above those of their closest competitors. However, in the short term, Latvia's proximity to its main export markets (Germany and Scandinavia) combined with its reputation for reasonable levels of skill and quality are key advantages, provided that Latvian companies can deliver their products faster than competitors in Romania and Bulgaria, two of the most important growth areas for garment subcontracting at present.

Foreign direct investment. Sources of foreign investment have been very limited to date. Swedish companies are the only foreign enterprises that have become involved on any significant scale. Some much smaller joint ventures have been established with German companies in the past, but without notable success. German companies tend to have better investment opportunities in former East Germany and have only been interested in providing relatively low-value CMT (cut, make, and trim) work to Latvia, without any longer-term commitment at present.

Certification problems have not been especially acute in the textile and clothing sector; however, the procedure of obtaining the necessary sanitary certificates can be cumbersome and costly.

Chemicals and Pharmaceuticals

For safety and environmental protection reasons, the chemical and pharmaceutical industry is much more constrained by legislation than other industries. Adaptation to constantly evolving requirements is not simple and demands huge financial resources and expert advice.

Incompatibility with GMP. Knowledge of GMP (Good Manufacturing Practice) is generally lacking and only one Latvian company (Grindex) manufactures products that meet GMP standards.

As far as short-term improvements are concerned, most technical efforts are devoted to upgrading products rather than improving process technology. Investments for the future tend to be geared to obtaining rapid payback on minor improvements. There is virtually no investment in major advances (novel products and processes), which carry a higher financial risk due to the longer pay-back period, but promise higher rewards through future competitive advantages.

Insufficient collaboration with scientific centers. Scientific research and technical skills are not being applied to benefit the Latvian chemical industry, particularly for the development of new products and processes. Some companies, such as the Center of Applied Biochemistry (CAB) and Grindex, have strong links with the academic world because they have retained and strengthened their connections with the institutes from which they originated. On the whole, however, links between companies and the academic community have been broken or are nonexistent, therefore no effective commercial use is made of the national academic resources. Evidence from a number of sources indicates that companies tend to be reluctant to collaborate with one another within this sector. This reluctance may be caused by mistrust based on the fear of competition for the same markets. However, there are many noncompetitive areas in which chemical and pharmaceuticals companies would do well to cooperate.

The problem of investments is acute in the chemicals and pharmaceuticals sector, because significantly more funds are needed for restructuring and the risk factor is also higher than in the woodworking or textile industries, for example. There are few possibilities for successful development without inflow of capital from outside. The most successful companies in the sector – Dautex, the only producer of man-made fibers in Latvia, and Grindex, a successful exporter of anti-cancer drugs – have received necessary funds from abroad. Dautex attracted foreign partners to purchase a new line for coproducing industrial filament yarns with an international fiber producer; these partners were able to raise the necessary overseas credits. Grindex received a World Bank loan of US$6.3 million that was crucial for setting up a packaging enterprise. The relative success of Grindex and Dautex demonstrates that state companies can also be quite successful.

In their current forms, monolithic companies such as Olaine Pharmaceutical Plant (the subject of one of our case studies) have little potential for future viability. Their oversized scales and centralized integrated systems of energy supply make it difficult for them to cut back to small, more flexible firms.

Mechanical Engineering Industry

The Latvian mechanical engineering industry is extremely diverse, comprising enterprises as varied as a producer of simple office equipment (Mangali) and producers of vehicles – RVR (trains) and RAF (minibuses). Moreover, the industry is highly stratified. Five large companies (RAF, RVR, Daugavpils Locomotive, Liepâjas Metalurgs, and Daugavpils Drive Chain) employ nearly two-thirds of the sector's labor force. The remainder of the industry is composed of medium-size and small companies that make a wide range of products, often with limited market opportunities.

Because it has a high proportion of former All-Union companies, this industry has suffered more than others in the wake of the collapse of Soviet Union, as the former distribution system has broken up and demand in many traditional markets has fallen.

Disruption of linkages with scientific centers. During the Soviet era, many organizations in the mechanical engineering industry had strong links to technical institutes and universities in Russia and Ukraine. Now most of these links have been disrupted, and companies have been separated from their sources of technical knowledge and innovation. Few firms have replaced these links with any substantial contacts with Latvian universities or institutes. This creates a particular problem, because the majority of these companies do not have their own facilities for research or product development. Almost no enterprises have computer-aided design (CAD) equipment.

Ill-considered diversification. Many companies in Latvia's engineering sector have not yet developed a viable long-term economic strategy and are reacting to events on a short-term basis. A number of companies were forced to diversify their product ranges when demand collapsed. Often, companies expanded from their core business into a variety of unrelated areas (such as agricultural implements, wood processing, and boilers) that required little engineering design capability and allowed the firms to compete in local markets. However, many of these product diversifications are low value-added and have little export potential. The expansion of these companies into the new products or new markets often came about by chance rather than through a planned or researched program.

Low productivity. Several indicators show that productivity in the mechanical engineering industry is extremely low by international standards. One cause of this is the inheritance of large, inflexible plants with high energy consumption, poor layout and maintenance, low-value products, high levels of inventory and work in progress, and poor quality. However, many of these causes of low productivity are related to management practices.

Quality. In many cases, mechanical engineering products are sold as components of larger systems, for example, hydraulic cylinders or automotive components. In this respect it should be mentioned that Western companies are unwilling to risk the reputation of their own products by buying parts from unknown producers. In some cases, Latvian companies have already developed elements of quality systems, including control of batches, production processes, metrology, and calibration. However, many other companies are far from having such an approach. There is little evidence of any knowledge of modern quality-control methods such as statistical process control, structured problem-solving techniques, or employee involvement programs.

Low-quality inputs. Despite the fact that Latvia has the only steel plant in the Baltics (Latvia Metalurgs), the majority of companies in the sector buy little of their raw materials and few of their component requirements from it. The majority of Latvian engineering companies import steel from Russia or Ukraine because it is relatively inexpensive; however, it has unreliable delivery and is of poor quality. These factors, together with the inflexible nature of many plants, have led to purchases of large batch quantities and to considerable stocks and work in progress in the plants.

Lack of close contacts with the West. Exports to nearby Western countries such as Finland, Sweden, and Denmark have been limited and in most cases have consisted of subcontracted machining operations for Finnish or Swedish companies. Joint ventures with Western companies were also relatively few in number. A few companies have limited licensing and other agreements with Western companies. The majority of firms apparently have no information about standards, certification, and metrology. Most companies have little or no information about EU directives such as the Machinery Directives or certification requirements. In addition, enterprises reported difficulties obtaining certification from Western certification bodies because of the high costs involved, but they also reported few arrangements for mutual recognition of certification systems with other countries.

Electronics and Electrical Engineering Industry

The electronics and electrical engineering sector, like the mechanical engineering sector, is quite diversified. Latvian electronics and electrical engineering firms used to be among the best in the industry in the Soviet Union. The companies of this sector can be divided into five large groups: telecommunications (exchanges, switches, military telecommunication systems, telephones, and printed circuit boards), electrical engineering (electric motors, electric rail equipment, and professional and consumer power tools), radio and audio equipment (portable radios, loudspeakers and cabinets, and turntables), lighting (electric lamps and fluorescent tubes), and microelectronics (microchips and microchip manufacturing equipment). Producers of radio and audio equipment and microelectronics are in the most difficult situations.

For the Latvian electronics and electrical engineering industry, the problems of transition to a market economy have been compounded by the distorted industry structure that remained after the separation from associated organizations in the FSU. The legacy of the old system is that Latvian companies frequently have only part of a product range, often with outdated product designs conceived to meet the needs of customers with whom they have had no direct contact. This is particularly true for RAR (a company covered in our case study), which continues to produce some instrument panels for Russia's car industry and which still has not successfully overcome the drop in demand for its products.

Disadvantages of excessive vertical integration. At the same time, in the electronics and electrical engineering sector the concept of full vertical integration (i.e., raw materials through to finished goods) is even more widespread than in the mechanical engineering sector. This situation has led to larger factories with a greater commitment to high-volume production than is the norm in the West. High-volume production tends to be inflexible and inefficient if operated below a threshold level. The virtues of vertical integration become liabilities at low volumes when it would be more efficient to obtain manufactured parts from a supplier serving a number of users. The most successful companies in this sector have realized this problem and have taken necessary steps to cope with it. For Vermerk, a producer of electric lamps included in our case studies, the steps for increasing operating profitability have included eliminating energy-intensive production of glass envelopes, which would have required huge investments to comply with environmental regulations, and switching production from xenon and quartz halogen lamps to filament lamps, which require less investment to be competitive. Manufacturing now consists of higher value-added activities, including filament winding and assembly. Similar strategies have been chosen by other successful companies in the sector, including a large number of joint ventures.

Unfortunately, the Latvian electronic factory VEF, a former show-piece, cannot be considered successful despite the remarkable improvement of its main product, telephone exchanges, resulting from effective cooperation with a research and development company formed from the former VEF Institute of Science and Technology. Among the main obstacles to recovery are state ownership, underdeveloped marketing functions, and disorder within management structure.

Incompatibility with standards. The companies surveyed claimed to be aware of Western market requirements for high quality, and many knew of and aimed for ISO 9000 standards. However, there seemed to be widespread misunderstanding about what the term "quality" means. Often, the ability to supply a batch of products to meet a demanding performance specification was confused with other characteristics implicit in the term quality. Only a few companies in the sector were able to produce products that had the characteristics of good quality, and even fewer had ISO 9000 accreditation. Some companies, however, lacked even basic information on EU regulations applied to a wide range of consumer and industrial products regarding aspects such as electrical safety and the need for compliance with regulations for electromagnetic compatibility (EMC).

4.7 Enterprise Efforts to Tackle Impediments to Exports

Export problems are often alleviated when an enterprise joins different business organizations. For instance, Ausma, a manufacturer of plastic goods, enjoys preferential treatment with respect to the import of raw materials from and the export of finished articles to Russia, because it somehow became a member of Russia's Union of Manufacturers.

Practically every one of the enterprises surveyed was a member of at least one employers organization. Most of these associations are very young; some are only now forming (for example, the Association of Pharmaceuticals Manufacturers). The most active of these include the Association of Textile and Clothing

Manufacturers, the Association Latvian Tree (mainly for furniture producers), and the Association of Wood Processors and Exporters. These organizations are important centers for information for potential foreign investors or importers. They are quite active in arranging seminars and workshops intended to encourage best practice in export marketing, design, training, and management, which are often organized in conjunction with the Latvian Development Agency.

Recently, industrial associations have started to help their members in other spheres as well; for example, some help organize the central purchase of raw materials, therefore ensuring more reasonable prices for producers. One example is the Association of Textile and Clothing Manufacturers, which assists in the centralized purchasing of fuel and helps find new sources of components and accessories.

Some manufacturers have begun to cooperate in sales efforts, opening joint retail outlets, which significantly reduces the costs of distribution. One example is Ausma, which co-owns two shops in Russia.

Manufacturers and their associations often initiate export-promoting treaties. One example is the agreement with Russia on Cooperation in the Sphere of Machine Building.

Latvian enterprises often try to attract foreign investors in order to settle financial problems that impede the development of exports. This has been the case with Vermerk, which has been successful even without investment in fixed assets.

For many enterprises, especially producers of garments, the easiest way to cope with working capital problems is to become a subcontractor for a foreign company. However, as indicated in the previous sections of this chapter, such work pays poorly and does not offer possibilities for further development. As a result, companies try to open retail outlets in major Latvian towns. Besides providing employment and increasing the value of the companies, such establishments are also important sources of market feedback on fabrics, colors, and designs. This information is essential for those companies seeking to develop beyond labor-only subcontracting; it is often considered a first step toward exporting the company's own products, because it allows the enterprise to accrue necessary funds.

Some companies ensure short-term financing needs (for the purchase of raw materials or for accomplishing export orders, for example) by simply delaying settlements of their own liabilities.

Barter arrangements are frequently used to sustain trade with FSU countries. The most imaginative use of bartering involves the creation of joint-venture agreements, where companies are established in the export country to manage both the receipt and onward distribution of finished products and the purchase and supply of materials and components.

Other examples of barter arrangements are the trade missions that were opened in Uzbekistan and Kazakstan to promote the exchange of Latvian minivans (produced by RAF) for cotton.

The company RVR, a railcar producer, chose an interesting way to settle payment problems. FSU railway companies have no money to buy new trains. However, these companies had previously granted large amounts of credit to their customers who, in turn, have no money to settle these debts. The railway companies sign contracts with intermediaries, in accordance to which mediators have right to collect these debts in kind (coal, fuel, and metal, for example); however, in exchange for this they must supply the railway companies with trains. As a result, RVR has contracts with these mediators, who transfer money to the RVR account; RVR, in turn, sends carriages directly to the FSU railway companies. These kinds of arrangements, which would be practically impossible if all partners were from the same FSU republic, give RVR an advantage in comparison with Russian producers.

An effective and widely used method of settling customs problems is bribery. Of course, none of the enterprises surveyed mentioned doing this, but such methods are extremely successful in exports to CIS countries. It has to be admitted that many of the export problems are also solved illegally, for instance, through tax evasion.

4.8 Conclusions and Policy Proposals

Our study demonstrated that the current environment for the development of Latvian exports is far from favorable. Latvian exporters face numerous challenges; some are demand related, but the largest obstacles are connected with internal problems of restructuring and adaptation. Many exporters have lost their only advantage in foreign markets, the ability to offer low prices based on a favorable (undervalued) exchange rate of the national currency.

The government and the business sector have different views on the most frequently discussed problems with respect to export development, exchange rate policy, and taxation. Frequently, exporters request a devaluation of the national currency in order to obtain better positions in foreign markets following the earlier sharp real appreciation of the lats. At the same time, the government has been adhering to the IMF-supported stabilization program, whose priorities are inflation suppression, exchange rate stability, and fiscal discipline. The main argument in favor of such a policy is that firms can best adapt to changes in demand, supply of inputs, and technology if they are able to plan and operate under stable and predictable conditions. The best proof of this assumption is the dismal economic performance of most CIS states.

Opposing views on taxation have provoked many discussions. Producers who pay taxes consider the present tax burden too high; however, the government often cannot perform even its basic functions due to widespread tax evasion. As a result, the government has made the improvement of tax administration one of its main priorities. It is not assured that the improvement in the budget will have the same positive impact on the export positions of Latvian producers. However, this measure will make conditions equal for Latvian companies competing with one another and will protect them from the penetration of illegal imports into Latvian markets. In this situation, the strongest enterprises will survive.

After the financial situation has been normalized, the State Revenue Service should be able to improve refunding of the VAT on inputs for exporters and correct shortcomings in the drawback system. Improvements in the fiscal system could allow the government to finish redistributing social functions between the state and business sectors, liberating enterprises from the responsibility of providing social services (local water supply and heating).

The speed of privatization should be accelerated by simplifying bureaucratic procedures and by allowing at least a part of old debts to be written off for those enterprises undergoing privatization. The government then must consider creating business promotion programs, particularly for developing exports. Financial support for the Latvian Export Crediting Company should be among the government's main priorities. This is needed for a rapid introduction of the export insurance and crediting mechanism.

Furthermore, the government will have to consider the possibility of providing state aid for research and development activities, which in the course of transition were practically stopped. A valuable contribution to the development of Latvian export possibilities would be at least partial state financing for participation of Latvian producers in international trade fairs. Government assistance in establishing permanent Latvian trade missions abroad is also needed.

At present there are many export promotion organizations in Latvia, both private and state run, but there is no coordination among them. Often, different organizations perform similar functions and provide similar services. As a result, the actual benefits to exporters from the activities of these companies are much lower than they could be. In such a situation the government has to elaborate a general concept to direct efforts of different export promotion organizations toward exporters' needs. A directory of export promotion organizations should be compiled to provide an exhaustive description of promotion services, because many exporters simply are not aware of the support they can receive.

Finally, the Latvian government must build on its achievements in the spheres of economic and political diplomacy. Special attention must be paid to political relations with Russia, which have a significant impact on economic relations between the two states. Ill-considered political actions must be avoided and political dialogue must continue.

References

Ilansson, A., 1995, The Baltic States: Battling over Financial Indiscipline, *Östekonomisk Rapport*, 5 May 1995, Vol. 7, Nos. 3–4, Stockholm Institute of East European Economies, Stockholm, Sweden.

Latvian State Committee of Statistics, *Monthly Bulletin of Latvian Statistics*, various issues, Riga, Latvia.

Latvian Development Agency, 1994, various working papers, LDA, Riga, Latvia.

Latvian Development Agency, 1995, various working papers, LDA, Riga, Latvia.

Ministry of Finance of the Republic of Latvia, 1995, Economic survey 1994, *Bulletin*, No. 1, Riga, Latvia.

Ministry of Finance of the Republic of Latvia, 1996, Economic survey 1995, *Bulletin*, No. 1, Riga, Latvia.

Palmstierna, R., 1995, Latvia's second coming?, in *Country Analysis*, Enskilda Securities, Credits.

Richard, A., and Tersman, G., 1995, Growth, Nontradables and Price Convergence in the Baltics, International Monetary Fund (IMF), Washington, DC, USA.

Shteinbuka, I., 1993, Issues of the Trade Policies in Latvia, paper prepared for the Thirty-third Regional Science Association European Congress held 24–27 August 1993, at Moscow, Russia.

Sorsa, P., 1994, Latvia: Trade issues in transition, *Trade in the New Independent States*, papers 141–155, World Bank/United Nations Development Programme, Washington, DC, USA.

Chapter 5

Romania

Vasile Pilat and Laurentiu Ciocirlan

This chapter relies extensively on information gathered during a survey of Romanian exporting enterprises. Fifty-five companies were asked to fill out in-depth questionnaires. The completed questionnaires were processed and 20 companies were selected for further investigation in case studies.

Detailed information on the 20 companies was obtained from the Romanian Ministry of Industry and the Department for Economic Reform. This information was complemented by press coverage. In addition, interviews were conducted with managers from most of the 20 companies during a conference of industrialists held in early 1995. The characteristics of these 20 companies are summarized in *Table 5.1*. In addition to the information collected from the case studies, the chapter also uses the literature and press reports to highlight actual impediments to export. The results of the survey are described in the Appendix to Chapter 5.

The rapid industrialization of the 1960s and 1970s, with a massive import of Western technology, did not bring about the achievement of efficiency targets; the natural outcome was an ever-growing foreign debt. After the second oil shock, the Romanian regime was the only one among the Communist countries that decided to repay its foreign debt at any price rather than liberalize the economy. Annual foreign trade surpluses in the range of US$1–3 billion became the rule in the 1980s.

The price paid was a severe compression of domestic absorption, an end to technology imports, virtually no important investment in modern infrastructures (except for those that were prestige driven), and the country's isolation from the outside world. At the outset of market-oriented reforms, of the socialist countries Romania was the least prepared both socially and intellectually to bear the sacrifices

Table 5.1. Profiles of companies covered in the case studies.

Company	Sector	Ownership[a]	Legal status[b]	Size[c]	Export/ sales ratio in 1994 (%)	Main markets[d]
COMP1	Porcelain	Majority private	JS	M	50	EU
Automobile Dacia	Compact cars	SO	JS	L	40	EU-associated countries, Latin America
ARO	Off-road cars	SO	JS	L	34	EU-associated countries, Latin America, China
Autocamione Roman	Trucks	SO[e]	JS	L	2.5	Latin America, China
Rocar	Buses	SO	JS	L	4	EU-associated countries, CIS, Middle East
COMP6	Fertilizers	SO	JS	L	67	Middle East
COMP7	Fertilizers	SO	JS	L	62	EU, EU-associated countries, China
COMP8	Man-made yarns	JV	JS	M	86	Middle East, EU-associated countries, EU, USA
COMP9	Porcelain sanitary equipment	SO	JS	M	27	EU
COMP10	Cement	SO	JS	L	26	EU
COMP11	Cement	SO	JS	L	7	EU-associated countries
COMP12	Equipment	SO	JS	M	25	China, CIS
COMP13	Wooden furniture	SO	JS	M	85	EU, Middle East, CIS
COMP14	Wooden furniture	SO	JS	M	80	EU, CIS
COMP15	Household refrigerating appliances	SO	JS	L	50	EU
COMP16	Wooden furniture	SO	JS	L	70	EU, CIS
COMP17	Men's suits	JV	JS	M	98	EU, Canada, EU-associated countries
COMP18	Men's trousers	Private	JS	M	95	EU
COMP19	Foreign trade ready-made clothes	Private	JS	S	32	EU, China
COMP20	Foreign trade ball bearings	SO	JS	M	68	EU, USA, Southeast Asia

[a]Ownership: classification based on nationality and control rights of majority shareholder; SO = *State-owned company* – majority owner is the State, via the State Ownership Fund; *Private* – private shareholders retain majority; JV = *Joint ventures* – majority retained by foreign private investors.
[b]JS = Joint-stock company.
[c]Size: L = Large; M = Medium; S = Small. Classification is not based on the absolute number of staff; rather, number of staff of the companies in the sample was related to staff sizes of other companies in the same sectors.
[d]EU = European Union; CIS = Commonwealth of Independent States.
[e]Included in the Mass Privatization Program.

Table 5.2. Development of trade flows in Romania, 1988–1994.

	1988	1989	1990	1991	1992	1993	1994	1995
	Value (in million US dollars)							
Export	11,329	10,487	5,775	4,266	4,363	4,892	6,151	7,520
Import	7,643	8,438	9,202	5,793	6,260	6,522	7,109	9,411
Trade balance	3,749	2,049	–3,427	–1,527	–1,897	–160	–958	–1,891
	Growth (in percent; 1988 = 100)							
Export	100	92.1	50.7	37.4	38.3	42.9	54.0	66.0
Import	100	110.4	120.4	75.8	81.9	85.3	93.0	123.0

Source: Authors' calculations using data from the *Romanian Statistical Yearbook 1995*, Tables 14.1.1 and 14.1.3, and the National Commission for Statistics.

required for the passage from a planned to a market economy. The explosion of domestic absorption after 1989 and the ensuing slump in foreign trade exceeded even the most pessimistic expectations.

The economic, social, and political transformation has had a strong impact on Romanian foreign trade, particularly on exports. Its impact has been greatest regarding the volume of foreign trade flows, the geographical orientation of exports, and the structure of commodity groups.

5.1 Export Evolution

Shortly after December 1990 Romania's new government decided to liberalize foreign trade, to end the state monopoly of hard currency, and to reorient the country toward the West both politically and economically.

In theory these measures seem sufficient to stimulate a sharp recovery for an economy in crisis and to support the growth of exports needed to drive both this recovery and Romania's integration into developed markets. However, what were the actual results of the measures taken?

5.1.1 Size of foreign trade flows

During the first year after the revolution, Romanian exports decreased dramatically, falling to almost 50% of the 1988 level (*Table 5.2*).[1] This decrease continued in 1991, when exports dropped to 37% of the 1988 level. This fall in exports in 1990–1991 was unprecedented in peacetime and exceeded even the most pessimistic expectations. Only in 1995 did exports rebound to 66% of the 1988 export level. In contrast, after a sharp increase in 1990 imports decreased to 76% of 1988 levels and gradually recovered through 1994, exceeding the 1988 level by 1995.

These changes in trade led to a rapid deterioration of the trade balance. In the 1980s the balance showed surplus varying between US$1.525 billion and US$3.719 billion; after 1990 the balance became negative. Between 1990 and 1994 the trade deficit averaged about 37.5% of total exports.[2]

5.1.2 Geographical reorientation of exports

The dramatic fall in exports throughout the period between 1989 and 1995 generated a new geographical orientation for Romanian foreign trade. A sharp increase (10.5 percentage points) was recorded in the share in exports held by developing countries. However, the highest growth (18.6 percentage points) was in the share of the developed countries, which occurred in conjunction with a dramatic fall (29.1 percentage points) in the share held by transition countries (see *Table 5.3*). The share in total Romanian exports held by Central and East European countries was only 10.1% in 1995, compared with 35.1% in 1989. Among developed countries, European Union (EU) member states account for most of the increase from 32.1% in 1989 to 53.2% in 1995. This shift in the geographical orientation of Romanian exports was primarily the result of the country's political decision to integrate into the economic structures of the developed world, particularly European structures.

It is worth mentioning that this reorientation was not caused by a geographical redistribution of existing exports, but by differences in contraction rates for various geographical areas. More precisely, the severe decrease of flows to transition countries (down by a factor of 5) and especially to Central and East European countries (down by a factor of 9) was not offset by flows to developed and developing countries.

By 1995 Romanian imports from developed and EU countries had increased 343% and 425%, respectively, compared with 1989 levels. As a result, the developed countries' share in total Romanian import volume increased from 19.3% in 1989 to 59.2% in 1995; that of EU countries increased from 13% in 1989 to 49.6% in 1995.

The significance of these foreign trade developments for the national economy can only be assessed through an analysis of the structure of exported commodities.

5.1.3 Changes in the commodity structure of exports

Five main groups of commodities, each with a share of total exports constantly over 10%, determined the basic structure of Romanian exports until 1989. These five groups were as follows:

- Mineral products (including cement and fuel);
- Chemical products;

Table 5.3. Romanian exports by groups of countries (fob).

	1989		1990		1992		1994		1995	
	Mln. US$	Percent	Mln. US$	Percent	Mln. US$	Percent	Mln. US$	Percent	Mln. US$	Percent
Total	10,487	100.0	5,775	100.0	4,363	100.0	6,151	100.0	7,520	100.0
Developed countries	4,427	42.2	2,595	45.0	1,874	42.9	3,446	56.0	4,571	60.8
EU	3,365	32.1	1,957	33.9	1,535	35.2	2,965	48.2	3,998	53.2
EFTA	186	1.8	97	1.7	104	2.4	56	0.9	74	1.0
USA	570	5.4	342	5.9	84	1.9	193	3.1	192	2.5
Japan	172	1.6	93	1.6	60	1.4	53	0.9	34	0.5
Transition countries	4,201	40.1	2,327	40.3	1,093	25.1	853	13.9	826	11.0
Cen./East. Europe[a]	3,686	35.1	2,102	36.4	1,082	24.8	813	13.2	762	10.1
USSR/FSU	2,374	22.6	1,422	24.6	604	13.8	405	6.6	420	5.6
Developing countries	1,859	17.7	853	14.7	1,396	32.0	1,852	30.1	2,122	28.2

[a]Central and East European countries plus European members of the CIS.

Sources: Authors' calculations using data from the *Romanian Statistical Yearbook 1992*, Table 277; *Romanian Statistical Yearbook 1995*, Table 14.1.4; *Romanian Statistical Yearbook 1994*, Table 7; *Foreign Trade Statistics Bulletin*, No. 12/1994, Table 3; and the National Commission for Statistics.

- Textiles and footwear;
- Base metals and metal articles;
- Machinery, equipment, and means of transport.

In 1989 these five groups accounted for over 82% of total Romanian exports. The data for the period from 1989 to 1995 highlight two essential structural features (see *Table 5.4*):

- The basic structure of exports was in fact maintained; in 1995 the five important groups (groups V, VI–VII, XI–XII, XV, and XVI–XVII) made up about 79% of the total exports, which shows that Romania's exports are still dominated by industrial goods.
- The real changes occurred among these main groups of industrial products.

More specifically,

- The share of the machinery, equipment, and means of transport group was 28.4% in 1989 and fell to 13.5% in 1995. The group's share dropped by 66% compared with a 28% decrease in total exports. This decline reflects the problems the machinery and equipment industry faces in reorienting its exports from former Council for Mutual Economic Assistance (CMEA) markets to other markets due to technological obsolescence, high costs, and low quality. Moreover, by any standards this group is excessively diversified, virtually lacking international specialization.
- A substantial decrease in exports was recorded for the mineral products group, from 18.6% in 1989 to 9.6% in 1995. Energy-intensive sectors such as the cement and oil processing industries are confronted with significant efficiency problems, mainly due to low-quality equipment and technology.
- The export share of the textile and footwear group increased dramatically, from 10.6% in 1989 to 25.1% in 1995; the share of the textile subgroup increased from 8.7% to 19.7% in the same period. This is the only commodity group whose exports in 1995 exceeded 1989 levels in nominal terms (up almost 70% in 1995).

The substantial increase in exports of textiles and footwear seems to reflect higher competitiveness in these industries compared with heavy industry branches. Still, we must take into account the fact that job-work production of textiles and knitwear is approximately 80% of total production. This explains the contradiction between the dramatic increase in exports of textiles and footwear and the drastic decline in the output of upstream industries (mainly yarns and fabrics, but also leather and skins); in 1994 this output represented only 44.2% of its 1989 level (NBR, 1994).

Table 5.4. Romanian exports by commodity group.

Code[a]	Commodity group	1989		1990		1992		1994		1995	
		Mln. US$	Percent	Mln. US$	Percent	Mln. US$	Percent	Mln. US$	Percent	Mln. US$	Percent
	Total exports	10,487	100.0	5,775.0	100.0	4,363.0	100.0	6,151.3	100.0	7,519.0	100.0
I–IV	Agricultural and food products, beverages	527	5.0	82.0	1.4	291.0	6.7	398.0	6.5	501.0	6.7
V	Mineral products (including cement and fuels)	1,947	18.6	1,136.0	19.7	572.0	13.1	714.0	11.6	724.6	9.6
VI–VII	Chemicals, plastic, rubber	1,037	9.9	407.0	7.0	506.0	11.6	630.0	10.2	899.9	12.0
VIII	Raw hides and skins, leather, fur skins and products	49	0.5	36.0	0.6	25.0	0.6	–	–	–	–
IX–X	Wood and paper products	364	3.5	213.0	3.7	172.0	3.9	222.4	3.6	332.3	4.4
XI–XII	Textiles and footwear	1,112	10.6	702.0	12.2	528.0	12.1	467.0	23.8	1,883.7	25.1
	Textiles	910	8.7	573.4	9.9	455.4	10.4	1,155.8	18.8	1,482.3	19.7
	Footwear	202	1.9	129.0	2.3	72.7	1.7	311.0	5.0	401.4	5.3
XIII	Glass and ceramics	127	1.2	78.0	1.4	88.0	2.0	111.0	1.8	142.0	1.9
XV	Base metals and base-metal articles	1,570	15.0	949.0	16.4	735.0	16.8	1,064.7	17.3	1,392.4	18.5
XVI–XVII	Machinery, equipment, and means of transport	2,977	28.4	1,717.0	29.7	981.0	22.5	910.0	14.8	1,012.0	13.5
	Machinery and equipment	1,546	14.7	946.5	16.4	528.1	11.7	519.1	8.4	607.2	8.1
	Means of transport	1,431	13.7	769.6	13.3	472.9	10.8	391.5	6.4	404.8	5.4
XX	Miscellaneous goods (including furniture)	573	5.5	413.0	7.2	366.0	8.4	436.0	7.1	501.6	6.7

[a]Commodities are categorized according to the Harmonized System of commodity description and coding.

Source: *Romanian Statistical Yearbook 1995*, Table 14.1.3; *Romanian Foreign Trade Yearbook 1994*, Table 5; and the National Commission for Statistics.

Table 5.5. Contribution of main commodity groups to export decline, 1989 to 1990 and 1989 to 1994 and 1995 (in percent).

Commodity group code[a]	Share in 1989 exports	Change versus 1989			Contribution to decrease of total export		
		1990	1994	1995	1990	1994	1995
Total exports	100.0	−45.0	−41.3	−28.3	–	–	–
V	18.6	−41.7	−63.3	−62.8	−7.8	−11.8	−11.7
VI–VII	9.9	−60.8	−39.2	−13.2	−6.0	−3.9	−1.3
XI–XII	10.6	−36.9	+31.9	69.4	−3.9	+3.4	17.9
XV	15.0	−39.6	−32.2	−11.3	−5.9	−4.8	−1.7
XVI–XVII	28.4	−42.3	−69.4	−66.0	−12.0	−19.7	−18.7

[a] See *Table 5.4* for commodity group description.
Source: Calculations based on *Table 5.4*.

The other sectors have roughly maintained their shares of total exports. This relative stability demonstrates that these groups have been more or less equally affected by the causes of the decrease in exports.

Differences in export performance for each main commodity group led to uneven "contributions" to the total decrease in exports. As can be seen from *Table 5.5*, the contribution of groups XI–XII changed from negative to positive between 1990 and 1995 (−3.9% in 1990 to 17.9% in 1995); in this same time period, contributions from groups VI–VII and XV diminished from −6.0% to −1.3% and from −5.9% to −1.7%, respectively. Trade of the commodities in the mineral products group and the machinery, equipment, and means of transport group changed dramatically: the contributions of these groups to the total decrease in exports increased from 19.8 percentage points in the total 45.0 percentage points in 1990 to 30.4 percentage points out of the total 28.3 percentage points in 1995. In other words, in 1990 these two groups were responsible for 44% of the total decrease in exports compared with 1989, but in 1995 they accounted for 107.4% of the total decrease. The causes of this critical evolution are numerous. The dismantling of the CMEA and increases in Western imports to former socialist countries contributed greatly to the catastrophic decrease in Romanian machinery and equipment exports to this region. By 1993 these exports were only 14% of the 1989 level and only 9% by 1995.

At the same time, exports of these commodities to EU countries decreased by 67% between 1989 and 1993, much more rapidly than export declines for other commodities. Whereas in 1989 the share of machine tools and transport equipment in total exports to the EU was 16.5%, it diminished to 10.6% in 1995. Even more dramatic was the fall of the EU's share in the export of mineral products, from 33% in 1989 to 3.8% in 1995.

It is worth mentioning that most of the reduction in exports to West European countries occurred during the first year after the revolution, when the trade cycle in these countries was still in its growing stage. Yet, whereas in 1990 total imports to Organisation for Economic Co-operation and Development (OECD) countries increased 7.4% in real terms, imports to these countries from Romania decreased 42%.

This trend shows that beyond the problems common to all sectors, the sectors in these two commodity groups (machinery and equipment and mineral products) face serious sector-specific problems.

As for Romania's exports to the EU, it is worth noting that although the Interim Agreement with the EU (containing the commercial section of the Association Agreement) entered into force in May 1993, in 1994 Romanian exports to the EU were still below the 1989 level. Only in 1995 was this level reached again. Paradoxically, in spite of restrictions, textile and footwear exports to the EU increased by a factor of 4.6 in 1995 compared with 1989 levels, and base metal exports to the EU rose to 187% of the 1989 level. In contrast, in 1995 exports to the EU from the machinery, equipment, and transport means and mineral products groups, for which tariffs were abolished, were only about 76% and less than 14% of the 1989 figures, respectively.

5.2 Impediments to Exports: Supply

5.2.1 Supply structure

The structure of Romanian export supply largely explains the dramatic problems outlined in Section 5.1.3. To better describe supply-related impediments, we first discuss the industrial structure inherited from the previous regime and attempt to explain why restructuring was stalled in the postcommunist era.

Inherited Structure

Romanian industry was designed and implemented along the Stalinist principle of "socialist industrialization" (which, in fact, reproduced classic nineteenth century concepts and industrial structures), in which priority was given to developing heavy industry, with metallurgy as a base and the chemical and heavy machinery industries as a backbone. Industry was oriented toward extensive development, was extremely resource and energy intensive, and, because it was oriented toward import substitution, offered an excessively diverse range of machinery and equipment. Thus it was able to meet the requirements of its export markets less and less often, even in the "planned" economies. Following the dismantling of the socialist economic system and the liberalization of prices, Romanian industry proved structurally inadequate to meet free-market demands. Some data directly and indirectly reflect the quality of the industrial structures inherited from the old system.

- The share of heavy industry (intermediate production) in the total industrial output averaged over 73% throughout the period from 1985 to 1989, compared with only a 27% share of consumer goods.
- Romania was highly dependent on imported energy and raw materials: energy-intensive sectors accounted for 82% of energy consumption, and the fuels, ores, and raw materials group accounted for 77.4% (Constantin, 1993) of the hard currency–denominated imports and 60% of total imports (Romanian Statistical Yearbook, 1995).
- Over 57% of the manufacturing output originated from 4 of the 16 industry branches of manufacturing:
  - Crude petroleum processing: low level of domestic crude production, mostly primary processing at low technical levels.
  - Chemicals: overwhelmingly manufactured in large-capacity facilities specialized for bulk production; old technology and high real costs.
  - Metallurgy: characterized by high costs and 40–60% higher energy consumption per unit of output compared with developed countries, partly due to old technologies.[3]
  - Machinery, equipment, and metal processing: a 30% share in total manufacturing industry production; mainly oriented toward heavy machines and equipment; production in large and very large plants; an extremely diverse range of products to ensure maximum import substitution; dated technologies and designs. In the last five years of the old regime (1985–1989), the annual hard currency–denominated import of machinery, equipment, and means of transport was only 8.5% of the total hard currency–denominated imports.

This forced, extensive, quasi-autarkic development of industry impeded development in agriculture, infrastructure (transportation and telecommunications, for example), and research and development. The situation was similar for education, health care, and culture, with serious negative effects on Romania's export potential.

Lack of Industrial Restructuring

One of the causes for the limited advances in the restructuring of Romanian industry over the past five years has been the systematic postponement of radical restructuring measures despite the obvious consequences. The acceleration of intercompany payment arrears, the high inflation and low investment, and the sharp fall in output indicated little willingness on the part of large industrial companies to adjust and suggested that they expected the government to support them when economic problems arose.

The increase in arrears has not had the same impact on all 6,000 state-owned companies. As expected, indebtedness is concentrated in a limited number of large and very large companies that have generated substantial losses, so-called black holes. To deal with this problem, the government selected the 32 Romanian companies with the highest debts and largest payment arrears to be included in its FESAL restructuring program. In 1993 these 32 companies accounted for 12.2% of the arrears and 8.6% of the total current debt of all state-owned companies.[4]

Financial constraints have severely affected the export potential of these companies: the proportion of exports in their turnover declined from 25.9% in 1993 to 5.2% in 1994.

As a consequence of growing intercompany payment arrears, in 1994 another 200 companies were put under financial surveillance by a newly-created institution, the Restructuring Agency. In 1993 these 200 companies accounted for 22.3% of the arrears and 16% of the current debt of all state-owned companies; these figures for 1994 were 19.2% and 17.9%, respectively. The 1994 decline of 3 percentage points in these companies' share in total arrears was not the result of an improvement in their financial situations due to better performance; rather, it was the result of old debts being written off and a general increase in the current debts of commercial companies (i.e., the companies that were targeted for privatization). The difficult financial situation of these 200 companies was reflected in the decrease in their share in the exports of all state-owned companies, from 36.3% in 1993 to 14.7% in 1994 (although Romanian exports increased 25.7% in 1994).

These steps toward industrial restructuring, including increasing the number of companies involved, were hardly convincing. The restructuring of the first group of companies has virtually stopped after more than two years. The numerous announcements of "definitive" solutions were generally viewed by the public as signals to the country's lending agencies or budgetary sources. Since the surveillance also included financial support from the government, many managers lobbied to be added to the list.

Arrears were "attacked" twice via global and partial netting out. In February 1995 an ordinance was issued compelling debtors to renegotiate their debts with suppliers, banks, and the state, and to reschedule, write off, or reduce them. The government accepted the write-off of some old penalties, including penalties for not having paid taxes on time, and allocated about 70 billion lei to a recovery fund to be used to pay the electricity and gas bills of those companies in the most difficult situation in order to generate a multiplier effect toward the reduction of arrears. The fund was a drop in the ocean compared with the total arrears (allegedly some 16,000 billion lei), and it was quickly exhausted without spectacular effect as companies used the money to pay outstanding salaries. More generally, the new surveillance regime perfectly fits the postponement pattern established in previous years.

5.2.2 Production costs

Relatively high production costs are the greatest impediment to full use of existing export capacities. The main factor impacting costs in the period after 1989 was the liberalization of prices. The alignment of energy prices and prices of basic raw materials with international prices quickly revealed a large number of export-inefficient products whose production costs were above world market prices.

Obviously, estimating the changes in costs brought on by the dramatic changes in relative prices of inputs is not possible in the framework of the present study. However, the information supplied by some of the managers during the case study interviews can serve as a guide.

According to the managers of the company ARO, the actual manufacturing cost of their off-road cars is up to 30% higher than the price obtainable on the international markct. This estimate was based on prices of products of comparable quality manufactured by ARO's main competitors, the Japanese company Suzuki and the Russian company AvtoVAZ, which according to the Romanian view are carrying out a dumping policy.

In the case of trucks manufactured by Roman Brasov, whose exports have decreased by a factor of over 5.5 compared with 1989 levels, costs exceed the average obtainable export price by 20–25%.

Cost of Material Inputs

When prices of intermediate goods increase faster than industrial prices, the competitiveness of industrial goods erodes, particularly products with medium-length and long manufacturing periods. According to a survey conducted by the National Bank of Romania, most Romanian companies associate the increase in their production costs with the increase in domestic prices of components (63.6% of all respondents) and raw materials (58.2%) (NBR, 1994).

The prices of all domestic inputs increased substantially after 1990; they were up 163.2% in 1991, 193.5% in 1992, 165.0% in 1993, and 140.5% in 1994. Given that in many cases the production processes are resource and energy intensive, such price increases can drastically erode the export capacity of companies, especially in products with narrow profit margins. This was demonstrated in the case studies of two fertilizer producers (companies 6 and 7) included in our study.

Another factor that in recent years has led to a sharp increase in unit costs is the drastic decline in capacity utilization. For example, in 1994 company 10 in our case studies, a cement producer, increased its specific consumption of fuel by 7% and its specific consumption of electricity by 10% at the same time it utilized only 46% of its capacity (compared with 71.5% in 1989).

The increase of costs was impacted by several additional factors:

- The division of some big companies into separate units, leading to a rise in fixed costs;
- The increase in the number of intermediaries, in many cases parasitic private limited-liability companies, an expected phenomenon resulting from earlier absolute dominance of state ownership in industry and trade;
- The exaggerated "inflationary expectations" of many managers, who increased prices to obtain a profit "cushion" while benefiting from their dominant positions in the domestic market.

Cost of Credit

For the vast majority of the companies surveyed the cost of credit is the foremost impediment to exports. Of the managers involved in our survey, 83.6% ranked it first in the hierarchy of export impediments (see Appendix to Chapter 5). This factor is of great importance for two reasons: there is a high share of credit in companies' working capital and the nominal interest rates are high.

Romanian enterprises inherited an extremely high degree of undercapitalization, because under the old system financial resources had been excessively centralized. According to evaluations made by the Romanian Commercial Bank, which manages the accounts of most of Romania's large industrial companies, the share of own sources in the total working capital of state-owned companies in 1992 was about 9%.[5] The remainder, about 91%, represents bank credit, commercial credit, arrears to suppliers, and tax arrears.[6] Inflation and the low profit rate in the years after 1992 prevented any improvement in this situation.[7]

We can consider the minimum credit needs for companies to be the amount of credit already contracted by the companies plus total net arrears.[8] In 1994 minimum credit needs were about 28% of the GDP, an amount exceeding the broad money (M2) by some 29%.[9] With minimum credit needs at this level, interest rates obviously become an important component of production costs. Moreover, a tough macrostabilization package was introduced in late 1993, and interest rates in 1994 for credits (short-term, and medium- and long-term) decreased from 280% to 150%, with the average interest rate fluctuating from 61.8% to 108%, while the inflation rate for 1994 was 61.7%. Such an increase in the cost of credit, at a rate much higher than the inflation rate during a time when financial resources were almost entirely from bank credit, could only lead to an increase in production costs in real terms and negatively impact the financial recovery of companies.

Wage costs did not negatively impact the cost structure: in 1994, as in previous years, the average yearly wage index was lower than the industrial price index, by about 7 percentage points in 1994, 53 in 1993, 40 in 1992, and by 53 in 1991. Only 5.5% of the managers who participated in the survey believed that wage costs had led to cost increases.

Exchange Rate

In April 1994, after a preparatory period during which the exchange rate was gradually depreciated in order to avoid inflationary "shocks" and ensure a "soft landing" to an actual market rate, the National Bank of Romania (NBR) announced that it was abandoning controls and moving to a free exchange rate. Current account convertibility went into effect. In April and May the interbank rate and the free market rate of the leu converged. We might say that, at the given price level, the interbank rate became an "equilibrium rate."

Between September 1993 and April 1994 the leu depreciated faster than the industrial price index (the difference between the two indexes was 5.6 percentage points). This largely eliminated the negative effect of cost increases on export competitiveness. Moreover, the consistency of this policy strengthened companies' confidence in the foreign exchange policy of the NBR. The liberalization of the foreign exchange rate on the interbank market allowed exporters to cover their costs by selling their hard currency revenues and holdings. Both factors induced companies to export. Consequently, compared with 1993 levels, 1994 exports increased 25.7% whereas imports increased by only 9%. In the period between April 1994 and December 1994, however, the leu depreciated by only 6.2% while the industrial price index increased by 26.9% (3.9 times more). The price evolution was quite different across commodity groups; for some sectors the price index was much higher than average. According to a producer of man-made yarns (company 8 in the case studies), the price of its raw materials increased 60% in this period.

Due to the NBR's anti-inflationary policy, the leu appreciated throughout 1994 and became an overvalued currency, as was evident by the increasing propensity to import. Consequently, although in the first half of 1995 the leu depreciated by 14.2% while the price index increased by 11.5%, the gap between imports and exports increased dramatically, to US$755.4 million from US$337 million in the same period in 1994. The growing deficit shows that the depreciation of the national currency in 1995 was insufficient to offset the effect of the increase in production costs after April 1994.

5.2.3 Product quality

Inferior quality is usually an impediment to exports in the machinery and equipment industry. Romania's long period of isolation led to continuous relative degradation of technical standards of products and technical capabilities of producers, with an extremely negative effect on export potential.

In the 1970s and early 1980s, Romania became known as one of the world's main producers and exporters of oil-field equipment for drilling and wells operations. It currently has all but disappeared from this market. In the 1970s and 1980s, Romania was also a well-respected producer and exporter of electric and diesel railroad locomotives (produced under Swedish license), with annual exports of 100 units. In 1992 Romania not only ceased to export but also ceased to manufacture these locomotives.

Even into the 1980s Romania was an important exporter of railroad freight and tank carriages (between 8,000 and 11,000 per year). However, it can no longer effectively export these products (only 436 pieces were produced in 1994), primarily because of their level of technology, which was already obsolete in the first half of the 1980s. According to the sales manager of the ARO company, manufacturing quality has played an important role in the drastic decline in exports of the well-known ARO off-road cars; exports decreased from 13,000–18,000 units in the late 1980s, to only 2,745 units in 1994.

These few, relevant examples give only a rough idea of the impediment to export expansion created by low product quality. The quality of the final product is directly related to the quality of the inputs it incorporates. Our survey revealed a high degree of discontent concerning the price/quality ratio of Romanian components.

There were no differences in terms of unfavorable price/quality ratios from one sector to another, which is probably largely the result of the already mentioned deterioration of Romania's entire industrial base in the 1980s because of the country's self-imposed isolation. The low quality of domestic inputs has led many companies to adopt a relatively dangerous strategy of making clear distinctions between quality for the Romanian market and quality for foreign markets. ARO, the off-road car producer, uses more than 90% domestically produced parts for cars delivered domestically, whereas the share of Romanian components in cars for export can be below 50%. The same situation occurs in the production of buses, furniture, and equipment. The danger implicit in this strategy is the risk of losing positions in the domestic market in the longer run because of dissatisfied customers who might turn to foreign competition.

5.2.4 General condition of companies

There are various parameters for quantifying the poor condition of companies, however, two of them are essential: indebtedness and the managerial crisis.

Indebtedness

High indebtedness is inevitable given the drastic undercapitalization inherited from the old regime, the very high inflation rate, and the limited use of existing capacities (industrial capacity utilized during the past four years hovered around 47–57%, and in some basic sectors such as chemical and petrochemical industries only 30–36% of the existing capacity is used).

At the end of 1994 the total value of arrears to banks, suppliers, and other fiscal authorities was 46% above the total value of credit to organizations other than the government. Clearly, Romanian companies are confronted with a debt crisis. Arrears exceeded the broad money supply (M2) by 8.9% and accounted for 23.1% of the GDP and 12.8% of total sales. By the end of June 1995 they exceeded the broad money supply by 4.6%.[10] Suppliers hold 64.5% of the arrears, reflecting a chain of arrears with serious effects on production and capacity to export. This is largely the result of the lack of restructuring, as shown above. However, it is also explained by the eagerness of commercial banks, especially those that are state-owned, to diminish their portfolio of bad loans as quickly as possible via an extremely conservative credit policy toward large industrial companies. The high risk premiums they charge these companies often result in a loss of export opportunities.

Thus, for example, despite the extremely favorable situation in the aluminum market starting in 1994, less than 50% of the industry's production capacities were in use. In that same year, output was 122.6 thousand tonnes (compared with 280 thousand tonnes in 1989), and exports accounted for 99.5 thousand tonnes (compared with 194 thousand tonnes in 1988). According to the managers of Conef s.a., a holding that de facto represents the nonferrous metallurgy sector, due to the high risk premiums for new credits to aluminum-related companies, foreign orders for about 30–40 thousand tonnes could not be filled.

Despite the more than 50% decrease in output of finished rolled-steel products, the steel industry could not satisfy some significant export demands for construction steel, especially for the Middle East, because of difficulties in mobilizing financial resources to obtain the necessary inputs. The same is true for oil refineries. The inability to obtain new financing prevented some refineries from securing important processing orders from Middle Eastern producers. According to managers of one foreign trade company (company 20 in the case studies), important export orders for ball bearings exist, yet producers are reluctant to apply for new credits to increase production because they are not sure they will be able to meet the repayment schedule. Moreover, they fear an increase in interest rates due to the accumulating arrears. This kind of increase actually occurred at the end of November 1995.

Managerial Crisis

The managerial crisis amplified by delays in privatization was probably one of the most important impediments to exports. To consider this obstacle, we must refer to the vacuum of authority and the embryonic state of business management in Romania.

The complete destruction of all authority structures in the December 1989 revolution led to a protracted authority crisis, which only ended in late 1993 when the State Ownership Fund finally began to function and the provisions of the Management Contract Law were implemented. The effects of the 1990–1993 crisis of authority distorted the economic behavior of Romanian companies. State-owned companies were oriented toward preserving employment, maximizing wages (regardless of whether investment fell to zero and debt accumulated), maintaining weak managers (as a result of the "workers' direct democracy"), outright theft, and arbitrary division of tightly vertically integrated companies. These practices resulted in a failure to introduce any substantial adjustment measures, rapidly deteriorating financial positions, and unrecoverable losses.

The Management Contracts Law provided for the organization of tenders in order to select the best managerial team for state-owned companies. However, in only 20% of the cases was there more than one bidder; in 6.7% of the cases there were two bidders, and in 13.7% of the cases there were more than two bidders. Of the 80% of the cases where there was only one bidder, in the vast majority of instances it was the managerial team already managing the company. There is obviously still a strong bias toward operation management, a heritage of the old system, when the biggest problem was not selling the output (since clients were already planned), but getting the inputs needed to achieve planned output targets. In the industrial sector 81% of the bidders for management contracts were engineers and 12.6% were economists; in agriculture, 82% were engineers and only 6.3% were economists. Such an overwhelming predominance of candidates with technical backgrounds could suggest a strong propensity to subordinate financial management to operations management.

5.2.5 Low quality of infrastructure

Among the elements of infrastructure the low quality of roads is seen as the most important barrier to exports. Respondents placed it eighth in the hierarchy of 43 barriers (see Appendix to Chapter 5). In 1993 the total length of national roads (including freeways and modernized European roads) was under 13,000 km – that is, 5.3 km for 100 km^2 of territory. County and municipal roads make up 23.5% (4,109 km) of the roads in Romania. If we add these to the national roads we obtain a territory density of 7 km/100 km^2. The next largest group of roads are those that have not been maintained for more than a decade and whose current situation is worse than precarious. The remaining 49% of the roads are not paved.

Somewhat surprisingly, the quality of telephone service is hardly a matter of concern for exporters, who rank it twentieth in the hierarchy of barriers. This favorable opinion of managers is in spite of the low number of telephone lines: 116 lines per 1,000 inhabitants, far behind Western Europe but ahead of most East European countries. This ranking is explained by RomTelecom's policy of granting priority to installing business telephone lines.

Railroad transport quality does not seem to be considered a significant obstacle to exports either; it was ranked twenty-third among the hierarchy of export barriers. Still, this ranking should be interpreted with care. After 1989 the share of railroad transportation in total transportation decreased from over 80% to some 30%, precisely because of the low quality of railroad transportation in the context of increasing quality requirements, especially from the newly emerging private sector.

Insufficient development of customs infrastructure and complicated bureaucratic procedures seem to be significant barriers to export, leading to substantial delays in export operations. In many cases, the customs examination of goods belonging to tourists and to business is not separated, leading to enormous delays. This might explain why exporters consider relationships with customs authorities to be as important as tariffs in foreign markets in terms of impediments to export.

A modern banking system is emerging, but many elements are still missing. In 1990 Romania had five state-owned commercial banks; currently there are 32 banks, most of which are privately owned. These changes have led to significant improvements in banking services. However, the period of payment, and especially the period and terms of credit disbursement, are still far from facilitating the foreign operations of Romanian companies. First, banks have a strong tendency to lengthen payment periods in order to take advantage of the money in transit. This is empirically confirmed by our survey, as this impediment was ranked sixth among all the impediments included in the research. Moreover, the numerous corruption scandals revealed in the press suggest that bribery to get credit resources has virtually become a rule of the game.

In addition, Romanian banks are reluctant to extend long-term credit, which leads to the loss of important export opportunities. There were several examples in our case studies. For instance, company 12, an important exporter of bottling lines to China, has had difficulties keeping its market without extending generous commercial credit arrangements to its Chinese partners (3–5 years). It might even lose the Chinese market because Romanian banks simply do not offer such credit arrangements and obtaining loans from foreign banks is still difficult.

Roman Brasov, a large truck producer, lost most of its export markets after 1989 as a result of the need to pay real prices for inputs. Although it desperately needs to accumulate resources in order to purchase new equipment and develop new products, it has increasing difficulties even in the domestic market to capitalize on its position. Attractive credit arrangements secured by foreign banks for the supply of second-hand trucks "stole" a large share of Roman's market in Romania.

Specialized infrastructure is also missing or is insufficient in Romania. For example, there exists only one specialized terminal for loading cement in the port of Constanta, Romania's largest port. This specialized terminal is controlled by a private company and, as testified in the case studies of companies 10 and 11, excessive loading costs make up a significant part of the total export cost for cement.

5.2.6 Lack of information

Lack of information is one of the most important factors responsible for Romania's insufficient use of export capacities. It can mainly be attributed to the emergence of several thousand private companies actively carrying out foreign trade operations, compared with approximately 40 exporting firms until 1989. Since the liberalization of foreign trade activities, many insufficiently trained producers, who in the past exported their products through specialized companies, have decided to export directly. This sudden increase in interest in foreign trade has made recruiting skilled personnel an extremely difficult task.

Our survey of companies with interests in foreign trade shows that of 43 impediments to foreign trade, the lack of a permanent representative abroad was ranked ninth (indicated in 45.5% of the responses); the lack of knowledge about price levels in export markets was ranked twelfth; the lack of knowledge about commercial legislation in foreign markets was ranked fourteenth; and the lack of knowledge of business rules abroad was ranked nineteenth (see survey analysis in the Appendix to Chapter 5).

At first glance, these rankings might suggest that these barriers are not overly important. Still, the rankings can be interpreted as demonstrating a low degree of awareness of how important good information is for exporting efficiently. This assessment is confirmed by the fact that the great majority of those interviewed, representing both state-owned and private companies, wanted to use fewer trade journals and specialized publications as sources of information. The managers of the joint-venture and chemical companies seem to be exceptions to this viewpoint.

Moreover, with the exception of joint ventures, state-owned and private exporting companies do not consider market research to be important. This is not because these companies have established their own market research structures capable of supplying the necessary data for decision making. The marketing departments, where established, are generally weak, have an insufficiently trained staff, and are heavily sales focused. Of the 10 marketing departments reported, 7 employ only two to three persons, and these employees deal primarily with current selling activities. Not only do these employees not have access to the most important of the specialized publications, they often do not know these publications exist. Also, only 3 of 10 companies reported market research programs for their products.

In the longer run, the lack of information will lead to excessive reliance on intermediaries (as was the experience of company 1 in the case studies) and to an exaggerated use of foreign labels for exporting. This practice is self-defeating, because the alternative, having a strong trademark of one's own, would be a key asset in the struggle to gain a foothold in the upper segments of the market.

5.2.7 Public policies as impediments to exports

Previous sections of this chapter have dealt with various effects of public policy. This section identifies and discusses additional policies that are related to trade.

Slow Pace of Privatization

Of the policies that have had a direct negative impact on the development of Romanian export potential, the slow pace of privatization is definitely the most significant.

As far as foreign trade is concerned, it is important to mention that during the past few years the private sector's percentage of the total export volume increased extremely slowly, from 27.5% in 1992 to 27.8% in 1993, to only 30% in 1994 (CNS, 1994a, 1994b). By 1995, this share had increased to 41%. These figures reflect the low level and slow pace of privatization, both in general and in industry in particular. At the end of 1993 private industrial enterprises made up only 6.4% of the total industrial work force (CNS, 1994a).

In 1994 the pace of privatization was still much slower than was possible and desirable.[11] The delays in privatization seriously affected the full use of export potential. Two types of behavior have developed among managers and employees as a result of pending privatization. Attempts to take companies over have been made by managerial teams during privatization. In some cases a policy leading to stagnation of output and falling profitability, or even real or apparent bankruptcy, has been adopted together with a campaign to discourage potential shareholders. This behavior is typical in small and medium-size firms and aims at reducing the value of the company to a minimum so managers will be able to gain at least a controlling share of stock.[12] A second type of behavior, found mainly in large companies, reflects a "take as much as you can" mentality. Among the tactics used to achieve this "goal" are the following: establishing private limited-liability companies, which are in fact parasitic companies through which the large companies buy their inputs and sell their output; establishing "joint ventures" with private companies, thus enabling the latter to acquire and use the fixed assets of the state-owned company; using bribery to obtain certain privileges; exerting influence on decisions that harm the larger company in favor of particular "business partners"; and white-collar stealing of tools, materials, and ready-made products. In some of the interviews, managers stated that in a few years the destruction of many state-owned companies that are currently potentially viable will be so serious that their recovery after privatization will be difficult or almost impossible.

Other negative effects of protracted privatization have been legislative inconsistencies and the outright breach of regulations during privatization by the very trustee charged with managing the state's possessions – the State Ownership Fund (SOF).

In 1993 the Management Contracts Law was passed by the Parliament. Management contracts were concluded for most state-owned companies by 1994. They provided a fixed monthly income for managers and an additional benefit in proportion with the amount of profit or reduction of losses achieved. Our interviews with managers confirmed that management contracts had a positive influence on managerial behavior. In 1994 positive macroeconomic results were related to the incentives provided by these contracts.

However, after the 1994 fiscal year, when managers were supposed to be paid according to the provisions of the managing contracts, the SOF began to worry that some managers were going to receive benefits far too high for Romania's standard of living (bonuses of tens of thousands of US dollars, in some cases over US$200,000). The SOF therefore decided to limit these bonuses to 12 gross monthly salaries, regardless of the contract (POF, 1994). According to several of the managers interviewed, this decision has had a significant inhibitive effect. "I am going to limit my efforts to assuring the 12 monthly remunerations, and if other opportunities of earnings [other than increasing the company's profit] occur I shall use them" said the manager of a nonferrous metal company. Also, many companies (for example, company 14, a furniture producer included in the case studies) accused the SOF of irresponsible portfolio management, because in many cases it has extracted dividends from relatively healthy companies and redirected the resources toward the so-called black holes of the Romanian economy.

In 1995 the so-called mass privatization was launched, based on the Law for the Acceleration of Privatization; it aimed at the free transfer of 30% of the equity in state-owned commercial companies to Romanian citizens. Over 90% of the citizens eventually subscribed their "privatization coupons." Still, the 30% of the nominal equity actually represents only 20–22% of the nominal state-owned capital (since commercial companies account for some 60% of the state-owned capital, while the so-called *regies autonomes* – the companies that are excluded from privatization – retain the remaining 40%). This raises doubts about whether the new owners will be able to break the established behavior of managers in state-owned companies and force them to focus on profit maximization, which may include expanding exports.

Tariff Policy

Romania's tariff policy has affected export potential indirectly, through the effect of low import tariffs for manufactured products and high import tariffs for raw materials. An example of this practice is the development of detergent production in Romania.

In 1989 Romania produced 109,000 tonnes of detergent, a certain quantity of which was exported. In 1995 the output was estimated to be around 20,000 tonnes and some 70% of the domestic market was supplied by foreign producers. Foreign detergents are definitely of better quality, but it is also worth pointing out that customs duties for imported detergents are 7%, whereas they are 15–20% for the raw materials used for the production of detergents. The government did not step in until September 1995, when it issued a decree exempting two basic raw materials from customs duties and sharply increasing the customs duties for imported detergents to 35%. These actions came too late, however. The national detergents industry is on the brink of collapse; the only chance of saving it is through joint ventures with foreign producers, a trend already well underway.

The situation is similar for computer components, where duties vary between 15% and 25%; duties on assembled computers range between 8% and 15%, and are sometimes removed altogether. Similar situations are also common for electronic consumer goods.

Obviously, such a tariff structure indirectly harms exports because it has negative effects on the costs and competitiveness of the manufactured goods in foreign markets.

Survey respondents also indicated that customs duties for modern manufacturing equipment are high regardless of whether there are similar Romanian products to be protected or not. The companies' efforts to modernize operations are thus harmed by the fiscal rather than commercial logic of the customs authority.

Implementation of Regulations that Facilitate Exports

The drawback on customs duties and the value-added tax (VAT) for inputs used in exported goods is useful in principle. Its utilization, however, creates serious cash flow problems for companies that are already short of cash (see Section 5.2.4). The company must block substantial resources, sometimes for long periods of time depending on the length of the manufacturing cycle. Moreover, the Ministry of Finance has an extremely complicated procedure for customs drawback, so acquiring the refunds often becomes an adventure. It is not easy to advance these payments with loans, even if the company can provide a guarantee: in many cases the companies already have arrears to their bank, which is not ready to give loans to pay the duties and VAT necessary to process exports.

Because the customs authority does not have an integrated computer network, it requires any company that wishes to benefit from the drawback system to export its finished goods through the same customs point where the imported inputs were registered. This requirement is considered absurd by all companies, as it artificially increases costs and creates enormous problems when, for example, inputs are imported from the West and the finished product goes south.

Although it is an important support, subsidized credit for export is only disbursed after a product is actually exported. This leads to serious financial problems for the companies, who suggest the disbursement of the subsidized credit on the grounds of the export contract.

5.3 Impediments to Exports: Demand

Demand-related impediments to export can be split into two groups: external impediments, which are outside the exporter's control; and impediments the exporter can overcome using its own resources.

5.3.1 External impediments

Structure of Export Markets

Export markets can be seen as an impediment to exports in terms of both structure and level of demand for specific products and for groups of products. These factors are directly related to the stage of development of the export market: the more developed the export market, the greater the demand for higher-quality products produced using more sophisticated technology.

As can be seen from the discussion in Section 5.1.3, for the Romanian economy there currently is an inverse relation between processing level and exportability: the more processed a product, the less exportable it is. This is a result of either outdated technology or an uncompetitive price/quality ratio. In terms of demand for Romanian products, the export markets can be divided into highly liquid markets and markets with limited liquidity.

Highly Liquid Markets

Developed countries. In highly liquid markets in developed countries there is low demand for the following Romanian products:

- Machinery and equipment, because of their low technical level and low price/quality competitiveness;
- Steel products, as a result of protective measures in foreign markets;
- Traditional building materials, because of massive substitution of new materials and the unsatisfactory price/quality ratio; and
- Fertilizers, because of the decrease in their consumption for ecological reasons.

There is high demand in these markets for high-quality Romanian consumer goods, including textiles, footwear, furniture, and machinery and equipment.

Developing countries. In highly liquid markets in developing countries there is high demand for goods requiring intensive post-sale service and products facing strict constraints of price/quality ratio, for example, construction and drilling equipment.

Markets with Limited Liquidity

Markets of former socialist countries [excluding Commonwealth of Independent States (CIS) countries]. These markets often have limited liquidity and are generally characterized by low demand because of their preference for imports from developed countries for both capital and consumer goods.

CIS markets. In these markets there is high demand for the following Romanian goods:

- Consumer goods: textiles, footwear, furniture, and foodstuffs, and
- Capital goods: boilers, machinery and equipment, electrical equipment, telecommunication equipment, railroad equipment, ships, and other vehicles.

Selling on this market is difficult due to serious transportation problems, which bring about long transportation delays, delays in receiving goods, and consequently delays in receiving payments. Such difficulties are mainly reported by small and medium-size enterprises, but occasionally large companies also encounter them.

Markets in developing countries. In markets in developing countries there is demand for both consumer and capital goods.

As is reflected in the survey above, the products Romanian producers can mainly offer for export are not demanded by markets that can pay in cash. Liquid markets demand products such as textiles, footwear, and furniture (that is, labor-intensive, low-technology, low-value-added consumer goods), or goods such as metals and bulk chemicals (products with a low level of technology that are energy and resource intensive and that have a narrow profit margin). The more-processed products that could easily be supplied by Romanian producers are demanded only by poor regional markets where the possibility of cash transactions is limited.

Protection Policies

High tariffs in export markets. According to our survey, 30% of exporters are harmed by protection policies. The sectors most affected in EU markets are the foodstuffs and textile industries, both of which are protected in the framework of the Association Agreement with the EU. Following these sectors closely is the furniture sector. It is worth mentioning that furniture and textile manufacturing currently are major basic export sectors, with a combined 25% share in total exports in the first half of 1995.

For markets outside the EU, exporters of motor vehicles and refrigerating equipment (including company 12 in our case studies) complain about the high tariff barriers.

Direct protectionism is practiced by EU countries via customs duties (albeit recently lowered) and import quotas, to say nothing of other nontariff barriers and instruments of indirect protectionism.[13] These measures are stipulated in the Association Agreements and are maintained in precisely those areas where EU producers might be outcompeted, that is, steel, agricultural, and textile products. The restrictions have hampered exports of EU-associated countries and have prompted bitter reactions from leading East European heads of state, including then Polish president Lech Walesa and Romanian president Ion Iliescu. The asymmetry of the mutual concessions provided by the Association Agreements and the opening of EU markets through unilateral elimination of customs duties and import quotas for the overwhelming majority of manufactured products are obviously positive measures. It is, however, worth mentioning that in Romania's case this free access is granted mostly for products that do not pose a threat to EU producers due to the insufficient competitiveness of East European producers or to specific nontariff barriers.

Quantitative restrictions and tariff quotas. Of the sectors that we included in our survey, foodstuffs, textiles, mineral products, and fertilizer seem to be the most harmed by quantitative restrictions and tariff quotas. Although companies that produce these goods make up only 16% of our sample, it is worth noting that these sectors account for more than half of Romania's exports. Consequently, these impediments may be quite important.

Difficulties Obtaining Import Licenses

Difficulties obtaining import licenses seem to be an important impediment to exports, especially in Chinese and Russian markets, where Romanian export supply could be matched by significant import demand. This barrier may be particularly relevant for the machinery and equipment industry, where low quality and technological levels have made it difficult for firms to penetrate other markets, such as the markets of developed countries.

Sanitary, Ecological, and Safety Standards

Meeting sanitary, ecological, and safety standards seems to be an extremely high hurdle, especially for producers of motor vehicles. With their present resources, companies such as Autocamione Roman and Rocar from our sample cannot satisfy the strict ecological and quality standards required for EU markets. They are left to trade in poor markets, where competitors can offer lower prices. However, they can try to diversify into other activities; this diversification might lead to renewed export potential, especially for auto parts, where Autocamione Roman in particular seems to have had some important breakthroughs. Although its main target used to be the softer markets of Eastern Europe and Latin America, Dacia, Romania's largest carmaker, was recently compelled to produce a totally new car to attempt to penetrate the European markets.

Another instance where meeting required standards constitutes a barrier is the case of Romanian cement producers, who find it very difficult to penetrate EU markets as they cannot always meet the strict packing standards.

Lack of Liquidity and Smooth Credit and Payment Arrangements

Producers of equipment, furniture, and household ceramics are the most harmed by liquidity, credit, and payment problems. These problems are an impediment to exports to developing and transition countries, especially China and Russia. This situation creates significant difficulties for Romanian exporters as they try to avoid the high cost of domestic credit resulting from the restrictive macrostabilization policy. As a result, Romanian exporters lobby the government for barter arrangements, although they do not believe this solution is very promising: most consider that they will no longer be using bartering by 2000.

Unfair Commercial Practices

The managers from state-owned and private Romanian firms see unfair commercial practices as an important barrier to exports; joint ventures with foreign partners seem to be less affected by them. Again, large firms that export equipment and vehicles claim that these practices harm them in developing markets and in the markets of Russia and China. For example, Autocamione Roman, the truck producer, asserts that the Russian company Kamaz and the Czech company Liaz compete unfairly in the Syrian market. Still, these statements must be taken with due caution. The weaker commercial abilities of state-owned and private firms in comparison with those of joint ventures might be a good explanation of the discontent they show vis-à-vis their foreign competitors. Moreover, it seems Autocamione Roman is tempted to accuse of product dumping any company that can offer significantly lower prices, although it can hardly prove that these practices really occur.

Another example of an unfair business practice is the production by unidentified Chinese producers of low-quality ball bearings falsely labeled "Made in Romania," thus capitalizing on the good reputation of Romanian bearings in Asian markets in the short run and destroying this reputation in the longer run.

5.3.2 Foreign impediments that can be overcome by exporters

Generally, foreign impediments that exporters can in principle surmount are associated with high entry costs, which unfortunately, most Romanian exporters currently can practically barely pay.

Lack of a Permanent Representative Abroad

The lack of a permanent representative abroad seems to be the most important in this category of impediments, because it is connected with the need for reliable, in-depth information. Almost half the companies surveyed, state-owned and Romanian private firms in particular, indicated that this was an important impediment to exports. According to data from the Ministry of Commerce, by the end of 1995 the total number of representatives abroad paid by Romanian companies was only 65. Glass and chinaware producers are the most affected by this impediment, followed by producers of equipment, vehicles, and furniture. Their financial resources do not allow them to hire representatives of their own; therefore, they lobby the government to support them in this respect. The representatives abroad currently work under extremely precarious conditions because of the high costs of renting adequate premises and obtaining the needed information about potential buyers and market opportunities.

Packaging and Labeling Standards

Exporters of foodstuffs are significantly affected by packaging and labeling standards for three reasons: not much attention was paid to packaging and labeling in the past; there are no competitive national producers of packaging materials in Romania; and exporters have limited financial resources for the purchase of necessary packaging equipment. Because of these impediments, Romanian exporters have been largely unable to establish a trademark and in many cases they produce under foreign trademarks in order to enter export markets. A good example of this situation is company 15 in the case studies, a producer of household refrigerating equipment that exports most of its output to EU markets under foreign labels. Another example is the textile and clothing industry, which recovered rapidly and had exceeded its 1989 export level by producing under job-work arrangements. In many cases, the conditions of these arrangements are such that apparel produced in Romania does not even bear the label "Made in Romania."

Costs and Sources of Promotion

According to current regulation Romanian companies cannot deduct more than 3% of their gross profit for promotion-related expenses. Thus, the resources available for launching a product in export markets are drastically limited. Insufficient resources for buying information results in limited knowledge of specific international and national legislation (indicated as an impediment by 37% of the companies surveyed), of business rules abroad (29%), and of prices in various markets (38%).

Distribution Channels

Difficulty in gaining access to distribution channels was indicated as an important impediment to exports by 42% of the companies surveyed. Exporters of foodstuffs are harmed the most, but exporters of equipment, vehicles, and mineral products are also affected.

5.4 Policies to Remove Impediments

5.4.1 Macrostabilization and investment recovery

The main objective of recent Romanian macroeconomic polices was to achieve macrostabilization as a prerequisite for placing economic activity (including exports) on a growth track. The average monthly inflation rate was in the double digits until 1994, and only in 1994 did the annual rate decrease to 61.7% from former rates between 200% and 300% (CNS, 1995a; NBR, 1994). In 1995 this was further curbed to the significantly lower rate of 27.8% (*OMRI Economic Digest*, 28 March 1996).

The positive evolution in 1994 was due mainly to the restrictive monetary policy of the National Bank of Romania (NBR). Resisting pressure from state-owned companies (often exercised via governmental institutions), the NBR promoted a positive real interest rate policy, leading to improved financial discipline among companies and diminishing inflationary pressures. The policy also led to an acceleration in the recovery of industrial production growth, up 3.3% in 1994 and up 14.7% in 1995, as well as to a 22.3% increase in exports in 1995 (*OMRI Economic Digest*, 28 March 1996).

The relative stability of the exchange rate was an effect of the attractive domestic interest rates and was maintained by the conversion of the hard currency reserves held by the public into lei and by the sale of the NBR's foreign exchange reserves. These two sources were exhausted in 1995, and after a period of implicit administrative controls (delivery in tranches of the hard currency exchanged, an increase in bank commissions) the exchange rate soared in November 1995. A US dollar was quoted to be worth 2,578 lei at the end of 1995, compared with about 2,100 lei at end of October 1995. Still, this depreciation did not lead to an increase in exports, clear proof of a very rigid correlation between imported inputs and exports, as determined by the present structure of the Romanian industrial sector.

A firm policy of budgetary austerity contributed significantly to the macroeconomic stabilization. Thus, in 1994 the budget deficit was limited to about 4.3% of the estimated GDP; certain rationalizations of expenses occurred, such as orienting budget expenses toward an increase in the share of capital investment and financing the deficit from non-inflationary sources.

The most important effect of the macroeconomic stabilization was the increase in export potential through revitalization of investments, which are crucial for restructuring production, upgrading equipment and technologies, and improving competitiveness.[14]

5.4.2 Interbank foreign exchange market

At the beginning of 1994, when commercial interest rates skyrocketed to over 150%, the shortage of lei forced companies to sell their foreign currency deposits; thus, a certain equilibrium exchange rate was achieved, with a beneficial effect on the inflation rate. Between April 1994 and March 1995 the exchange rate depreciated in nominal terms by only 9.7% (from 1670.71 lei/US$ to 1832.6 lei/US$) compared with 165.2% in the period from April 1993 to March 1994. The relative equilibrium on the foreign exchange market paved the way for the introduction in August 1994 of a modern interbank foreign exchange market. This system facilitated transactions without administrative intervention. Thus, companies could more easily import inputs in order to export.

5.4.3 Foreign trade policy

Economic Diplomacy

Economic diplomacy contributes to the creation of a legal framework for expanding potential external markets and to the identification of possibilities for further extension of foreign commercial relationships. The following are major fields of this diplomatic activity: concluding commercial agreements with various countries (20 agreements in 1993, 44 in 1994); activities of governmental joint commissions with various countries (20 sessions in 1993, 44 in 1994); organizing economic missions abroad where a large number of companies' representatives participate (21 in 1993, 55 in 1994); organizing missions for foreign businesspersons in Romania (17 in 1993, 41 in 1994); and organizing commercial representative offices or economic agencies within Romanian embassies abroad (over 80 in 1994).

Of utmost importance were the conclusion of the Europe Agreement for Romania's Association with the European Community and the free trade agreement with the European Free Trade Association (EFTA). Also important were the free trade agreements concluded with the Czech and Slovak Republics and the agreement about to be concluded with Poland. The conclusion of a free trade agreement with these EU-associated countries is the first step toward renegotiating with the EU the clause for the cumulation of origin including all associated countries. The cumulation of origin is currently only agreed within the Visegrád Four, on one side, and between Romania and Bulgaria, on the other. Regional cumulation of origin would accelerate the emergence of an integrated economic area, much in the spirit of the Rome Treaty of 1957, and enhance the export opportunities of each of the associated countries.

Development of the Institutional Framework

In 1995 the Romanian Center for Foreign Trade was created within the Ministry of Trade. Its goal is to help companies develop their export capabilities.

Continuous Export Liberalization and Export Facilities

The following measures have been important for further liberalization of exports.

- There was a decrease in the number of products whose export was temporarily banned (from 388 in 1993 to 154 in 1995) or was controlled by export quota (from 117 in 1993 to 52 in 1995);
- Zero VAT was introduced for export of goods and services; drawback of import duties was established for goods incorporated into products to be exported;
- Subsidies were given for interest paid on export credits and budget allocations were made for export credit insurance against country risk (in 1993 the equivalent of US$92.1 million, in 1994 US$42.3 million, and in 1995 some US$62 million was paid from Ministry of Trade funds); low-interest export credits were given (at the NBR's refinancing interest level); in 1994 credits worth 250 billion lei (US$151 million) were distributed to exporters (Government of Romania, 1994); and in 1994, 10 billion lei (US$6 million) was granted in the framework of a favored credit regime with guarantees for exports of equipment and machines with long manufacturing periods.

Even if these measures and allocations are welcome, they cannot be considered sufficient to support strong growth of exports. The Ministry of Trade considers the following to be priorities for further development of the legal framework for export promotion.[15]

- Assistance for private and state-owned companies through partial compensation of the costs of participating in international fairs and expositions. In 1994 this compensation was US$1.5 million.
- Logistical support for companies involved in export operations (for example, information, consulting, and contacts) from the Ministry of Trade through its 122 representatives in 106 countries.

In addition, special arrangements are used for the export of complex equipment and turnkey plants, products with a long manufacturing cycle. These special provisions include guarantees for attending international tenders and guarantees for credits, subsidized credits, and export insurance. The main shortcoming of this support is the limited resources allocated for its enforcements. In 1995 a special fund amounting to approximately US$11.2 million was established for the implementation of this initiative.

5.5 Conclusion

The most important conclusion of this study is that Romanian exporters face much more serious problems domestically than they must cope with abroad. Our empirical research, our survey, and the case studies all confirmed this finding.

The direct implication of this "hierarchy" of impediments to export is that the usefulness of any export-promotion arrangement is limited in the absence of resolute measures to correct the industrial structure. Thus, the best export-promotion policies would be the acceleration of privatization in order to release important production potential that is now underutilized and the restructuring of large companies, which are more difficult to privatize, in order to stop them from wasting national resources. Improving the operation of these companies would decelerate the accumulation of intercompany payments arrears, would curb the inflationary expectations of participants in the capital market, and would encourage investment as the only source of both strong export and GDP growth.

Notes

[1] Two things are worth noticing. Exports in 1988 were only 1.9% higher than exports in 1981. Also, the approximately 8% decrease in exports in 1989 compared with the 1988 figure was not caused by a purposeful reduction in forced exports (which had expanded throughout the 1980s); it was the result of the economic crisis Romania was already encountering in 1989.

[2] The sharp deterioration of the trade balance was due to the fall of exports, not to the sharp increase in imports resulting from their liberalization, as Radulescu (1994) claims.

[3] Although in Western Europe and Japan Siemens-Martin technology was entirely abandoned by the end of the 1970s, in Romania even in 1989 almost one-quarter of the output was produced in Siemens-Martin ovens.

[4] Information for this section was supplied by the National Commission for Prognosis.

[5] Information based on discussion at the Romanian Economic Society's meeting.

[6] There are no statistics concerning working capital or its share in total assets.

[7] For the economy as a whole, the profit rate declined from 4.50% in 1992 to 3.14% in 1994. In the state-owned sector, which held 90% of industry in 1994, the profit rate fell from 2.70% in 1992 to 0.05% in 1994, according to data from the Ministry of Finance.

[8] Minimum credit needs here refer to the approximate amount needed to maintain economic activity at the same level.

[9] Calculated on the basis of data from the Ministry of Finance.

[10] Calculated on the basis of data supplied by the Ministry of Finance and the 1994 annual report of the NBR, Tables 12 and 16.

[11] According to the provisions of the Privatization Law (Law 58/ 1991), the trusteeship for state-owned enterprises was transferred from the Government (Ministry of Finance) to two new types of institutions: 70% to the State Ownership Fund (SOF), and 30% to so-called Private Ownership Funds (POFs). The latter temporarily manage the ownership rights of over 15 million citizens (the owners) under a scheme of free distribution of ownership certificates. POFs manage share capital of state-owned companies until the certificates are converted into shares. The SOF is a nongovernmental economic organization subordinated to the Parliament, which appoints the members of the SOF's Board. It was created to organize the privatization of its 70% quota and, as the majority shareholder of the commercial companies, to supervise the management of state property. Thus the privatization process was taken away from the government. The recently promulgated Law for the Acceleration of Privatization, which completed Law 58/ 1991, actually effects the distribution of the 30% quota to the citizens in a manner that permits the attainment of majority private ownership. This is done through the free distribution of the POF quotas and part of the SOF quotas to the companies. Privatizing the 70% quota of state-owned shares is exclusively the task of the SOF.

[12] In a "strictly confidential" discussion, the manager of a well-known state company in Bucharest, a major producer of metal products for which exports make up an important share of total output but which has a relatively modest share of capacity used, was asked whether limited export demand and competition are the main restrictions to export expansion. He answered, "Not at all. We are competitive and we are able to double the exports. Look, I have on my desk a great deal of potential orders and I do not intend to answer them. Why? Because I am not naive. We would become very profitable. It might call the attention of those with money to our company and its market value will rise. Practically, we might be put off the game. For us, the management team, it is a decisive moment to obtain control together with the employees." The company was recently privatized via a management buy-out and has launched an aggressive advertising campaign.

[13] During a recent conference in London, British Foreign Secretary Malcolm Rifkind, advocating a policy of openness toward European countries in transition, stressed that the antidumping measures taken by Western countries against East European countries "are nothing but hidden protectionism" (*Curierul National*, Oct 26, 1995, p. 13).

[14] Under these circumstances, not only is it important that the level of investment in 1994 was 15.3% higher than that in 1993, but it is also significant that of total investments, the percentage of investments in equipment, which in recent years constantly decreased to 37.1% (1992), grew to 44.7% (calculated based on CNS, 1995a).

[15] Of the arrangements mentioned, the most important are (1) the customs commission of 0.5% for job-work operations on imports and only on VAT for exports; (2) easing of the conditions under which the commodity may be subject to compensation or

barter operation, arranged by companies; (3) elimination of the VAT payment and depositions of guarantees equal to the customs duties due on imports for job-work operations irrespective of the foreign partner to whom the commodity is re-exported; (4) elimination of the VAT payment and guarantee deposits for customs duties on imports for leasing operations.

References

CNS, 1994a, Statistic Yearbook of Romania.

CNS, 1994b, Statistic Bulletin of Foreign Trade No. 12.

CNS, 1995a, Romania – The present stage of the economic and social development, National Commission of Statistics, Bucharest, Romania.

CNS, 1995b, Statistics Bulletin of Prices, No. 4.

CNS, 1995c, Statistics Bulletin, Industry, No. 8.

Constantin, I., 1993, *The System Crisis of the Command Economy*, Bucharest, Romania, pp. 80 and 83.

Government of Romania, 1994, Two Years of Governing, Bucharest, Romania.

NBR (National Bank of Romania), 1994, *Quarterly Bulletin*, No. 4, Bucharest, Romania.

NBR (National Bank of Romania), 1995, *Monthly Bulletin*, No. 9, Bucharest, Romania.

POF (Private Ownership Fund), 1994, Address No. 3.

Radulescu, E., 1994, *Fiscal and Monetary Policy*, Bucharest, Romania.

Romanian Statistical Yearbook various volumes.

Appendix to Chapter 5: Analysis of the Country Survey

5A.1 Methodology

This analysis is based on responses from questionnaires filled out by 55 Romanian companies in various sectors with different types of ownership. Although the composition of the sample does not necessarily reflect the actual proportions of various sectors in total Romanian exports, the size and export capacity of the firms in the sample ensure that the empirical data obtained have a high level of reliability.

The results were processed according to two criteria, type of ownership and field of activity. Three kinds of ownership were identified: state ownership (36 firms), joint ventures (7 firms), and private ownership (12 firms). There were eight major fields of activity, classified according to the Harmonized System: agriculture and food products, and beverages (2 firms); mineral products, including cement (5 firms); chemicals, plastics, and rubber (8 firms); textiles (11 firms); glass and ceramics (2 firms); machinery and equipment (17 firms); means of transport (6 firms); and miscellaneous goods, including furniture (4 firms).

Qualitative assessments were made by the respondents on scales of 1 to 5 or 1 to 3 representing the level of importance of each of the factors listed. We first analyzed the ranking of importance that firms attached to the various barriers, counting only the number of firms that reported that a certain factor had a negative or very negative impact on their export performance (see Section 5A.2). The levels of importance attributed to these factors were subsequently weighed with the number of respondents. The results, i.e., the pronounced differences between firms with different types of ownership on the one hand, and in different sectors on the other, are analyzed in Section 5A.3.

5A.2 Analysis of Ranking of Barriers

An overwhelming majority of the firms (46) declared the cost of domestic credit to be the top barrier to exports (see *Table 5A.1*). The second most significant barrier, customs duties for inputs (raw materials, consumables, components, equipment, and technologies) lagged far behind the first, indicated by 36 firms. An interesting finding is that the price of Romanian inputs was ranked third and the quality of these inputs was ranked fifth in importance. The price of the raw materials was ranked fourth on the list. In contrast, the price of imported inputs was only ranked tenth and the quality of these components was ranked last, because no firms reported being harmed by it.

Among the most interesting findings are the low importance attributed to high tariffs abroad (only 17 firms reported being seriously harmed by them) and the surprising importance ascribed to relations with the customs authority (17 firms reported being seriously harmed by poor relations with it). The latter result should be compared with the barrier represented by relations with the Ministry of Commerce and the Chamber of Commerce, each of which was indicated by only one firm. Quantitative restrictions also received surprisingly low ratings (regarded as an important barrier by only six firms).

It is also worth remarking that only one firm reported being harmed by the low quality of the work force and that only three reported being harmed by the cost of labor.

5A.3 Pronounced Differences

Domestic barriers to export

None of the firms seemed to be troubled by Romanian export duties, although exporters of textiles were somewhat more sensitive to this barrier than enterprises in the other sectors.

State-owned and private firms seemed to be fairly dissatisfied with the procedures for obtaining export licenses; however, joint ventures consider this barrier to be of little importance. The most sensitive enterprises are again in the textile sector.

There was quasi-unanimity concerning the substantial barrier to exports represented by customs duties for imported inputs. State-owned firms seemed to be the most affected in this respect. Exporters of miscellaneous goods (mainly furniture) were significantly affected, whereas exporters of mineral products were only affected to a limited extent.

All firms agreed that the high cost of credit greatly affects exports; private firms were the most discontented. At the sector level, the dissatisfaction was highest in the area of glass and ceramics.

The lengths of time required for banking transactions substantially affected the operations of all firms; joint ventures were the most discontented. Exporters of chemicals, plastics, and rubber seemed to suffer most from this barrier.

State-owned and private firms seemed to be greatly dissatisfied with price controls for inputs, whereas the dissatisfaction of joint ventures was moderate. Exporters of glass and ceramics headed the ranks of the dissatisfied.

Table 5A.1. Ranking of barriers to exports by the 55 firms included in the survey.

Rank	Type of barrier	Number of firms harmed
1	Cost of domestic credit	46
2	Customs duties for imported raw materials, consumables, components and equipment	36
3	Price of Romanian components	35
4	Price of raw materials	32
5	Quality of Romanian components	30
6	Duration of banking operations	26
7	Price controls	25
8	Low quality of roads	25
9	Lack of a permanent representative abroad	25
10	Price of imported components	24
11	Difficult access to distribution channels	23
12	Lack of knowledge of price level in the export markets	21
13	Frequent alterations of Romanian commercial legislation	20
14	Lack of knowledge of commercial legislation in foreign markets	20
15	Technological level of equipment	20
16	Distance from export markets	20
17	High tariffs abroad	17
18	Relationship with the customs authority	17
19	Lack of knowledge of business rules abroad	16
20	Low quality of telecommunication services	15
21	Long waiting periods at border crossings	15
22	Stagnating or declining demand	
23	Low quality of railroad transport	12
24	Antagonistic commercial practices	12
25	Own manufacturing technologies	10
26	Duration of export insurance formalities	9
27	Duration of process for obaining export licenses	8
28	Limited supply of transport capacities	8
29	Quantitative restrictions	6
30	Packaging and labeling standards	6
31	Foreign importer's difficulty obtaining import licenses	6
32	Capacity to satisfy specific standards required on foreign market	6
33	Sanitary and security standards	5
34	Difficult delivery conditions	5
35	Importers impose use of a certain bank	4
36	Tariff quotas	3
37	Cost of labor	3
38	Export commission	2
39	Qualification of work force	1
40	Relationship with the Chamber of Commerce	1
41	Relationship with the Ministry of Commerce	1
42	Importers impose use of a certain carrier	0
43	Quality of imported components	0

Source: Results of survey carried out by the authors.

Joint ventures were comparatively more dissatisfied by the frequent alteration of Romanian commercial legislation than state-owned or private firms. However, all three groups reported being substantially harmed by these frequent changes.

Most surprisingly, the low quality of telecommunication services was perceived as only "a limited" barrier by joint ventures, whereas the same barrier was considered "pretty" harmful to export performance by state-owned and private firms.

Joint ventures were comparatively less dissatisfied by the long waiting periods at border crossings than state-owned or private firms, although all three groups considered this barrier "pretty" harmful to exports. Exporters of chemicals, plastics, and rubber reported being "much" harmed by this barrier, whereas mineral products exporters were only affected to a limited extent.

Of the three kinds of enterprises, state-owned firms were the most dissatisfied with the quality of railroad transport; joint ventures were the least concerned with this barrier. This disparity clearly reflects the relatively higher dependence on railroad transport of state-owned firms. Of the firms surveyed, exporters of chemicals, plastics, and rubber products were the most dissatisfied with railroad transport.

Joint ventures, which are relatively dependent on roads for transportation, were more dissatisfied with the quality of roads than either state-owned enterprises or private firms. Furniture exporters reported being most harmed by the conditions of the roads; those who reported being least harmed were exporters of mineral products.

Concerning the variety of means of transportation available, joint ventures reported being affected only to a limited extent, whereas state-owned firms reported being substantially harmed by this export barrier. Exporters of mineral products were the most dissatisfied with the methods of transportation available.

In general, state-owned firms reported being harmed most by customs duties for imported inputs, price controls on inputs, low quality of telecommunication services, long waiting periods at border crossings, low quality of railroad transport, and the limited variety of transportation means available. Joint ventures generally reported being most affected by the duration of banking operations, frequent modifications of commercial legislation, and low quality of roads. Private firms seemed to be especially bothered by the procedure of obtaining export licenses and the cost of domestic credit. In general, the sector most sensitive to domestic barriers appeared to be the chemicals, plastics, and rubber sector; the sector least harmed by these barriers seemed to be the exporters of mineral products, including cement.

Foreign barriers to export

Joint ventures reported being substantially harmed by high tariffs in export markets, whereas private firms appeared sensitive to these barriers. Those who were by far the most affected by foreign barriers were producers of agricultural and food products, followed by producers of textiles and furniture; these are precisely the key exporting industries in Romania.

Quantitative restrictions seriously harm private firms. Among the sectors most harmed by quotas were the food products and mineral products sectors. Private firms were still the most affected by the tariff quotas, state-owned firms were less affected. Tariff quotas seemed to pose a substantial problem for exporters of food products and transportation equipment.

Somewhat surprisingly, sanitary and safety regulations seemed to bother joint ventures the most, whereas they affected the export capacity of state-owned and private firms to only a limited extent. These regulations were fairly harmful to exporters of transport means and food products.

Packaging and labeling regulations only affected joint ventures to a limited extent; however, they affected private firms substantially, due to the lower financial capacity of these firms, which cannot always afford the equipment needed for competitive packaging. Again, exporters of food products and means of transport were the most affected.

Antagonistic or hostile commercial practices seemed to be a serious barrier for both private and state-owned firms. Exporters of glass and ceramics were significantly affected by antagonistic practices, far more than exporters of food products and means of transport, which were only affected to a limited extent.

As expected, joint ventures have easier access to distribution channels than private firms that are completely Romanian owned. This access was an important concern for most of the sectors, with exporters of food products being the most discontented.

Foreign importers' difficulties obtaining import licenses affected private exporters considerably, but affected joint ventures only to a limited extent. Here, exporters of means of transport followed by food products exporters were the most dissatisfied.

Both private firms and joint ventures were substantially affected by the lack of information on price levels in export markets; state-owned firms were greatly affected by this factor (which is related to the lack of a system for monitoring competitors that seems to prevail among state-owned firms – see discussion below). Glass and chinaware producers complained most about the lack of information, followed by exporters of machinery and equipment, means of transport, and furniture.

Private firms and joint ventures were considerably affected by their ignorance of business rules in export markets. Exporters in the machinery, means of transport, and furniture sectors reported being substantially affected by this barrier.

The lack of a permanent representative in the export market posed a serious problem for private and state-owned firms. Of firms in the sectors studied, glass and chinaware exporters were by far the most affected.

Most surprisingly, insufficient knowledge of commercial legislation in export markets affected joint ventures more substantially than state-owned firms.

The barrier presented by stagnant or declining demand for exported products affected all three groups of firms to a certain extent, with joint ventures in a relatively better position than state-owned or private firms. The sectors most affected seemed to be food products followed by textiles; glass and ceramics were only affected to a limited extent.

Overall, state-owned firms were relatively more sensitive to difficult access to distribution channels, to difficult delivery conditions, and to the lack of information on price levels, business rules, and commercial legislation in export markets, as well as to the lack of a permanent commercial representative abroad. High customs duties, quotas and tariff quotas, as well as difficulties importers encounter obtaining import licenses bother private exporters more than the state-owned firms or joint ventures. Probably as a result of their better knowledge of foreign markets, joint ventures were less concerned by the various demand barriers than were Romanian state-owned and private firms: the only exceptions to this were sanitary and security norms.

Of the sectors studied, food products were definitely the most harmed by tariffs and quotas, and glass and ceramics were the most affected by the lack of price information and legal information about export markets.

Factors of competitive advantage

The 55 enterprises included in our survey also assessed their competitive strengths and weaknesses in terms of the following factors: cost of labor, cost of raw materials, qualification of work force, level of technology, distance to export markets, capacity to satisfy specific customer needs, and relations with influential Romanian authorities.

The results show that, with the exception of cost and quality of labor, state-owned firms felt that they were at a competitive disadvantage with respect to the factors considered. Private firms were particularly dissatisfied with the quality of relations with the customs authority. Joint ventures indicated the fewest factors, reporting only the price and quality of Romanian components and the price of foreign components as having a negative impact on their competitiveness.

Differences in terms of input usage

A surprising discovery was that the vast majority of the respondents use the same quality of inputs for exported and domestically sold products, an obvious result of competition in the domestic market made possible by the liberalization of foreign trade flows. It must be stressed that in none of the cases were the inputs used for the domestically delivered output superior to those used for the exported outputs; however, a certain number of firms used inputs of a higher quality for exported products. Overall, joint ventures were slightly more inclined to use better inputs for exports. State-owned and private firms used work forces and equipment of virtually the same quality for both exports and domestically sold goods, while joint ventures clearly used a better work force and equipment for export production.

At the sectoral level only a minority of firms used better inputs for exported output than for domestically sold goods. The exceptions are that food products for export are manufactured from better raw materials and with better technologies than domestically consumed goods, and chemicals, plastics, and rubber are produced by a better qualified work force for exports than for domestic use.

Importers' involvement in realizing the exported output

Several entries in the questionnaire inquired about importers' involvement in supplying specifications and designs, providing cofinancing for product or process development, supplying raw materials or components, leasing equipment, providing their trademarks, and arranging transport insurance. The answers reflect that, in this respect, joint ventures have a noticeable competitive advantage because they are able to fine-tune their product to the constraints of the export market, either by capitalizing on their distribution network there or by using their existing business relationships. At the branch level, it seems that those most dependent on importers' support for market fine-tuning are textile and glass and ceramics exporters.

Exporters' bargaining capacity

All three groups perceived the limitations in exporters' capacity to bargain over prices. Joint ventures were in the best positions; state-owned firms were the most vulnerable. This disparity is a logical result of joint ventures' better knowledge of the export markets, as one of these markets is normally the foreign partner's home country. This finding might also support the idea that in many cases the importer and the foreign partner in the joint venture are the same.

Competitor intelligence system

A vast majority of the firms interviewed did not have a competitor intelligence system (CINS) in place. Joint ventures performed better than state-owned or private firms. The exporters most satisfied with their CINS were in the food products sector; those most unhappy with theirs were in the means of transport sector.

Information sources

The nature and importance of information sources showed very different patterns for joint ventures than for state-owned and private firms. State-owned and private firms were excessively dependent on information provided by business partners, suggesting that they might persistently be in a weak position and that they might lack a strong long-term business strategy. Joint ventures had alternative or complementary sources of information (specialized publications and information provided by the firm's representative abroad), which offered them a competitive edge in comparison with other Romanian firms.

Influence of Romania's Association Agreement

The vast majority of the firms surveyed believed that the Association Agreement with the EU has a positive effect on exports. However, state-owned and private firms estimated that the Agreement's overall effect is neutral to positive, whereas joint ventures were much more optimistic, considering the Agreement's effects positive to very positive. This is an understandable opinion, as some 70% of foreign investment comes from the EU and many large investments are made by non-European firms that are primarily targeting the EU market but do not want to bear the EU's high labor costs. Private firms seemed to be the least enthusiastic about the Agreement, probably because they have only recently emerged and still consider it necessary to consolidate their positions behind the present commercial barriers. At the sectoral level, producers of food products, textiles, and furniture considered this Agreement to be very positive; the other sectors considered its influence on their exports to be neutral.

Chapter 6

Slovakia

Ján Fidrmuc and Jarko Fidrmuc

6.1 General Conditions of Export Development in Slovakia

Slovakia is among the smallest nations in Central and Eastern Europe. Its present domestic industrial structure was influenced by the creation of a nation-state, both in prewar and postwar Czechoslovakia, and by the autarky it pursued vis-à-vis other neighboring nations.[1] With the addition of strong ideological elements after World War II, this policy of autarky was intensified and the country's isolation from its West European neighbors increased. Slovakia now must find a place in the international division of labor based only on its comparative advantage without attempting to maintain the pattern that was established over the past 40 to 80 years.

The organization and regulation of Slovak foreign trade relations prior to 1990 reflected the characteristic features of Czechoslovakia's centrally planned economy. The structure and organization of Czechoslovak industry was the result of the nationalization of virtually every sector of the economy after World War II and the gradual centralization and concentration of decision-making powers. Enterprises were created from several plants or factories, some of which were previously independent enterprises themselves. The new enterprises from one industry branch or a few related branches were associated into Production Units. Each Production Unit was managed by its own ministry, either at the republic

We would like to acknowledge the many useful comments provided by János Gács and Jaroslav Fidrmuc. Any mistakes are the responsibility of the authors. We would also like to express our gratitude to the managers of the 20 enterprises surveyed, who shared their experience with us and gave us information necessary for completing this project. Although this study was prepared and edited with great care, no liability can be assumed for the enterprise data it contains.

or federal level. Each level of management had precisely determined, limited authority for decision making, coordinating, and planning. The coordination of exports was usually the responsibility of the Production Units, which used so-called foreign trade enterprises (FTEs) or in some cases had their own foreign trade departments.[2] In either case, individual enterprises had few opportunities to influence the flows of exports. Furthermore, as prices were set centrally, an enterprise could do very little to affect its profitability through its export policies.

The division of Czechoslovakia into the Czech Republic and Slovakia resulted in a high level of economic openness. The introduction of standard procedures for trade flows between the two countries leading to higher transaction costs and some administrative impediments prompted Slovakia to replace a substantial part of imports from the Czech Republic with domestic products or imports from elsewhere. The development of Slovak exports was similar to that of imports although it did not exhibit so radical a shift (see Section 6.4).

Slovak foreign trade was approximately balanced at the beginning of the reforms.[3] However, Slovakia's export performance deteriorated during 1992 and 1993. Although exports accounted in domestic currency remained nearly constant, there was a 10% decline in US dollar terms because the domestic currency was devalued during 1993. The decrease in foreign demand was even greater if the 1993 decline in bilateral trade with the Czech Republic is considered. This decrease necessitated currency devaluation and the implementation of import restrictions (for general trade data see *Table 6.1*).

Despite negative expectations after the split of the federation, foreign trade developments have shown more or less unabated improvement since then. The trade balance (excluding trade with the Czech Republic) was negative in 1993 and 1994; however, the 1993 deficit would have been substantially lower had the positive bilateral balances with the Czech Republic been included, and the overall balance in 1994 was actually positive.[4] In 1995, the overall trade balance was positive (US$60 million), mainly due to the trade surplus with the Czech Republic (US$678 million).

Additional foreign exchange revenues were generated by transit fees for gas and oil transported from Russia and Kazakstan (US$450–500 million a year). The pipeline going through Slovakia is the only pipeline linking Western Europe with the gas fields in the Commonwealth of Independent States (CIS). The balance of tourism, which increased from US$164 million in 1992 to US$302 million in 1995, has also improved the current account of the balance of payments. The current account amounted to US$649 million in 1995.

When the economic transition began, Slovakia had a trade structure that was dominated by a few important trade partners and a limited number of commodities. Hence, a reorientation of foreign trade in both regional and sectoral terms has

Table 6.1. Foreign trade of the Slovak Republic.

	Total trade excluding the Czech Republic						
	Exports		Imports		Trade Balance		
Year	CSK/SKK[a] (bln.)	US$ (bln.)	CSK/SKK (bln.)	US$ (bln.)	CSK/SKK (bln.)	US$ (bln.)	Avg. exchange rate: CSK/SKK per US$
1970	11.280	0.418	17.108	0.634	–5.828	–0.216	27.00[b]
1980	40.553	2.844	44.866	3.146	–4.313	–0.302	14.26[b]
1989	54.790	3.641	51.642	3.431	3.148	0.209	15.05[b]
1990	52.032	2.899	61.258	3.413	–9.226	–0.514	17.95[b]
1991	101.672	3.441	106.360	3.599	–4.688	–0.159	29.55
1992	98.594	3.488	100.705	3.562	–2.111	–0.750	28.27
1993	97.303	3.155	124.372	4.033	–27.069	–0.878	30.84
1994	135.510	4.255	148.820	4.673	–13.310	–0.418	31.85
1995	164.553	5.533	182.931	6.151	–18.378	–0.618	29.74

	Trade with the Czech Republic						
	Exports		Imports		Trade Balance		
Year	SKK (bln.)	Clearing ECU (bln.)	SKK (bln.)	Clearing ECU (bln.)	SKK (bln.)	Clearing ECU (bln.)	Avg. exchange rate: SKK per ECU[c]
1993	71.12	1.94	70.04	1.92	1.09	0.03	36.568
1994	80.01	2.01	62.64	1.57	17.37	0.44	39.822
1995	89.55	2.33	69.38	1.80	20.17	0.52	39.680[d]

[a] CSK = Czechoslovak koruna; SKK = Slovak koruna.

[b] Official commercial rate; parallel black market rates were estimated as 40.89 (1970), 26.18 (1980), 42.39 (1989), 38.01 (1990).

[c] Official average exchange rate (SKK per clearing ECU) applied for the clearing account between the Czech Republic and Slovakia.

[d] Average exchange rate for January to October 1996 (end of clearing system). Corresponding ECU values for 1996 were computed using the average exchange rate of 1 ECU (38.45).

Sources: Slovak Statistical Office; International Monetary Fund; and the Czechoslovak National Bank.

been a priority of Slovak economic and foreign policies. Slovak foreign trade was seriously affected by the dissolution of Czechoslovakia in 1993, and new markets were sought to compensate for the loss of traditional markets. Moreover, the implementation of consumption and value-added taxes (VATs), which are related to imported goods, also negatively influenced foreign trade flows.[5]

6.1.1 Foreign trade liberalization and exchange rate regime

An important part of Slovak economic reforms was the introduction of currency convertibility in January 1991, when the country was still part of the Czech and Slovak Federal Republic. The leaders of economic reform in Czechoslovakia considered a convertible national currency crucial for an economy in transition because it could help reveal the economy's comparative advantages in relation to its foreign trade partners, thereby providing orientation for the restructuring of the economy. Currency convertibility in Czechoslovakia was based on the introduction and targeting of monetary anchors. In 1993, when the Slovak currency was being established, the International Monetary Fund (IMF) recommended a flexible exchange rate system. Despite this advice, the National Bank of Slovakia (NBS) chose a policy of fixed exchange rates. After overcoming difficulties in early 1993, this policy has been successful in the sense that the Slovak koruna maintains its limited convertibility with considerable exchange rate stability.

The exchange rate has been fixed since 1991. On 10 June 1993 the NBS devalued the Slovak koruna by 10% as part of an agreement with the IMF. This devaluation occurred in the aftermath of strong devaluation expectations and followed previous devaluations of the Slovak koruna against the Czech koruna within the exchange rate bounds given by the payment agreement between these two countries. This exchange rate policy kept the Slovak currency undervalued in comparison with all West European currencies and the US dollar.

From the beginning, the Slovak koruna has suffered under the lack of credibility of the NBS, leading to sharp losses of foreign reserves. This situation improved in the second half of 1993, when the governor of the NBS was finally approved by the Parliament and the NBS defended its independence vis-à-vis the government. This improvement in credibility was also evident in the rebuilding of foreign exchange reserves, which increased from a level of US$0.3 billion in June 1993 to US$3.4 billion at the end of 1995.

In February 1993 the NBS introduced some restrictions on certain types of payments abroad in order to improve its exchange reserve position. Among the restrictions were the obligation for traders to consult with the NBS on payments of more than 1 million Slovak koruny, the introduction of a three-month payment delay for non-investment imports above 1 million Slovak koruny, and an obligation to set aside the paid amount 14 days before the payment in a commercial bank. These restrictions were fully abolished in November 1993. However, balance of payments problems occurred in late 1993 and early 1994 and were treated with short-term trade restrictions.

Certain measures restricting imports were implemented in an effort to improve the trade balance, which showed a deficit of 27 billion Slovak koruny in 1993, and to raise the hard currency reserves of the NBS, which were approximately US$330 million on 15 February 1994, excluding gold. In February 1994 a regulation requiring quality certificates to be issued by Slovak authorities for imported foodstuffs was introduced, replacing the former policy of recognizing some foreign quality certificates. This measure affected Czech exporters in particular, as it led to additional paper work and delays. In March 1994 a 10% import surcharge on consumer goods went into effect in Slovakia. According to the original proposals, the surcharge should have been decreased to 5% after September 1994; however, it was reduced to 7.5% only in July 1996. According to government plans, it will be reduced to 0% (but not removed) in January 1997. This arrangement would give the authorities the opportunity to increase the import surcharge again in the face of adverse developments in the current account after easier negotiations with the World Trade Organization (WTO) and the European Union (EU).

6.1.2 Regional reorientation

The changes in foreign trade flows after 1990 are characterized mainly by shifts from former Council for Mutual Economic Assistance (CMEA) markets to Western market economies. These developments are similar to developments in other Central European countries in the early 1990s (see *Tables 6.2* and *6.3*). Slovakia, like its neighbors, managed to shift exports away from regions characterized by a loss of demand. The reorientation was also made possible by the exchange rate policy after 1990, which was determined by the initially strongly undervalued exchange rates.

Slovakia's largest trade partners are the Czech Republic and the EU. In 1994 the Czech Republic accounted for 37% of Slovakia's total exports and 30% of total imports. The EU accounted for 29% of total exports and 26% of total imports in the same year. The importance of the EU increased further after January 1995, when Austria, Sweden, and Finland became EU members. Trade with European Free Trade Association (EFTA) countries accounted for 7% and 9% of total exports and imports, respectively, in 1994. In 1992 exports to the EU grew sharply (16%) and imports from the EU grew 37%; in 1993 exports decreased slightly and imports increased by 17%.[6] The economic recovery in EU countries and further liberalization of trade allowed a 54% growth in exports to the EU in 1994,

Table 6.2. Distribution of exports of selected Central European countries by region (in percent).

Year	Region	Slovakia	Czech Rep.	Hungary	Poland
1991	CMEA	42	35	19	19
	EU	34	43	46	56
	Other	24	22	35	25
1994	CMEA	27	18	19	14
	EU	47	55	52	62
	Other	26	27	29	24

Source: Nomura Research Institute, Vienna, Austria, in *Hospodárske noviny*, 1995/04/05, p. 10.

while total exports increased only 28% in that year. Of the EU nations, Germany is Slovakia's most important trade partner (with 17% of total exports and 14% of total imports), followed by Italy (5% exports and 4% imports), France (2% both exports and imports), and the Netherlands (2% both exports and imports). Of the former EFTA countries, Austria is the most important trade partner, accounting for 5% of total exports and 6% of total imports in 1993.

Czechoslovakia signed an Association Agreement with the EU on 16 February 1991. An interim agreement allowed for trade liberalization as of 1 March 1992 and was extended after the division of Czechoslovakia. The Association Agreement between the EU and Slovakia went into effect on 1 February 1995. Slovakia officially submitted its application for EU membership in June 1995. However, several times the EU has expressed concerns about recent political developments in Slovakia and about certain aspects of the government's economic policy (in particular privatization). These disagreements may worsen Slovakia's position in negotiating EU membership.

According to the Association Agreement, exports of most industrial goods to the EU are exempt from tariffs, although the export of selected commodities is still restricted by quotas. The quotas to the EU were divided between the Czech and Slovak Republics with respect to commodity exports to the EU in 1990 and 1991, or according to production capacities where exports in those years differed significantly. However, the trade of some sensitive commodities (for example, steel tubes) was restricted in 1993, mainly through antidumping regulations, which decreased the traded quantity of these commodities to levels below those of 1992.[7]

At the June 1993 meeting of the European Council in Copenhagen, the EU declared that it would speed up the liberalization of trade with associated countries in sensitive commodities. One result of this meeting was the acceptance of the view that tariffs on textiles processed in Eastern Europe in order to take advantage of cheap labor should be abolished as soon as possible. Slovakia could benefit

Table 6.3. Slovak foreign trade by SITC category and region (in mln. Slovak koruny[a]).

	Total	SITC category[b] 0	1	2	3	4	5	6	7	8	9
1991:											
Exports	101,672	6,954	721	4,665	1,124	96	12,199	37,095	22,739	16,042	37
EU	35,267	2,920	14	2,436	245	71	4,717	15,429	4,280	5,155	0
EFTA	8,189	512	7	913	566	21	1,603	2,760	967	840	0
CEFTA	14,583	754	637	713	223	2	1,883	6,001	2,823	1,547	0
USSR/NIS	24,847	1,124	47	141	46	0	2,295	7,371	9,360	4,463	0
Imports	106,360	4,551	861	12,564	38,370	99	9,318	8,650	25,820	6,123	4
EU	25,116	1,468	273	1,354	300	45	4,487	2,302	12,902	1,981	4
EFTA	12,207	348	210	440	112	32	1,698	1,279	6,476	1,612	0
CEFTA	7,086	726	112	694	854	9	858	1,487	1,779	567	0
USSR/NIS	47,134	98	103	7,365	33,522	0	1,341	2,328	2,104	273	0
1994:											
Exports	215,522	9,711	2,011	10,962	9,991	218	27,611	84,506	41,746	28,633	133
EU	62,906	1,641	15	2,784	90	67	7,124	26,931	14,064	10,177	13
EFTA	15,074	377	21	1,261	2,117	1	1,720	5,333	1,863	2,379	2
CEFTA	103,244	6,166	1,469	6,644	7,613	144	16,229	36,958	19,197	8,733	91
NIS	15,854	1,220	496	130	168	5	1,476	3,267	4,357	4,713	22
Czech Rep.	80,012	5,074	1,372	3,709	4,295	128	12,411	28,866	16,633	7,458	66
Imports	211,463	14,709	2,731	11,167	40,777	608	28,098	35,656	58,627	18,723	367
EU	55,492	4,525	495	1,413	308	158	9,514	8,559	24,034	6,347	139
EFTA	18,727	1,025	97	373	352	30	3,809	3,407	7,405	2,185	44
CEFTA	74,323	5,409	1,925	2,712	8,105	410	11,409	21,126	16,566	6,494	167
NIS	44,985	462	13	5,159	31,905	10	2,355	1,727	1,976	1,368	10
Czech Rep.	62,644	4,251	1,844	1,830	6,198	322	9,132	18,783	14,595	5,528	161

[a]Figures for 1991 are in Czechoslovak koruny.
[b]SITC category 0 = Food, live animals; 1 = Beverages, tobacco; 2 = Crude materials except fuels; 3 = Mineral fuels, energy; 4 = Animal and vegetable oils; 5 = Chemicals; 6 = Manufactures (by material); 7 = Machinery, transport equipment; 8 = Miscellaneous manufactures; 9 = Others.
Abbreviations: CEFTA = Central European Free Trade Agreement; NIS = Newly independent states of the former Soviet Union.
Source: Slovak Statistical Office.

from these changes because of its proximity to the EU and its labor costs, which are even lower than in other East European countries.

The Association Agreement between Czechoslovakia (and now Slovakia) and EFTA has been in effect since March 1992. Since then, trade of industrial goods has been nearly liberalized. The structure of the EFTA agreements was similar to that of the EU agreements. Austria, Sweden, and Finland's admission to the EU limited the importance of the agreement with EFTA for current trade.

The countries of Central Europe have been affected by the shock of the collapse of the CMEA, which triggered their mutual cooperation and policy coordination and led to the creation of the Central European Free Trade Association (CEFTA). The CEFTA includes Poland, Hungary, the Czech Republic, Slovakia, and since January 1996, Slovenia.

Trade among CEFTA countries was to be liberalized within eight years according to the original CEFTA proposals; this time frame was reduced to five years in February 1994. However, urgent balance of payments problems in all Central and East European countries created pressure to maintain trade restrictions. Nevertheless, the growth potential of these economies in the near future and their common aim, participation in European integration, can be viewed as important motivations for trade liberalization in the region. There is, however, no feeling of regional solidarity among these countries: Central and East European countries are trying to find a foreign trade regime that ensures balanced bilateral trade.[8] CEFTA's foreign trade policy (including its negotiations with the EU) remains uncoordinated, in part because of similarities in the structure of trade between the EU and individual Central and East European countries (Fidrmuc *et al.*, 1995).

Despite standstills in the liberalization of trade in Central and Eastern Europe, in recent years Slovakia has reached relatively high growth rates and shares in exports to other Central and East European countries. In 1994 trade with Poland represented 2.8% of total exports and 2.4% of total imports, and trade with Hungary accounted for 5.4% and 1.7% of total exports and imports, respectively. No significant revival of exports to the newly independent states (NISs) of the former Soviet Union (FSU) was seen in 1994, although the earlier decline of exports stopped.

6.1.3 Commodity restructuring

The structure of Slovak exports by commodity group remained surprisingly stable between 1991 and 1995, especially in comparison with the important shifts in the regional structure of exports.

As can be seen from *Table 6.4*, the structure of Slovak exports is dominated by manufactured goods [Standard International Trade Classification (SITC) groups 6, 7, and 8]. Manufactured goods accounted for about 75% of total exports from 1991

Table 6.4. Commodity structure of Slovak foreign trade by SITC category (in percent).[a]

SITC category	0	1	2	3	4	5	6	7	8	9
Exports										
1991	6.8	0.7	4.6	1.1	0.1	12.0	36.5	22.4	15.8	0.0
1992	7.3	0.5	5.5	0.8	0.1	11.4	42.6	17.3	14.4	0.0
1993	5.5	0.9	4.9	4.9	0.1	12.0	38.8	19.4	13.4	0.1
1994	4.5	0.9	5.1	4.6	0.1	12.8	39.2	19.4	13.3	0.1
1995	5.0	0.9	5.0	4.2	0.1	13.2	40.5	18.8	12.2	0.0
Imports										
1991	4.3	0.8	11.8	36.1	0.1	8.8	8.1	24.3	5.8	0.0
1992	4.6	0.8	6.8	29.5	0.0	9.8	8.7	31.9	8.0	0.0
1993	7.3	1.5	5.2	20.9	0.2	11.4	15.1	29.3	9.0	0.2
1994	7.0	1.3	5.3	19.3	0.3	13.3	16.9	27.7	8.9	0.2
1995	6.8	1.1	5.8	17.9	0.2	13.5	17.6	29.0	8.0	0.1

[a] See *Table 6.3* for description of SITC categories.
Note: Figures for 1991 and 1992 do not include trade with the Czech Republic; for 1993 to 1995 data include trade with the Czech Republic. Source: Slovak Statistical Office.

to 1995 (excluding trade with the Czech Republic). This corresponds to about 72% of total exports (i.e., exports including the Czech Republic) since 1993.

Exports of intermediate and minimally processed products (SITC 6) represent the most important item on the export side. This commodity group accounted for 36.5% of total exports in 1991 and 40.5% in 1995. In 1995 nearly 40% of these exports went to EU countries.

Exports of machinery and transport equipment (SITC 7) accounted for 18.8% of Slovak exports in 1995. Here the USSR had been the most important trading partner at the beginning of economic reform, accounting for 41% of the machinery and transport equipment exports in 1991. The collapse of demand in this market could not be fully offset by sales to other countries; however, exports of machinery and transport equipment to the EU (including its new members) reached 40% of exports in this category by 1995.

Contrary to general expectations concerning the favorable prospects of the chemical industry, Slovak exports of chemicals and related products (SITC 5), which accounted for 12% of total exports in 1991, did not increase until 1994, when earlier declines were reversed. In 1995 exports of chemicals again increased substantially, by 21.8%, mainly due to expansion of sales in the European Union.

The share of exports of miscellaneous manufactured articles (SITC 8) show a continuous fall in recent years, from 15.8% in 1991 to 12.2% in 1995. The share of exports of mineral fuels, lubricants, and related materials (SITC 3) increased substantially in 1993. This increase, however, was mainly due to the inclusion of earlier deliveries to the Czech Republic in export sales after the split of Czechoslovakia.

The share of exports of foodstuffs and live animals (SITC 0) decreased during the transition, from 6.8% in 1991 to 5.0% in 1995. Over half of Slovak agricultural exports are sold to CEFTA countries, mainly the Czech Republic (40% in 1995), while sales to the EU made up only 20% of Slovak agricultural exports in 1995.

The structure of exports to the Czech Republic does not differ significantly from the structure of total exports: exports of manufactured goods (SITC 6, 7, and 8) are lower by about eight percentage points, a difference that is mainly related to similarities between the two countries in the manufacturing structure of final and intermediate products. Slovakia exports slightly more machinery and transport equipment (SITC 7) to the Czech Republic than it does to the rest of the world (19.4% and 18.5% in 1995, respectively), which suggests a high share of intra-industry trade in the automobile industry. As indicated above, Slovakia exports almost as many agricultural products to the Czech Republic as to the rest of the world. Following a rapid growth of trade in chemicals between Slovakia and the Czech Republic in 1995, export in this category (SITC 5) has also become more intense to the Czech Republic than to the rest of the world.

The changes in import structure from 1991 to 1994 were less important than the changes in export structure. The most important items were mineral fuels, lubricants, and related materials (SITC 3), which declined from 36.1% of total imports in 1991 to 17.9% in 1995. The decline in shares corresponded to an absolute decline in the value of these imports as well. The importance of the FSU, which accounted for 92% of imports of mineral fuels, lubricants, and related materials in 1992, remained nearly unchanged (77.5% in 1995).

Imports of machinery and transport equipment (SITC 7) increased substantially after 1991, accounting for 29.0% of total imports in 1995. The increase was mainly in imports from EU and EFTA countries, with a corresponding decline in imports from the FSU and Eastern Europe. Similar developments can be observed in intermediate and minimally processed products (SITC 6), which accounted for 17.6% of total imports in 1995, and miscellaneous manufactured articles (SITC 8), with 8.0% of total imports in 1995. Imports of chemicals and related products (SITC 5) increased substantially, to 13.5% of total imports in 1995.

6.1.4 Industrial exports

With regard to industrial exports, the metal products and metal processing industry branch is the most important in Slovakia (see *Table 6.5*). In 1994 it accounted for 24% of total industrial exports, and the export share of this industry's sales reached

Table 6.5. Exports by industry, 1991–1994.

Industry	1991 Exports (mln. Slovak koruny)	1991 Exports /sales ratio (%)	1994 Exports (mln. Slovak koruny)	1994 Exports /sales ratio (%)
Mining: Fuels	110.1	0.44	80	1.51
Mining: Other raw materials	210.9	5.02	1,172	30.47
Foodstuffs	4,102.8	6.57	5,363	8.69
Textile and clothing	6,450.3	40.34	8,864	54.31
Leather processing	2,983.2	37.70	2,546	45.32
Wood processing	1,866.9	25.73	2,888	49.83
Paper and printing	3,828.2	25.15	9,657	48.29
Coke, mineral fuels, atomic fuels	3,267.0	11.04	13,612	45.04
Chemical products	8,839.3	32.02	19,239	63.28
Rubber and plastic products	2,754.7	22.56	7,752	58.58
Ceramics and mineral materials	2,989.0	21.77	7,988	52.43
Metals and metal products	21,537.3	40.27	41,033	67.17
Machinery	13,352.7	31.32	11,340	43.76
Electrical and optical equipment	2,973.6	15.60	8,857	51.48
Transport equipment	3,037.1	14.64	12,444	74.23
Other manufacturing	2,279.4	29.11	2,876	34.23
Utilities	411.8	0.89	15,534	17.83
Total	80,994.2	19.71	171,245	40.37

Source: Slovak Statistical Office.

67%. This branch is also one of Slovakia's most important employers and producers, with 11% of total industrial employment and 14% of total industrial sales.

The chemicals industry is the second largest export industry in Slovakia, with a 63% export-per-sales share and 11% of total industrial exports. At the beginning of the transition in 1991, machinery accounted for 16% of industrial exports. The decline of demand in other former communist countries resulted in a decline in Slovak exports, and by 1994 machinery accounted only for 7% of industrial exports.

Transfer fees for the transit of mineral gas and oil (listed as utilities in *Table 6.5*) increased from less than 1% to 9% of industrial export revenues in 1994. Exports of automobiles also increased substantially during the transition, presumably as a result of Volkswagen's investment in BAZ Bratislava, which began to produce cars oriented to foreign markets.

The automobile industry received 14% of the total stock value of foreign direct investment (FDI) in Slovakia in 1993. The chemicals branch also received a high share of investment (16% of the stock value in 1993), but the production of this sector is oriented to the Czech and Slovak markets (as evidenced by our case study of the company Henkel Palma). No other important exporter in Slovakia received higher shares of foreign capital.

The structure of industrial exports remained stable during the transition (1991–1994). Although the value of exports more than doubled during this period (including industrial exports to the Czech Republic for the period from 1993), the correlation coefficient calculated for the export structures of 1994 and 1991 (with SITC two-digit industries data) was quite high (0.825). The changes in exports were only slightly more important than the changes in the domestic market (the correlation coefficient for total sales was 0.860 during the same period).

6.1.5 Structural problems

A critical problem for Slovak foreign trade is the economy's high dependence on certain commodities and trade partners. Moreover, the most important export items are so-called sensitive commodities, trade of which is conducted with only a few foreign partners. Therefore, because of the high share of sensitive commodities in total exports, a decline in demand or import restrictions in one target country might significantly reduce the trade of specific commodities and have a negative influence on the trade balance.

We used four-digit trade data classified according to the tariff list in order to analyze the cross dependence of Slovak exports. As the results show, in 1993 the top 30 commodities accounted for about 33% of total exports.[9] The most important export item was iron and steel plates, accounting for 12% of total exports. In 1993 average total export dependence on the three most important partner countries was 69%. After excluding the Czech Republic, because trade relations with that country have a different historical background and are more intensive than relations with other countries, trade dependence of the main commodities in exports decreased to 47%. Of the top 30 commodities, iron and steel products and machinery were the most dependent on exports to the Czech Republic.

6.1.6 Factor contents of foreign trade

For the analysis of trade aggregates with respect to production factors used, it must be assumed that in different countries the same technology is used to produce the same goods, which means that the factor proportions are the same in all countries. We used the classification of SITC three-digit groups described by Schulmeister

Table 6.6. Factor content and revealed comparative advantage in Slovak foreign trade, 1991.

	Factor content		Revealed comparative advantage
	Share in imports (%)	Share in exports (%)	
Human-capital intensive	8.58	3.22	–0.45
Production components	16.39	15.46	–0.03
Capital intensive	0.62	1.60	0.44
Labor intensive	7.29	19.32	0.45
Resource intensive (weak)	2.31	9.37	0.60
Resource intensive (strong)	6.57	25.92	0.60
Other industrial exports	4.75	11.19	0.40
Agricultural products	5.42	7.68	0.17
Raw materials	12.93	5.08	–0.44
Fuels	35.16	1.14	–0.94

Note: Foreign trade excluding trade between Slovakia and the Czech Republic.
Sources: Czech and Slovak Statistical Offices; authors' calculations.

(1990), which consists of seven industrial trade groups according to their factor contents created from the SITC three-digit groups (*Table 6.6*). Furthermore, we divided nonindustrial goods into three aggregates: agricultural products (SITC 0, 1, and 4), raw materials (SITC 2), and fuels (SITC 3).

As the reclassification of Slovak trade aggregates into these categories shows, in 1991 Slovakia imported mainly raw materials and fuels.[10] Production components represented the most important group of industrial goods, while products intensive in human capital accounted for 9% of total imports. On the export side, natural resource–intensive products represented the most important item. The high share of labor-intensive products in Slovak exports (19%) confirms the orientation of the Slovak economy toward labor-intensive goods.

Moreover, we computed the index of revealed comparative advantage (RCA) adjusted for unbalanced trade: $\text{RCA}_i = (X_i - \alpha M_i)/(X_i + \alpha M_i)$, where X_i and M_i are exports and imports of products of industry i; respectively, and α is the ratio of total exports to total imports. This measure lies between -1 and 1 and equals 0 if the export–import ratio of industry i corresponds to the average. A positive value for the RCA index indicates that a country has a revealed comparative advantage in that sector; a negative value indicates a comparative disadvantage.

The RCA index shows the importance of labor- and resource-intensive products for Slovak exports in 1991 (see *Table 6.6*). A high coefficient for capital-intensive commodities can also be seen.

6.2 Demand-Side Impediments to Exports

The following analysis is based on 20 enterprise case studies prepared for Slovak companies in 1995. Most of the enterprises are industrial producers; some specialize in trade or other services. The basic data for the enterprises covered are presented in *Table 6.7*.

6.2.1 Direct and indirect foreign restrictions

The most difficult structural problem of Slovak exports is the inherited high concentration of sensitive commodities. This phenomenon developed as a result of strong ideological pressure placed on heavy industry and mining, as well as of the overall policy of autarky pursued by the communist governments. Moreover, the almost total integration of Slovak and Czech industry within Czechoslovakia resulted in differences in the relative importance of particular sensitive sectors, with the steel and iron industry being the most important sector for Slovak exports and coal and agricultural exports being of relatively little importance. Unlike in other former communist countries, the location of certain industries in Slovakia was not the result of central planning; rather, it stemmed from a more or less random distribution. Nevertheless, the overall share of sensitive sectors in former Czechoslovakia and the Slovak Republic was at about the same level as in the other former communist countries: in 1991 the share of sensitive products in these countries was 69–70% in the Czech and Slovak Republics and in Poland, and was 61% in Hungary; the share of strongly sensitive products in these countries stood at 40%, 38%, 46%, and 41%, respectively (see Fidrumc *et al.*, 1994).

With the exception of barriers to sensitive commodities, direct foreign restrictions (tariffs and quotas) do not currently represent a significant impediment to Slovak exports to developed countries. However, sensitive commodities, in particular iron and steel, account for a significant part of total Slovak exports. The 1991 Association Agreements with the EU provided for the gradual elimination of tariffs and quotas. However, new quotas for sensitive commodities were introduced in 1992. The quotas allowed for a gradual annual increase over 1991 levels and were supposed to have been reconsidered or eliminated altogether after 1995. The quotas forced Slovak enterprises to seek exports to other, more remote territories, often with lower profitability due to higher transport costs.[11]

In addition to the direct effects of reducing tariffs and quotas, the Association Agreement also had an indirect effect on exports of Slovak enterprises. Even industries that were not significantly affected by the Agreement experienced an increase in the level of interest West European firms showed in making trade contacts with Slovak enterprises.

Table 6.7. Profiles of the companies covered in the survey.

Company	1993 Turnover (mln. SKK)	1993 Gross profit (mln. SKK)	1993 Labor force	1994 Turnover (mln. SKK)	1994 Gross profit (mln. SKK)	1994 Labor force	1994 Exp. share[a] (%)	FNP share (%)	Privatization method	Main product	Main export markets
Chemolak	1,288.35	176.82	779	1,467.07	175.82	n.a.	37.2	0.0	VP	Chemicals	CR, Russia
Chirana Prema	2,696.10	156.30	n.a.	3,131.50	162.80	4111	77.7	0.0	VP	Medical equip.	CR, CIS, CEE
Chirana Exp-Imp	760.62	19.80	130	1,810.40	26.93	128	30.3	2.3	VP/Hldg	Trade	Former USSR
Gumon[b]	216.13	–5.11	380	181.47	–21.17	343	31.7	35.1	VP	Elec. insulation	D, WE
Henkel Palma	n.a.	n.a.	n.a.	1,015.60	34.10	250	30.0	0.0	JV	Detergents	CR
Hirocem	1,390.00	153.00	1020	1,496.00	129.00	874	60.0	29.0	JV/VP	Cement	D, NL, B, A
Hydronika	125.79	–60.87	468	166.45	–10.77	420	43.7	13.9	VP	Machinery	CR, D, F, Russia
Incheba[c]	386.40	78.80	n.a.	734.90	61.90	n.a.	59.9	0.0	DS/VP	Services	Europe
Kablo Bratislava	825.05	–154.17	500	1,038.28	–198.00	542	60.0	0.0	JV	Cables, conductors	CR, D, A
Kerametal	14,983.43	349.86	240	33,724.51	275.69	241	50.0	0.0	DS	Trade	n.a.
Omnia	1,217.40	21.50	212	1,797.00	41.85	220	56.4	0.0	DS/MBO	Trade	n.a.
Ozeta[b]	1,736.51	140.40	5809	1,990.79	101.29	5929	93.4	7.5	VP	Clothing	NL, US, D
Palma-Tumys	1,777.58	66.12	909	2,263.49	166.72	915	3.3	0.0	MBO	Vegetable oils	CR, CIS, CEE
Plastika	1,494.75	139.07	1320	1,647.40	143.71	1264	55.0	0.0	VP	Plastics	CR, PL, D
Protetika	100.33	12.62	n.a.	126.49	11.98	303	29.6	43.8	VP	Rehabil. aids	CR
Slovakofarma	3,008.00	727.00	2073	3,650.00	674.00	2100	73.0	0.0	MBO/VP	Pharmaceuticals	CR, D, Russia, PL
Slovnaft	27,988.00	1,611.00	6653	33,144.00	3,143.00	5716	49.3	73.0	SP/VP	Petrochem. prod.	CR, H, A, D
TOS Trencín	495.20	n.a.	1791	575.30	–4.12	1394	95.0	49.3	VP	Machine tools	Europe, dvlpg coun.
VW Bratislava[d]	1,668.00	n.a.	467	4,000.00	n.a.	806	94.6	0.0	JV	Auto. assembly	I, D,
VSZ Kosice	25,518.58	1,904.48	25624	29,404.27	3,841.15	25242	84.2	25.0	VP/MBO	Metallurgy	CR, EU

Abbreviations: SKK = Slovak koruny; n.a. = Not available; FNP = Fund of National Property; VP = Voucher privatization; DS = Direct sale to a selected investor or investors; Hldg = Enterprise is part of holding company, significant stake owned by mother company; JV = Joint venture with significant foreign participation; MBO = Management buy-out; SP = Significant state participation; CR = Czech Republic; CIS = Commonwealth of Independent States; CEE = Central and Eastern Europe; EU = European Union; WE = Western Europe; D = Germany; A = Austria; NL = Netherlands; PL = Poland; H = Hungary; I = Italy; Turnover = Sum of revenues from ordinary business activities; Gross profit = profit before tax, excluding extraordinary items.

[a] Unless otherwise specified, exports share includes exports to the Czech Republic. [b] Exports not including the Czech Republic. [c] Exports share calculated on basis of total rented exhibition area. [d] Exports share calculated on basis of number sold.

Trade restrictions have recently been intensified in some Central and East European countries. Despite the CEFTA agreement, Slovak enterprises frequently find it more difficult to export to Hungary or Poland than to other countries in Western or Central and Eastern Europe. Both countries recently introduced import surcharges; yet even without these, the overall levels of tariffs are substantially higher in Poland and Hungary than in the Czech Republic and Slovakia.[12] Finally, whereas the exchange rate of the Slovak koruna has been relatively stable since 1991, the currencies of Hungary and Poland have steadily depreciated, at least in nominal terms.

In developed countries, indirect restrictions are often more important than direct ones. Among the most significant indirect restrictions are the requirements of quality certificates and registration of the product with certain central authorities in the country of destination. The most common quality certificate is the International Organization for Standardization's ISO 9000, which has been required for exports to EU countries since 1996. In general, enterprises that currently export to developed countries produce products whose quality corresponds to the ISO 9000 requirements. However, as a rule, obtaining the certificate takes several months and presents an additional expense.[13] For some firms, especially smaller enterprises, the difficulties and expenses related to obtaining the certificate can be quite high relative to the volume of exports.

Moreover, a certificate awarded by one country often is not recognized in other countries. A separate certificate or registration must be obtained for each destination country. This is the case for exports to the FSU, for example, where each successor country now requires a separate registration procedure. Other administrative impediments are created by environmental and health protection standards. However, these are not particularly important with respect to the volume of exports affected.

6.2.2 Payment arrangements and buyers' inability to pay

Among the greatest difficulties Slovak enterprises face with respect to exports are unacceptable or burdensome payment arrangements. For many enterprises this problem began when they switched from indirect exporting through foreign trade enterprises to direct exporting, because the foreign trade enterprises often took partial or complete responsibility for export financing.

Foreign enterprises often require longer payment periods than is usual in Slovakia. Frequently payment is made 30 to 90 days after delivery. Moreover, domestic suppliers of inputs often require a guaranteed payment or payments prior to delivery. This disparity between payment conditions applicable to inputs and those applicable to outputs further increases the Slovak enterprises' need for funds.

When the interest rates charged for loans by domestic banks are also taken into account, the exported products often prove uncompetitive. During our interviews with managers of selected Slovak enterprises, we found that several firms had been forced to decline otherwise attractive export contracts because of unacceptable payment conditions (see Section 6.6). In certain cases, especially in some developing countries, local enterprises are compelled by law to require long payment periods and payment conditions that are especially unfavorable for the exporter.

Because they are unable to accept long payment periods (which are sometimes of several months' duration) and because of the high interest rates charged on export credits, Slovak enterprises are losing their traditional positions in the markets of Central and Eastern Europe, the FSU, and some developing countries. Slovak exports to these markets are being replaced by products of exporters from Organisation for Economic Co-operation and Development (OECD) countries, who are able to offer better financing arrangements.

In many cases, the problem is not the payment conditions but the trade partner's ability to pay at all. In particular, this has been the case in the FSU since the collapse of the CMEA. When the Soviet government ceased to provide payment guarantees and coordinate the trade flows, many deliveries of goods from Slovak enterprises were left unpaid.[14] At present, it is common for Slovak enterprises to require an advance payment or a bank guarantee when exporting to the FSU. Only the most reliable traditional trade partners enjoy better payment conditions.

6.2.3 Entry barriers

The costs of entering a foreign market are a significant determinant of an enterprise's ability to export. In general, there are two kinds of entry costs faced by enterprises: advertising costs and costs of establishing representation abroad. Because the present exchange rate of the koruna is well below the purchasing power parity, both advertising costs and costs of establishing a foreign representation are significant impediments to Slovak enterprises. The inability to finance extensive advertising of their products is a significant competitive weakness of Slovak enterprises.[15]

The costs of establishing representation abroad are unbearable for many Slovak enterprises. The ability to create a representation abroad is further adversely affected by foreign regulations restricting employment of domestic (i.e., Slovak) employees abroad. Finally, in some countries a foreign enterprise must obtain permission from governmental authorities to establish a joint venture or a fully owned affiliation.[16]

Another entry barrier is the enterprises' limited ability to obtain information about foreign markets. This is an area where the government could be quite helpful by supporting the trade departments of Slovak embassies abroad. However, according to the experience of some of the managers we interviewed, Slovak trade departments abroad are quite ineffective at present.

Some enterprises face a significant entry barrier where there are strong formal or informal relations between the local producers and distributors in the foreign market. In such cases, penetrating the local distribution networks can prove quite difficult. Another problem pertaining specifically to the FSU, and to a lesser extent to some other Central and East European countries, is corruption.[17] When a transaction is subject to approval by governmental authorities, it is often necessary to bribe the person or persons approving the transaction. Even then there is no guarantee that the transaction will eventually be approved and the contract fulfilled.

6.2.4 Effects of the CMEA's demise

Prior to 1990 the Czechoslovak economy was predominantly oriented toward trade relations with other countries of the CMEA. In 1989, for example, 63% of total exports and 58% of total imports were realized with other socialist countries. However, in 1994 the shares of Slovak exports to and imports from former socialist countries declined to 28% and 39%, respectively. This dominance of trade with other socialist countries meant that many Slovak enterprises were tailored to the needs of CMEA members. This dependence on exports to and imports from CMEA countries was more pronounced in Slovakia than in the Czech Republic. Whereas Czech industry is based on industrial traditions from the Austro-Hungarian Monarchy and the prewar republic, the majority of Slovak industry is from the postwar period. Also, Slovakia's orientation toward trade with the CMEA was stronger than was the case with Hungary or Poland, as is apparent from *Table 6.2*.[18]

The demise of the CMEA in 1991 caught most Slovak enterprises off guard. Moreover, the Czechoslovak government, and later the Slovak government, undertook virtually no measures to mitigate the effects of the change.[19] There were several factors underlying the subsequent collapse of trade. First, trade relations under CMEA coordination were never really commercially based. The actual extent of price controls differed among CMEA countries in the late 1980s, but the degree of regulation was nevertheless high. After the mechanism for settling payments within the CMEA was abandoned, the effective prices changed dramatically.[20] Second, decisions concerning CMEA trade were made centrally, regardless of real economic incentives. The lack of governmental coordination and promotion of exports starting from 1991 forced enterprises to secure exports on their own, something they had little experience doing.[21] Third, the elimination of central coordination of trade resulted in more intense competition among producers from the CMEA and other countries. Fourth, the economic transition undertaken in most former CMEA countries was reflected in rapid and substantial deterioration of the financial soundness of many enterprises. Hence, Slovak enterprises often were unable to collect payments for their exports.

6.3 Supply-Side Impediments to Exports

6.3.1 Organization of exports

Foreign trade was subject to rather strict regulation until 1990. With few exceptions, industrial enterprises were not allowed to export directly, but were compelled to use so-called foreign trade enterprises (FTEs). In general, FTEs had a centrally mandated commodity structure for exports and imports. Hence, a particular industrial enterprise had little or no choice in the selection of a trading company for its exports.[22] Furthermore, because prices were determined by the central authorities, producers had no impact on trade policies or export prices.

In 1990 this foreign trade regulation was eliminated and nearly all restrictions on exports were removed.[23] In response, many enterprises chose to organize their exports directly, circumventing the FTEs. The switch to direct exporting was frequently mandated by the FTEs' inability to adapt quickly to the changed conditions and seek new contacts in both traditional and new markets (this factor, in particular, was emphasized during our interview with VSZ Kosice); however, it also brought on a number of problems. Direct exporting was new for industrial enterprises and they lacked many of the prerequisites. Their employees had neither the knowledge nor the experience needed to secure exports. The enterprises did not have the network of foreign representatives and affiliations that the former FTEs did, nor did they have the FTEs' established relations with foreign trade partners. The move to direct exporting also had positive effects, as many enterprises were able to increase their export orientation substantially after this change (the case study of VSZ Kosice is also an example of this).

In addition to these changes in the institutional setup of exports, in 1991 both the CMEA and governmental planning and coordination of exports ceased to exist. Exports to former CMEA markets collapsed. For these reasons, many enterprises experienced a decrease in exports in 1990 and 1991, especially in real terms.[24] Moreover, exports were frequently secured on an ad hoc basis during this period.

The situation has improved since then, but low levels of experience and knowledge are still a problem in many Slovak enterprises. There appear to be large differences across industry branches. While some enterprises have been able to reorient their production to exports, and thus make up for the decline in domestic demand, others have failed to do so. A significant factor seems to be the quality and competence of management. The ability to export appears to be crucial for the development of an enterprise's financial position: enterprises that were able to redirect their production toward exports were more likely to produce high profits than firms that were not able to do so.[25] A good example of such a relationship is VSZ Kosice. This enterprise's share of exports (excluding those to the Czech Republic) increased from 36% in 1989 to 69% in 1994. During this period VSZ Kosice was able to overcome the financial problems it faced in 1991 and 1992, and its gross profit more than doubled between 1989 and 1994. Other such examples from our case studies are the companies Slovnaft and Ozeta. Although several other factors may have contributed to the improvements in the financial positions of these enterprises, including privatization, restructuring, and downsizing, the increase in exports seems crucial.

6.3.2 Quality and prices

The enterprises in our study usually evaluated the quality of their products as being quite good. However, there were differences across industry branches. The use of advanced production technologies is often decisive for product quality; this is especially true in the case of products with a relatively high degree of processing. In general, products with a low degree of processing compare favorably with foreign products. Products with a high degree of processing are more often deficient in quality. Nonetheless, the differences in quality of Slovak and foreign products often involve features that are not essential for the function of the product: design, packaging, or certain luxury features. Frequently, even when the quality of the exported products is high there are deficiencies in the level of service accompanying the exports, for example, timeliness of deliveries, uniform and reliable quality of products, and availability of after-purchase maintenance.

According to information from the enterprises we surveyed, prices of Slovak exports are in most cases lower than or equal to prices of competing foreign products of the same quality. Hence, the general price-to-quality ratio is usually quite favorable.

The quality of Slovak exports is perceived differently in different regions. Customers in developed countries, especially in Western Europe, have a certain aversion to products from Central and East European countries (among our case studies, the company Chemolak faced this phenomenon). This aversion could be caused by the greater emphasis buyers in these countries place on the level of accompanying services and on attributes such as design and other features not essential to the general function of the product. In contrast, buyers in Central and East European countries, the FSU, and developing countries emphasize low price (as was evident from the case studies of the companies Chirana-Prema and

Chirana Export-Import).[26] Moreover, Slovak exports can build on positions already established in former socialist countries.

These differences in quality have been reflected in the changing commodity structure of Slovak exports. Overall, a substantial portion of exports are products with a relatively low degree of processing during production. Furthermore, between 1991 and 1995 the share of such products increased and the share of products with a high degree of processing declined. In terms of SITC classification (see *Table 6.4*), the percentage share of exported products in the intermediate and simply processed products category (SITC 6) increased from 36.5% in 1991 to 40.5% in 1995. Similarly, the share of mineral fuels (SITC 3) rose from 1.1% in 1991 to 4.2% in 1993. Smaller increases were also recorded for crude materials except fuels (SITC 2) and chemical products (SITC 5). In contrast, the export shares of machinery (SITC 7) and miscellaneous manufacturing products (SITC 8) declined from 22.4% and 15.8%, respectively, to 18.8% and 12.2%, respectively.

The interviews often pointed to a link between the degree of processing and the regional orientation of exports for particular Slovak enterprises. Companies that export both finished goods and intermediate products frequently export the former mainly to Central and East European and developing countries and export the latter to developed countries. Examples among the enterprises included in our case studies are Slovakofarma, whose exports to West European countries are mainly chemical substances used for the production of medicaments and whose finished pharmaceuticals are exported mainly to CIS and Central and East European countries, and Chirana Prema, whose medical and dental equipment is exported mainly to CIS and developing countries and whose exports to Western Europe are almost exclusively disposable medical supplies such as syringes.

6.3.3 Availability of export financing

In general, exporting usually implies additional financing requirements for the enterprise involved. The payment periods are frequently longer and an enterprise's negotiating power is reduced in foreign markets. Most Slovak enterprises do not have sufficient internal resources to cover these financing needs. An enterprise's ability to obtain credits for financing exports depends on its individual conditions. A financially sound enterprise often finds it easy to obtain credits from domestic banks. Similarly, an enterprise in which a powerful foreign enterprise owns a significant share tends to have relatively few problems obtaining credits (this is demonstrated in the case study of Kablo Bratislava). In contrast, an enterprise that currently has financial problems or has had them in the past may encounter serious difficulties obtaining new credits. The application process may involve considerable bureaucracy and banks often have quite strict requirements with respect to liens or other forms of guarantees (this is the case for Gumon, a company included in our case studies).

Even when an enterprise is able to obtain credits from domestic banks, the interest rates are quite high, frequently reaching 18–20%, which makes the export too expensive.[27] Theoretically, it is also possible to obtain credits from foreign banks, which could be a source of financing at favorable interest rates. However, approval from the Slovak National Bank is required before credits can be received from abroad. In addition, foreign banks are mainly interested in large-volume transactions. Thus, only the largest Slovak enterprises have access to this kind of financing (for example, VSZ Kosice in our case studies has been using foreign credits).

Slovak commercial banks offer only a limited number of credit schemes specifically for financing exports. Moreover, currently there is no comprehensive, state-supported program for financing exports (see Section 6.7). Some enterprises have been using factoring. In general, many enterprises do not distinguish between export financing and other financial needs.

6.3.4 Impact of an enterprise's overall financial situation

During 1991 most Slovak enterprises recorded substantial declines in output in real (not nominal) terms. The economic transition based on a shock-therapy model brought about a substantial decline in domestic demand; the demise of the CMEA caused a sharp fallback in exports; and, not coincidentally, many Slovak enterprises started to have serious liquidity problems. Many enterprises failed to find ways to handle this situation and their financial positions deteriorated. In the absence of effective bankruptcy legislation, such enterprises continued to produce even after they had become insolvent. In this manner the liquidity problem was transferred to other enterprises, which were unable to collect payments on their deliveries to insolvent firms. Furthermore, several enterprises incurred significant liquidity problems because from 1991 they never received payment for their exports to the USSR/FSU.

Although these problems frequently originated externally, they had a major impact on the enterprises' ability to produce and hence also affected their exports. Indebtedness and mediocre financial situations made it nearly impossible for certain enterprises to obtain new credits. Many enterprises responded to the growing problem of interenterprise arrears by requiring advance payments; in contrast, as indicated above, exporting enterprises often must allow foreign buyers a payment period of 30 or more days. These disparities have led to temporary or permanent liquidity problems, causing interruptions in production due to a lack of funds for purchasing necessary inputs. In turn, enterprises suffering from production interruptions have often failed to fulfill negotiated export contracts. For example, this situation occasionally occurred in Gumon and Protetika, two companies included in our case studies. In the case of the company Hydronika, liquidity problems caused by unrecoverable export claims nearly brought the enterprise to bankruptcy and resulted in a sharp fall in turnover in 1993. Nonetheless, as the general financial situations of Slovak enterprises improve, this kind of problem is becoming less important.

6.3.5 Pre-privatization uncertainty

Not much information is available about how pre-privatization uncertainty affected enterprises' ability to export. It is quite difficult to identify the effects of this particular factor, because they can only be isolated from the effects of other factors with difficulty. Indeed, there is some evidence that enterprises with more or less concentrated private ownership (as opposed to state ownership or ownership by thousands of shareholders) tend to perform well in exports (an example from our case studies is Slovakofarma). However, there are several state-owned enterprises or enterprises with dominant state participation (for example, Slovnaft in our case studies) that also perform well.

Pre-privatization uncertainty prompted enterprises to search intensively for foreign investors. There is evidence that in Slovakia, as well as in other Central and East European countries, the participation of a foreign partner substantially improves an enterprise's ability to export to OECD countries.[28]

6.3.6 Availability of inputs

In the past availability of inputs was a problem. The price liberalization in January 1991 virtually eliminated the shortage economy, and obtaining inputs is no longer a real difficulty. What remains an issue is reliability of delivery contracts, in particular the timeliness of delivery and the delivery of the contracted quality and amounts. Flexible adjustments of contracts according to the current market situation may not always be easy to achieve.

6.3.7 Impact of legislation and government regulation

As described above (see Section 6.1.1), nearly all restrictions on international trade were removed in 1990–1991. At present the government does not directly restrict exports; however, several indirect impediments to exports are stipulated in Slovak law.

Tax System

The value-added tax (VAT) regulation directly affects enterprises that export a significant part of their total output. Under the VAT regulation, enterprises pay the VAT on inputs and receive payments for the VAT from buyers when the output is sold. The difference between these two values is then paid to (if positive) or refunded from (if negative) the state budget. Exports are exempt from the VAT. Nevertheless, enterprises are obliged to pay the VAT on exported goods at the time of delivery; they can claim a refund once they prove the goods have been exported. Thus, enterprises that export a large portion of their output constantly file refund claims. It generally takes about two months until the money is actually refunded, which increases the financial burden on exporters and forces them to seek additional financing. Although this bureaucratic procedure may be justified as a measure to restrict tax evasion, the delay seems unnecessarily long.

There is also a disparity in the recognition of VAT liabilities and claims. On the one hand, a VAT liability exists whenever a sale of goods takes place, regardless of whether the goods will eventually be paid for or not. On the other hand, a VAT claim is only recognized if a payment has occurred as well. Similarly, the VAT on imports must be paid immediately, whereas for exports the VAT refund is received after two months.

Another impediment to exports is implied by the eligibility conditions under which exports can be exempt from the VAT: an exporter must be a Slovak enterprise or an entrepreneur registered with the tax authorities. Hence, this regulation prevents foreign persons and enterprises from collecting a VAT refund if they export directly, that is, without a Slovak intermediary or a joint venture in Slovakia. Nonetheless, the effect of this is not particularly significant, as it probably only affects small-volume transactions, particularly shopping tourism.

The income tax laws also incorporate certain restrictions that can affect an enterprise's ability to export. In particular, this includes restrictions on what expenses are exempt from taxes.[29] For example, the tax law places restrictions and limits on tax exemptions for promotion and advertisement expenses, including direct-mail marketing (sending information and offers to prospective buyers).[30]

Limited Convertibility and Foreign Exchange Regulation

Foreign trade liberalization in 1991 and the accompanying introduction of limited currency convertibility with unified exchange rates substantially below the estimated purchasing power parity provided a strong incentive to export. The devaluation of the currency in 1990 was reflected in a substantial increase in exports;

exports rose from US$2.899 million in 1990 to US$3.441 million in 1991 (see *Table 6.1*).

As is apparent from *Table 6.1*, the exchange rate has remained relatively stable since 1991, with the exception of a 10% devaluation in June 1993. Although there is no doubt that this exchange rate regime contributed significantly to the low inflation rates recorded after 1991, the incentive to export provided by the devaluation is gradually fading away. The annual inflation rates in Slovakia ranged between 10% and 24% from 1992 to 1994, and it is expected that the price growth will remain around 10% in the medium-term future, as well. Thus, the Slovak currency is constantly appreciating in real terms against major Western currencies. The regulation concerning the limited current account convertibility stipulates that Slovak exporters must convert their hard currency receipts into Slovak koruny. This restriction increases the transaction costs for enterprises that engage in both exports and imports, because they must purchase the hard currency from commercial banks although they already have substantial hard currency receipts.

6.3.8 Quality of infrastructure

Although the quality of infrastructure in Slovakia is still rather poor, not many of the enterprises surveyed considered this to be a significant impediment to exports. Nevertheless, the unreliability of telecommunications can cause unnecessary problems and delays. Thus, although infrastructure problems do exist in Slovakia, they probably have only a secondary impact on the ability of Slovak enterprises to export.

6.4 Impact of the Division of Czechoslovakia

Economic and political developments resulted in Czechoslovakia's splitting into two successor republics in 1993. Although this act was actively discussed from the first reforms in 1989, when it actually occurred it was faster and even more surprising than anticipated.[31] Its legislative preparation left much economic uncertainty in early 1993, which resulted in a lack of credibility and goodwill of Slovak firms.[32] For example, Austrian imports from and exports to Slovakia in January 1993 were only 40% and 60% of their respective levels in January 1994. Only after the summer of 1993 did foreign trade reach previously established levels.

After the split of Czechoslovakia, the Czech Republic and Slovakia created a currency and customs union. This step not only ensured lower trade losses after the division, but also simplified the international positions of both countries and the negotiations with the EU (including the extension of the Europe Agreement for both republics).

Because of massive intercountry trade, the high amounts of transfers on the both sides in the past, and the limited amount of foreign reserves, the Czech and Slovak Republics agreed to a clearing payments settlement system after the dissolution of the currency union in early February 1993. The legal and technical framework was provided in the Payment Agreement between the two republics. According to this agreement, the payment settlement was to be carried out without any flows of foreign exchange (given balanced trade). Obligations that originated before 8 February 1993 were to be settled through the Old Account. The "account clearing koruna" (XCS) was to be used as an accounting unit with a fixed exchange parity determined according to the exchange rate of the Czech koruna to the ECU on 5 February 1993. The New Account was created for settling any obligations originating after 8 February 1993. The exchange rate of each of the national currencies to the clearing ECU (XCU) was to be determined independently by the National Bank of Slovakia and the Czech National Bank. According to the Agreement, each central bank could adjust the exchange rate of the XCU to the ECU within 5% bands. The exchange rate difference has been used as an important economic policy instrument by both the Czech National Bank and National Bank of Slovakia, although the former ceased to use it in 1994.

Another important aspect of the Agreement was the credit limit, set at ECU 130 million. Sums above this limit were to be settled in hard currency within 15 days after the end of the target period. The Payment Agreement could be terminated by either side by a written statement at least three months prior to the proposed ending date. The Czech Republic used this option in June 1995, after a series of informal negotiations with Slovakia. The clearing system was thus dismantled as of 1 October 1995. As of 1995, when both the Czech Republic and Slovakia adopted full current-account convertibility, mutual trade can also be settled in national currencies.

The division of Czechoslovakia brought with it transaction costs and trade barriers that led to a decline in levels of cooperation; moreover, in each republic goods from the other republic were largely replaced by domestic products or imports from third countries. Both republics signed a number of agreements to simplify bilateral trade; the most important of these are the agreement on the customs union and the clearing agreement. However, the adjustment systems built into these agreements and the changes that were made to them indicate that the levels of uncertainty in specific areas of these trade relations (for example, exchange rates) are higher than in trade relations with other countries. This uncertainty is a strong incentive to redirect exports to other markets. As reported above, the first half of 1993 in particular was characterized by uncertainty about future development, including the foreign trade regime and the exchange rate level. In the second half of 1993 bilateral relations were stabilized, solutions were found for all controversial issues, and property division was nearly completed. However, for the most difficult problems (for example, the division of some property items), instead of finding a compromise the representatives from the two republics merely stopped negotiating, which suggests that these problems may re-emerge in the future.

The stabilization of overall relations between the two countries in 1993 led to a slight increase in bilateral trade in 1994, although trade remained below the levels achieved when the republics cooperated closely. However, the more rapid growth of Slovak imports from the Czech Republic and the corresponding deficit within the clearing payments system led to a worsening of trade relations in the spring of 1994 and the introduction of new trade barriers. First, importers of food products were required to obtain product quality certification from Slovak authorities; originally a quality certificate issued by Czech authorities sufficed. This administrative measure mainly restricted Czech food exports to Slovakia. Second, the overall 10% import surcharge in Slovakia was also applied to Czech products. In 1994 and 1995 Slovakia had a positive balance of trade and a positive balance of clearing settlements with the Czech Republic. However, Czech and Slovak trade statistics differ substantially. According to Slovak statistics, Slovakia reached a trade surplus of 17.4 billion Slovak koruny (US$0.5 billion) in 1994. Czech trade statistics show a trade surplus of 6.8 billion Czech koruny (US$0.2 billion) in favor of the Czech Republic in trade with Slovakia. To some extent, this discrepancy is due to differences in the methods of data collection, but it may also have been caused by the evasion of import taxes, phony exports, and speculative transactions (see Section 6.5).[33]

6.5 Temporary and Artificial Incentives to Exports

Slovakia is a small country located near other economic centers of different sizes and importance, including Vienna, Budapest, Brno (Czech Republic), and Cieszyn (Poland). Moreover, Bratislava and Kosice, Slovakia's economic centers, are located in border regions. These factors allow for significant border tourism, which implies trade in both directions that is often not recorded in national statistics. For imports by Slovak citizens, the most popular items are consumer goods with high VAT rates that can be refunded at the Austrian borders by intercountry shoppers. On the export side, tobacco products, beverages, petroleum (which carries high taxes), and products whose prices deviate considerably from world prices (for example, some foodstuffs, textiles, and services) are the most popular. The foreign and domestic press have also reported cases of weapons exports and exports to countries that were under international embargo (Serbia), but no case was sufficiently documented. Although it is quite likely that some of these reports of illegal trade are based on fact, the amount of this trade is rather low and it does not play an important role.

Artificial or temporary incentives to export exist in Slovakia. A particularly pressing export incentive is tax evasion. This is especially the case with commodities that carry a high consumption (excise) tax: mineral fuels and related products, tobacco and cigarettes, and alcoholic beverages, for example. Exported products are exempt from the excise tax; therefore, a delivery can be declared "exports" but be sold on the domestic black market instead. These kinds of phony exports often involve the active participation of customs officials who do not check certain deliveries. It should be noted that the same phenomenon occurs with imports, where imports of products that are subject to the excise tax are not declared or are purposely misdeclared.

Another form of tax evasion is misdeclaring exported products. Unlike the case of phony exports, here the tax evasion takes place with respect to the country of destination, not Slovakia. Such cases are particularly common in trade with the Czech Republic, probably because of its relatively lenient customs controls and the large volumes of trade in both directions, making a particular misdeclared delivery more difficult to discover. In this manner, for example, diesel can be declared as heating fuel, which in the Czech Republic is subject to a lower excise tax.

Tax evasion can also occur when VAT refunds are claimed for misdeclared exports. In this case, the exporter inflates the value of the exported products (which are VAT exempt) in order to receive a larger VAT refund. Such transactions are often made through phony firms that are liquidated shortly after the transaction occurs. A firm thus exports worthless goods purchased from a phony domestic firm. The VAT evaded in the transaction is 25% of the price allegedly paid to the phony firm for the goods. The goods are then exported and are thus tax exempt. In the country of destination, they either disappear altogether or are sold to a phony foreign firm. Such tax abuse is especially likely in trade with the Czech Republic; however, these kinds of phony exports have so far been discovered only in cases of Czech exports to Slovakia.

A temporary incentive to export was prompted by the Payments Agreement between the Czech Republic and Slovakia, which enabled the creation of two different exchange rates for the Slovak koruna: one vis-à-vis the Czech koruna and another vis-à-vis other currencies. This system of two exchange rates existed from February 1993 until May 1995. Czech and Slovak enterprises apparently took advantage of the two exchange rates; whereas the clearing account was used for Slovak exports, Czech exports in some cases were paid for in convertible currencies, mostly by settling the payments through a foreign firm, often established specifically for this purpose.

A temporary export incentive was also prompted by the implementation of an import surcharge in March 1994. Because barter trade is not subject to the surcharge, foreign companies often attempt to find Slovak firms that can engage in barter transactions. In this way, both the foreign company and the Slovak enterprise can achieve better results from the transaction than without barter arrangements. It is likely that the increasing share of barter transactions contributed to the fact that only about 13% of total imports were effectively subject to the import surcharge in March through December 1994.

6.6 Enterprise Efforts to Tackle Export Impediments

In this section, we address selected impediments to exports that have been analyzed in more detail in the preceding sections. This section will illustrate how these impediments are tackled by Slovak enterprises, in particular those we visited.

6.6.1 Export financing

Credits designed specifically for exports are not always available from Slovak commercial banks (see Section 6.3.3). Moreover, the interest rates charged are quite high, especially when compared with interest rates common in developed countries. Currently, there is no government or government-supported institution offering export credits with low interest rates.

Some of the Slovak enterprises we interviewed have explored ways of obtaining financing from foreign banks. Another way an enterprise can secure export financing is by negotiating financing arrangements with its foreign affiliates. This is primarily the case with joint ventures founded abroad by Slovak enterprises. As a foreign enterprise, the foreign affiliate has access to credits offered by foreign banks; these credits can be transferred to the Slovak mother company. Finally, some enterprises take advantage of financing arrangements provided by foreign trading firms.

6.6.2 Payment arrangements

After the collapse of the CMEA, many Slovak enterprises experienced sharp declines in their exports, caused in part by increased difficulties with and higher transaction costs of making payments among former CMEA countries. In some cases, foreign buyers have enough cash in their own currency but are not able to secure hard currency to make the payment. This situation can be solved by establishing a joint venture in the foreign country (Hydronika, a company included in our case studies, adopted this approach for its exports to Russia). This solution is particularly attractive when a Slovak enterprise has not only export but also import transactions with the other country. The joint venture then secures both the imports and exports of the Slovak enterprise, and only the net difference between the costs of imports and receipts from exports must be settled in convertible currencies. The need for such measures arose after Czechoslovakia split into the Czech Republic and Slovakia: the creation of the new border and especially the separation of the currencies brought new administrative difficulties, problems with collecting payments in the Czech Republic, and payment delays. These problems could be eliminated or significantly reduced by founding a joint venture. Moreover, a joint venture in the Czech Republic with sufficient warehouse capacity can often help retain trade contacts with small and medium-size enterprises that otherwise would be lost (this pattern was followed by Ozeta and Chemolak, two companies included in the case studies).

6.6.3 Name recognition and other entry barriers

Several of the enterprises interviewed said they often felt a consumer bias against products from Central and Eastern Europe, particularly in Western Europe and other developed countries. Consumer reluctance may be due to a product's country of origin, or what is perhaps more common, to the make of the product, regardless of the country of origin. Products from Central and Eastern Europe are often sold at prices below levels appropriate for the product's quality. There is currently little hope that Slovak enterprises will quickly achieve credibility based on name recognition: the competition in most of their markets is intense and Slovak enterprises do not have sufficient resources for financing active marketing and advertisement strategies. Some Slovak enterprises have solved this problem by entering into partnerships with large international producers. In this way Calex, a Slovak producer of refrigerators, was acquired by Samsung, and Tatramat, a producer of washing machines and related products, was acquired by Whirlpool. Among the enterprises included in our case studies, this approach was adopted by Volkswagen Bratislava and Kablo Bratislava.

Other enterprises have attempted to tackle this problem by entering into agreements with foreign companies on a temporary basis. In these cases, both enterprises usually cooperate only in production, remaining completely independent with respect to ownership. The degree of cooperation varies: the foreign partner may provide technology and know-how and certain input materials, or it may participate in the final phases of production. In some cases the foreign partner only takes care of packaging (for example, Chemolak in our sample). The final products are then sold under the foreign firm's name; in some cases the country of origin listed on the product label is the foreign firm's home country. The foreign firm is then also responsible for product advertising and distribution. Such cooperation may either be a one-time engagement or may last for several years (in the past, Omnia in our sample intermediated the sale of Slovak-made television sets and refrigerators through German department store chains under the store's trademark). A Slovak enterprise may work in this way with several foreign firms simultaneously.

Finally, some enterprises have solved the problem of decreasing sales by engaging in outward processing traffic (OPT). This kind of cooperation is often used by Slovak enterprises in the textile and apparel industry (for example, Ozeta in our case studies).

6.7 Government Policies Regarding Exports

In 1990 and 1991 government subsidies were nearly eliminated from the Czechoslovakian economy; currently there is little government coordination of economic activities of the enterprises. In general, there would be little objection to such an approach if it were applied in all countries; however, that is certainly not the case. In fact, most developed countries support certain industry branches, such as agriculture, or selected enterprises that are in trouble. Moreover, many countries have programs and institutions to support exports. The absence of such programs and institutions in Slovakia is a significant competitive weakness for the country's exporters. In fact, the Slovak government has attempted to support exports: several large-volume export contracts were negotiated by the members of the government during their official visits to the FSU in 1991. Many of these contracts actually were fulfilled. However, a large number were never paid by Soviet enterprises, and the Slovak government took no responsibility for the payments.

Nevertheless, the Slovak government did attempt to solve the problems of individual enterprises on a case-by-case basis. However, it focused on general financial problems, not export-related problems. The so-called Consolidation Bank was founded, which took bad credits over from commercial banks and converted them into long-term credits with favorable interest rates. The Ministry of Finance also forgave the income tax liabilities of several enterprises that had become insolvent.[34] The Czechoslovak federal government founded the Export Guarantee and Insurance Company (EGAP), with representatives in the capitals of both the Czech and Slovak Republics. This institution was supposed to provide guarantees and insurance on export credits against political risks and the risk of default. After Czechoslovakia split into two countries, the EGAP continued its activities as a Slovak government–supported institution. Nevertheless, according to feedback from the enterprises we visited, the activities of the EGAP did not have a particularly significant effect on Slovak exports. The EGAP is currently being transformed into the Society for Export Insurance (SPE). The transformation is expected to continue into the future and the SPE is likely to be transformed into a regular import-export bank. However, because the SPE is currently a 100% state-owned institution, it is questionable whether the government will be able to provide sufficient funds to enable it to operate effectively in the future. Nevertheless, participation of commercial banks and other institutions or enterprises is also being considered.

Certain measures in support of exports were also undertaken by the NBS. In May 1993 the NBS issued a measure that allows enterprises to obtain refinancing for exports. Within this program, the NBS purchases the bills of exchange issued by commercial banks in order to refinance the credits given out for export financing. The measure also stipulates that the maximum interest rate on export credits provided by commercial banks cannot exceed the discount rate by more than 30% of the discount rate. The maturity period of the bills of exchange can be between 30 and 180 days. Finally, the measure is limited to exports to only 31 countries, mainly developed countries but also a few developing countries.

The degree of government support of exports is clearly insufficient at present. There are several areas where active involvement by the government would be in order, particularly in building effective commercial departments within Slovak embassies abroad. These departments could promote Slovak products abroad and provide Slovak enterprises with information about foreign markets. There is also a pressing need for measures in support of export financing; for example, the creation of a special export bank. The government could also become involved in selective support of exports of high-value-added products, through tax incentives for example. Finally, the government should undertake changes in the regulation of VAT refunding and the regulation of currency convertibility so as to minimize transaction costs and further liberalize the flows of payments.

6.8 Enterprise Perceptions

The results of our research reported above have been based on the case studies prepared for 20 Slovak enterprises. However, the importance we attributed to individual impediments might differ from the perceptions and direct experience of the managers of Slovak enterprises. Therefore, we drew up a simple questionnaire listing the main impediments to exports. Managers from the various enterprises were asked to rank the individual items as being very important (3), important

(2), of little importance (1), or not important (0). Impediments pertaining to the foreign environment were further separated into three main regions: Western Europe, Central and Eastern Europe, and the FSU. All barriers were listed in each of the three sets. The questionnaire also listed a set of impediments pertaining to the domestic environment and to the enterprise itself. The managers of all 20 enterprises were asked to fill out the questionnaire; however, in the short time that was available, only 10 responses were received. We believe this sample provides interesting insight into the perceptions about export impediments, despite the fact that the outcome may not be representative because of the small sample size. The results of the questionnaire, including the average rank for each item, are summarized in *Table 6.8*.

As expected, in each of the three regions analyzed the managers indicated different foreign impediments to exports as being the most important. In Western Europe, the greatest importance was attributed to intense competition from foreign firms (2.50); this impediment was closely followed by quality requirements and certificates (2.40) and the high cost of market entry (2.10). For comparison, for Central and Eastern Europe intense competition from foreign firms had a ranking of 1.90; quality requirements and certificates, 1.50; and the high cost of market entry, 1.60. These rankings for the FSU were 1.67, 1.33, and 1.89, respectively. In Central and Eastern Europe, the three most important impediments were the buyers' inability to pay (2.50), unreliability of relationships and contracts (2.00), and intense competition from foreign firms (1.90). This implies that the problems Slovak enterprises encounter when exporting to Central and East European countries have more to do with the unreliability of trade partners than with government-imposed restrictions. Nevertheless, the importance of direct restrictions, particularly tariffs, was higher in Central and Eastern Europe (1.30) than in Western Europe (1.00).

The pattern of unreliability of buyers was even more evident in the case of the FSU than for Central and Eastern Europe. The three most important export impediments in the FSU were buyers' inability to pay (2.78), long payment periods (2.22), and unreliability of relationships and contracts (2.11). Interestingly, corruption (1.89) was ranked fourth in the FSU, whereas it was considered much less important in Central and Eastern Europe (1.40) and unimportant in Western Europe (0.50).

Finally, although the average rankings of domestic impediments were not as high as those of foreign barriers, many items were considered relatively important (rankings greater than 2.0). The most important domestic impediments were high interest rates (2.30), high prices of imported inputs (2.30), and availability of export credits (2.20). Several other items received rankings near 2.00. It is apparent that enterprises consider problems obtaining financing for exports to be extremely important. However, the managers are not overly critical when judging

Table 6.8. Enterprise perceptions about importance of impediments to exports in different regions.

Export impediments	WE avg.	CEE avg.	FSU avg.
Foreign environment			
High tariffs	1.00	1.30	1.11
Quotas	0.50	0.40	0.56
Quality requirements/certificates	2.40	1.50	1.33
Threat of antidumping procedures	0.90	0.60	0.44
Low demand	1.56	1.67	1.50
Long payment periods	1.40	1.60	2.22
Buyers' inability to pay	1.70	2.50	2.78
High cost of market entry	2.10	1.60	1.89
Insufficient information about markets	1.60	1.50	1.78
Difficulties in establishing contacts	1.20	1.50	1.56
Intense competition from foreign firms	2.50	1.90	1.67
Unreliability of relationships, contracts	1.40	2.00	2.11
Corruption	0.50	1.40	1.89
Domestic conditions			
Low quality of products	0.89		
High prices of products	1.67		
Insufficient level of service	1.40		
Insufficient advertisement abroad	1.70		
Insufficient experience with exports	1.10		
Bad financial situation of enterprise	1.30		
Availability of credits in general	2.00		
Availability of export credits	2.20		
High interest rates	2.30		
Foreign exchange regulations	2.00		
Slow VAT reimbursement	2.00		
High prices of domestic inputs	2.00		
High prices of imported inputs	2.30		
Quality of inputs	1.70		
Quality of infrastructure	1.40		
Quality of telecommunications	1.20		

Abbreviations: WE = Western Europe; CEE = Central and Eastern Europe; FSU = Former Soviet Union.

Note: Survey was conducted by mail/fax during June 1995; 10 enterprises responded to the questionnaire; not all enterprises answered all questions.

the impediments that pertain to their own enterprises: low quality of products was ranked as the least important impediment (0.89). Insufficient experience with exports was also given a relatively low value (1.10). This conflicts somewhat with our findings and shows that the enterprises may be a little overconfident. However, it could also indicate that while these two parameters have not reached the optimal levels, great improvements have been made during the past few years.

6.9 Summary and Conclusions

In a small country like Slovakia, which has a population of 5 million, foreign trade necessarily plays an important role in the economy. The relative importance of Slovak foreign trade increased substantially in the wake of recent political and economic changes. The liberalization of the economy, and of foreign trade in particular, allowed for a major increase in the volume of foreign trade transactions. The fall in domestic demand effected by the economic transition further increased the importance of exports, which had to offset lost sales in the domestic market.

The division of Czechoslovakia resulted in a high level of openness and led to the introduction of a standard procedure of trade flows between the Czech Republic and Slovakia. Increased transaction costs and some trade impediments led Slovakia to replace imports from the Czech Republic with domestic products or new imports, and simultaneously to make up for Slovak losses on the Czech market. Impediments to exports seriously restrict Slovakia's participation in the international division of labor according to its comparative advantages and needs of economic growth. The barriers are not only present in trade with West European countries, where they are aimed at protecting markets in sensitive commodities, they also exist in trade with transition countries, which deepens the decline of exports to these traditional markets.

Direct foreign restrictions such as tariffs and quotas are particularly important for the export of sensitive commodities. The most important indirect restrictions are requirements for quality certificates. The export possibilities of Slovak enterprises are also significantly affected by payment conditions and limited opportunities for securing export financing with favorable interest rates. Uncertainty of payments is a serious barrier, especially to exports to countries of the FSU and to Central and East European countries.

Slovak exports are also limited by existing entry barriers, especially the high cost of breaking into foreign markets and the lack of brand name or producer name recognition. Overall, the most important supply-side impediments to exports are probably the low levels of experience and competence on the part of the export staff. The quality of exported products and their price levels vary among industries; however, a large portion of Slovak exports are goods with a low degree of processing. Finally, an important export limitation is the financial situation of the enterprises. Less important but quite common are the impediments implied in tax and foreign-exchange laws.

Temporary or artificial incentives to exports are mainly related to illegal and "semilegal" activities such as tax evasion, speculative transactions, and arbitrage.

Regarding government policies toward exports, some measures have already been accepted, but the majority of the job must still be done.

Notes

[1] The trade structure of prewar Czechoslovakia was particularly affected by the creation of authoritative regimes in neighboring countries.

[2] Chirana Export–Import, one of the companies included in our case studies, was founded when the former foreign trade department of Chirana Prema, another company in our sample, was turned into an independent enterprise.

[3] The Statistical Office of the Czech Republic and the Statistical Office of Slovakia split the foreign trade data for Czechoslovakia back to the 1970s according to registration numbers of importing or exporting companies. In the text the foreign trade data for the Slovak Republic refer to these estimates.

[4] The Czech statistics, in contrast to those from Slovakia, showed trade surpluses for the Czech Republic in both years.

[5] The introduction of new VAT rates, in particular, impeded imports of foodstuffs, books and newspapers (from the Czech Republic), and other commodities that under the old system were taxed according to a zero (or even a negative) turnover tax rate.

[6] In US dollar terms, exports declined by 9% and imports increased by only 7% because of the 10% devaluation in June 1993. In other years growth rates of exports and imports denominated in different currencies are similar. Therefore, we refer to growth rates in the domestic currency.

[7] In fact, Czech and Slovak exports of these commodities, such as steel, were liberalized considerably during 1992. However, after a substantial increase, new quotas were implemented for 1993. The quota for steel products was the 1991 volume plus 20%. Thus, the quotas were actually well below the 1992 volumes for particular products.

[8] The lists of commodities that are to be fully or partly liberalized are agreed on bilaterally between every pair of countries. This can mean that, at least during the introductory period, the commodity lists will be defined so that bilateral trade is balanced between every pair of countries.

[9] From a list of the 222 most important four-digit tariff items representing about 50% of total Slovak trade in 1993, we identified the top 30 commodities from their list ranked according to the value of exports.

[10] Unfortunately, we do not have comparable data for later years.

[11] For example, in 1993 exports to Thailand of the iron and steel products of VSZ Kosice, an enterprise included in our case studies, were more than double the 1992 level, making it the second most important destination of total sales in that year.

[12] In fact, Slovakia also introduced a 10% import surcharge in March 1994. Nevertheless, several transactions are excluded from the use of the import surcharge such as the import of strategic raw materials like oil and natural gas, and barter transactions. According to the Slovak Ministry of Economy, only about 13% of total imports were subject to the import surcharge from March through December 1994.

[13] The ISO certificate is awarded for a fee by selected consulting companies from the EU.

[14] Hydronika, one of the companies included in the case studies, is an example of an enterprise with substantial financial difficulties caused by unpaid exports to Russia.

[15] This is true in domestic markets as well. Managers of several of the enterprises we visited complained that they were not able to keep pace with the advertisement activities of foreign competitors and that their domestic sales had declined since the opening of the domestic market.

[16] This is the case in Austria, for example.

[17] In fact, the Slovak press recently reported that in certain countries foreign cars and buses are stopped by the police to collect a so-called environmental fee. The fee can be paid in hard currency, cigarettes, or alcoholic beverages.

[18] It should be taken into account that political and economic reforms started in Poland and especially in Hungary much earlier than in former Czechoslovakia. Hence, the reorientation of foreign trade relations started earlier as well.

[19] Nevertheless, it should be noted that almost no one at the time expected the decline in trade to be so massive and rapid.

[20] This effect was further intensified by price liberalization and the changes in currency regulation in most former CMEA countries.

[21] In post-CMEA trade, the deregulation of foreign trade probably overshot its target. In fact, extensive regulation of foreign trade relations was replaced by the complete absence of active government involvement in promoting exports (see Section 6.7).

[22] However, large enterprises, in particular, occasionally had their own foreign trade departments. Nevertheless, the area for their activities was quite limited.

[23] There are a few exceptions, such as exports of military products.

[24] The currency devaluations in 1990 and the price liberalization in 1991 led to a substantial nominal increase in sales and exports recorded in 1991. Nevertheless, the development in real terms of both total sales and exports was quite different.

[25] However, this linkage works the other way too: a poor financial position for an enterprise may preclude its increasing exports (see Section 6.3.4).

[26] There is evidence that for certain consumer products the medium price/medium quality orientation may prove ineffective. Instead, aiming at either the lower or the upper range of price and quality may prove more successful in developing countries.

[27] The annual inflation rate was 11.7% in 1994 and 7.2% in 1995.

[28] In certain enterprises a majority stake by a foreign investor resulted in a substantial reorientation of the enterprise's exports from Central and East European countries and the FSU to Western Europe. This happened, for example, with Kablo Bratislava, the subject of one of our case studies.

[29] Under the Slovak law on accounting and financial reporting, certain expenses can be recorded as a "bookkeeping expense" but cannot be recognized as a "tax expense."

[30] In general, the Slovak income tax law is conservative with respect to allowing expenses to be exempt from taxes. For example, writing off doubtful and unrecoverable claims and amortizing the start-up losses of an enterprise are prohibited. The income tax is thus often levied on unrealized profits, which contributes to a further deterioration of the financial situations of affected enterprises. The impact on certain enterprises has been quite substantial in the past.

[31] In 1993 about 80% of the Slovak population thought that the dissolution of Czechoslovakia was too rapid and that it was worsening the living conditions in Slovakia.

[32] Some firms that had been created earlier as subsidiaries of Czech enterprises changed their firms' names and export brands (for example, glass producers exporting under the brand name Glas Bohemia).

[33] The main difference lies in the registration of re-exports.

[34] Hydronika, the subject of one of the case studies, is an example of an enterprise with export-related liquidity problems that was eventually bailed out by the government.

References

Fidrmuc, J., Foltin, J., Huber, P., Jarosova, M., Kohutova, J., Kosir, I., Kovac, R., Ochotnicky, P., Szerdahelyiova, S., and Wörgötter, A., 1994, The Slovak Republic: After One Year of Independence, Bank Austria, Vienna, Austria.

Fidrmuc, J., Helmenstein, C., and Huber, P., 1995, Investigating Disaggregate East-West Trade Data: The Reshaping of the International Division of Labour, Institute for Advanced Studies, East European Working Paper 23, Vienna, Austria.

Schulmeister, S., 1990, Das technologische Profil des österreichischen Außenhandels, Austrian Institute of Economic Research (WIFO) Monatsberichte 12, Vienna, Austria.

Chapter 7

Slovenia

Franjo Štiblar

At the beginning of the 1990s Slovenia's political and economic systems underwent substantial changes; at the same time the Slovenian economy's institutional framework and behavioral characteristics changed dramatically. These changes are especially evident in foreign economic relations. Since Slovenia's proclamation of independence in June 1991, foreign economic relations have become a primary force behind the country's successful economic development. For this reason, an in-depth analysis of exports and imports is extremely important (Bole, 1994; Landesmann, 1995). This chapter includes analyses of Slovenian macro- and microeconomic performance, as well as an analysis of the impediments to exports experienced by Slovenian companies.

Although the lack of sufficiently long and consistent time series prevents a thorough time-series analysis, certain conclusions can be drawn on a comparison of major trade indicators in the periods before and after Slovenian independence.

This study of Slovenia's macroeconomic performance begins with an analysis of changes in the balance of payments and its components between 1988 and 1995 and the consequences of these changes for Slovenia's foreign exchange reserves and external debt. The investigation focuses on the trade of goods, which made up over 80% of the current balance of payments. However, trade of services should not be disregarded, because although it makes up only a small part of the volume of external payments, it is important for the determination of the overall balance of current payments.

Two fundamental questions are addressed in this chapter: How were Slovenian foreign economic relations affected by the country's separation from Yugoslavia, its shift from a socialist to a capitalist market system, and its abandonment of self-management? Also, which impediments prevent Slovenian enterprises from increasing their exports?

Slovenia has a population of 2 million spread over 20,225 square kilometers. In 1995 its per capita GDP was US$9,352. The republic's separation from former Yugoslavia in 1991 and the subsequent transformation of its economic system caused a serious economic depression: between 1987 and 1992 the GDP fell 22%. However, since 1993 the economy has been growing.

In 1995 the GDP grew 3.5%, the inflation rate was 8.6%, the current account of the balance of payments was US$36 million, and the high unemployment rate continued to decrease slowly. The official unemployment rate in 1995 was 13.9%, but it is estimated to be around 7% by International Labour Organization standards. The state budget had a deficit of 0.2% of GDP, and public debt is below 30% of GDP. Investments are reviving, albeit from a very low level. The average standard of living is increasing; however, differences between the standards of living of different groups of the population have increased significantly since Slovenia's economic transformation, which has negatively affected the aggregate welfare of the Slovenian people.

The domestic currency, the Slovenian tolar, was introduced in October 1991 with a successful monetary reform. It appreciated from mid-1993 to mid-1995 against the US dollar and to a lesser extent the Deutsche mark. This appreciation was a result of the excess supply of foreign currency after 1993 (both from a surplus in the current account and from the net inflow of foreign exchange – "hot money" – into the capital account). The excess of foreign currency led to a rapid increase in foreign currency reserves. Continuous real appreciation of the tolar has caused losses for exporters and has increased the trade deficit.

Achieving a single-digit inflation rate was a primary goal of the economic policy for 1995. By the end of 1995 the growth of retail prices was 8.6%. This moderate increase in prices, together with an interbank agreement on limits to passive interest rates for deposits, brought the central bank's nominal discount rate down to 10%, the real interest rate for short-term deposits to banks down to 6%, and the average active bank rate for credits down to 12%.

Exports have been a major driving force behind the revival of economic activity, but domestic demand was also strong in 1994–1995. In this respect, an important weakness of the economy is that wages are too high, which reduces the competitiveness of the Slovenian economy in international markets. In the summer of 1996 average net monthly wages were around 80,000 tolars (DM 895); labor costs were close to double that figure. Slovenian wages are significantly higher than wages in other economies in transition. Higher productivity cannot justify all of this difference.

7.1 Macroeconomic View

7.1.1 General framework for international economic relations

Institutional and Legal Framework

Under Slovenian legislation, foreign economic relations are much more liberal than they were in Yugoslavia before its collapse.[1] Slovenian legislation is currently among the more liberal in the world.

Before its break from former Yugoslavia, Slovenian international trade was restricted by the domestic institutions that governed trade, credit, and the foreign exchange regime. This restrictive framework was both a cause and consequence of the permanent lack of foreign hard currency (Štiblar and Vidovic, 1993).

As of June 1991 the new Slovenian constitutional laws on foreign-exchange businesses and foreign credit transactions abolished the administrative regulation of foreign economic relations inherited from former Yugoslavia. Full internal convertibility of the currency was established, replacing the previous practice of distributing "rights to foreign exchange." Administrative determination of the exchange rate was replaced by determination by the market. When the tolar was introduced in October 1991, the market exchange rate became the basis for calculating the official exchange rate (the central bank's current official rate is a weighted average of business exchange rates from the previous 60 days) (Štiblar, 1993a; 1993b). The central bank and the government opted for a flexible (floating) instead of fixed exchange rate for several reasons, the most important of which was the lack of foreign currency reserves needed for intervention at the time independence was proclaimed, because almost all hard currency reserves had been kept in the Yugoslav central bank in Belgrade.

Currently, legal entities can freely borrow abroad. In the spring of 1995 this provision was limited when the central bank requested borrowers of foreign credits to make deposits in domestic currency of 40% of the amount of credit if the loan was not given for over a seven-year period. The reason for this limitation was not a lack of liquidity, which was in fact almost too high, but the problem of monetization and sterilization of such excessive foreign exchange liquidity.

The constitutional laws, and later the law on foreign trade enacted in March 1993, fully liberalized and simplified foreign trade transactions. Thus, for instance, there is no need for special registration for exporting or importing goods and services. National treatment of foreign enterprises is fully in place. Some domestic businesspersons assert that the liberalization of Slovenian trade went too far – from total control at one extreme to the absence of control at the other. More recently, standardization rules were introduced to exert minimal control over trade flows.

The Customs Law and the Law on Customs Tariffs were enacted in 1995 and came into force in 1996. These laws modernize the administration of customs, the only remaining classical instrument of trade policy allowed, thus bringing it closer to standards of developed countries. The Law on Customs Tariffs introduced a combined nomenclature (using up to eight digits for classification) and synchronization with the European Union (EU) system. The use of nontariff measures (except standards) is slowly being eliminated in accordance with requests from the General Agreement on Tariffs and Trade (GATT) and the World Trade Organization (WTO).

Significant contributions to the liberalization and normalization of the domestic market for foreigners came from the antimonopoly legislation enacted in 1993 (The Law on Protection of Competition and Establishment of the Agency for Protection of Competition), from increased protection of industrial (intellectual) property rights, and from tax legislation, according to which national treatment is valid for foreigners.

In the establishment of economic relations with foreign countries and international organizations, Slovenia's achievements are already far above those of former Yugoslavia. With regard to the number of economic agreements, however, Slovenia still lags behind former Yugoslavia. Slovenia receives general system of preferences (GSP) treatment from seven of the world's most developed countries, including the USA but excluding the new members of the EU.

Slovenia concluded a special cooperation agreement with the EU in September 1993. Its most important element is a trade agreement that permits Slovenia to use most of the quotas given to all of former Yugoslavia for exports of sensitive products to the EU.

Slovenia is the most economically developed of the countries in transition. Therefore, the EU's long-standing reluctance to treat Slovenia as it treats other transition countries indicates that political, not merely economic, criteria in part determine how countries are treated with respect to future EU membership. The Association Agreement between Slovenia and the EU was finally signed in June 1996 but needs to be ratified by the parliaments of Slovenia and the EU member countries.

Negotiations with European Free Trade Association (EFTA) countries were successfully concluded in June 1995, leading to a free trade zone agreement between the members of EFTA and Slovenia. Of these countries, currently only Switzerland is a significant trade partner, with more than 1% in Slovenia's trade.

Free trade agreements were also concluded between Slovenia and the members of the Visegrád Group; Slovenia formally became a member of CEFTA in 1996. Likewise, a free trade agreement was signed with Macedonia, where impediments

Table 7.1. Selected indicators for Slovenian foreign trade.

Indicator	1989	1990	1991	1992	1993	1994	1995
Average exchange rates							
Tolar/DM	–	7.00	16.60	52.10	68.40	79.40	82.66
Tolar/US$	–	11.30	27.60	81.30	113.20	128.80	118.51
DM/US$	–	1.61	1.66	1.56	1.65	1.62	1.43
Growth rate of tolar/DM (%)	–	–	137.70	213.80	31.30	16.10	4.15
Annual average inflation rate (retail prices, %)	1,306.0	549.70	117.70	201.30	32.30	19.80	12.6
Unit value index (previous year = 100)							
Exports	–	116	101	102	100	103	–
Imports	–	110	95	99	90	103	–
Terms of trade (previous year = 100)	–	105	106	103	111	100	101

Note: Trade data for 1992–1995 includes trade with former Yugoslav republics.
Sources: *International Financial Statistics*, IMF, Washington, DC, various issues; *Bilten Banke Slovenije*, Ljubljana, various issues.

to its implementation still exist. Negotiations on free trade zone agreements are currently taking place with two Baltic countries and with Romania.

After it proclaimed its independence, Slovenia became a member of all major international financial and economic organizations and associations with exception of the Organisation for Economic Co-operation and Development (OECD). It is member of the GATT and a founding member of the WTO. The country is still only an observer in the Bank for International Settlements in Basel.

Parameters of Slovenian International Trade

Figures for basic indicators of prices and exchange rates are given in *Table 7.1.* Because several trade aggregates in the subsequent tables are given in current US dollars, it is important to take into account the following factors, which have an impact on US dollar values:

- Changes in the tolar/US dollar exchange rate;
- Intercurrency changes among major international currencies;
- Currency structure of exports and imports;
- Export and import prices of goods and services;
- Physical volume of trade.

The tolar depreciated in real terms in 1991 and 1992, but appreciated in 1993 and 1994. Real appreciation also took place in the first half of 1995, but stopped in the second half of that year.

In the currency structure of Slovenia's trade, the share of the US dollar remains at about 18% for both exports and imports. If, as an extreme assumption, all other currencies are represented by the Deutsche mark, then the weakening of the US dollar leads to increases in the value of exports and imports expressed in current US dollars. Despite quite significant changes in the Deutsche mark/US dollar ratio within each year, the average ratio (around 1.6) remained roughly unchanged in the the early 1990s. Before the 1990s the US dollar was significantly stronger; however, in the first half of 1995 the dollar was weakened, regaining some strength at the beginning of 1996.

The physical volume of international trade can be estimated by dividing current value amounts of exports and imports by indices of import and export prices.

Calculations for the index of terms of trade (the ratio of export price index to import price index) show that during the observation period (1990–1995) Slovenia's terms of trade remained equal to or above 100, indicating continuous improvement. This was in sharp contrast to conditions in other countries of Central and East Europe in this period.

To summarize, external conditions for Slovenia's international economic relations, represented by prices and exchange rates, were relatively favorable, even improving constantly between 1988 and 1995. The only negative factor was the appreciation of the tolar in the period from 1993 until the first half of 1995.

7.1.2 Permanent surplus in the current account

An overview of Slovenia's international economic relations is given in the balance of payments in *Table 7.2*.

During the period between 1988 and 1994 Slovenia achieved a surplus in the current balance of payments; however, before its separation from Yugoslavia this surplus was not transparent, nor was it available to Slovenia for use because of the centralization of all resources. In the current account, the primary source of surplus lies in the balance of services. Data for 1992 are presented according to both the old and the new methodologies. In 1995 the surplus in the current account showed a negative balance (–US$36 million) and the net inflow in the capital and financial account balance was US$84 million.

There is a significant tendency toward increased exchange of goods, which doubled during the observation period; trade of services was almost stagnant during this period. The ratio between trade in goods and trade in services changed from 58%:42% in 1988 to 85%:15% immediately after independence. This indicates considerable potential in the trade of services after the Balkan conflict is settled.

During the period from 1988 to 1994, the total current turnover (inflows and outflows of foreign currency based on current balance transactions) increased from

Table 7.2. Slovenian balance of payments, 1988–1995 (in millions of current US dollars).

	1988	1989	1990	1991	1992	1992[a]	1993[a]	1994[a]	1995[a]
Current balance	1,352	1,089	518	129	759	926	192	540	−36
Trade balance	365	192	−608	−262	50	791	−154	−338	−956
Export FOB	3,278	3,409	4,118	3,869	4,184	6,683	6,083	6,830	8,312
Import FOB	−2,914	−3,216	−4,727	−4,131	−4,135	−5,891	−6,237	−7,168	−9,269
Balance services	966	922	1140	483	754	180	375	723	744
Export	1,341	1,355	1,699	1,013	1,370	1,219	1,393	1,852	2,028
Import	−375	−433	−560	−530	−616	−1,039	−1,017	−1,128	-1,284
Net income of factors	−94	−100	−119	−106	−91	−91	−51	108	130
Net transfers	115	74	106	15	46	46	22	47	47
Capital and financial accounts	−113	103	−48	−291	−650	−645	−202	−545	84
Capital account	–	–	–	–	–	–	4	−4	-13
Financial account	−113	103	−48	−291	−658	−645	−206	−541	97
FDI	−5	−14	−2	41	113	113	111	131	170
Inflow	0	3	4	65	111	111	113	128	176
Outflow	−5	−17	−6	−24	2	2	−2	3	−6
Securities	0	0	3	–	−9	−9	3	−33	−9
Other flows	−108	118	−48	−225	−121	−117	−209	3	151
Foreign exchange reserves	–	–	–	−107	−633	−633	−111	−642	-215
Statistical errors and omissions	−1,238	−1,192	−470	162	−109	−289	10	5	-48
Total hard currency reserves[b]				409	1,164	1,164	1,567	2,764	3,426
Total external debt[b]				1,866	1,741	1,741	1,873	2,258	2,970

[a]From 1992 former Yugoslav republics are considered new foreign countries and trade with them is considered foreign trade, in this period job work is moved from services to the trade in goods category.
[b]Measured at the end of the year.
Sources: *Bilten Banke Slovenije*, Ljubljana, various issues.

US$8 million to US$16.5 million. Almost half the increase is the result of former Yugoslav republics' being considered foreign countries.

Although the capital account remains negligible, significant net inflow of foreign currency has entered the financial account in every year since 1991. Before its separation from former Yugoslavia, Slovenia's surplus remained hidden in the total Yugoslav balance of payments deficit.

After 1992, data on net foreign direct investment (FDI) and on investment in securities appear in the financial account. FDI is becoming quite significant, with over 1% of GDP annually. There are still few foreign portfolio investments, partly due to legal restrictions.

The primary reasons for a strong net inflow to the financial account were the appreciation of the tolar since 1993 and the relatively high real interest rates in Slovenia compared with those in other countries, especially Slovenia's neighbors. Slovenia's national credibility increased and its country risk decreased; moreover, its overall economic performance has been among the best of the countries in transition. In the spring of 1996 three leading international credit rating agencies gave Slovenia the highest credit rating of all countries in transition. Therefore, foreign "hot money" flowed in to be changed into domestic currency and deposited for only a short period of time (usually 31 days), thus earning significantly more than it could have earned at home. At the same time, high lending rates forced Slovenian enterprises to borrow abroad.

The surpluses in both the current and financial accounts led to a strong inflow of foreign currency. Initially this was beneficial, because in 1991 Slovenia had practically no foreign currency reserves. However, as of June 1996 Slovenia's hard currency reserves were over US$3.4 billion and the amount of external debt was around US$2.9 billion. Reserves are sufficient to cover at least four months of imports of goods and services.

Thus, with respect to external liquidity, there is no need to further increase foreign currency reserves, even after former Yugoslavia's share of unallocated commercial (private) debt is allocated to Slovenia. According to the agreement between Slovenian negotiators and representatives of foreign banks, US$835 million (US$710 million if repayment to so-called connected entities is excluded) will be added to Slovenia's external debt. This is the price Slovenia must pay to be excluded from the "joint and several liability" clause that applies for all of former Yugoslavia's commercial debt. For this debt, long-term Slovenian government bonds were issued on the Luxembourg Exchange.

Even with added debt, Slovenia's indicator of external debt to GDP is still below 20%; the ratio of debt to exports of goods and services is below 40%; and the ratio of debt service to exports is below 10%.

Further accumulation of foreign reserves is causing serious problems for monetary authorities. The central bank (Bank of Slovenia) is not able to monetize and sterilize all net inflow of external currency, which leads to more significant appreciation of the tolar. This currency appreciation hurts domestic exporters. Since the ratio of exports to GDP is over 50% in Slovenia, this unfavorable impact of the exchange rate on exports has a broader effect on the whole economy.

Confronted with these problems, the government is trying to help exporters using additional stimuli presented below (see Section 7.2.6).

Table 7.3. General openness of the Slovenian economy (in million US dollars unless otherwise indicated).

Year	GDP	Eg	Ig	(Eg+Ig)/ GDP[a] (%)	Egs	Igs	(Egs+Igs)/ GDP[b] (%)
1988	16,278	3,278	2,913	38	4,618	3,288	49
1989	15,985	3,408	3,216	41	4,763	3,649	53
1990	15,234	4,118	4,727	58	5,817	5,287	73
1991	13,817	3,874	4,131	58	4,886	4,661	69
1992	12,988	4,184	4,134	64	5,553	4,749	79
1992[c]	12,988	6,683	5,892	97	7,902	6,931	114
1993[c]	13,170	6,083	6,237	94	7,440	7,284	112
1994[c,d]	14,140	6,830	7,168	99	8,682	8,296	120
1995[c,d]	18,600	8,313	9,269	95	10,340	10,553	112
1996[c,e]	19,200	8,604	9,780	96	10,690	11,140	114

[a]Eg = Export of goods; Ig = Import of goods.
[b]Egs = Export of goods and services; Igs = Import of goods and services.
[c]Includes trade with former Yugoslav republics; import f.o.b.; factor incomes and transfers not included since they account for less than 1%.
[d]Estimated figures.
[e]Projected figures.
Sources: *Monthly Report*, Statistical Office of Slovenia, Ljubljana, various issues; *Statistical Yearbook of Slovenia 1994*, Statistical Office of Slovenia, Ljubljana, 1995.

7.1.3 Increasing openness of the Slovenian economy

The openness of a national economy is usually measured by the ratio of exports plus imports to GDP. The data in *Table 7.3* indicate that at the beginning of the observation period the Slovenian economy was quite open and that during the observation period this openness increased. This finding is not surprising for a small, open economy where exports are a strategic force behind growth and development. However, the numbers listed in the table should be qualified. Namely, if flows of goods crossing the Slovenian border are taken as a criterion for openness, and if flows to and from other republics of former Yugoslavia before Slovenia's separation in 1991 are also taken into account, the situation appears to be quite different. According to calculations based on input-output tables made by the Slovenia Statistical Office, the total flow of goods over the Slovenian border in 1994 was still around 18% lower than in 1987. However, because data on flows of services between the republics of former Yugoslavia cannot be obtained, the finding concerning declining trade flows holds only for the narrowly defined concept of openness related to trade in goods.

Slovenia's GDP peaked in 1986. In the period between 1987 and 1992 the country experienced a 22.5% cumulative decrease of GDP. The cumulative GDP growth in 1993–1994 was around 7%; therefore, the GDP remains around 16% below its peak level. With the expected 5% yearly growth in GDP under a favorable economic climate in the EU, the historical maximum can be reached again in 1997. If conditions are less favorable, only 3–4% growth can be expected and the achievement of the historical maximum will be delayed.

These estimates – that the 1994 GDP was 16% below its peak level and that the 1994 flows of goods over the Slovenian border were 18% below their peak level – seem realistic and consistent with other experiences.

According to the government's strategic prognosis (Potočnik *et al.*, 1995), in the years until 2000 growth in trade of services should exceed growth in trade of goods, and both should exceed growth of GDP. Thus, the openness of the Slovenian economy should increase further. According to these calculations, in the year 2000 the index of trade (exports plus imports) of goods to GDP should increase to 106 from its 1995 level of 95, while the wider index of trade of goods and services to GDP should increase to 131 from its 1995 level of 112.

Slovenia's openness exceeds that of almost all other countries in transition. Among developed and newly industrialized countries, there is greater openness in small countries such as Luxembourg and in the so-called Asian Tigers than in Slovenia. Although there is no optimal level of openness, in principle, the more economic openness the better, because trade increases product availability and thereby increases the welfare of states, regardless of whether or not the theory of absolute or comparative advantages is used. However, limits to openness do exist, and they are not only of an economic, but also of a social, political, and ecological nature.

7.1.4 Structure of trade of goods

Export and Import of Goods by Degree of Processing

The relatively high proportion of processed goods in Slovenia's imports and especially in its exports indicates that with regard to international trade Slovenia already has the status of a developed economy.[2] According to the theory of absolute and comparative advantages, Slovenia, as a relatively less-developed country in comparison with West European countries, should export minimally processed goods to and import highly processed goods from Western Europe (EU countries account for 68% of Slovenia's trade of goods). In fact, Slovenia trades highly processed goods and even achieves a surplus with the EU. Slovenia's pattern of trade fits Linder's (1961) theory (according to which more developed countries trade predominantly

Table 7.4. Exports and imports by degree of processing (in percent of total exports and imports, respectively).

Year	Exports			Imports			
	Low	Moderate	High	Low	Moderate	High	$A_x - A_m$[a]
1989	5.7	18.6	75.7	11.4	20.3	68.3	270–257=13
1990	4.5	14.9	80.6	12.6	17.3	70.1	276–258=18
1991	4.6	13.2	82.2	11.1	18.1	70.8	278–260=18
1992[b]	4.8	14.2	81.0	11.5	22.4	66.1	276–255=21
1993[b]	6.1	13.2	80.7	10.9	19.9	69.2	275–258=17
1994[b,c]	2.6	14.0	83.4	7.6	22.1	70.3	281–263=18

[a]Difference of aggregate level of processing for exports (A_x) and imports (A_m). For further explanation see main text.
[b]Includes trade with former Yugoslav republics.
[c]Figures are for January through November.
Source: *Statistical Yearbooks of Slovenia*, Statistical Office of Slovenia, Ljubljana, various volumes.

among themselves; i.e., intra-industry trade exceeds inter-industry trade), only in the case if Slovenia's being considered to be a relatively more-developed country.

The classification of products by degree of processing in *Table 7.4* was done by the Slovenian Statistical Office; Standard International Trade Classification (SITC) was used as a base and goods were grouped as having low, moderate, or high levels of processing. The criterion was the Statistical Office's internal estimation of the level of processing of each good related to the detailed SITC. The results show that at the beginning of the observation period, the share in exports of highly processed goods was 76%; its share at the end of the period was 83%. This group's share in imports was 68% at the beginning of the period and 70% at the end.

By assigning weights to the different levels of processing (low level = 1, moderate level = 2, and high level = 3) and multiplying them by the percentages in *Table 7.4*, the aggregate levels of processing (A_x and A_m) were calculated. As *Table 7.4* shows, the value of this indicator was 270 for exports and 257 for imports in 1989, the beginning of observation period. By the end of the period, both these values had increased; moreover, the difference between exports and imports of processed goods had also increased. This trend corresponds to the development of a developed economy. When flows to and from the successor states of Yugoslavia were included in exports and imports after 1991, there was a moderate decrease in the degree of processing. This decline was more pronounced in imported than in exported goods, which confirms the view that Slovenia, as the most developed of the republics of former Yugoslavia, primarily imported less-processed goods from the other republics and exported more-processed goods to them.

Geographic Trade Patterns of Slovenia: Orientation toward the EU

The geographical composition of trade by groups of countries is presented in *Table 7.5*. The patterns reflect the Slovenian economy's Western orientation in its trade of goods. The large concentration of trade with developed countries, especially those in Western Europe, increased during the observation period. According to Mencinger (1994) intra-sectoral (intra-industry) trade is currently prevailing. An end to the conflict in the Balkans will probably stop a further increase in the concentration of Slovenia's trade with the EU (Aiginger *et al.*, 1994).

Trade of goods with developed countries makes up more than 75% of all trade. The share of the EU 12 was close to 60%, and when the number of EU members increased to 15 in 1995, this share increased to over 68%. The addition of three new members to the EU changed the former Slovenian trade surplus with the EU into a deficit. With the exception of Japan, the EFTA countries are those with which Slovenia has the most negative trade balance.

Trade with the Visegrád Group (part of the developing countries listed in *Table 7.5*) retained a less than 5% share in total trade, with Slovenia experiencing a small trade deficit. This share could double at most after the impact of Slovenia's membership in CEFTA is felt. The share of trade with less-developed countries decreased, most recently due to smaller volumes of trade with the successor states of Yugoslavia. With a less than 25% share in trade for all developing countries, including European countries in transition and the successor states of Yugoslavia, trade in this region has probably reached a level below which it could be undesirable to go as it would lead to overconcentration of trade with West European countries.

In the late 1980s Slovenia traded with the rest of Yugoslavia more than with foreign countries: in this period the ratio was 42% for foreign countries to 58% for the rest of Yugoslavia; in 1994 the ratio was 89% to 11%, respectively. Peace in the Balkans could lead to the reestablishment of some of this trade; however, no more than a 20% share in total Slovenian trade directed toward the successor states of Yugoslavia can be expected in even the most optimistic scenario. Slovenia has decisively oriented itself toward the developed West.

The Structure of Trade According to SITC

Slovenia's exports and imports show considerable product diversity. Slovenia's top 10 export items for 1993 are shown in *Table 7.6*.

The top four import items were passenger motor cars, woven cotton fabric, parts for motor vehicles, and data processing machinery.

Major changes in the structure of Slovenian exports and imports by SITC groups are given in *Table 7.7* using SITC one-digit categories. The highly processed

Table 7.5. Geographical patterns of Slovenian trade (in percent).

	Exports							Imports						
	1989	1990	1991	1992[a]	1993[a]	1994[a]	1995[a]	1989	1990	1991	1992[a]	1993[a]	1994[a]	1995[a]
Total[b]	100	100	100	100	100	100	100	100	100	100	100	100	100	100
Developed	68	74	80	67	71	73	73	78	81	82	67	74	78	78
EU	51	58	64	55	57	59	67	57	58	60	50	56	57	69
EFTA	9	9	9	7	7	8	1	13	13	14	11	12	15	3
Other	8	7	7	5	7	5	5	8	10	8	6	6	6	7
Developing	32	26	20	33	29	27	27	22	19	18	33	26	22	22
Europe	24	20	14	30	26	25	25	17	12	12	29	20	17	17
Form. Yugo.[c]	–	–	–	23	16	15	15	–	–	–	20	11	8	7
Other	24	20	14	7	10	10	10	17	12	12	9	9	9	10
Asia	6	5	4	3	2	2	1	3	5	4	2	3	2	2
Africa	1	1	1	0	1	0	2	1	0	0	1	1	2	2
America	1	0	1	0	0	0	0	1	2	2	1	2	1	1
Oceania	0	0	0	0	0	0	0	0	0	0	0	0	0	0

[a] Includes foreign trade with successor states of Yugoslavia.
[b] Disparities due to rounding may occur.
[c] Form. Yugo. = successor states of Yugoslavia.
Sources: *Monthly Reports*, Statistical Office of Slovenia, Ljubljana, various issues; *Statistical Yearbook of Slovenia*, Statistical Office of Slovenia, Ljubljana, various volumes.

Table 7.6. The top 10 export items in Slovenia in 1993 and their shares in exports in 1993 and 1995, in percent.

	1993	1995
1. Motor cars	5.2	8.4
2. Medicaments	3.4	3.5
3. Furniture and parts	2.7	2.6
4. Women's suits, dresses, jackets	2.6	2.2
5. Seats and chairs	2.5	2.7
6. Refrigerators and freezers	2.0	2.0
7. Parts for motor vehicles	2.0	1.7
8. Wood for construction	1.8	2.1
9. Electric water heaters	1.7	1.7
10. Men's suits, jackets	1.7	–

products of SITC groups 5 to 7 are dominant in trade, which is again a sign of an economy with developed trade. The share in imports of machines and equipment has overtaken this group's share in exports. The share of food and energy in imports has increased because these products, which traditionally came from former Yugoslavia, are now considered imports. As Mencinger (1994) reported, the increase in exports of fuels is related to re-exports. The decrease in exports of machines and equipment is connected with the lack of credit support (the Slovenian export-import bank is only in its initial stage of operation, and its capital funding is too small for it to play a decisive role in international economic relations).

The increase in the share of miscellaneous and unclassified products (SITC groups 8 and 9) could in part be caused by the increasing globalization of production. The division of production, according to which only certain parts of a final product are produced in individual countries, seems likely to increase in the future, especially for smaller countries like Slovenia. However, a large share of Slovenian exports of products from SITC group 8 consists of clothing, footwear, and furniture, and most of this trade is carried out in the framework of outward processing traffic (OPT).

7.2 Microeconomic View

Slovenia differs significantly from the other countries covered in this book in many ways (Kimball, 1994); however, exports are at least as important to Slovenia as to the other small transition economies. It should be stressed that the loss of the former Yugoslav markets affected Slovenia much as the collapse of the Council for Mutual Economic Assistance (CMEA) impacted other East European countries.

Table 7.7. The structure of Slovenian exports and imports by SITC group (in percent).

	Exports						Imports					
SITC group	1985	1990	1992[a]	1993[a]	1994[a]	1995[a]	1985	1990	1992[a]	1993[a]	1994[a]	1995[a]
0 Food, live animals	7.0	4.6	5.1	3.9	4.0	3.2	2.7	6.0	7.5	7.4	7.6	6.7
1 Beverages, tobacco	0.7	0.8	1.3	0.7	0.7	0.6	0.1	0.4	1.0	0.7	0.6	0.6
2 Crude materials	3.0	3.0	2.1	1.8	1.9	2.1	15.9	9.4	6.8	5.3	6.5	6.6
3 Mineral fuels	0.9	0.1	2.6	5.1	1.1	1.0	10.7	7.2	11.0	11.0	7.1	6.5
4 Animal and veg. oils	0.2	0.1	0.1	0.1	0.1	0.1	0.8	0.3	0.4	0.4	0.4	0.4
5 Chemicals	9.7	8.9	9.1	9.1	10.3	10.5	18.9	14.0	12.0	11.0	12.2	12.1
6 Goods by material	27.0	28.0	27.0	26.0	27.3	28.6	17.4	18.0	20.0	18.0	19.4	19.8
7 Machinery, equip.	34.0	38.0	29.0	27.0	30.3	31.5	30.2	35.0	26.0	30.0	31.8	33.8
8 Miscellaneous	17.0	16.0	23.0	26.0	24.0	22.5	3.3	8.5	10.0	12.0	11.0	10.6
9 Other	0.0	0.2	0.0	0.2	0.2	0.2	0.0	0.3	4.6	4.0	3.3	2.8
Total[b]	100.0	100.0	100.0	100.0	100.0	100.0	100.0	100.0	100.0	100.0	100.0	100.0

[a]Includes trade with successor states of Yugoslavia.
[b]Discrepancies due to rounding may exist.
Sources: Statistical Office of Slovenia, 1994; Internal data of the Statistical Office of Slovenia, Ljubljana.

Soviet (CMEA) markets ceased to be important for Slovenia in the early 1970s. Until then up to one-third of exports had been made under a clearing (barter) arrangement, usually with East European socialist countries, among which the most important was the Soviet Union. In the mid-1980s exports under clearing payment arrangements dropped to about 15% of Slovenian exports. In the 1990s exports to countries of the former Soviet Union (FSU) have made up only around 3% of total exports, while exports to small East European countries in transition have accounted for 5% of total exports. To summarize, Slovenia's exports (and trade) to Eastern Europe had a 32% share in the 1970s, a 16% share in the 1980s, and a paltry 8% share in the 1990s; that is, the trade share decreased 50% each decade.

Unlike the other countries discussed in this book, Slovenia was not an institutionally closed economy at the start of its transition (Kumer, 1995). Starting in the mid-1960s Yugoslavia was quite open with regard to trade of goods and services and was closed only to a limited extent with regard to flows of production factors. Slovenia was the most liberal of the Yugoslav republics in what was a fairly decentralized economic system. The principles of central planning were abandoned in former Yugoslavia in the early 1950s. It seems that many of the economic transformations regarding liberalization of trade that are currently occurring in most economies in transition took place in Slovenia some 20 to 30 years ago, during the former Yugoslavia's economic reforms.

Some recent studies (Gros and Vandille, 1995, for example) have shown that of all the countries in transition the structure of Slovenian exports and imports is closest to the average structure of trade of EU countries; moreover, Slovenia's trade structure comes closer to the average than those of some less-developed members of the EU. From this finding the authors conclude that Slovenia's accession to the EU would cause it only a moderate adaptation shock. According to Baldwin's (1994) calculations, of the countries in transition aspiring to EU membership Slovenia would cost the least for the EU (200 million ECU per year). This factor speaks for Slovenia as the best candidate for membership to the EU. However, political considerations predominantly determine the order of accession. For this reason it is not surprising that nine countries in transition had already signed Association Agreements with the EU before Slovenia signed one in June 1996.

7.2.1 Subjects of the empirical study

The 21 enterprises in our sample were selected according to the following criteria:

- For the most part, the selected enterprises are nonmarginal exporters that export a significant portion of their production. They are from both the manufacturing and service sectors. Firms that export to the West are predominant, but those that export to former CMEA countries are also included. Some of the companies selected are new and tend to be smaller, but there are also medium-size and large firms. Some firms are privately owned "greenfield" firms; others were former socially owned firms that have been or are being privatized. Social ownership still prevails in some firms. Many of the selected firms operate outside the capital, Ljubljana. In some of the firms the minority or majority owners are foreigners.

- With regard to commodity orientation of the companies' production programs, we attempted to include companies representing Slovenia's major manufacturing and export industries. Thus, the sample includes two manufacturers of chemicals, the country's largest iron and steel concern, a manufacturer of finished metal goods and tools, a manufacturer of electrical machinery, several manufacturers of ready-made clothing and accessories, a producer of knitted goods, a manufacturer of mass-produced footwear, several manufacturers of wooden furniture, manufacturers and traders of foodstuffs (including meat), and firms that process and preserve fruit and vegetables. For manufacturers of parts for motor vehicles, only one producer is included (a producer of car tires). Also included in the sample are a producer of cosmetics and washing detergents and a producer of pharmaceuticals, both of which are among the most important exporters in Slovenia.

For further characteristics of the enterprises in our sample see *Table 7.8*.

7.2.2 Impediments to exports: Demand

Lack of Orientation to Low-demand Regions and Commodity Groups

Slovenian exports are not predominantly oriented toward low-demand regions and commodity groups for several reasons.

First, for at least the past three decades Slovenia has been exporting most of its products to developed countries in the West. Therefore, its exports (and, indirectly, its domestic activity) have been sensitive to trade cycles in world markets, more so than those of other countries currently in transition.

Second, the outflow of goods to the rest of former Yugoslavia can be treated as exports to poorer regions with lower demand. Despite considerable liberalization of trade, a certain level of protection from outside competition existed in this region, which led to relatively high prices for low-quality products. With the loss of markets in former Yugoslavia most of these flows were redirected to Western markets. Various studies show that this redirection was quite smooth and was accompanied by an improvement in the quality of exported products and, even

Table 7.8. Profiles of the companies covered in the survey.

Company	Sector	Owner-ship[a]	Legal status[b]	Size[c]	Export/sales ratio (%)	Main markets
1. PETR	Footwear	So	JCS	L	92	USA, Germany, Italy, Russia
2. SAKR	Tires	So	JSC	L	81	Austria, Germany, Italy Hungary, Netherlands
3. SLLJ	Furniture and unrelated trade	M	JSC	L	65	Russia, USA, Italy, Hungary, Germany
4. LIMA	Metal products	So	JSC	L	44	Western Europe (94%)
5. MELJ	Food and trade of food	P	JSC	L	6	Germany, Croatia, Ukraine, Italy, Austria
6. ZLMA	Cosmetics	M	JSC	M	43	Austria, Germany, Switzerland, EC-Europe
7. IEKR	Electric meters	P	JSC	L	90	Germany, W. Europe, S. America, Asia
8. TTOV	Textiles	So	JSC	M	77	Germany, Italy
9. SVMA	Textiles	So	JSC	M	81	USA, Germany, Italy
10. LELJ	Pharma-ceuticals	P	JSC	L	66	USA, Croatia, Poland Russia, Canada, Czech R.
11. SVKA	Textiles	P	JSC	M	60	Germany, Austria, Italy
12. STKA	Furniture	M	JSC	M	45	Germany, Czech R., Hungary, Scandinavia
13. TRKA	Electronics	P	LLC	S	40	Hungary, Germany, Czech R., Finland
14. FEMA	Machinery, metal equip.	P	LLC	S	10	Germany
15. ERLJ	Furniture, wooden accessories	P	LLC	S	100	Germany, Switzerland, Italy, Austria, Japan
16. HEDO	Chemicals	So	JSC	M	50	Russia, Hungary, Poland, Belorus R, Czech R.
17. KOLJ	Food processing	P	JSC	M	28	Spain, Austria, Germany Switzerland, Russia
18. INJA	Impregnated textiles	So	JSC	M	57	Netherlands, Germany, Poland, Russia, Croatia
19. TODO	Textiles for health and hygiene	So	JSC	M	40	Croatia, Russia, Poland
20. SŽLJ	Steelworks	St	JSC	L	55	Germany, Italy, USA, Austria, Croatia
21. TDRU	Chemicals	St,M	JSC	M	65	Germany, Austria, Italy

[a] So = Social, P = Private, M = Mixed, St = State.
[b] JSC = Joint-stock company, LLC = Limited-liability company.
[c] L = Large (>1,000 employees), M = Medium-sized (50–1,000 employees), S = Small (<50 employees).

more important, by a reduction in their prices. According to the companies we surveyed, with few exceptions prices in the domestic market are currently around 20% higher than prices in foreign markets. The prices of Slovenian exports to former Yugoslav markets are somewhat lower than domestic prices, but are still higher than prices achieved in Western markets. This pricing strategy is merely the continuation of the earlier practice by Slovenian exporters of using the higher prices achieved in Yugoslav markets to finance penetrations into Western markets by product dumping.

With regard to commodity groups, the structure of exports presented in *Tables 7.4*, and *7.7* indicates that the commodity groups of moderately to highly processed products prevail in Slovenian exports, although the share of miscellaneous products is significant. This distribution of exports was one of the main reasons for concluding that Slovenia behaves as a mature, developed economy with regard to its international economic relations. Slovenia's role as an economic front-runner in former Yugoslavia and its vicinity to highly developed Austria, Italy, and Germany are among the reasons for such development.

Moderate Foreign Protection

As part of former Yugoslavia, Slovenia enjoyed all the preferential treatment which that country achieved in international economic relations. Thus, for instance, it received special treatment within the GATT for agricultural products and goods from other sectors with respect to which Yugoslavia was treated as an underdeveloped country. A special cooperation agreement *sui generis* was signed between Yugoslavia and the EU with nonreciprocal treatment for the former. During the confrontations of the Cold War, Yugoslavia was always treated favorably by the West because it was considered one of the renegades of the Communist bloc; this treatment had certain effects on economic relations, as well.

At the same time, Yugoslavia was one of the founding members of the Nonaligned Movement, which also had positive consequences for its economic relations with these countries. For instance, oil could be sometimes bought on favorable terms. Usually the possibilities were not fully exploited; however, of all the former Yugoslav republics, Slovenia used these opportunities most effectively.

Despite its openly declared independence from the Eastern bloc after 1949, the eastern part of Yugoslavia, mainly Serbia, maintained good economic relations with Eastern bloc countries. Here, Slovenia was not dominant.

Thus, during the Cold War former Yugoslavia (and Slovenia) used its "in-between" position to obtain economic support from, and maintain good relations with, both the Eastern and Western blocs and the group of nonaligned nations.

However, with the collapse of communism and as the Non-aligned Movement lost its reason for existence, Slovenia's situation changed dramatically. In an economic sense, this has meant an end to the country's preferential status in the West, the East, and in the "Third World." Foreign (Western) protection against entry by Slovenian exporters is currently as harsh as for exporters from other countries in transition, if not harsher. This treatment was obvious during negotiations for Slovenia's membership in the GATT and later the WTO, when stricter conditions were placed on Slovenia than on other new members, in particular regarding liberalization of trade and the creation of a transparent export system.

There is one temporary situation that benefits Slovenia with regard to foreign protection. In economic relations with the EU, Slovenia is allowed to use all the quotas allocated to former Yugoslavia for sensitive products exported to the EU, because the other former republics have recently been exporting little or nothing due to the Balkan conflict. This treatment will cease with the signing of the Association Agreement between Slovenia and the EU, and with the revival of the economies of the other successor states of Yugoslavia, which would like to have their share of these quotas.

From the first days of its independence in 1991, Slovenia has made efforts to adapt production and legislation regarding quality, health, and environment to Western and above all EU standards. Therefore, no special tariff or nontariff barriers are in use or planned against Slovenia abroad.

One example of a foreign protection impediment is the series of investigations made by Italian authorities into the domestic (Slovene) origin of exported chemicals to substantiate eligibility of exemptions from import taxes in Italy; the company TDRU in the sample has been the subject of this type of investigation. As almost everywhere in the world, imported ore is used in the production of these intermediate chemical products. According to the opinions of Slovenian producers, intermediate products produced from this ore in Slovenia should not be treated as products of foreign origin.

Another form of sophisticated foreign protection is the requirement to register products that enter countries targeted for Slovenian exports. Pharmaceuticals typically encounter this kind of protection. For example, one Slovenian factory (LELJ, included in the sample) registered a single medicine in the USA, which helped to increase its exports by US$40 million. Similar obstacles are standards requested by the authorities of countries that import Slovenian products. This was emphasized by several of the companies interviewed, such as LELJ in pharmaceuticals; TODO in health and beauty products; IEKR which produces electric meters; and SVKA which produces towels.

Credit and Payment Arrangements Abroad

Our survey shows that on average payment arrangements are more difficult for the imports of Slovenian companies than for their exports, especially for smaller companies like TRKA and FEMA included in the sample. It is interesting that for some of the companies interviewed, payments from abroad are obtained in a shorter period of time than payments from domestic clients.

Before Slovenia became an independent country, its enterprises made use of credit lines abroad granted for former Yugoslavia (with special favorable treatment) and clearing payment arrangements that were in place in trade with most of the CMEA countries; the exceptions were Czechoslovakia and, at a later stage, Hungary.

After its proclamation of independence in 1991, political recognition of the newly established country was not easy to achieve, and thus credit was not readily available abroad for Slovenian imports and exports. Credit and guarantee lines were slowly reopened, with Germany in the forefront (Hermes). At the same time the country risk rating improved greatly, and already there is probably too much credit available in international markets for Slovenian enterprises and banks.

The idea of a payment union or some type of clearing arrangement among the successor states of Yugoslavia was proposed in recent international conferences. It was clearly stated, however, that Slovenia, which has an excess and not a lack of foreign currency, is not interested in these kinds of arrangements.

One way to solve payment difficulties that arise in the East is for Slovenian exporters to use intermediaries from the West to support their exports, namely, businesspersons born in Eastern countries who have established trading companies in the West. With their connections in the East, these intermediaries are able to arrange payments much more easily than Slovenian firms that export directly. A drawback to this approach, however, is the additional cost of such intermediation. In our sample, MELJ trading company uses a Swiss intermediary with a Romanian background for exporting to Romania.

Since 1993 foreign credits have been available to Slovenian companies, including exporters, in increasing amounts. At the beginning of Slovenia's economic transition, when domestic interest rates were extremely high, these credits were less expensive than domestic credits. However, the practical experience of the companies we interviewed (TODO and SVKA in textiles, INJA in impregnated textiles, and IEKR in electric meters) indicates that by mid-1995, with all additional costs of credits (provisions for bank guarantees, and manipulation and intermediation costs) taken into account, the costs of domestic credits were similar to those of foreign credits.

High Entry Costs

Entry costs frequently are important impediments to exports, particularly for Slovenian producers of medicines such as LELJ in our survey, whose products must be registered abroad through costly procedures. Producers of furniture and other wooden products, part of an important industry in Slovenia, often encounter difficulties entering foreign markets; two firms included in the sample, STKA and SLLJ, reported facing such obstacles. Firms like these perceive that, for all practical purposes, many Western markets are closed to them.

With strong economic relations with the West and a significant presence in Western markets already established, Slovenian firms in most cases have no special new entry costs. The exceptions are former "exporters" to Yugoslav markets that have recently redirected their exports to the West and new exporters (TODO, LIMA, and HEDO in the sample).

In order to further ease these entry barriers, business conferences have frequently been organized between Slovenia and other countries. Since 1990 there have been at least 30 such conferences, with certain countries hosting more than one meeting.

Building a good reputation for Slovenian products is a slow process. Only some brands are well-known abroad. Among the companies we interviewed, firms such as PETR (shoes), ZLMA (cosmetics), SVKA (textiles) and, ERLJ (service tables) have been the most successful at creating a good reputation in foreign markets.

Comparative Attractiveness of Domestic Market

The appreciation of the tolar between mid-1993 and mid-1995 has made the domestic market more attractive than foreign ones. However, a serious problem exists: in Slovenia's small, open economy, which has lost its principal market (former Yugoslavia), production capacities are too large for the domestic market, which cannot absorb all the domestic production potential. Therefore, exports are vital if Slovenia's growth is to continue.

As has already been mentioned above, prices in the domestic market are on average about 20% higher than those in highly competitive foreign markets; this is true, for example, for tires produced by the company SAKR and for goods produced by all the textile manufacturers in the sample. Only a few companies (probably the most successful ones) claimed to reach the same or higher price levels abroad; however, these price levels were only achieved for individual products produced under special order (ERLJ for service tables and LELJ for pharmaceuticals). The way out of this discrepancy is to decrease costs of production, not to devalue the domestic currency or try to redirect production to domestic markets. In this respect, exporting helps many companies expand toward the optimal scale of production, a point that was emphasized by companies in our sample like PETR in footwear, SAKR in tires, LELJ in medicines, and SVKA in textiles. This approach leads to lower average total costs and enables companies to survive with lower prices in exports. Moreover, full capacity utilization, including labor employment, is desirable from a purely social point of view as well.

It is obvious that the only products that can reach the highest price levels abroad are those with excellent quality, that have a new idea in design, or that are the result of a company's own research and development. Thus, it is not surprising that the food-processing company KOLJ is striving to create a totally new product that can be marketed all over Europe. Such a product would solve all the company's problems but is not easy to create. The company ERLJ may succeed in creating a special product with its production and marketing of movable service tables.

7.2.3 Impediments to exports: Supply

Costs, Exchange Rates, and Risks

Wage-related costs in Slovenia account for more than 60% of all production costs; in this respect, Slovenian wages are too high, which hampers the country's competitive position. The net average monthly wage in 1996 is nearly DM 900, significantly higher than in any other country in transition. Taxes and social security contributions appended to wages make labor costs more than double the net wages. Thus, labor costs are excessive, even if the high productivity of the country's relatively skilled work force is taken into account. A social contract for regulating wages was recently adopted to serve until, following privatization, new active private owners are able to control wages. This shift of control will not take place easily, because currently in most cases of privatization insiders obtain dominant ownership of the enterprise, especially in enterprises that perform well and in enterprises whose activities are labor intensive. For capital-intensive enterprises that perform well, the second best way for management to retain de facto control is to use the public sale of shares (through vouchers). The labor-intensive companies in our sample (SVKA, SVMA, and TODO in textiles) are especially affected by labor costs.

Even with stricter control of wages, Slovenian labor will remain relatively expensive compared with labor in East European countries. Thus in the future job work will move from the West of Europe (and out of Slovenia) to the less-developed areas of the FSU and to Asia. Job work might also shift to Africa. Some of the companies in the sample are already trying to move their factories to

Russia, the Caribbean, and North Africa; for example, electric meters produced by IEKR, pharmaceuticals produced by LELJ, and furniture manufactured by STKA are products whose production is to be relocated by the companies in our sample.

The share of job work in Slovenian exports and imports has constantly decreased since the country's independence, thus confirming that high labor costs are an impediment to its exports. The share of job work in exports was 19% in 1993, 14% in 1994, and around 11% in 1995.

Although they account for less than 10% of all production costs, interest rates (real and nominal) are still too high. However, Slovenia's interest rates probably do not exceed those in other countries in transition by much. Their high level is due to restructuring problems in the financial sector and a lack of competition in the financial market, as well as to relatively high inflation. Some recent developments, including an interbank agreement to keep upper limits for passive interest rates, and significantly decreased inflation (at the end of 1995 prices grew by only 8.6%) could help bring interest costs down.

Regarding the exchange rate, as has been stated above, administrative devaluation is technically impossible under the current regime of determining the official exchange rate using past market rates (Kožar and Cimperman, 1995). Moreover, from an economic point of view, it would not be the best solution for helping exporters in a small, open economy like Slovenia's. As shown by Bole (1994), this approach would work better in larger economics where the domestic market is not yet saturated and exports represent a smaller ratio of GDP. In Slovenia depreciation would lead to an increase in interest rates, thus increasing other costs and damaging growth prospects.[3]

The only way to increase the attractiveness of exports and improve the competitive position of Slovenian enterprises in international markets is by decreasing the costs of production. The option of fully replacing domestic inputs with imported ones because of price differentials stemming from the appreciation of the domestic currency would have negative consequences for domestic producers of raw materials. Hopefully, an increasing trade deficit combined with a decreasing inflow of "hot money" will stop appreciation, thus helping domestic producers of raw materials.

To increase their exports, some of the companies surveyed (for example, the chemical manufacturer HEDO) are willing to take higher risks when exporting to Eastern Europe than their competitors from the West. These risks are related to payments, since exporters are bound to encounter a lack of financial discipline when doing business in less-developed Eastern countries, especially the successor countries of the Soviet Union.

Information about Potential Customers and Trading Practices

Lack of information about conditions of trade is not a major obstacle to Slovenian exports because of Slovenia's longtime experience in Western markets, the efforts of the Slovenian Chamber of Commerce and other government institutions, and the general openness of the country. Western trading practices are relatively well-known in Slovenia, although additional education and experience is needed, especially with regard to new trading practices (leasing and franchising, for example).

Among the companies surveyed, the smaller and newer exporters in particular expressed the need for more organized support from the Chamber of Commerce for making contacts with potential buyers abroad and for attending fairs and business conferences. Two such examples from the sample are ERLJ, which produces furniture and wooden accessories, and TRKA, which produces electronic goods. Due to their small size, these companies are not able to develop all their business functions to the same extent as large companies, and marketing is usually the one that is not well represented.

Slovenian domestic intermediaries are still used to help export goods and services, especially by smaller producers and manufacturers of textiles. For example, the company PETR from our sample uses the services of a specialized export-import enterprise, KOTO, in its exports of footwear to Eastern markets; TTOV uses an intermediary from Ljubljana in exports to the West.

Quality, Quality Control, and Reliability

The quality of most Slovenian exports is in the upper-middle range. Experience with exports to the West has helped to improve the reliability of business connections. Although the lack of reliability is not a significant impediment to exports, efforts are needed to further improve reliability. Improving the quality of production seems to be one of the most important strategic goals for all the enterprises in the survey. The more advanced companies in the sample (for instance, IEKR, which produces electric meters, and SAKR, which manufactures rubber tires), have already obtained certificates of ISO 9000, ISO 9001, or other standards that they see as imperative for prospering in developed markets.

Most enterprises in our survey (including SVKA and SVMA in textiles and HEDO and TDRU in chemicals) listed quick reaction time and short delivery time among their competitive advantages, partly because of the smaller series they produce and partly because of their excellent geostrategic positions. These competitive advantages, when coupled with reliability, can push Slovenian exporters ahead of their counterparts from Eastern Europe.

Small, newly established exporters suffer from Slovenia's low rating as a business partner (entailing high risk) more than larger exporters with long-term business relations with foreign clients. Thus the company TRKA, which produces electronics, has not been able to obtain satisfactory payment conditions abroad for exports, whereas larger enterprises such as HEDO in chemicals were supported by the German export insurance company Hermes immediately after independence of Slovenia because of their performance record and their size.

Underdeveloped Public Infrastructure

Much should be done with respect to public infrastructure, both because of Slovenia's geographic position and because its public infrastructure is underdeveloped in comparison with equally developed countries in the West. This need for development concerns roads, railways, and telecommunications.

The current upturn of investments was started by the government in 1992 with investments in these areas of infrastructure; investments are growing with around 15% real growth rates, but they started from a very low level. The construction of almost 300 kilometers of highway by the year 2000 is planned; for a country with an area of 20,225 square kilometers, this is a significant extension of the existing network of roads. Slovenian railways should be modernized. In telecommunications, foreign competition has been allowed to enter the Slovenian market.

With regard to financial services, Slovenia currently lags behind equally developed countries in the West. Rehabilitation of the banking system is well under way and should help significantly improve this sector and make Slovenian business competitive in the West.

Access to Inputs

Slovenian exporters have no problems obtaining inputs, as was confirmed by our survey. Imports are completely liberalized, and no shortage of foreign currency impedes their purchase. However, enterprises that are not overly successful may have trouble obtaining domestic financing (working capital). This difficulty was mentioned by textile companies like SVKA in the sample.

Producing smaller series of special, higher-quality products frequently induces Slovene exporters to import high-quality raw materials, which are both more expensive and more difficult to obtain. This problem was reported by companies in our sample like ERLJ, a manufacturer of wooden products; SVKA, which produces textiles; and INJA, which manufactures impregnated textiles.

Disruptions in the supply of cheap raw materials to Slovenia from the successor states of Yugoslavia poses a major problem for many of the exporters surveyed (for instance, LIMA, a producer of steel products). New supply lines must be established and these supplies are usually more expensive than the old ones.

Present Conditions of Enterprises

The restructuring of enterprises is well under way, despite the fact that privatization is not yet complete and thus new, active private owners are not yet in control of many enterprises. In Slovenia the rehabilitation of the enterprise sector was decentralized and banks played an important role by pressuring enterprises to repay debts and to restructure in order to remain liquid and solvent.

New legislation prevents the enterprises from accumulating high levels of debt. To a certain extent, the legislation forces creditors to participate in the debt consolidation program and sometimes even to swap their claims for shares in the debtor company.

Decapitalization of enterprises that are distress borrowers and distress exporters has been used as a short-term, transitional solution for many companies with weak financial positions.

Slovenian companies lag behind those in the developed West more with respect to their institutional weaknesses than their levels of technological development. Privatization is not yet complete, and there are many unresolved ownership claims made by those who owned the companies before they were nationalized. Among the companies observed in this study, this is true for SVKA, INJA, HEDO, and PETR, for instance. Usually the share of these claims in the companies' total assets is very small, but it must be admitted that in this respect Slovenia seems to be behind many countries in transition.

The subsidiaries and factories of some Slovenian enterprises were taken over by Serbs and Montenegrins in their respective countries. The unpaid bills and the loans that are not serviced by these two countries are worsening the financial conditions of these Slovenian exporters. Companies such as SLLJ in furniture, PETR in footwear, and MELJ in food trading from the sample reported experiencing these kinds of problems.

7.2.4 Temporary or artificial incentives to exports

Among the temporary and artificial incentives to exports are domestic energy prices that are still below the estimated equilibrium price derived from world market prices. These low prices enable profitable exports of chemicals and steel. The pricing disparity is related to government control of prices and to the government's insistence on continuing to operate the country's only nuclear power plant, which produces 25% of the country's electrical energy.

Generally speaking, some so-called strategic industries are still supported by the Slovenian government to a certain extent. An example is the steel industry, which has been given subsidies and relief in the past. These subsidies enabled firms in the sector to export, but such support is artificial and should be only temporary in nature. A gradual phasing out of this support should be announced and made transparent.

Other incentives such as the opportunity to re-export smuggled materials or exports used for tax evasion are not common in Slovenia. However, Slovenian companies are making an effort, which is probably only transitory, to keep the country's ecologic standards below those in Western Europe. Maintaining lower ecological standards was one way certain Slovenian textile exporters of special materials managed to survive (this was the case with a manufacturer of tents, INJA, and a producer of textiles for medical use, TODO). In these cases, economic and social criteria are at odds with ecological criteria of welfare. Luckily this solution is not used as frequently in Slovenia as it probably is in other countries in transition.

Evidence of Slovenia's lower ecological standards in comparison with those of developed economies includes the high level of sulfur dioxide in the air, the pollution of Slovenia's waters (according to a recent analysis, exporters causes an above-average amount of this pollution), and the fact that certain toxic substances in paint produced in Slovenia are not allowed in the paint that Slovenia exports.

7.2.5 Efforts to tackle impediments to exports

The general conclusion from this study is that Slovenian enterprises are apparently trying to find a place in European markets between competitors from the West, with higher quality and higher prices, and those from the East, with lower quality and lower prices. The financially stronger companies often try to achieve standards very close to Western standards and expand exports by offering slightly lower prices. The financially weaker companies often engage in mass production and try to vanquish Eastern competitors with better quality and a more professional business approach. The future strategy of Slovenian exporters is also related to this dilemma; companies must either engage in mass production, even expanding their production facilities to countries of export destinations, or they must further improve product quality and invent new products and designs (and thus continue to produce in small series) to justify higher prices.

The following are among the efforts enterprises typically make to tackle impediments to exports:

- Enterprise downsizing was a typical reaction to transitional difficulties on the part of the exporters in this analysis. For example, two of Slovenia's best performing enterprises, the pharmaceuticals manufacturer LELJ and IEKR, which produces electric motors, were among the firms in our sample that turned to downsizing to cope with problems during the transition. Downsizing usually means dividing former "artificial" conglomerates into smaller separate enterprises, not just reducing production and laying off workers.

- Enterprises try to decrease labor costs, because wages are not competitive and most contributions for social security and taxes are attached to net wages; from the sample, the textile companies SVKA, SVMA, TODO, and INJA have pursued this approach. High wage-related taxes have also encouraged illegal employment, with a consequent savings of social security contributions.
- Privatization brings changes in management. Better educated, ambitious managers are taking over the less-successful exporting companies, which leads to or intensifies restructuring. Among the surveyed enterprises, SŽLJ in steel works, SVKA in textiles, MELJ in food trading underwent these kinds of management changes.
- In the rehabilitation procedure or the process of privatization, it is not uncommon for a foreign strategic investor to be brought in, as was the case of the company ZLMA, a producer of cosmetics. With the inclusion of a foreign investor, increased efficiency, improved management, and, usually, modernization of technology are expected.
- Lowering the prices on foreign markets is an important instrument for increasing competitiveness of exports; this approach was used by all the companies in the sample except LELJ and ERLJ. In former Yugoslavia, this kind of quasi–dumping policy was financed by higher prices in Yugoslavian domestic markets. Since Slovenia's independence, such massive cross financing is not possible. Furthermore, when privatization is completed low prices in sales abroad will cease to be financed through decapitalization, because new private owners are not expected to allow their enterprise to deplete its assets.
- Barter trade is used frequently when it is not possible to sell goods for cash payments. Thus, for instance, the chemical factory HEDO imports cars from Russia in exchange for its products.
- Job work, even if it is losing its share, is still quite important in exports, especially in labor-intensive industries such as textiles and footwear.
- Increasing specialization and production in small series is a strategic way for an exporting company to increase its competitive position, thus achieving higher prices. This factor was emphasized in the survey by the companies SVKA, a manufacturer of textiles, and KOLJ, which is active in food processing, among others.
- Efforts to improve the quality of products and shorten the reaction time to changes in world markets were also identified as measures that help an

enterprise improve its competitive position. These efforts are relevant for production that is closely connected with fashion, such as footwear (PETR), textiles (SVKA and SVMA), and cosmetics (ZLMA).

- It is important for larger companies to develop their own networks abroad because the costs of intermediation are high and increasing. Moreover, such a network can be extremely helpful for executing some of the company's other functions (marketing and research), as more advanced companies have already found out. This new strategy includes investment abroad as a way to consolidate an exporter's position on a foreign market. The trading companies SLLJ and MELJ in the sample reported attempts to develop networks abroad.

  According to macroeconomic criteria Slovenian investments abroad are desirable as a way to balance the excessive inflow of foreign currency with appropriate outflow. Many of the companies surveyed had these intentions but complained about the extensive formal procedures required by domestic authorities before permission to open subsidiaries abroad is granted. This red tape is partly related to the circumspection of authorities (capital flight) and is partly a residual of the old administrative bureaucracy.
- The smaller and newer the exporter is, the more important personal contacts are for success in exports. These contacts include the fulfillment of professional obligations, but also individual communication that increases credibility and thus eases payment conditions. This factor was emphasized by companies like ERLJ, TRKA and FEMA, all of which are small limited-liability companies that have been in existence only a short period of time.
- New forms of strategic cooperation that do not include capital investment by foreigners (i.e., the form of cooperation usually chosen by weaker domestic exporters) are being developed by more advanced Slovenian exporters. They include cooperation in production, research and development, marketing, and advertising, where fixed costs are too large for enterprises of this size. In this way the economy of scale is used effectively. The pharmaceutical company LELJ, one of the most advanced enterprises in our sample, emphasized this factor.

Other efforts made by companies in the sample include signing long-term cooperation agreements (SŽLJ and IEKR); designing and introducing one's own models (ZLMA, PETR, and SVKA); creating new products or penetrating new product markets (such as the introduction of production of cinema seats by STKA); moving production to less-developed countries (IEKR, SLLJ, and HEDO); establishing parallel joint ventures with foreign partners in Slovenia (HEDO and LELJ); and reorienting to strong markets away from former Yugoslavia (INJA, TODO, and LIMA).

7.2.6 Government policies creating or removing impediments to exports

Only rarely is the Slovenian government directly involved in creating export deals. Still, in some specific sectors (for example, strategic military products, pharmaceuticals, and electric meters) the direct involvement of the Slovenian government is warranted, especially when the importer of Slovenian products is a state enterprise or the state itself (importing products for infrastructure, military needs, or health protection).

A short survey was made of the enterprises in our sample regarding the quality of those aspects of the domestic environment of exports, that are predominantly determined by government measures. Answers were graded on the following scale: 1 = very bad, 2 = bad, 3 = moderate or neutral, 4 = good, and 5 = excellent. The average values of answers were the following:

- Situation with respect to permissions for exports or imports: 3.5;
- Situation with respect to subsidies for exports: 1.5;
- Situation with respect to tax relief for exports: 1.3;
- Existence of credit support for exports: 3.3;
- Availability of guarantees for exports: 3.25;
- Overall evaluation of measures of supporting exports: 2.44.

The overall situation is unsatisfactory in the opinion of exporters. In particular, small, up-and-coming enterprises, such as the companies ERLJ, TRKA, and FEMA in the survey, feel the lack of state support in conducting business at home and especially abroad. Clearly, at the time the survey was made no special subsidies existed for supporting exports and the tax system did not include any relief for Slovenian exporters.

According to results of the poll, the situation is better with respect to three other measures: availability of guarantees for exporters, availability of credits (here many of the complaints were about interest rates that were considered too high), and especially export and import permissions. With few exceptions, no special permission is required to export.[4]

With regard to the continued appreciation of the tolar in 1994 and 1995, in the spring of 1995 the government tried to persuade the central bank to change its exchange rate policy to one that was more "neutral," probably meaning one that would preserve purchasing power parity. However, the Bank of Slovenia did not make the requested changes.

The Slovenian government introduced two measures in May 1995 to support exporters. First, subsidies were proposed for labor-intensive exporters in the amounts of 5 billion tolars in 1995 and up to 10 billion tolars in 1996 (DM 60 and

DM 120 million, respectively). The subsidies should cover up to 40% of the social security contributions of enterprises that are net exporters and that have suffered losses due to exchange rate risk (exporters to Italy and areas where the payment currency is the US dollar). This measure was welcomed by exporters, but the amount, which was around 6% of the monthly value of exports, seemed to be far too small to have a significant impact.

Second, the government proposed an additional injection of capital into Slovenska izvozna družba (SID, the Slovenian Export Company), a kind of export-import bank. SID was established in 1992, but has not yet had much impact on exports because of its limited size. With increased capital, SID should cover commercial risks for foreign banks that give credits to foreign importers for buying Slovenian products. It is clear that the role of this bank should be increased in the future: recently, exporters of various products, not just those from the narrowly defined class of equipment, showed an interest in using its services. In general, SID currently seems willing to guarantee exports that are already secured, but unwilling or unable to help with credits and guarantees for exports to high-risk destinations.

SID currently has 25 employees. Its balance sheet showed US$60 million in total assets at the end of 1994. Its involvement in risk insurance is US$50 million insurance for political risks, US$35 million for commercial risks, and US$120 million in other insurance. The amount of outstanding guarantees currently is US$13 million. Altogether US$300 million of exports (around 5% of total exports) is covered in different forms by SID: SID's involvement is 50%, the rest is covered by banks. Besides issuing risk insurance and guarantees, SID is also involved in interest rate subsidies for credits for exports.

In 1996, in order to enhance exports, tax reliefs were introduced by the Slovenian government for all exporting enterprises, especially for labor-intensive producers.

Economic Diplomacy: Approaching the EU Institutionally

Many of the companies surveyed believe the Slovenian government should require reciprocity in free trade agreements with foreign countries. Liberalization of imports to Slovenia went so far that many enterprise managers feel that in the more recent agreements reciprocity was not established.

Several enterprises complained that Slovenia's diplomacy neglected their interests in negotiations about free trade areas and other economic agreements with foreign countries and associations. One such example from the sample is TRKA in electronics, which feels neglected in free trade arrangements with Visegrád Group. It seems that smaller exporters with weaker lobbying positions were sometimes sacrificed in the bargaining process of the free trade area agreements. Although obviously not all agents will be better off in a free trade agreement, these exporters should at least be consulted with on a regular, institutionalized basis before negotiations with foreign countries or associations start.

In the spring of 1995 an extensive poll was taken of the main Slovenian exporters about their perspectives on Slovenia's membership in the EU. More than 100 of the 200 largest exporters surveyed responded to the questionnaire. Of those enterprises that answered, 82% belong to the manufacturing sector, 14% to the trade sector, and 4% to other sectors of the economy. They represented around half the Slovenian exports and one-quarter of the imports in 1994. The results of the poll indicated that almost 92% of those questioned think that Slovenia should become a member of the EU.

The managers of large exporting firms estimated the productivity of their enterprises in comparison with the average productivity of enterprises in EU countries: 9% of enterprises have productivity below 50% of the EU level; 24% have productivity between 50% and 69% of the EU level; 51% have productivity between 70% and 81% of the EU level; and 16% have productivity above 90% of the EU level.

A quarter of the enterprises questioned think that the role of state intervention in the economy is emphasized more in the EU than in Slovenia; according to 31%, the roles in both are equally strong; and according to 44%, government intervention in the economy is stronger in Slovenia than in the EU.

Exactly 49% of those questioned think that insider ownership, which seems to be the prevailing form of privatization in Slovenia, will hamper the competitive position of these enterprises. Among the reasons given for such a conclusion were conflicts due to the dual role of workers who are also owners and preservation of the old, self-management way of thinking.

Legal Regulation

There are still many areas where the lack of Slovenian legislation and the absence of Slovenian membership in international associations present impediments to exports (Ministry of Economic Relations and Development, 1994). For example, in the pharmaceuticals industry many regulations on production and distribution of pharmaceuticals that are required in destination countries have not yet been enacted in Slovenia, which has prevented Slovenia from becoming a member of international pharmaceutical associations. As a consequence, Slovenian exporters must go through an especially complex process to obtain approval for certain medicines for export to foreign countries. The company LELJ in the sample reported experiencing these difficulties.

Through their legal activities, Slovenian authorities sometimes even increase impediments to exports. One example of a government-induced export barrier is the recent introduction of a special 5% tax rate for earnings from export services.

Foreign Exchange Regime

When in 1991 Slovenia adopted the Law on Foreign Exchange Business and the Law on Credit Transactions with Foreign Countries, two of the so-called Independence Laws, it abolished the administrative regulation of foreign trade operations. Internal convertibility of the tolar in relation to foreign currencies (introduced 7 October 1991) gave all citizens the right to open their own foreign currency accounts. Enterprises must exchange foreign currency into domestic currency within 48 hours after inflow. At the same time, with few exceptions, firms are not allowed to have foreign currency accounts. External convertibility has been formally taking place as of 1 September 1995.

Instruments of Foreign Trade Policy

The Law on Credit Transactions with Foreign Countries allows legal entities to borrow money from abroad. For banks to borrow from abroad, appropriate authorization from the Bank of Slovenia is needed.

Currently, import restrictions are applied in Slovenia only on some textile and agricultural products, and even these restrictions are weak.

A new Law on Customs Services and the Law on Customs Tariffs were adopted in 1995 and came into force in 1996. With these new laws, the Slovenian customs system is moving closer to the regulations of developed Europe, simplifying customs procedures and including internationally agreed rules on customs procedures.

Currently the uniform tariff rate is 15% and its scope is from 0–15%. However, several products are exempted from the tariffs; the average tariff rate in 1993 was 12%, while the rate effectively paid in 1994 was close to 6%. A special decree in 1994 stipulated the exemption from customs duties of imported raw materials and production materials that are used for export production if the goods are exported no later than one year after the import of these materials. In 1996, import tariffs were reduced further. This process will continue in 1997 in accordance with the requirements of the Association Agreement with the EU.

Export duties were introduced as a temporary measure to prevent disturbances on the domestic market in the supply of certain raw materials. For example, duties were introduced for wood (up to 15% of the customer value for some kinds of unprocessed wood and 10% for processed wood) and for certain metal waste (amounting to 25%).

Exports are not subject to any internal taxation. Internal turnover tax rates in Slovenia range from 5–32% for products and from 1–20% for services. The turnover tax is the only major tax instrument in place, but preparations are being made to introduce the value-added tax.

One impediment to Slovenian exports (and imports) is the lengthy duration of customs procedures at Slovenian borders. Compared with the customs authorities of its neighbors, such as Austria, Slovenian authorities require twice as much paper work and twice as much time and money to complete the documents necessary for exports or imports.

It is important that reverse preferential treatment not be given to foreign exporters to Slovenia; that is, foreign firms should not receive better treatment than domestic companies in the domestic market with regard to taxes, for instance. The companies in the sample frequently observed that in different areas foreign exporters to Slovenia receive better treatment in the form of customs duties and information about markets than Slovenian exporters to these countries. This situation was reported by SVMA, SVKA, and TODO in textiles; LELJ in medicines; and KOLJ and MELJ in food processing and trade. The Slovenian authorities' desire to increase competition in the domestic market apparently goes too far at times.

Notes

[1] For more information on the evolution of the Slovenian economy's legal framework, see, for example in Gray and Štiblar (1993).

[2] Section 7.1.4. is based on Štiblar (1995).

[3] Namely, by depreciating the exchange rate the foreign balance surplus would increase. Consequently a larger part of the total amount of national savings would be needed to finance the external surplus. Accordingly, the source of funds for domestic investment would be reduced, which would push up interest rates in domestic markets. Thus, only increasing the total amount of national savings (through real wage decreases, for instance) would provide adequate sources for investments, both external (investment abroad because of the surplus) and domestic, without raising interest rates.

[4] The only complaint among some of the interviewed enterprises was that no special permission is required for importing, either; at least some of these firms would like to see some restrictions. They consider the present situation too liberal, with many firms importing and no requirements for standards.

References

Aiginger, K., Peneder, M., and Stankovsky, J., 1994, The explanatory power of market-based trade theories for the trade between market economies and reform countries, *Empirica*, **41**:197–220.

Baldwin, R.E., 1994, Towards an Integrated Europe, Centre for Economic Policy Research, London, UK.

Bole, V., 1994, Sektorski učinki realne apreciacije tečaja in "menjalnost" proizvodnje (Sectoral effects of real appreciation and tradability of production), GG 12/1994, EIPF Ljubljana, Slovenia: 25–37.

Gray, C., Štiblar, F., 1993, The evolving legal framework for private sector activity in Slovenia, *Journal of International Business Law*, Spring, XIV/2: 119–167.

Gros, D., and Vandille, G., 1995, Slovenian and European Trade Structures, Centre for European Policy Studies and University of Frankfurt, ACE Project, Frankfurt, Germany: 1–18 [mimeograph].

Kimball, J.D., 1994, East-Central Economies in Transition [mimeograph].

Kožar, A., and Cimperman, F., 1995, Medvalutna razmerja in stvarna podoba o blagovnih tokovih Slovenije s tujino (Relations among currencies and the true picture about trade flows of Slovenia) (1), *Bančni Vestnik*, 1-2: 22–26.

Krugman, P., 1991, Rethinking International Trade, Cambridge, MA, USA.

Kumer, A., 1995, La Liberalisation du commerce et l'Union Europeénne, June.

Landesmann, M.A., 1995, Balance of Payments Constrained Growth in Eastern Europe, paper presented at LINK Meeting, in March 1995 at New York, NY, USA.

Linder, K., 1961, *An Essay on Trade and Transformation*, John Wiley, New York, NY, USA.

Mencinger, J., 1994, Slovensko – nemška trgovinska menjava (Slovene–German trade), GG, 5/1994 EIPF: 21–35.

Ministry of Economic Relations and Development, 1994, Foreign Trade Regime of the Republic of Slovenia, April, Ministry of Economic Relations and Development, Ljubljana, Slovenia: 1–54.

Potočnik, J., 1993, Input-output tabela Slovenije za 1988, ZMAR, Ljubljana, Slovenia.

Potočnik, J., Senjur, M., and Štiblar, F., 1995, The Strategy for Economic Development of Slovenia: Approaching Europe – Growth, Competitiveness and Integration, Institute of Macroeconomic Analysis and Development, Ljubljana, Slovenia.

Statistical Office of Slovenia, *Statistical Yearbooks of Slovenia*, various issues, Statistical Office of Slovenia, Ljubljana, Slovenia.

Statistical Office of Slovenia, 1994, *Slovenia in Figures*, Statistical Office of Slovenia, Ljubljana, Slovenia.

Statistical Office of Slovenia, 1995, *Statistical Data on International Trade of Slovenia*, Statistical Office of Slovenia, Ljubljana, Slovenia (internal materials).

Štiblar, F., 1993a, Slovenia's Independence, Economic Transition and International Reaction, September, Woodrow Wilson Center, Washington, DC, USA: 1–49.

Štiblar, F., 1993b, Strategija Slovenije v ekonomskih odnosih s tujino (Slovenia's Strategy in Foreign Economic Relations), GG 9/1993, EIPF, Ljubljana, Slovenia: 21–35.

Štiblar, F., 1995, Spremembe zunanje menjave v preobrazbi Slovenije, Gospodarska gibanja (Changes of Foreign Trade in Transformation of Slovenia), EIPF, 1995/2 Ljubljana, Slovenia.

Štiblar, F., and Vidovic, H., 1993, Slovenia's External Position, Special Studies Series, July, WIIW, Vienna, Austria: 1–33.

Part II

Topical Studies

Chapter 8

Impediments to the Recovery of Russia's Trade with East European Small Economies

Vladimir Drebentsov

In recent years Russia's trade with East European countries has decreased drastically. For decades this region was by far the Soviet Union's main trade partner, accounting for about 60% of Soviet foreign trade in the 1980s. Yet in 1995 this region accounted for just under 10% of Russia's trade, and it seemingly continues to lose importance for both Russian exporters and importers. These radical changes raise some serious questions. Is the extraordinary speed at which trade between former Council for Mutual Economic Assistance (CMEA) partners has collapsed a sign of a temporary decline? Or is this contraction (or more precisely, its steepness) evidence of the former artificial character of all economic relations within the CMEA bloc?

If the causes of the collapse are only temporary, the effects of the short-term shock caused by the one-time dismantling of the mechanisms of the USSR's economic cooperation with its European allies should level out with time. After the inevitable transition period, there could be a revival of trade relations between Russia and Eastern Europe, bringing with it if not the record-high trade volumes of the past then at least a much higher level of such trade than exists in the current slump.

The views presented in this chapter are those of the author and cannot be attributed to the World Bank.

Conversely, the recent contraction in trade may reflect the artificial character of trade relations within the CMEA. One can recall, for instance, that the countries of this region contributed less than 10% to Soviet foreign trade during the period between the two World Wars.[1] If this view is correct, it should become apparent that the extremely high level of mutual economic dependence within the CMEA, of which trade was just one component, was only a consequence of a "socialist fortress" policy that enforced ties between the bloc's members. Because it was conceived in order to achieve maximum self-sufficiency (with little regard to the economic feasibility of such a goal), this policy in effect restricted trade between the USSR and Eastern Europe on the one hand, and the rest of the world on the other, thus limiting the international division of labor primarily to members of the "club." If this ideological reasoning truly was the main driving force behind the USSR's extensive trade with East European partners, then elimination of this factor would obviously cause the entire system to collapse. Moreover, in this case Russia's trade with Eastern Europe could potentially decline further.

To determine which of the suggested arguments (or what combination of them) is relevant to reality, it is necessary first to analyze trade data at a disaggregated level. This analysis will provide us with more accurate insight into what exactly the general collapse of Russia–Eastern Europe trade has meant for each individual country and consequently show the main impediments to revitalizing exports to Russia faced by eight small East European economies: Bulgaria, the Czech Republic, Estonia, Hungary, Latvia, Romania, Slovakia, and Slovenia. In making this analysis, attention should be paid to some obvious distinctions between the six from these eight countries that did not belong to the former Soviet Union (FSU) and the two FSU countries that did. The countries currently belong to the same region, but the historical differences between them are numerous, including their different classifications in Russian trade statistics, the different levels of "transparency" of their customs borders with Russia (at least during a significant part of the period under analysis), and peculiarities of the Russian government's commercial policy toward them. With this in mind, the eight economies under consideration are split into two groups for this analysis. As a result, the chapter discusses the following topics: the dynamics, composition, and main features of Russia's imports from the six non-FSU economies between 1985 and 1994; short- and long-term reasons for recent trade restructuring between Russia and non-FSU East European economies; the dynamics and peculiarities of Russia's imports from the two Baltic FSU economies in the 1990s; and chances for eliminating the current impediments to trade within the region and the prospects of expanding Russia's imports from the eight East European economies.

8.1 Non-FSU Economies: Eliminating the CMEA Legacy and Searching for a New Specialization

As *Table 8.1* shows, several countries' contributions to Russia's imports have declined on average by a factor of five during the period from 1988 to 1995.[2] It is also quite evident that this contraction has been uneven among countries. Bulgaria and Romania have lost the largest proportions of their exports to Russia. Hungary and Slovenia clearly have done better: their share of the Russian import market has shrunk by a factor of three, which is quite an achievement compared with Romania's almost 10-fold decrease. These differences in the standings of East European countries can be traced to each nation's specialization in the Russian market, or more precisely, to the extent to which such specialization matched the changing requirements of the Russian economy (at both the enterprise and household consumer levels).

In fact, some of the problems of socialist countries' specialization in the Russian market had already surfaced prior to 1988. This can be seen in *Table 8.2*, which shows the somewhat different patterns of Russia's import requirements and the socialist countries' exports to Russia between 1985 and 1989. In many cases where Russia's reliance on imports grew during that period the share of imports from socialist countries in Russian consumption declined.

In fact, of the 12 product groups for which an increase in Russia's reliance on imports was recorded for that period, the socialist countries maintained their positions in just 3 (railroad cranes, railroad cars, and trolleybuses); moreover, these countries remained exclusive suppliers of these goods to Russia. For three other product groups, industrial robots, sewing machines for home use, and detergents, imports from socialist countries grew more slowly than those from other regions (particularly for detergents) so that although the niche of socialist countries in the Russian market increased, it expanded less than the niches of other countries. As for the rest of the commodities with potential for import growth, the socialist countries definitely dropped out as serious exporters during these years. The increase in the share of imports in the Russian market benefited the developed countries and, to a lesser extent the developing countries. Socialist countries were crowded out of Russia's lucrative imports market.[3] It is important to note that this situation developed prior to the breakdown of the CMEA, and thus was not due to factors associated with this event, but to other disadvantages of importing from the socialist bloc.

The six East European small economies (EESEs) have not been exceptions to the above-mentioned trend. The experiences of the companies surveyed for this chapter clearly illustrate this fact.[4] By the end of 1994 none of the 10 companies

Table 8.1. The share of selected East European countries in Russian imports (in percent).

Country	(*A*) 1988	(*B*) 1995	Decline by factor (*A*)/(*B*)
Bulgaria	10.57	1.42	7.4
Czechoslovakia	10.48	1.32/0.88[a]	4.8
Hungary	7.60	2.50	3.0
Romania	3.74	0.39	9.6
Slovenia	3.30[b]	1.02	3.2
Total	35.69	7.54	4.7

[a]Czech Republic/Slovakia.
[b]Figure is for all of Yugoslavia.
Sources: Calculated on a basis of *Foreign Economic Relations of the USSR in 1989* (1990) and State Customs Committee (1995, 1996).

Table 8.2. The share of selected imported commodities in Russian consumption by type of country of origin (in percent).

	1985 (domestic consumption)		1989 (domestic consumption)	
Item	Share of total imports	Share of imports from socialist countries	Share of total imports	Share of imports from socialist countries
Industrial robots	5.3	4.4	11.8	8.3
Railway cranes	22.5	22.5	30.5	30.5
Textile equipment	52.9	47.6	57.8	37.2
Knitting equipment	52.2	46.4	68.4	20.9
Sewing equipment	42.2	33.4	78.9	13.4
Fur/leather/footwear equipment	73.0	40.0	82.1	17.9
Chemical machinery	55.5	31.6	61.4	20.4
Railway cars	24.8	24.8	33.3	33.3
Trolleybuses	10.7	10.7	14.8	14.8
Detergents	3.7	3.4	22.7	4.3
Sewing machines for home use	3.3	3.3	8.5	4.9
TV sets	0.4	0.0	1.6	0.0

Note: Calculations were made by the Ministry of Foreign Economic Relations' Institute for Economic Analysis; the imports selected were major commodities in imports whose share in domestic consumption grew between 1985 and 1989.
Source: *Foreign Economic Relations of the USSR in 1989* (1990).

surveyed maintained the high level of dependence on EESE imports that had been typical for them in 1988. In 1988 imports from EESEs contributed 40–90% to these companies' total imports, with five companies having shares of EESE imports over 70%; by 1994 this range had contracted to 0–35%, with eight companies having shares of EESE imports below 6%.

To grasp the basic features of this process and to recognize common problems and individual peculiarities more generally, it is necessary to take a more detailed look at the EESEs specialization on the Russian market. With this purpose in mind, we have analyzed the structural dynamics of Russia's major imports from EESEs beginning in 1985.[5] The results show that the structure of major imports remained fairly stable across all EESEs between 1985 and 1988. In fact, with only a few exceptions (imports of drilling equipment from Romania and ships from Yugoslavia), changes in the structure did not exceed a few percentage points during this period.[6] Moreover, even these exceptions were understandable: because of the high unit value, even minor changes in the volume inevitably caused quite noticeable changes in the value of these particular import items. This relative inflexibility was just another manifestation of the growing inconsistency between Soviet import requirements and patterns of earlier EESE exports to the Soviet Union. Most likely the impetus for this trend came from both ends: on the one hand the USSR switched its demand for new imports from traditional CMEA partners to the West; on the other hand the EESEs were not very interested in the Soviet market at this time.

The rather stable structure of Soviet imports from particular EESEs in the second part of the 1980s allows us to define each EESE's specialization on the Russian market. For this purpose we have regrouped the four-digit data into six broader categories:

I. Agricultural products/foodstuffs;
II. Chemical products;
III. Nonfood consumer products;
IV. Industrial machinery;
V. Transport machinery;
VI. Nonindustrial equipment.

This breakdown shows that in 1988 group IV products dominated major imports from Bulgaria (32% of total imports; see *Table 8.3*). Group IV products also led imports – though with a narrower margin – from Romania (30%), Czechoslovakia (22%), and Yugoslavia (19%). Group V products led imports from Hungary (18%), and were the second most important for shipments from Czechoslovakia (13%) and the third most important from Yugoslavia (13%) and Romania (12%). Group III products were second in importance in Romania (18%) and in Yugoslavia

Table 8.3. Aggregated structure of Russia's imports from EESEs.

	1988		1994	
	Aggregated commodity group	Aggregated commodity group's share in total imports (%)	Aggregated commodity group	Aggregated commodity group's share in total imports (%)
Bulgaria	I	8.9	I	27.6
	II	5.4	II	15.7
	III	0.9	III	3.4
	IV	32.0	IV	10.2
	V	1.3	V	4.5
			VI	1.4
Czechoslovakia/ Czech Republic	III	8.5	I	5.4
	IV	21.7	II	6.6
	V	13.4	III	9.6
			V	13.7
			VI	5.8
Hungary	I	14.0	I	18.6
	II	7.5	II	15.7
	III	5.5	III	0.6
	IV	4.2	IV	7.2
	V	18.0	V	16.4
	VI	3.9	VI	1.0
Romania	I	2.5	I	35.9
	III	18.1	II	1.8
	IV	29.5	III	11.4
	V	12.0	IV	27.7
			V	0.6
			VI	2.6
Yugoslavia(1988)/ Slovenia(1994)	II	7.5	I	4.1
	III	15.2	II	30.2
	IV	19.1	III	17.1
	V	13.1	IV	5.0
			V	5.8
Czechoslovakia/ Slovakia	III	8.5	I	5.0
	IV	21.7	II	8.8
	V	13.4	III	10.1
			IV	11.2
			VI	8.1

Sources: *Foreign Trade of the USSR in 1988* (1989) and State Customs Committee (1995).

(15%). Group I products were the second most important among imports from Hungary (14%). Each of the groups mentioned above has contributed over 10% to imports from at least one of the EESEs; other combinations of commodity group and country have not reached this 10% threshold.

Looking at the same data from a slightly different angle, one may notice three other interesting features: in 1988 imports from Romania and Yugoslavia were the most concentrated, with three aggregated groups of major imports contributing 60% and 47% to total imports from these countries, respectively; imports from Hungary were the most diversified (all six aggregated groups were present), and imports from Czechoslovakia were the least diversified (just three groups were present); and aggregated imports from Bulgaria were the most unevenly dispersed, ranging from less than 1% to almost 32%. Finally, if one sums the aggregated groups across EESEs, it becomes evident that machinery for industrial use was the primary area of specialization of these countries, with everything else lagging behind. A detailed analysis of the main causes of the drastic reduction in Russian imports from EESEs will be provided later in the chapter. For now it is sufficient to mention that the EESEs' sheer overconcentration of exports on investment goods to Russia was bound to have a severe impact on their trade with Russia when the latter fell into a deep economic crisis.

A more subtle picture of EESE specialization in the USSR/Russian market can be seen through the calculation and analysis of the so-called relative specialization (revealed comparative advantage) indicator and the countries' shares in Russian imports of specific commodity groups (see *Table 8.4*).[7] Specialization indices calculated for four-digit trade data show that in 1988 *Bulgaria* was the most specialized of all exporters to Russia in the following products (given in descending order by level of specialization): cigarettes, forklift vehicles, computer components, fortified wines, and preserved fruits. As the import shares indicate, Bulgaria was also the main (in some cases almost the exclusive) source of Russian imports of these goods: its shares in total imports of the commodity groups mentioned above were 98%, 97%, 69%, 67%, and 40%, respectively.

In 1988 *Czechoslovakia* mainly specialized in trucks, textile machinery, metal-rolling mills, power-generating equipment, railroad locomotives, spare parts for trucks, leather footwear, and furniture; its shares in Russia's imports for these commodity groups were 87%, 47%, 37%, 32%, 30%, 30%, 27%, and 25%, respectively. Also in 1988, *Hungary* specialized in the following products (its share in Russia's imports of the respective commodity group is given in parentheses): buses (96%), frozen poultry (76%), frozen meat (71%), vegetable preserves (65%), and fortified wines (38%). *Romania's* main specialization was drilling equipment (67%), furniture (21%), frozen meat (17%), railroad rolling stock (16%), and apparel (12%). *Yugoslavia's* comparative specialization was in car batteries (31%),

Table 8.4. Changes in East European countries' specializations and their shares in Russian market, 1988 and 1994.

Country/Item	Country's share in imports of comm. group (%)	Relative specialization (revealed comparative advantage)
Bulgaria (1988)		
Total	10.57	3.68
Fruits/berries, preserved	40.03	3.79
Fortified wines incl. sparkling	67.46	6.38
Cigars/cigarettes/cigarillos	97.59	9.23
Pharmaceuticals	17.28	1.64
Perfumery/cosmetics	27.73	2.62
Apparel	3.85	0.36
Forklift vehicles	96.69	9.15
Agricultural machinery	15.13	1.43
Metal-cutting machine tools/ press-forging equip.	15.73	1.49
Computer components	68.69	6.50
Electrotechnical machinery	11.69	1.11
Ships/vessels and shipping equip.	4.95	0.47
Bulgaria (1994)		
Total	1.22	10.11
Citrus fruit, fresh or dried	1.08	0.88
Prepared/preserved meat products	3.57	2.93
Pickled vegetables/fruits/nuts	20.19	16.57
Prepared/preserved tomatoes	29.98	24.60
Vegetables prepared without vinegar/not frozen	16.49	13.53
Sauces, condiments, mustard, flour, and meal	20.07	16.47
Fortified wines incl. sparkling	10.98	9.01
Spirits/hard liquors	3.60	2.95
Cigars/cigarettes/cigarillos	5.32	4.37
Pharmaceuticals	3.89	3.19
Dental pharmaceuticals	25.71	21.10
Printed books/brochures/leaflets	5.30	4.35
Steam/vapor-generating boilers	20.32	16.68
Forklift vehicles	20.33	16.69
Electro-mechanical tools	24.19	19.85
Parts/accessories for excavators, bulldozers, etc.	2.83	2.32
Car batteries	13.31	10.92
Medical equipment	2.63	2.16
Furniture and parts thereof	2.14	1.75
Czechoslovakia (1988)		
Total	10.48	2.55
Apparel	11.98	1.14

Table 8.4. Continued.

Country/Item	Country's share in imports of comm. group (%)	Relative specialization (revealed comparative advantage)
Leather footwear	27.48	2.62
Tubes/pipes	7.71	0.74
Power-generating equip.	32.14	3.07
Chemical machinery	16.05	1.53
Hoisting and conveying equip.	8.86	0.85
Agricultural machinery	15.42	1.47
Food-processing machinery	16.20	1.55
Textile machinery	46.60	4.45
Metal-rolling mills	36.51	3.48
Metal-cutting machine tools/ press-forging equip.	9.54	0.91
Railway/locomotive rolling stock and parts thereof	29.81	2.84
Trucks	86.97	8.30
Parts/accessories for motor vehicles	29.59	2.82
Furniture	25.47	2.43
Czech Republic (1994)		
Total	1.41	11.34
Cane/beet sugar	1.28	0.91
Chocolate/cocoa foodstuffs	2.27	1.61
Pharmaceuticals	1.17	0.83
Footwear with rubber sole and leather upper	5.69	4.03
Table/kitchen/office glassware	40.83	28.93
Steel/iron tubes/pipes/hollow profiles	2.10	1.49
Parts of engines	11.21	7.94
Air/vacuum pumps	5.84	4.14
Refrigerators/freezers	5.68	4.02
Industrial/laboratory equipment	1.69	1.20
Self-propelled bulldozers	1.49	1.05
Equipment for food-processing industry	1.32	0.94
Machinery for pulp and paper industry	20.25	14.34
Electrical lighting/signalling equipment for motor vehicles	32.37	22.93
Electric apparatus for telephone/telegraph lines	1.39	0.98
Locomotives/trams, components and parts	34.31	24.31
Buses	4.90	3.47
Trucks	13.81	9.78
Chassis fitted with engines	55.78	39.51
Parts/accessories for motor vehicles	6.61	4.68
Light ships, dredgers, etc.	83.74	59.33
Prefabricated building components	7.44	5.27

Table 8.4. Continued.

Country/Item	Country's share in imports of comm. group (%)	Relative specialization (revealed comparative advantage)
Slovakia (1994)		
Total	0.74	8.64
Sugar confectionery not containing cocoa	1.33	1.80
Chocolate/cocoa confectionery	0.86	1.16
Pitch/pitch coke	11.69	15.87
New pneumatic rubber tires	25.37	34.43
Footwear with rubber sole and leather upper	3.24	4.39
Other footwear	1.98	2.69
Iron/non-alloy steel flat-rolled products	11.32	15.36
Parts of engines	5.75	7.80
Pumps for liquids	0.83	1.13
Derricks/cranes/straddle carriers	2.79	3.79
Self-propelled bulldozers	1.95	2.64
Electric motors/generators	14.90	20.23
Electric current adapters	12.09	16.41
Cars	1.26	1.71
Parts/accessories for motor vehicles	2.69	3.65
Cruise ships/similar vessels	12.38	16.80
Medical/veterinary instruments/appliances	2.63	3.56
Furniture and parts thereof	1.53	2.07
Hungary (1988)		
Total	7.60	4.35
Meat, frozen	71.23	9.37
Poultry, frozen	75.70	9.96
Wheat	7.41	0.97
Preserved vegetables	64.99	8.55
Fortified wines incl. sparkling	38.27	5.04
Pharmaceuticals	20.93	2.75
Insecticides/herbicides	21.70	2.86
Knitted goods	10.24	1.35
Apparel	6.02	0.79
Leather footwear	11.86	1.56
Agricultural machinery	9.86	1.30
Food-processing machinery	12.05	1.59
Buses	95.80	12.61
Parts/accessories for motor vehicles	44.04	5.79
Laboratory equip.	16.66	2.19
Medical equip.	22.02	2.90

Table 8.4. Continued.

Country/Item	Country's share in imports of comm. group (%)	Relative specialization (revealed comparative advantage)
Hungary (1994)		
Total	2.69	5.21
Pork, fresh/frozen	2.96	1.10
Apples, pears, and quinces, fresh	11.87	4.42
Corn	21.83	8.13
Vegetables/fruit/nuts	30.36	11.30
Vegetables prepared without vinegar/not frozen	26.74	9.96
Fruit/vegetable juices	17.67	6.58
Pharmaceuticals	9.54	3.55
Insecticides/fungicides/herbicides	6.25	2.33
Fur coats/apparel	12.59	4.69
Leather footwear	1.40	0.52
Parts of engines	13.68	5.09
Electric ignition/starting equip.	20.63	7.68
Equip. for food-processing industry	3.99	1.48
Specialized mechanical appliances for industrial use	1.79	0.67
Taps/cocks/valves for pipe tank	20.29	7.55
Buses	29.42	10.95
Cars	7.14	2.66
Parts/accessories for motor vehicles	26.48	9.86
Medical equipment	1.04	0.39
Romania (1988)		
Total	3.74	3.87
Meat, frozen	16.99	4.55
Knitted goods	11.46	3.07
Apparel	11.71	3.13
Leather footwear	5.89	1.58
Iron/steel rolls	4.89	1.31
Tubes/pipes	4.29	1.15
Drilling equip.	67.15	17.96
Agricultural machinery	6.59	1.76
Metal-cutting machine tools/ press-forging equip.	3.60	0.96
Railway/locomotive rolling stock and parts thereof	16.26	4.35
Ships/vessels and shipping equip.	4.39	1.17
Furniture	20.55	5.50

Table 8.4. Continued.

Country/Item	Country's share in imports of comm. group (%)	Relative specialization (revealed comparative advantage)
Romania (1994)		
Total	0.52	15.38
Pork, fresh/ frozen	20.94	40.55
Vegetables/fruit/nuts	0.86	1.68
Fruit/vegetable juices	0.24	0.46
Pharmaceuticals	0.23	0.44
Steel/iron tubes/pipes/hollow profiles	1.14	2.21
Iron industrial reinforcement, structures/parts	4.14	8.02
Reservoirs/tanks/vessels	44.24	85.68
Central heating boilers	38.02	73.64
Parts/accessories for excavators, bulldozers, etc.	1.29	2.49
Drilling/boring/milling machine-tools	4.91	9.50
Machine-tools for wood/cork/bone industry	1.17	2.26
Industrial equipment parts/ accessories for tools of groups 8456-8465	1.14	2.21
Sorting/screening/washing machinery	1.27	2.46
Machinery for special purposes	0.66	1.28
Taps/cocks/valves for pipe tank	22.31	43.22
Television sets	0.25	0.49
Television and radio equip. parts/accessories	3.63	7.03
Parts/accessories for motor vehicles	0.48	0.92
Furniture and parts thereof	3.92	7.59
Yugoslavia (1988)		
Total	3.30	3.38
Pharmaceuticals	3.84	1.16
Paints/varnishes	7.70	2.33
Plastic materials	4.35	1.32
Carpeting	27.01	8.18
Knitted goods	5.84	1.77
Apparel	2.12	0.64
Leather footwear	26.75	8.10
Iron/steel rolls	4.01	1.21
Drilling equip.	6.60	2.00
Food-processing machinery	6.22	1.88
Metal-cutting machine tools/ press-forging equip.	8.76	2.65
Industrial reinforcements/ metal structures	22.89	6.93
Electrotechnical machinery	5.73	1.73
Car batteries	30.61	9.27
Ships/vessels and shipping equip.	13.21	4.00
Furniture	2.71	0.82

Table 8.4. Continued.

Country/Item	Country's share in imports of comm. group (%)	Relative specialization (revealed comparative advantage)
Slovenia (1994)		
Total	0.81	8.66
Sugar confectionery not containing cocoa	0.85	1.05
Chocolate/cocoa confectionery	0.49	0.61
Cereal, flour, starch, milk products	10.55	13.02
Pharmaceuticals	4.79	5.91
Paints/varnishes	12.34	15.22
Mastics/paints' fillings	11.23	13.85
Semifinished plastic products	18.19	22.44
Footwear with rubber sole and leather upper	1.66	2.04
Iron industrial reinforcement, structures/parts	8.05	9.94
Wooden and iron tableware and cooking tools	17.43	21.51
Derricks/cranes/straddle carriers	1.96	2.42
Equipment for food-processing industry	1.36	1.68
Car batteries	4.88	6.02
Electric ignition/starting equipment	25.35	31.28
Electric apparatus for telephone/telegraph lines	2.58	3.19
Trucks	0.93	1.15
Parts/accessories for motor vehicles	1.12	1.39
Trailers/semitrailers	7.94	9.79
Furniture and parts thereof	3.60	4.44
Lamps/lighting equipment	5.03	6.21

Explanation of the relative specialization (revealed comparative advantage) index is given in note [7].
Source: Author's calculations based on *Foreign Trade of the USSR in 1988* (1989) and State Customs Committee (1995).

carpeting (27%), leather footwear (27%), industrial reinforcements/metal structures (23%), and ships (13%).

It is noteworthy that with exception of Yugoslavia EESEs fulfilled the bulk of Russian import needs for most of the commodity groups in which they specialized. Consequently, it is apparent that any decrease in Russian demand for these products would have an adverse effect primarily on EESEs. Moreover, bearing in mind that these were the EESEs' major exports to Russia, one could rightly assume that such an event would influence the entire pattern of EESE trade with Russia, which is exactly what was observed over the past three to five years.

The substantial restructuring of exports of EESEs is indicated by the disappearance of many of the 1988 major four-digit commodity groups by 1994. For instance, as *Table 8.4* shows, of Bulgaria's 12 major exports to Russia in 1988, only

6 four-digit commodity groups remained on the list of Russia's major imports from Bulgaria by 1994. The most drastic revision occurred in imports from Romania, where over this same time span only 4 commodity groups of 12 continued to be major imports for Russia. This drop in major exports was not left uncompensated: new major exports to Russia have replaced those that have dropped from the list.

It is no surprise that the pattern of EESE specialization in 1994 was significantly different from the pattern of 1988. This change is reflected in the statistics for 1994. The following list, based on revealed comparative advantage indices, presents those commodity groups that the countries were most specialized in their exports to Russia. The figures in parentheses show the respective country's share in total Russian imports of a commodity group. In 1994 *Bulgaria* appeared to specialize in preserved tomatoes (30%), dental pharmaceuticals (26%), electro-mechanical tools (24%), and forklift vehicles (20%). By 1994, the *Czech Republic* was specializing in lighthouse vessels (84%), chassis fitted with engines (56%), table glassware (41%), and locomotives (34%). In that year *Slovakia's* specialization was in tires (25%), electric motors and generators (15%), cruise ships (12%), and electric adapters (12%). For *Hungary* the products of specialization in 1994 were fruits and vegetables (30%), buses (29%), vegetable preserves (27%), and parts and accessories for motor vehicles (26%). *Romania* specialized in reservoirs and tanks (44%), central heating boilers (38%), pipe taps and valves (22%), and pork (21%). *Slovenia* specialized in electric ignition equipment (25%), semifinished plastic products (18%), wooden and iron tableware and cooking tools (17%), and paints and varnishes (12%).

The lists of commodities constituting the EESEs' major exports to Russia in 1994 indicate a considerably lower Russian reliance on imports from EESEs in 1994 than in 1988. Our enterprise survey provides more evidence of this shift. In addition to a drastic contraction of the surveyed companies' reliance on EESE imports, practically none of the 10 companies surveyed was importing the same products from EESEs in 1994 as it had imported in 1988. Even more interesting, the survey explicitly demonstrated a shift in the pattern of imports from industrial products to consumer goods. While most companies reported only industrial products among their major imports from EESEs in 1988, as of 1994 five of them had consumer goods on this list (two firms had completely ceased to import from EESEs). One of the most striking anecdotal examples in this respect is the case of Prommashimport, a company that, as its name implies, specializes in imports of industrial equipment. In 1988 its imports from EESEs consisted mainly of equipment for the wood processing and construction industries, which contributed 25% and 20% to the company's total imports, respectively. By 1994 its sole import from EESEs was canned vegetables (2% of total imports). The reasons for this radical reorientation will be analyzed later in the text, but in general they are primarily related to economic restructuring within Russia itself.

The trends described above were particularly noticeable in the four EESEs that were CMEA members.[8] In 1988 their shares in Russian imports of specific commodity groups ranged from two-thirds to almost complete reliance; these shares dropped to around 20–25% by 1994 (see *Table 8.4*). Another noteworthy change is the substantially increased indices of EESE relative specialization in major exports to Russia. Between 1988 and 1994 the average index grew from 3.7 to 10.1 for Bulgaria; from 2.6 to 11.3 and 8.6 for the Czech and the Slovak republics, respectively; from 4.3 to 5.8 for Hungary; from 3.9 to 15.4 for Romania; and from 3.4 to 8.7 for Slovenia. The case studies also reflect this trend toward declining diversification. For 1988 five companies from our sample each reported five product groups as their leading imports from EESEs; two firms reported four groups; and one firm had six groups on its list. In contrast, only two companies had four product groups on their lists of leading imports from EESEs in 1994; the remainder of those that were still importing from EESEs had just one to three items on their lists.

This basically means that the concentration of EESE exports to Russia has increased. Moreover, for items belonging to the specialization of each EESE, this specialization increased relative to the average share of the respective commodity group in exports to Russia from all other suppliers. Hence, while Russia has become less dependent on imports from EESEs, each EESE has become less diversified in its trade with Russia. As a result of this trend, EESE exports to Russia have become more vulnerable to potential changes in Russian demand for these goods than the exports from other countries. In this respect, Hungary has been better off than other EESEs, because it has experienced the smallest increase in the relative specialization index.

Changes in specialization patterns can also be grasped at a more aggregated level. Returning to the data in *Table 8.3*, one might notice that the structure of imports from Bulgaria moved in favor of foodstuffs at the expense of industrial machinery. In cases of the Czech Republic and Slovakia, imports of industrial machinery gave way to imports of foodstuffs and chemical products, which were not among major imports in 1988. In imports from Hungary, clothing lost ground to foodstuffs and chemical products. In Romania's exports to Russia the main trend was similar, with transport machinery losing its place on the list of major export items. Among Slovenia's major exports, industrial machinery was replaced by chemical products.[9]

One can conclude that the immense decline in the EESE shares of total Russian imports has not meant an across-the-board restructuring of Russian imports away from East European partners. Some EESE exports to Russia have actually been crowded out by other suppliers and have consequently dropped off the lists of EESE major exports to Russia. Yet other goods have gained importance; even if they are imported at a lower absolute level (which is not surprising, given the general slump in Russian imports), there is still a rather high level of Russian reliance on the supply of these commodity groups from EESEs. Thus, it is apparent that impediments to EESE exports to Russia have not affected all commodity groups to the same extent. This suggests some questions: what barriers did imports recently confront? And what impediments might block the trade of those goods that currently constitute the bulk of EESE exports?

8.2 Major Impediments Facing EESEs in Russia

The main reasons for the decline and drastic restructuring of Russian imports from EESEs fall into three broad groups. The first group is associated with the collapse of the CMEA (particularly, the trade and payments system); the second, with liberalization of Russian foreign trade and the opening of the country for trade with industrial nations; and the third, with the radical restructuring of the Russian economy itself. Each of those three groups of explanations not only determines the nature of the barriers that EESEs confront, but also draws a distinction between them with respect to the time horizons of their existence and their scales of magnitude. It is worth noting that the factors mentioned above have affected imports in all EESEs; in fact, it seems most impediments to imports from EESEs are product specific, not country specific. Bearing this in mind, we will speak of specific obstacles facing particular countries only to the extent that these countries specialize (or used to specialize) in exporting particular commodity groups to Russia.

8.2.1 The collapse of the CMEA

At first glance the factors associated with the collapse of the CMEA seem to be the most disadvantageous for imports from EESEs. Of the 10 Russian importers surveyed for this study, 7 named the collapse of the CMEA as a decisive event in the contraction of imports from EESEs. Moreover, 2 of the firms singled it out as the most important cause for the breakdown of Russian trade with EESEs. Trade between members of the former CMEA experienced an inevitable serious shock from the rapid economic changes that accompanied its dismantling. In essence, these economies moved away from a system resting on three pillars, namely, politically rooted intergovernmental agreements on cooperation, payments in transferable (exchange) rubles, and discretional price setting by central planners. The system toward which they moved is characterized by an international division of labor and hence trade flows between countries governed by economic reasoning;

payments denominated in hard currencies; and prices set or impacted by the world market. Under the old system price or non-price competitiveness of goods shipped to Russia was not the highest priority for EESE exporters. In fact, in most cases they did not even have a choice of whether to ship goods to Russia or not; everything was decided for them in intergovernmental agreements on mutual shipments. By the same token they did not have to worry about payments for their exports. Whether or not anybody really needed their products in Russia, payments flowed into their accounts until the late 1980s, when EESEs started to experience problems with defaulted payments from the USSR. Similarly, pricing mechanisms for EESE exports to the USSR were highly distorted.

After the demise of the CMEA, all these arrangements changed rapidly. The agreements of the past basically had no sound basis; rather they were part of the "grand vision" of socialist planners and their understanding of the guiding principles of the international division of labor. Nonetheless, these agreements served at least one EESE goal quite well: via the system of special accounts run by the Soviet authorities, EESEs linked part of the proceeds from Russian exports to EESEs with Russian imports from the region. Thus, many EESE exports had a guaranteed market for products that had never been tested for international competitiveness. Clearly, when this system collapsed many imports from EESEs lost their basis of financing.[10]

It appears, however, that as important as the guaranteed market of Russia for EESE products was it was not the most significant factor to impact EESE exports. It is quite obvious that the elimination of the old centralized payments system and institutionalized trade contracts has had an equally important effect on trade in most commodity groups. However, as *Tables 8.3* and *8.4* show, contraction of Russian imports from EESEs has varied significantly among exporters, which is precisely why the EESE specialization in the Russian market has changed. This means that the recent dynamics of EESE trade with Russia cannot be explained by the dismantling of the CMEA's economic mechanisms alone.

In fact, the consequences of excluding political considerations from economic relations between Russia and EESEs have been much farther reaching than the consequences of the CMEA's demise. There is no doubt that the CMEA was merely an economic extension of the Warsaw Pact created to serve specific purposes, namely, to increase the military power of the Warsaw Pact countries and to facilitate the bloc's self-sufficiency. Consequently, trade in defense-oriented goods was considerable; according to estimates from experts in Russia's Ministry of Foreign Economic Relations, direct cooperation between the USSR and EESEs in arms production alone accounted for 10–15% of overall trade (even excluding all goods used in defense-oriented industries or having a dual use).[11]

Since the dismantling of the Warsaw Pact, most military trade between EESEs and Russia has stopped. Imports from EESEs have been affected, inter alia, by the withdrawal of large contingents of the Soviet Army from military bases in Central and Eastern Europe. In the past, substantial volumes of various goods that in most cases were reported as Russian imports from EESEs were actually supplies of armaments and a variety of other goods for Soviet troops deployed in the "exporting" countries. These imports completely vanished after the Soviet Army's withdrawal. Moreover, current moves by EESEs toward accession to North Atlantic Treaty Organization (NATO) raise serious doubts about the chances of resumed cooperation between Russia and EESEs in defense production on any significant scale. The opening up of former CMEA economies to the rest of the world has also caused a noticeable reshaping of EESE specialization along lines of newly discovered real comparative advantages. In particular, the opening up of these economies has revealed unnecessary past development of heavy industry in most EESEs and the FSU, and the consequent oversized trade with Russia in capital goods for heavy industry.

However, unlike military-related commodities or investment goods for heavy industry, not all Russian imports have been doomed to contraction in absolute terms. The levels of some imports, consumer goods in particular, have risen. Although, this trend is reflected in the changing structure of EESE exports to Russia (see *Table 8.3*), consumer imports from Eastern Europe have been also doing much worse than similar imports from other countries, and consequently have been losing ground to the latter (as reflected in the EESEs' falling share in total Russian imports of these products, see *Table 8.4*). The reasons for this are numerous, but they can be generally grouped into a cluster of factors associated with the liberalization of Russia's foreign trade and the opening of the Russian economy. These factors have primarily affected consumer imports, yet even imports of those capital goods whose trade has not been completely eliminated have been influenced by them.

8.2.2 Liberalization of Russia's foreign trade

The most important event in the liberalization of Russia's foreign trade is the seemingly simple fact that Russian importers have gained freedom in choosing suppliers. The abolition of the state monopoly on foreign trade has made nongovernmental importers the main actors in the market. These importers make choices based on the preferences of individual Russian consumers, not on geopolitical considerations. In this regard, EESE exporters have been reduced to the level of other potential suppliers, lacking privileges vis-à-vis exporters from the industrial or developing regions. This might suggest that EESE exports have been crowded out of the markets by shipments from elsewhere because these products have fallen out of favor with Russian consumers. With the gradual but steady dwindling of centralized imports, this explanation seems to be increasingly warranted. As our case studies show, imports from suppliers from Germany, USA, Italy, and Japan have replaced imports from EESEs for most of the companies surveyed.

Exactly why have Russian consumers and customers of industrial goods lost interest in products from EESEs? The answer to this question is complex and we will try to give an answer using the example of consumer products. At the broadest level, Russian consumers are experiencing a desire to "test the West" (in fact, the word "West" here represents not only the industrial West, but anything outside the former Soviet realm). For years choice has been limited to goods produced domestically or originating in socialist countries. Even if traditional brands had met all consumer requirements – which they apparently did not – people might have developed a kind of product "fatigue." It is understandable that once Russian consumers gained free access to "Western" goods – which have been symbols of style and quality for years – they shifted demand in that direction. World-famous brand names, particularly in clothing, foodstuffs, alcohol, and tobacco, have conquered the Russian market without any real struggle.

This shift in demand has had disastrous consequences for some EESE major exports to Russia. For instance, Bulgarian cigarettes, which used to be one of the leading Russian imports from this country and virtually the only type of imported tobacco on the Russian market, have vanished from stores and street vendors. It is interesting, though not unexpected, that many Russian consumer goods have had the same problems on the Russian market as EESE products. It might be said that most former "socialist" products – whether Russian or not – have lost appeal in the eyes of Russian consumers. As a result of this reclassification, imports from EESEs have become the primary competition for Russian products, facing all corresponding difficulties. Whereas more expensive Western brands have satisfied the demand of upper-level consumers prepared to pay extra for quality, imports from EESEs and domestically produced goods, which are generally valued less by consumers, both appear to have targeted the same group of low-income consumers.[12] Thus, while high-quality Western products appear to be beyond competition (at least for the time being), EESE products currently must compete with Russian goods of more or less the same quality. Given that Russian producers of consumer goods continue to lose ground to imports from the West, particularly in apparel and foodstuffs manufacturing, the competition is fierce. Because the quality of many comparable EESE and Russian consumer goods is approximately the same, price has become an important factor in this competition. This problem will be discussed in more detail below. Here it is sufficient to mention that because they are subject to import duties – currently ranging from 15% for most foodstuffs to almost 30% for many durable consumer goods – EESE products have a clear disadvantage in this area compared with domestically produced goods.[13]

It is worth mentioning that some Western imports have been (and are) higher in quality than those from EESEs. In all the case studies conducted for this analysis, the respondents assessed the quality of EESE products as inferior to that of comparable imports from the West; four companies assessed it as satisfactory (which was a lower-end mark), and one assessed it as poor. Russian consumers' fairly low opinion of the quality of many EESE imports remains one of the main impediments EESEs face in recovering their positions on the Russian market.

Moreover, this opinion also concerns products other than consumer goods. As one of the managers interviewed for this study said, the only reason his enterprise has entirely dropped imports from EESEs was the availability of higher-quality products from the West.[14] In other words, when Russian managers were finally ready to buy in the West, the West was ready to sell to them; this trade was also supported by the continuing liberalization of Coordinating Committee on Trade with Communist Nations (COCOM) restrictions. As one might guess, imports of obsolete "high tech" goods from EESEs were doomed to be dropped the minute Russian customers gained access to advanced Western technologies and state-of-the-art equipment.

Not all "Western" products have actually been of high quality (this is particularly true for cheap Chinese clothing, footwear, electronics, and home appliances, which usually bear prominent brand names – or names phonetically close to them – irrespective of patent law in most cases). It has not taken long for Russian consumers to realize that high quality is not guaranteed by a "Western" brand name. However, this realization does not necessarily mean that consumers will switch back to EESE products as easily as they disregarded them. For example, when answering a question about Russian consumers' attitudes toward EESE goods, only 4 of 10 companies surveyed assessed them as good. Six others gave them lower marks. Moreover, there are other reasons imports from EESEs have fallen out of favor with Russian consumers. Clearly, inability to offer better prices for supplied goods has been one of the important ones (although, our case studies admittedly have revealed fairly high levels of satisfaction with prices on the part of the companies surveyed). For purposes of illustration, some average import contract prices registered in 1992 are provided in *Table 8.5*.[15]

As *Table 8.5* shows, for most goods imported from EESEs Russian customers have been able to find less expensive substitutes. This has been true across the board, from the simplest consumer goods to complex machinery. Also, according to experts in Russia's Ministry of Foreign Economic Relations, EESEs have charged prices above world levels for agricultural products and foodstuffs. These higher prices come as no surprise, though, because governments in EESEs have made

Table 8.5. Average contract prices for selected Russian imports in 1992 (in US$ per unit).

Injectors for liquid fuel (841610)[a]				*Home refrigerators* (841821)				*Vertical freezers, less than 900 liters* (841840)			
CSFR	Germany	USA		CSFR	Germany	France	Belgium	Hungary	Yugosl.	France	UK
100	82	65		2,667	819	1,000	852	236	181	95	254
Home dishwashers (842211)				*Bulldozers* (842911)				*Sowing vehicles* (843230)			
Hungary	Germany	Belgium	Sweden	CSFR		Germany		CSFR	Yugosl.	Germany	France
625	546	500	448	15,500		11,000		23,667	16,077	10,670	9,224
Automatic washing machines for less than 10 kg of laundry (845011)				*Sewing machines for home use* (845210)				*Cash registers* (847050)			
Bulgaria	Austria	Sweden	Singapore	Bulgaria	Yugosl.	Germany	Finland	Hungary	Yugosl.	Germany	Austria
1,000	684	857	917	229	266	163	172	1,489	4,000	1,292	500
Direct-current generators (850132))				*Lead-based car batteries* (850710)				*Electric chain saws* (850820)			
Bulgaria	Austria	Romania	Italy	Bulgaria	S. Korea	Hungary	Germany	Hungary	Germany	Greece	China
1,045	1,000	542	500	64	47	84	83	222	191	200	110
Home vacuum cleaners (850910)				*Electric irons* (851640)				*Electric kettles* (851671)			
Hungary	USA	Taiwan		Hungary	Belgium	Finland	Netherlands	Hungary	Ireland	Switzerl.	
33	33	33		21	20	16	21	50	45	42	
Tennis balls (950661)[b]				*Toothbrushes* (960321)				*Ballpoint pens* (960810)			
CSFR	Germany	Israel		Hungary	Germany	France	Finland	CSFR	Yugosl.	Netherlands	Austria
13	6	7		3	1	1	2	2	1.44	1.01	0.86

[a] Six-digit TN VED (Harmonized System) classifications given in parentheses.
[b] Per kilogram.
Abbreviation: CSFR = Czechoslovakia.
Source: Roscomstat (1994).

the elimination of agricultural subsidies a cornerstone of economic reform. The plausibility of such actions' increasing the efficiency of national economies is undoubtable. Yet industrial nations have always subsidized agricultural producers and continue to do so. Consequently, EESE food suppliers are doomed to lose price competition in the Russian market to exporters from European Union (EU) countries, USA, and Canada.

These price disadvantages are only part of the reason exporters from EESEs have been losing the Russian market to exporters from industrial nations; another significant problem is the almost total lack of marketing of EESE products. The absence of EESE marketing was mentioned in our survey by managers of former major importing firms in Russia. Marketing efforts were unnecessary in the past, when trade was conducted on the basis of long-term direct ties or cooperation established at the intergovernmental level. Such ties and agreements no longer exist, yet no active marketing policy by EESE suppliers has replaced them. Nowhere is this more apparent than in the area of commercial advertising.

Since the beginning of economic reform in Russia, commercial advertising has been among the most rapidly developing fields. There is no doubt that foreign firms have unilaterally dominated the most "aggressive" sector of visual advertising in Russia: TV commercials and outdoor advertisements. (By the author's count, foreign firms contribute up to 70–80% of all TV and outdoor advertisements.) It should be pointed out that foreign firms in this case do not include exporters from EESEs. Thus it is no wonder that the trade companies surveyed gave EESEs their lowest marks for advertising: on a scale of 1 to 5, with 5 being the highest and 1 being the lowest, EESEs received seven "3s," two "1s", and one "2." EESEs do not advertise on TV or radio, and they do not distribute fliers in magazines or mailboxes (which in Moscow are currently no less jammed with junk mail than anywhere else in the world) or on counters in supermarkets or drug stores. Some Russian consumers might recall that, say, Hungarian salami or Tokaji wine is actually better than cheap imitations from the Netherlands, Denmark, or Germany. But, EESE exporters to Russia should invest in at least some advertising as it is critical for their success in Russian markets, particularly bearing in mind that the share of Russian consumers that have not been accustomed to EESE products grows every day.

Other areas where EESE exporters face considerable obstacles are import financing and insurance, and trade management. Trade financing as it is usually understood was almost unknown in the CMEA (and still is, according to our cases studies: all 10 respondents claimed that trade credit lines were unavailable in EESEs). Credits at the enterprise level were not necessary in Russia–EESE trade, because this trade was based on an intergovernmental, transferable-ruble-denominated clearing system where enterprises acted as mere subcontractors for the state trading organizations, institutions that served their government in implementing its monopoly on foreign trade. Our case studies provide explicit evidence in this respect. In 1988, 8 of 10 companies surveyed conducted almost 100% of their trade with EESEs on the basis of intergovernmental agreements (for the two others this share was 60% and 80%, respectively). There were also some joint-investment projects in the 1970s and 1980s (for instance, construction of the Yamal–Western Europe gas pipeline) under which EESEs shipped investment goods to the USSR with no immediate payment. Such EESE exports were to be compensated later by shipments of Russian natural gas. Yet due to a steep contraction in joint-investment activity, such financing schemes are now of the past. The same is true of financing under intergovernmental agreements. As the case studies show, by 1994 the share of trade with EESEs conducted on the basis of intergovernmental agreements was down to nothing for 9 of 10 companies.

Unlike trade financing, trade insurance existed in the CMEA. In all the case studies company managers reported that insurance was available in both 1988 and 1994. The state-run company Ingosstrakh – the foreign operations affiliation of Gosstrakh, the country's sole insurance company during the Soviet era – provided insurance for shipments from abroad. This insurance was mandatory; however, it was only the most basic insurance against damage in transport, with no coverage for any financial risks or delays in delivery.

After the collapse of the CMEA's trade system, real market mechanisms appeared to be in great demand; however, neither the EESEs nor Russia had appropriate institutions in place. At the time the CMEA was dissolved EESE financial institutions were only in their initial stages (which is one of the main reasons Russia–EESE trade intermediation has almost completely gone to West European intermediaries). Both Russia and EESEs are still either struggling through or slowly recovering from economic recession, which is exactly why exporters and importers urgently need trade financing and insurance, particularly due to widespread insolvency. These firms could not wait until national institutions in these areas matured. In the first place, national banking and insurance happened to be relatively weak, at least initially. Exim banks, which would promote exports, have only recently started to emerge in EESEs: Hungary established an export–import bank to help finance trade with Russia only in late 1994; a similar bank for settling payments in national currencies has also been created jointly by Bulgaria and Russia.

Western intermediaries have won dominance in dealing with Russia and have been active in financing imports from EESEs; however, they have been even more active in promoting imports from industrial nations. Institutional intermediaries such as the Group of Seven, the EU, the European Bank for Reconstruction and Development, and others have not been exceptions to this rule. In fact, a plan was discussed in which international donors' money for emergency relief aid to Russia could be used to buy EESE products; however, nothing significant has come of this idea. Instances like the Hungarian exports to the Commonwealth of Independent States (CIS) financed by the EU in 1992 are the exceptions. Most of the money has been spent shipping foodstuffs and pharmaceuticals to Russia from North America and the EU (which is hardly surprising given that major donors of international financial institutions have their own interests at stake).

A final reason EESE imports have lost ground in Russian markets is that EESE exporters appear to have been unprepared for necessary revisions in the management of trade with Russia after that country lifted the state monopoly on foreign trade. In the past Russian state-run foreign trade organizations imported goods in huge quantities; however, the new Russian importers were interested only in small shipments. This change in demand required adaptation on the part of EESE exporters (for instance, beginning to trade in small volumes through the use of bonded consignment warehouses); according to experts at the Ministry of Foreign Economic Relations, this adjustment unfortunately has not yet occurred.

8.2.3 Russia's economic restructuring

The economic recession that has affected the solvency of Russian importers falls into the third group of factors that have caused drastic changes in the Russia–EESE pattern of trade.[16] This group can be further subdivided into two sets of factors: the first is associated with the current general economic slump and hence is of a more or less temporary nature; the second comprises more basic, structural shifts and peculiarities and, consequently, is of a more lasting character. As expected, economic recession has caused a rather drastic reduction in investment, resulting in shrinking demand for capital goods. EESEs that predominantly specialized in exactly these products on the Russian market could not avoid the immediate adverse effects of this change. Moreover, the impact has been more severe than that of a normal economic recession because of the greatly oversized investment program that previously existed in the Soviet Union. This chapter is not an appropriate occasion for discussing the unnecessarily high level of investment in the USSR. For our purposes it is sufficient to note that EESE export capacities targeting Russia were developed to fit an industrial colossus whose continued existence is of little interest to Russians today.

Even graver consequences for imports from EESEs have been brought about by another peculiarity of Russia's industrial restructuring. Two negative impacts that the contraction of military cooperation between former Warsaw Pact countries has had on EESE exports to Russia have already been mentioned: a reduction in Russian imports formerly consumed by Soviet troops deployed in EESEs and a reduction in defense-oriented production in Russia. Moreover, the latter has not only had a direct downsizing effect on imports from EESEs due to decreased demand for armament components and other intermediate inputs, but has had an even more important indirect effect through the conversion of Russian defense enterprises, or more precisely through the way this conversion has taken place.

In the first place, the majority of enterprises undergoing this conversion have not yet managed to find any export markets for their nonmilitary products. Consequently, *import substitution* has become one of the main goals of converted industries. Moreover, the Russian government has officially proclaimed that import substitution is part of Russia's industrial policy. A good example of this commitment to import substitution is the federal government's program for developing the manufacture of locomotives, which used to be one of Czechoslovakia's major exports to Russia. This program stipulates the complete substitution of imports in this area by the year 2000. There are numerous other examples of import substitution programs that are similar to this one.

Interestingly enough, import substitution has affected suppliers from EESEs to a greater extent than those from industrial nations. Moreover, one of the very factors that EESEs tended to consider their principal advantage in exporting to Russia has turned out to be their main disadvantage. EESE products fit Russian technical requirements perfectly, because in many cases products have been manufactured according to blueprints developed by Soviet engineers. These high levels of *equipment compatibility* and product compliance with Russian standards, which EESEs have constantly pointed to as something Russian customers should be interested in, have actually had the opposite effect.

The fact that EESE products are virtually identical to Russian products has proved detrimental to EESE exporters. Unlike imports from industrial countries, most of the products EESEs have been able to offer to Russian customers (particularly industrial goods) can be manufactured just as well by Russian enterprises. Moreover, due to the need to integrate into civilian markets, the Russian military-industrial complex has been aggressively seeking new areas of production. One of most notable examples of the displacement of EESE imports by domestic products is the shifting of AvtoVAZ orders from EESE imports to Russian former military enterprises. This shift has affected almost all EESEs because of their extensive cooperation with AvtoVAZ in the production of components, equipment, and spare parts for Russian-made Lada passenger cars in the past (see *Table 8.4*). Yet there are numerous examples like this one; the fact that about 80% of Soviet manufacturing was directly or indirectly defense oriented provides a rough idea of the potential scope of EESE product displacement.

It is true that such import substitution is a step back toward Russian economic isolationism. Unfortunately, this policy has influential supporters in the Russian government, and there is little chance that in leading manufacturing industries advocacy of international cooperation will outweigh growing protectionist sentiments.

The various impediments that EESE imports have encountered on the Russian market over the course of the past three to five years have been of different durations. Some have already exhausted their effect, some will stop being an issue in the next few years, and some will continue to exist for a long time to come. However, before turning to the analysis of impediments from this angle, we should complete our picture of the decline of EESE imports by looking at imports from the two Baltic EESEs.

8.3 Estonia and Latvia: Reshaping Trade with Russia After Regaining Independence

As *Tables 8.6a* and *8.6b* show, two Baltic EESEs have faced basically the same problems as non-FSU EESEs. Their trade with the FSU, and Russia in particular, has been steadily contracting: according to World Bank staff estimates, for instance, Russia's share in Estonian exports declined from 56.5% in 1991 to 22.9% in 1993; the total FSU share in Estonian exports fell over the same period from 94.8% to 43.2%. Simultaneously, their exports to Russia have become even more concentrated on a handful of commodity groups, predominantly foodstuffs, making their trade extremely vulnerable to minor fluctuations in the Russian market. There is only a formal difference between FSU and non-FSU EESEs in this regard: it was the collapse of the CMEA that caused a drastic restructuring of trade patterns for the latter, while the breakup of the USSR (and its centrally planned, mutual, interrepublican supplies) led to the same consequences for the former. The reshaping of Russia's trade regime and the restructuring of the Russian economy have brought about similar impediments for both groups of EESEs.

Admittedly, the two Baltic EESEs have faced some extra impediments in their trade with Russia. One such impediment was associated with their acute desire to break with the legacy of the Soviet past; the other was related to their relatively complicated political relations with Moscow.

The first of these impediments to trade were initially related to two peculiarities of domestic economies inherited from the communist era: constant shortages, particularly in the consumer market, and numerous "smoke stacks," enterprises built in the Baltics according to a grand vision of planners in the Kremlin, often serving only the Russian market. Shortages initially led the Baltic EESEs to establish restrictions on exports to other republics of those goods for which Russia was, no doubt, the primary consumer, a policy that emerged prior to the USSR's breakup within the so-called economic experiment in the Baltics. Also, it was

Table 8.6a. Product structure of Estonian exports to Russia, 1991 and 1994.[a]

	1991		1992/1991			1994	
	Volume in physical quantities	Value (mln. rubles)	Change in physical volume of exports (%)	Commodity group (TN VED code)	Item	Value (thsd. US dollars)	Structure of exports (%)
Meat and meat products (1,000 tons)	21.0	261.7	–98	0405	Butter	10,214	5.17
Milk and milk products (1,000 tons)	233.3	175.0	–90	1604	Canned fish	21,928	11.09
Furniture	n.a.	67.0	n.a.	1704	Confectionery	3,595	1.82
Excavators (units)	811.0	45.7	n.a.	1801	Cocoa	4,356	2.20
Plastics (1,000 tons)	61.6	45.0	n.a.	1806	Chocolate	2,520	1.27
Sulfuric acid (1,000 tons)	252.0	40.4	n.a.	2009	Juices	4,520	2.29
Knitted goods (mln. units)	2.5	25.2	–60	3004	Pharmaceuticals	4,198	2.12
Cigarettes	n.a.	24.0	n.a.	3811	Chemicals	1,584	0.80
Leather footwear (mln. units)	0.8	18.0	–75	7304	Metal pipes	1,054	0.53
Apparel	n.a.	17.6	n.a.	8413	Pumps	1,516	0.77
Confectionery (1,000 tons)	4.0	16.0	–98	8702	Buses	1,423	0.72
Perfumery/cosmetic goods	n.a.	11.4	n.a.	8703	Cars	13,403	6.78
Carpets (mln. sq. m)	0.6	10.6	–93	8705	Special. motor vehic.	7,383	3.73
Hosiery (mln. units)	1.9	8.8	–79	8708	SP for motor vehic.	22,719	11.49
Portland cement	n.a.	8.1	n.a.	9026	Manometers	1,505	0.76
Yeast (1,000 tons)	1.6	4.8	n.a.	9403	Furniture	2,219	1.12
Wheat flour (1,000 tons)	8.1	3.6	–72		Total of major exports	104,137	52.68
Office products	n.a.	3.4	n.a.				
Eggs (mln. units)	0.9	1.6	–100		*Total exports*	197,676	100.00
Pianos, units	36.0	1.5	–100				
Rubber footwear (mln. units)	0.1	1.0	–100				

[a]Between 1993 and 1994 the methods of statistical reporting were revised, which led to differences in commodity breakdowns.

Abbreviations: n.a. = Not available; SP = Spare parts; Fruit/veg. pres. = Fruit and vegetable preserves.

Sources: Calculated on the basis of unpublished Roscomstat data (Roscomstat, 1992a, 1992b, 1993a, and 1993b) and Roscomstat (1995).

Table 8.6b. Product structure of Latvian exports to Russia, 1991 and 1994.[a]

	1991		1992/1991			1994	
	Volume in physical quantities	Value (mln. rubles)	Change in physical volume of exports (%)	Commodity group (TN VED code)	Item	Value (thsd. US dollars)	Structure of exports (%)
Meat and meat products (1,000 tons)	30.4	257.1	−85	0303	Frozen fish	6,161	3.12
Milk and milk products (1,000 tons)	285.4	248.3	−88	0405	Butter	1,379	0.70
Knitted goods (mln. units)	4.9	104.4	296	1604	Canned fish	13,489	6.84
Ferrous-metal rolls (1,000 tons)	183.3	55.0	−80	1704	Confectionery	5,159	2.61
Hosiery (mln. units)	11.5	42.2	−63	1806	Chocolate	2,491	1.26
Apparel	n.a.	13.5	n.a.	3004	Pharmaceuticals	11,221	5.69
Rubber footwear (mln. units)	0.6	13.4	−33	4403	Unsawn timber	1,128	0.57
Fertilizer spreaders (1,000 units)	2.4	8.3	n.a.	8508	Electric hand-tools	8,283	4.20
Cigarettes	n.a.	7.9	n.a.	8517	Telephones	3,772	1.91
Vegetable oil (1,000 tons)	5.3	7.6	−85	8548	SP for elec. appl.	2,870	1.45
Fruit/veg.pres. (mln. equiv. jars)	8.1	5.4	−17	8607	SP for railway stock	2,351	1.19
Yeast (1,000 tons)	1.6	4.8	n.a.	8702	Buses	11,985	6.07
Confectionery (1,000 tons)	1.1	4.6	−82	8703	Cars	2,347	1.19
Leather footwear (mln. units)	0.3	4.5	−67	8705	Special. motor vehic.	3,227	1.64
Radios (1,000 units)	n.a.	n.a.	n.a.	8708	SP for motor vehic.	1,064	0.54
Newsprint (1,000 tons)	0.8	2.4	n.a.	9403	Furniture	3,585	1.82
Sparkling wine (1,000 deciliters)	18.5	1.5	−69		Total of major exports	80,512	40.81
Portland cement	n.a.	1.2	n.a.				
					Total exports	197,297	100.00

[a]Between 1993 and 1994 the methods of statistical reporting were revised, which led to differences in commodity breakdowns.
Abbreviations: n.a. = Not available; SP = Spare parts; Fruit/veg. pres. = Fruit and vegetable preserves.
Sources: Calculated on the basis of unpublished Roscomstat data (Roscomstat, 1992a, 1992b, 1993a, and 1993b) and Roscomstat (1995).

decided to substantially downsize overdeveloped industries, many of which the new governments in the Baltics did not want to see as a part of their national economies. Consequently, products from these industries immediately fell out of potential Baltic exports to Russia.

Continued political bickering with Russia has meant that, unlike all other EESEs, the two Baltic states still do not enjoy most favored nation (MFN) status in trade with Russia. An MFN agreement with Latvia was signed in 1994, almost three years after Russia's MFN agreements were signed with other EESEs, and is still not ratified by either Parliament. To date no MFN agreement between Russia and Estonia has been signed. Thus imports from Estonia and Latvia are subject to the regular Russian import duty rates multiplied by a factor of two (which is how Russia treats all non-MFN nations).

By the beginning of 1995 these differences between Russia's treatment of the Baltic EESEs and other EESEs had diminished and the Baltic states have joined the main group of Russia's former close partners who were actively seeking ways to revive some of the broken ties and at least prevent further contraction of their exports to Russia.

8.4 Can EESE–Russia Trade Recover?

This discussion of the reasons behind the decline in Russian imports from EESEs has not touched on what the Russian media have dubbed the "psychological rejection of Mother Russia" by EESEs. We have decided to omit from our analysis the EESEs' deliberate policy of not conducting business with Russia because they had been forced to do so during the communist era. After the Kremlin loosened its ideological control over EESEs in the 1980s, the striving for political independence had a strong, destructive impact on international economic relations between EESEs and the USSR and subsequently Russia. By the mid-1990s this political motive had faded substantially; the benefits of obtaining a place in the potentially lucrative Russian market now overshadow the offenses of the past. Another strong stimulus for developing trade with Russia has emerged in the form of foreign investment in EESEs. There is convincing evidence that many companies from Organisation for Economic Co-operation and Development (OECD) countries have invested in EESEs in order to develop production that will eventually be targeted at FSU markets, the Russian market in particular. (For instance, according to estimates from the Russian Ministry of Economy, about one-fifth of all foreign investments in the Czech economy were made with this purpose in mind.) As a result, keeping (or regaining) a place in the Russian market has become the primary goal of

EESEs. Hence, we will continue to concentrate on those obstacles for reviving EESE–Russia trade that are of economic origin.

There is, however, one political factor that bears examining, the economic consequences of the reshaping of military alliances in Europe. This reorganization has almost completely eliminated the military-industrial complex, which was once an extremely significant sector for EESE–Russia trade. The ongoing accession of most EESEs to NATO – however gradual – will almost inevitably lead to a shift in the standards used by EESE defense industries to those used in NATO countries. This adjustment will further separate those industries from potential Russian partners. Bearing this in mind, there appears to be little if any hope for revitalizing EESE–Russia trade in this sector.

The same is true for much of the trade in capital goods. However, after the economic recession in Russia bottoms out there will be potential for increasing imports of investment goods, albeit on a much more modest scale than in the past.

Russia seems determined not to return to the inefficient, oversized investment programs that were typical during the Soviet era. Moreover, given the need to convert the Russian military-industrial complex, import substitution is likely to continue to be one of main features of the contemporary Russian economy. In addition to the federal program of locomotive manufacturing mentioned earlier, a federal program aimed at developing urban transport manufacturing, whose goal is the complete elimination of imports of buses by 2000, has been developed and is ready for consideration by the government. If approved, this program would be disastrous for imports of Hungarian-made Ikarus buses, which continue to be among Hungary's leading exports to Russia despite an already steep decline in the number of shipments (from 10,000 a year during the Soviet era to just 789 in 1994). Heavy industries that once contributed considerably to Russia–EESE trade are not likely to regain their former importance in the Russian economy (see *Table 8.4* for the types of metallurgical and primary metal products processing equipment that were high on the list of EESE major exports to Russia in 1988). Hence, no considerable upward movement from the current low level of trade in these goods is expected. Finally, demand for imports of capital goods for light industries and food industries will depend on the fate of those industries in Russia, which at the moment is fairly uncertain (if not gloomy, particularly for textile and apparel manufacturing).

EESE exporters will have to offer something that, unlike supplies of the past, cannot be easily produced by Russian industrial capacities that are currently standing idle. This observation applies to capital goods that still have some potential on the Russian import market and to manufacturing products in general. Moreover, it concerns in particular equipment compliance with technical requirements of modern, state-of-the-art manufacturing: in other words, the quality of supplied goods. Product quality is apparently no less relevant to consumer products than to industrial goods. Without a substantial increase in quality (and style) of clothing, footwear, wine, and tobacco (particularly from Bulgaria and Romania), imports from EESEs will continue to lose in the Russian market to suppliers from industrial nations. For obvious reasons, some products have less favorable prospects in this respect, at least for the time being; for instance, computers from Bulgaria or electronics from Hungary. Conversely, some products have clear potential for a greater share in the Russian market.

Trade figures illustrate the changing prospects of EESE products in Russia. Slovak exports of light industry products and foodstuffs to Germany reached US$900 million in 1993; for the same year total Russian imports from Slovakia were slightly over US$200 million. It is not likely that the tastes and requirements of Russian consumers are on average higher than those of German consumers. Hence, once it has "tested" the West, the Russian market will be able to absorb much larger volumes of quality consumer goods from EESEs.

Quality will no doubt be vital for trade, but EESE success in this area will also depend on the countries' abilities to promote competitively priced exports in Russia with the same vigor as rival OECD suppliers. This promotion will require a completely new attitude toward doing business in Russia. Hopes of increasing the efficiency of old mechanisms that some EESEs and Russia are currently trying to reintroduce are likely to disappear. Although many of the intergovernmental sectoral commissions and agreements that were dismantled after the break up of the CMEA in 1991 have been re-established over the past two years (for instance, a program of cooperation in 27 areas, including production of components for cars, agricultural machinery, and medical equipment, was signed with Bulgaria in 1993), one can hardly expect that they will have any significant influence on Russia–EESE trade. Without other elements of the CMEA mechanisms (the old system of payments, in particular), the activities of such commissions are largely just wishful thinking with no specific means of implementing the desired programs. What is needed more than the reintroduction of old mechanisms is the development of new types of institutions to promote mutual trade, such as export-import banks, flexible trading companies, insurance funds, and finally, multinational corporations.

It is also quite obvious that if EESE exporters want to regain at least part of their former share in the Russian market they must realize that dated, overpriced products will not find their way onto Russian markets, which, unlike in the communist era, are no longer characterized by constant shortages; on the contrary, many markets have approached the point of saturation.

The current impediments for EESE exports mentioned above are not product specific. However, some commodity groups are definitely in better positions than others, or at least have that potential. For instance, imports of commodity groups belonging to the investment cluster are in a much shakier position than consumer imports. Our case studies illustrate this point quite clearly.

There is little doubt that the Russian agricultural sector will need much more time to recover from the legacy of central planning and state ownership than the industrial enterprises. Therefore, there still will be more room for imports of foodstuffs than for manufacturing imports; this trend has already become apparent in Russia's foreign trade and imports from EESEs are no exception (see *Table 8.3*). Yet it is almost certain that EESEs will continue to face price disadvantages in this sector relative to OECD agricultural exports. There is little any EESE exporter can do about this situation; unless EESE governments resume subsidies to agriculture, which were almost completely abandoned over the course of economic reform, OECD exporters will easily beat any price EESE exporters can offer for almost any type of food. (Technically speaking, another option is to lobby the Russian government to introduce antidumping duties on EU and North American Free Trade Agreement (NAFTA) agricultural exports to Russia; this approach is not likely to succeed though.) Concerning the imports of various types of clothing, it seems EESEs, like many developing nations, will have to manufacture and export consumer goods under internationally recognized brand names. In order to sell any product using a national brand name, firms will have to spend a considerable amount on advertising.

With respect to product advertising it is illuminating to look at imports of pharmaceuticals from EESEs. By 1994 this commodity group had moved into the category of major exports to Russia for almost all EESEs (see *Table 8.4*). The potential for these products' staying in favor with Russian consumers is also fairly high; Russians, like many people, are more or less conservative when it comes to health. When they go to a drug store they tend to look for medicines they have used for many years, and many of these medicines have traditionally been imported from EESEs. Yet all that anyone entering a drug store currently sees are dozens of colorful advertisements and leaflets praising the merits of medicines imported from the USA, Switzerland, UK, or Finland; there are no similar advertisements for any product from EESEs. Many new consumers have entered the market since the era when EESE-made medicines were the only imported medicines in Russian drug stores. Moreover, the number of such consumers increases with time. If EESE producers of pharmaceuticals continue to disregard advertising, they will probably lose those consumers to OECD competitors.

EESE producers will also have to develop trade from regional bonded consignment warehouses to stay in the Russian market. The Hungarian company Gedeon Richter has apparently realized this: agreements to open such warehouses in Krasnoyarsk (Western Siberia) and Rostov (southern part of European Russia) were signed with the respective local governments early in 1995. Yet it took this company, and others like it, several years to finally accept the necessity of this revision in their approaches to trade with Russia. EESE suppliers of industrial equipment should also adjust trading practice to meet the current requirements of the Russian market, especially the needs of new small and medium-size businesses. In particular, this would mean developing leasing operations, which to the best of our knowledge have not yet become part of the activities of EESE exporters in Russia.

Aside from changing their approach to marketing goods in Russia, EESE exporters can reverse this trend by investing in the Russian economy. Perhaps common sense prevents EESE companies from committing themselves to investments in a country whose climate for foreign investment is currently not overly favorable. Yet if they want to keep an equal footing with firms from OECD countries in the Russian market, they had better not linger too far behind. A commitment to large investment programs (over US$100 million, with own contribution of not less than US$10 million) yields immediate advantages for shipments to Russia: companies involved in such investment programs enjoy a 50% reduction in import duty rates for the final products they currently export to Russia.

No EESE company enjoys these benefits so far. Unfortunately, negative attitudes toward new investments in Russia are typical. A clear illustration of these attitudes can be seen in Yaroslavl locomotive works' unsuccessful attempt in early 1995 to convince the Czech company Skoda to invest in a joint venture to repair Skoda electric locomotives – the backbone of Russia's electric locomotive fleet, which accounts for three-quarters of all long-distance passenger rail service in the country. Skoda was expected to take a 48% share in the venture, which would set up and run repair shops. However, the company refused to put up any new funds, offering instead to write off part of the Russian debt to the Czech Republic as its contribution to the joint venture's capital. Perhaps it was a generous offer as far as debt servicing was concerned, but it definitely was not plausible as far as Czech participation in repairing Skoda-made CS-7 high-speed engines (and, consequently, potential imports of spare parts for what constitutes 90% of Russia's hauling stock) was concerned.

Most likely, this venture will now follow the path taken by the Samara Transport Machinery Factory, which has already oriented part of its capacities to periodic maintenance or capital repair of Ikarus buses. (The agreement for capital repair of the city's fleet of Ikarus buses was signed with the municipal government of Samara in January 1995; one might speculate that this factory may eventually get orders for the capital repair of Ikarus buses in the entire Volga River basin.) The economic efficiency of such import substitution may be doubtful, yet it is absolutely clear that without involvement of EESE producers this fate may await the majority of equipment imported from EESEs in the past.

There is another important change EESE exporters must undertake in their trade practice in Russia. The old scheme in which EESE companies dealt primarily with authorities in Moscow is no longer valid. EESE companies now must do business directly with regions, an inevitable consequence of Russia's federal decentralization. Evidently not all EESE companies realize this yet; even those that do seem to be picking regions fairly randomly, without a strategy for market penetration. The repair of Ikarus buses may again serve as an illustration. In March 1995 the Hungarian Ministry of Industry and Trade signed an agreement with the administration of Rostov oblast (region) to build shops for Ikarus capital repair. One might well ask why agreements were signed only with Rostov. Apparently this city is home to the Hungarian prime minister's alma mater. Imports of Ikarus spare parts would have benefited more had this ministry also directed attention to Samara and many of Russia's 88 other oblasts and republics. In essence, success can be achieved only by putting effort into developing trade ties with all Russian regions.

These ties are particularly important because there is not much hope that the Russian federal government will contribute anything significant to facilitating imports from and trade with EESEs in general. Interestingly enough, by mid-1995 Russia's influential Security Council had become interested in trade with EESEs and its role in Russia's economic security. However, the memorandums prepared for this occasion by two core ministries in the area (the Ministry of Economy and the Ministry of Foreign Economic Relations) have reflected a certain contentment with the current state of trade relations with EESEs. The Ministry of Economy's memorandum explicitly states that Russia's current level of trade with EESEs is not below normal, as many think, but fits perfectly with these countries' share in the world economy and world trade. Thus, any efforts to change today's situation could be justified by geopolitical considerations, but certainly not by purely economic ones. Officers from the other ministry have developed this thesis even further by saying that, "due to radical political and economic changes that have taken place in Russia, as well as in countries of Central and Eastern Europe, over recent years, rebuilding of traditional trade and cooperation ties in many areas is not only impossible, but also would contradict this country's long-term economic interests."

In conclusion, it should be noted that although some of the impediments to EESE exports to Russia that have detrimentally affected trade have already vanished, others (especially those associated with the restructuring of the Russian economy in general and the radical reshaping of its trade regime in particular) continue to adversely affect Russian imports from EESEs. Our case studies indicate that EESE producers will have to use all their creativity to overcome these impediments or they will be almost completely displaced from the Russian market. All 10 companies surveyed implied that increasing their imports from EESEs from the current low level is impossible without government subsidies, which effectively means that unless new mechanisms of trade financing and facilitation are found (not necessarily in the form of state support), imports from EESEs are doomed to stagnate.

Notes

[1] It should be acknowledged that using this period as a basis for comparison is somewhat dubious. There is little doubt that Soviet trade with Central and East European countries was highly politicized even then. Yet comparisons with the last century would make even less sense.

[2] Obviously, accurate analysis requires that consistent statistics be used. However, the only data available for Russian foreign trade prior to 1991 are those concerning Russia's share in the USSR's trade. Hence, we must make some generalizations about basic features of Russia's foreign trade when it was one of the republics of the Soviet Union. In particular, it is assumed that both country and product breakdowns reported for the whole USSR are representative for Russia's trade during those years. [A fairly complete analysis of problems arising from attempts to create a single time series for Russia's trade that uses both data for the USSR and later for Russia is available in Tabata (1994)]. In other words, for the years prior to 1992 all country and product structures shown for Russian foreign trade are, in fact, structures of the USSR's foreign trade. This might seem to be a fairly bold assumption at first glance. However, at least in the case of a country breakdown, it is supported by Soviet/Russian statistical authorities: in 1991 the USSR's Goskomstat and the Russian Committee on Statistics reported exactly the same breakdown of foreign trade by type of country for USSR and Russia, respectively. For one acquainted with the weaknesses of trade statistics at both of these institutions, this may seem not to be a strong base to build on. However, the author currently is not aware of a better way to assess the parameters of Russia's trade during the Soviet era. For the purpose of consistency, for the years after 1992 trade with CIS countries is excluded from Russia's foreign trade totals. With these reservations in mind, Soviet trade hereafter is treated as being completely equivalent to Russian trade during those years. Given that Russia accounted for about 80% of the USSR's imports, this assumption should not lead us to utterly incorrect conclusions.

[3] There is no doubt that the advantages of exporting to the Soviet Union had shrunk significantly for East European countries by the end of the 1980s, largely because of nonpayment by Russian partners. Still, all exporters to the USSR faced similar problems at that time, the only difference was in the type of financing: whereas imports from the West were funded primarily by loans from donor countries, East European exports to the USSR lacked government support. For whatever reason, Eastern Europe was crowded out of the potentially vast Russian market; as it turned out, it was much easier to lose markets than to regain them.

[4] A survey was done on the activities of 10 specialized Russian foreign trade companies that had intensive trade relations with suppliers from CMEA countries prior to 1991.

[5] Major imports have been defined as commodity groups (four-digit TN VED aggregation, similar to the Harmonized System classification at this level) that have been among the top 12 imports during at least one of the years covered in the study.

[6] Because statistics for Russian imports from Slovenia are not available for the period prior to 1993, data for all of Yugoslavia have been used as representative information for Slovenia during those years.

[7] The relative specialization indicator is calculated as

$$\frac{X_{ij}/\Sigma_i X_{ij}}{\Sigma_j X_{ij}/\Sigma_{ij} X_{ij}} ,$$

where X_{ij} is imports of good i from country j; $\Sigma_i X_{ij}$ is total imports from country j; $\Sigma_j X_{ij}$ is total imports of good i; and $\Sigma_{ij} X_{ij}$ is total Russian imports. Thus, this indicator compares the share of a particular commodity group in imports from a given country with the share of this product group in total imports. If the result is close to 1, the particular country does not differ from other countries in supplying this group of goods. If it is close to 0, the country is dwarfed by other suppliers of a particular good. If it is greater than 1, the country enjoys a comparative advantage in supplying this group of goods – the larger the number, the more specialized in such shipments the country is relative to other supplying countries. One should of course use the term "comparative advantage" with caution when applying it to East European countries prior to the collapse of the CMEA. Strictly speaking, comparative advantages could not be realized then due to distortions associated with central planning. Nonetheless, we use the above indicator and the term "revealed comparative advantage" for the purpose of comparing characteristics of trade in the years before and after the collapse of the CMEA. Revealed comparative advantage is merely an indicator of an actual structure of trade, with no indication of whether the decision-making process is economically sound or is just an outcome of the "grand vision" of socialist planners. This characteristic should be borne in mind when using this indicator for the years preceding the collapse of the CMEA.

[8] Romania has always played a much less important role as Russia's trade partner than have the other EESEs, mainly due to political tensions between Moscow and Bucharest during Ceausescu's reign.

[9] Slovenian figures should be considered with the same kinds of reservations as those called for in the USSR/Russia comparisons. See note [2].

[10] This analysis does not consider another clearly important impediment that imports from EESEs encountered immediately after the demise of the CMEA trading system, namely, Russia's considerable debts to EESEs. According to experts in Russia's Ministry of Economy, by the beginning of 1995 Russia owed US$3.9 billion to the Czech Republic, US$1.6 billion to Slovakia, the same amount to former Yugoslavia, US$800 million to Hungary, and US$100 million to Bulgaria.

[11] In fact, some items in Russia's imports from EESEs that might seem purely civilian had military origins. In footwear, for instance, imports from Czechoslovakia included large volumes of boots supplied to the Soviet Army. Many other goods that the army required fit into this category as well.

[12] Experts and enterprise managers who attended Soviet–EESE contract negotiations in the 1970s and 1980s reported that Soviet importers usually asked for lower-quality goods in order to minimize costs. Hence, EESEs developed a two-tiered system of exporting similar goods with different levels of quality: the higher-quality goods were shipped to the West and Soviet consumers received the lower-end products. (Communication from János Gács.) It is interesting to note that EESE exporters failed to adjust when the *nouveau riche* emerged in Russia at the beginning of the 1990s. EESEs did not compete with Western suppliers in targeting this group.

[13] It is also worth mentioning that the prestige of consuming certain Western products has played a crucial role in the contraction of the market for EESE goods. Newly wealthy Russians do not willingly smoke Bulgarian Shipka cigarettes instead of Marlboros, or drink Slynchev Bryag brandy instead of scotch. In fact, image in this case becomes a more important factor than product quality; some Russians would rather buy fake French cognac than genuine Bulgarian brandy.

[14] That is, in addition to the fact that he has been allowed to spend foreign exchange on his own.

[15] Due to broad differences in the nature of goods falling into the same groups, even at the six-digit TN VED (Harmonized System) level, one should use caution when interpreting the results of such a price comparison. By choosing fairly narrow price ranges, one can safely assume that the comparison is being made between more or less the same products.

[16] The insolvency might be slightly exaggerated if we consider that of the 10 companies surveyed for the study only 1 reported moderate arrears for imports from EESEs in 1994. The other 9 companies had no arrears for such imports.

References

Foreign Economic Relations of the USSR in 1989, 1990, International Relations Publishing, Moscow, USSR [Vneshnie Ekonomicheskie Svyazi SSSR v 1989].

Foreign Trade of the USSR in 1988, 1989, International Relations Publishing, Moscow, USSR [Vneshnaya Torgovlya SSSR v 1988].

Roscomstat, 1992a, Interstate Shipment of Consumer Goods according to Agreements between the Russian Federation Agreements and Other Countries in 1991, Roscomstat, Moscow, Russia [Mezhgosudarstvennye postavki tovarov narodnogo potreblenia v schet protokolov-soglashenii Rossiiskoi Federatsii s drugimi gosudarstvami v 1991].

Roscomstat, 1992b, Fulfillment of Intergovernmental Agreements Dealing with the Shipment of Industrial Goods to Russia in 1991, Roscomstat, Moscow, Russia [Vypolnenie mezhpravitelstvennykh soglashenii v chasti postavok produktsii proizvodstvenno-tekhnicheskogo naznachenia v Rossiiskuyu Federatsiyu za 1991 god].

Roscomstat 1993a, Inflow and Outflow of Consumer Goods within the Russian Federation in 1992, Roscomstat, Moscow, Russia [Zavoz i vyvoz tovarov narodnogo potreblenia po Rossiiskoi Federatsii za 1992 god].

Roscomstat, 1993b, Intergovernmental Shipment of Industrial Goods into the Russian Federation in 1992, Roscomstat, Moscow, Russia [Mezhgosudarstvennye postavki produktsii proizvodstvenno-tekhnicheskogo naznachenia v Rossiiskuyu Federatsiyu za 1992 god].

Roscomstat, 1994, *Average Foreign Trade Prices in 1992*, Vol. 1, Roscomstat, Moscow, Russia [Srednie Vneshnetorgovye Tseny v 1992 godu, Vol. 1, Rosinforcentr, 1994].

Roscomstat, 1995, *Statistical Yearbook of Russia 1994*, Roscomstat, Moscow, Russia [Rossiiskii Statisticheskii Ezhegodnik, 1994].

State Customs Committee, 1995, *Customs Statistics of Russian Federation's Foreign Trade in 1994*, State Customs Committee, Moscow, Russia [Tamozhennaya Statistika Vneshnei Torgovli Rossiiskoi Federatsii v 1994].

State Customs Committee, 1996, *Customs Statistics of Russian Federation's Foreign Trade in 1995*, State Customs Committee, Moscow, Russia [Tamozhennaya Statistika Vneshnei Torgovli Rossiiskoi Federatsii v 1995].

Tabata, S., 1994, The anatomy of Russian foreign trade statistics, *Post-Soviet Geography*, **35**(8):433–454.

Chapter 9

Government Policies in Support of Exports in Small Transition Economies

János Gács

Introduction

Traditionally exports were not of primary importance for centrally planned economies. Given the system's ideological base, which determined the countries' isolation from the world market, as well as its inherent autarkic tendencies, total exports were simply the residual over domestic balance, or merely the means to ensure necessary imports calculated in the central plan's system of material balances. In the 1980s, countries such as Poland, Hungary, Romania, and the German Democratic Republic permitted their imports from the West to expand too quickly and subsequently fell heavily into debt. For these countries, exports became increasingly significant because of the need to ensure debt service or debt reduction. Here export promotion was carried out either in the framework of central planning (for example, the forced redirection of existing domestic commodities abroad at the expense of domestic consumption, as happened in Romania), or through the creation of short-term incentives for the expansion of exports (such as providing bonuses to managers or exempting enterprises from wage controls to reward good export performance, as was done in Hungary). However, for achieving a better external balance the control of imports was a much more obvious and frequently used tool than the promotion of exports.

As far as Council for Mutual Economic Assistance (CMEA) markets were concerned, the promotion (or reduction) of exports either was not a problem at all or was carried out primarily via direct government control.

Once economic transition began, international trade gained importance in small transition economies. In 1994, exports averaged about 40% of the gross domestic product (GDP) in the eight countries covered in this book.[1] Moreover, in contrast to the pretransition situation, these trade flows are already having a real, organic impact on production processes. Following the decline of domestic demand – reflected in a cumulative average 20% decline in GDP and a 40% decline in industrial production in the region – exports became crucial for maintaining production. It has also increasingly been acknowledged that trade is important for the process of adjustment to relative prices in the world market, for developing specialization according to changing comparative advantages, for improving national welfare in general, and for obtaining external financing for transition. Paradoxically, the importance of trade and the perception of this importance by policy makers increased substantially just as governments were forced to relinquish almost all the authorization they previously had for intervening in trade. Clearly, among the many tasks resulting from transition, the governments of the countries of Central and Eastern Europe must learn how to evaluate developments in trade, how to orient their economies with respect to global trade, and how to develop and implement trade strategies under the new circumstances.

This chapter contains an analysis of the recent evolution, scope, and future potential of export policies in small transition economies. Four countries were selected as examples: the Czech Republic, Hungary, Slovakia, and Slovenia. Because the author is most familiar with policy making and real developments in Hungary, more data and examples are presented from this country than from the others.[2] For the sake of simplicity, the chapter does not deal with the support given to agricultural and food exports.

Section 9.1 discusses how different components of the transition process impact trade policy. Section 9.2 contains an analysis of how East European governments perceived the importance of exports during the first years of transformation. In Section 9.3, the different fields of governmental action are reviewed in detail. Conclusions are summarized in Section 9.4.

9.1 Main Components of Transition and Their Consequences for Export Policy

In Central and East European countries the trade policies of the mid-1990s have evolved as a result of a complex transformation process. In this section we attempt to identify the different, sometimes conflicting, pressures the governments of these countries have experienced in recent years with respect to their roles in influencing trade flows, particularly exports.

Economic transition in Central and Eastern Europe means simultaneous transformations in many areas of the society and economy. For our purposes, it is useful to distinguish between marketization, trade reform, macrostabilization, and restructuring.

By 1994–1995 the process of *marketization* (i.e., the establishment of basic market institutions) had shifted these economies to a position somewhere between a centrally planned and a market economy. Accordingly, if we take the usual justifications for (limited) government intervention in market economies (basically derived from the existence of market imperfections such as increasing returns to scale, externalities, learning by doing, and excessive risk aversion on the part of private agents with respect to research and development, for example) and their application to trade intervention, we have to realize that these principles cannot be mechanically used in transition economies. On the one hand, the imperfections of signals and the working of the market are probably more significant in these countries than in standard market economies because here the market is still only in its nascent state. Property rights are blurred and financial intermediation, capital markets, and many other institutions of the market are underdeveloped. On the other hand, transition economies are burdened with the heritage of the central planning system, which was dominated by government failure. This experience legitimizes cautiousness. Here government intervention involves the risk of triggering a chain of further intervention: there is no tradition of intervention with a limited amount of provision (direct or indirect support) and limited coverage, and no experience of efficient monitoring of policy implementation.

Trade reform in Central and Eastern Europe, which has basically been a part of marketization, has shown many similarities to trade reforms in developing countries. Trade liberalization involves a decrease in government intervention in trade flows; a move from direct government regulation through rationing (quantitative restrictions) toward the use of price mechanisms (tariffs); and a reduction in both the dispersion of the protection rate system and the level of protection, eventually leading to the establishment of equal incentives for exports and import substitution (Michaely *et al.*, 1991; Balassa, 1982).

Although the trade reform measures that were applied in the countries of Central and Eastern Europe resemble those applied in developing countries, an important distinguishing feature is that here they were introduced at an exceptionally fast pace, particularly in the field of imports (Gács, 1994). Another difference from the usual trade liberalization episodes was that, given the peculiarities of the old system in Central and Eastern Europe, it was extremely difficult to quantify changes in the level of protection of domestic production that resulted from the trade reform. There was a shift from rationed imports based on central plans or licenses, price equalization funds, export directives, and direct export subsidies to free trading with minimal control, moderate tariffs, and minimal export subsidies.[3] The changes in the level of protection were, however, undoubtedly enormous, even if they were partially compensated by the substantial currency devaluations in almost all the countries concerned.

Obviously, the philosophy of trade liberalization conflicted with government intervention in both imports and exports. However, because the outcome of the large-scale liberalization measures was uncertain, corrective measures could have been conceived, either in the form of transitional protection of domestic production or in support of exports (see McKinnon, 1991; and Hughes and Hare, 1991). This seemed all the more rational because, in addition to the drop in the level of protection of import substitution, the conditions of exports also drastically deteriorated due to the external shocks originating from the disappearance of the CMEA trading system. The internal and external shocks that hit the transition economies could not be compared with incremental changes in the protection levels of *either* import substitution or production for exports, particularly because conditions of *both* these activities deteriorated.[4] Accordingly, the agenda could have included the elaboration of new, horizontal forms of support for exports that would have been both less distortional and more acceptable to the international trading community than protection from imports. However, the elaboration of this system would have required much more time than was allotted for the elimination of earlier direct intervention.

The primary tasks of *macrostabilization* have been the establishment of equilibrium on product markets, the reduction of government budget deficits, and the curbing of inflation. Because of the special phenomenon of excessive and protracted output decline in transition economies, macroeconomic policies subsequently also had to pay attention to halting this recession. Stabilization has many consequences for trade policies, particularly due to the special role exchange rates play in curbing inflation as well as to the governments' decreasing abilities to give outright budgetary subsidies (like export subsidies in a direct or indirect form) and to forego tax or customs revenues.

A significant consequence of marketization and stabilization was the disappearance of the shortage economy: most markets in transition economies are no longer sellers' markets but have become buyers' markets. Consequently, it is the sellers who must make efforts to establish contacts with future customers, to inform them about their products, and to persuade them to make deals. This considerable change in business culture was bound to be the most difficult to accomplish in external markets, where enterprises had the least presence and the least information. Governments had a role to play here for making up for this deficiency.

Restructuring in trade and production is a response to stabilization, to systemic changes including trade reform, and to external impacts such as the collapse of former dominating foreign markets (the CMEA and the USSR) and easier access to other markets [like those in European Union (EU) and European Free Trade Association (EFTA) countries]. It implies a rapid, massive relocation of factors of production in an environment where market actors have just begun to learn their roles, where signals are not easy to identify, and where intermediators are weak and inexperienced. In this situation, the government has a major role to play in assisting intermediation, smoothing abrupt consequences of the shocks, identifying the long-term goals of the society, and assisting the agents in realizing the associated tasks.

With respect to exports, the government is responsible for securing new external markets and improving access to old ones (through economic diplomacy), helping to organize the institutions of intermediation (credits, guarantees, and insurance), and giving temporary assistance to keep alive industries, firms, production cultures, and research and development potential that seem viable in the long run but are temporarily in jeopardy. Naturally, the qualifications concerning the dangers of government failure mentioned above also apply here.

9.2 Perception of the Importance of Exports

From the outset, the transition agenda in East Central Europe was full of important tasks; sustaining or expanding exports was only one, and it was not high on the list of priorities.

The alarming collapse of trade with former CMEA members was partly self-inflicted, and thus foreseeable and politically acceptable. The first democratically elected governments of these newly independent countries did not want to devote much of their efforts to reviving trade relations with former allies. In any case, realistically there was not much they could have done to improve the situation (see Section 9.3.4).

In the early years of transition, apart from the dissolution of the CMEA, trade liberalization and improving access to Western markets were the primary activities of the governments with respect to the management of international trade. How the complete shake-up of the system would impact trade was hardly predictable, especially because of the unforeseeable effects of wide-scale price liberalizations coupled with restrictive macroeconomic policies. Forethought was replaced by trial and error.

The careful introduction of new currencies in newly emerging countries (such as Slovenia, Estonia, and Latvia) as well as the substantial devaluations at the outset of stabilization programs (in all the countries except Hungary) seemed to give a sufficient boost to exporters, enabling them to overcome the hurdles of limited access to and lack of knowledge about Western markets, as well as problems of financing, quality, and marketing.

The uniform conviction that devaluation would sufficiently support exports did not seem to be shaken by diverse export performance. For instance, the first two years of transition led to vastly different export performances in Czechoslovakia, Hungary, and Slovenia, on the one hand, and Bulgaria and Romania, on the other. The former showed stagnant total exports in the first two years, while the latter suffered an almost 50% export decline (calculated for 1990–1991, except for Slovenia where this calculation was made for 1991–1992).

The bold and rapid campaigns of trade liberalization demonstrated the governments' commitments to relinquishing intervention in trade and to pursuing a hands-off approach in remedying the problems of enterprises through trade policy measures. In each country hundreds (or even thousands) of enterprises found themselves in serious trouble, and many were given temporary government support. As a rule, in most countries these measures were not trade measures, even if the source of trouble many times was the loss of export markets or the need to sell exports at cost (or even at a loss).

Still, if there were instances of trade intervention, they were more to protect domestic industries through temporary barriers to imports, and much less to provide across-the-board or discretionary support to exports. Import surcharges were introduced in Czechoslovakia, Poland, Slovakia, and Hungary (in that order); stricter control of the use of foreign exchange was applied in Slovakia; additional quality certificates were requested for imported food products in Slovakia, and for food and consumer products in Hungary; and certain tariff adjustments and new quotas were introduced in each of the countries.

This focus on protection from imports at the expense of support to exports is not a surprise if the political economy of trade policy formulation is taken into account. Government policies usually focus on domestic issues and are impacted by domestic interest groups. As far as imports are concerned, collective action possibilities favor domestic producers and representatives of employees that push for saving domestic jobs. Protection from imports also brings direct customs revenues for the budget (or rents to importers or quota-allocating administrators). Although exports may also ensure domestic jobs, the mechanism of lobbying for export support is less obvious than demanding protection against imports. Moreover, the direct budgetary consequences of export promotion are negative.

In addition, there seems to be a perception that in practice export policies are inferior to import control in case of imminent trade balance or liquidity problems. This was demonstrated, for example, in Slovakia and Hungary by the relatively hasty introduction of measures to control imports or limit the use of foreign exchange for imports even when these measures endangered exports.

In February 1993, just after Czechoslovakia split into two separate republics, in response to a sharp fall in foreign exchange reserves, the National Bank of Slovakia (NBS) introduced exchange restrictions on selected payments abroad by domestic commercial banks and importers. Obligatory consultations with the NBS, a payment delay of three months, and advance deposit for payments were required for the purchase of, among other goods, production inputs from abroad. Obviously, these measures might have hindered the implementation of the enterprises' export plans. The measures were used for nine months, although some payment restrictions were still in effect in 1995.[5]

In March 1995, following two years of hefty trade deficits in the order of 8–10% of the GDP, the Hungarian government introduced an 8% import surcharge for all imports except for energy sources, complete machines for investment purposes, and materials purchased for job work. This meant that, at least in the first weeks of the import surcharge system, most production inputs were subject to additional taxes, for which the producers, including the exporters, received no refund. Later the enterprises were informed that reimbursement was possible using the same cumbersome method used for reimbursing normal import duties for exporters.

From the point of view of their effect on exports, the import surcharges introduced in Poland and Slovakia took the development of exports into consideration more than those in Hungary. In these countries exporters were either reimbursed from the start (Poland) or were not affected at all (Slovakia) (Foreign Trade Research Institute, 1993; Fidrmuc *et al.*, 1994).[6]

In recent years the fortune of exports in East and Central Europe and its possible dependence on government policies has gradually attracted increasing attention in the respective administrations. The persistence of general output decline and the emergence of trade imbalances, in particular, have contributed to this export awareness.

It became clear that in most countries the original benefits of currency undervaluation for trade balances had faded; however, because of the need for further control of inflationary pressures, there was only limited room for adjustments in the exchange rate. Of the eight sample countries covered in this book, alarmingly large trade deficits (35–50% of exports) characterized the first two years of transition only in Romania (whose deficit later gradually decreased); however, trade deficits emerged in Bulgaria and Hungary in 1993, and in Estonia and Latvia in 1995. In 1995, which was otherwise a favorable year of the trade cycle in the West, trade deficits developed in each of the countries in our sample except Slovakia.

The continuing real appreciation of the domestic currencies, unless compensated by productivity improvements, implied declining cost competitiveness in external markets. The expansion of those exports that relied on non-cost factors also met serious barriers in Western markets, such as entry barriers, reputational and marketing barriers, and disadvantages in financing. East European exporters have been forced to recognize that they have only limited market power in both the successor states of the USSR and in the West. Compared with competitors from mature market economies, they are at a disadvantage with respect to financing, commanding the necessary information, marketing, brand names, and reputation.[7] In each of the countries in our investigation, there is intense discussion about the current and future competitiveness of their own products and producers from different sectors. The chances of development in different sectors are discussed according to whether the products are high or low value added; unprocessed or highly processed; cost or reputation competitive; and natural resource, simple labor, skilled labor, or research and development intensive. These deliberations always provoke debates about the rationale behind creating some kind of industrial policy; but in practice none of the countries has yet created a definite and sophisticated industrial policy.

By 1993–1994, export promotion programs had been drawn up in some of the countries, which at least at the level of declarations substantiated government efforts to support exports.[8] In the Czech Republic, however, at the end of 1993 the government still rejected the draft of a law on export promotion because it did not agree with the idea of governmental activity in this field (Sass, 1995). In most of the countries, export promotion is implemented in a pragmatic way. Between 1994 and 1996, the focus in each country has been on economic diplomacy and export financing, and in some countries also on the exchange rate.[9]

It is indicative that while this chapter was being written, three of the four countries that it focuses on experienced major political disputes reflecting strong disappointment with the current hands-off stance the governments have taken toward exports. In Slovenia the prime minister met with managers of leading export companies, who demanded much stronger actions in support of exporting activities. They discussed the provision of sufficient financing to the Slovene Export Company (the national export-import bank), a postponement of the payment of sales taxes, and other issues. In the Czech Republic a conflict emerged between the minister of trade and industry, Vladimir Dlouhy, on one side, and the prime minister and other ministers, on the other. Dlouhy was dissatisfied with the government's stance on exports and urged the recapitalization of the Czech Export Bank and the Export Guarantee and Insurance Company (EGAP). He also initiated an individualized approach for those companies whose claims for payments for exports to the Soviet Union were not honored by the buyers in the last year of Czechoslovak–USSR trade.[10] In Hungary, although high-level politicians liked to speak about the existence or even the operation of an export promotion package, the most competent ministry official publicly complained about the lack of such a package and called for changes.[11]

9.3 Fields of Government Action

9.3.1 Exchange rate policies

Early trade liberalization in Eastern Europe was coupled with liberalization of foreign exchange regulations and with massive nominal devaluations in almost all the countries involved. The trade-related goals of these devaluations were to provide protection for domestic production after most nontariff barriers were abolished and to promote exports following the phasing out of most export subsidies. In recent years much of the strength of this protection/promotion has evaporated because, irrespective of the exchange rate regime in place (of which there was a wide variation), the currencies of the small East European countries experienced continuous real appreciation.[12] Although there may be several interpretations of this uniform real appreciation, it is indisputable that the exporters in these countries perceived it as a loss of competitiveness on foreign markets that could only be partly compensated by improvements in market access and productivity.

The detrimental effect of the real appreciation of the domestic currency was most apparent in Hungary. Here the effect of a substantial real appreciation (35% between 1990 and 1994 according to International Financial Statistics) was amplified by the fact that, unlike in the other countries, the process of real appreciation had not been preceded by a substantial devaluation.[13]

Another component contributing to changes in competitiveness was the growth of wages. Hungary and Slovenia abandoned administrative wage regulations relatively early; Slovakia partially relaxed wage regulations in 1993; and in the Czech Republic, brakes on wages were still in effect in 1995. In part because of these differences and in part because of differences in starting positions and real appreciation, in 1994 Slovenia and Hungary showed relatively high average monthly wages in comparison with the Czech Republic and Slovakia (see *Table 9.1*). Comparing the wages in these four countries with those in Bulgaria (where the monthly average wage in 1994 was US$87), Poland (US$234), or other countries shows that Hungary and Slovenia had the highest wages in East Central Europe. Accordingly, wage competitiveness is no longer a means for their penetration of Western markets.

As official documents and government actions show, policy makers in Hungary are less willing to accept deteriorating wage competitiveness than those in Slovenia, particularly because Hungary's current account balance in 1993–1995 was much worse than Slovenia's.

In Slovenia, the Bank of Slovenia is trying to contain the further real appreciation of the tolar, but the government has no plans to explicitly improve the competitiveness of Slovenian exports with the help of exchange rate policies. Policy

Table 9.1. Average gross monthly wages (in US dollars).

	1990	1991	1992	1993	1994
Czech Republic	183	129	164	199	240
Hungary	213	240	282	295	317
Slovakia	179	128	161	174	196
Slovenia	899	610	628	666	735

Sources: Dietz (1995), Havlik *et al.* (1995), *Slovenian Economic Mirror* (March 1995), and WIIW (1995).

makers are certain that the competitiveness of Slovenian exports can be improved other ways: by improving quality and design, by introducing trademarks, by targeting higher price ranges, and by building the reputation of exporters (Potocnik *et al.*, 1995). The productivity increases in 1993 and 1994 more or less compensated for the appreciation of the tolar and seem to justify the optimistic belief that the restructuring of exports is on the way.[14]

In Hungary the long process of real appreciation was arrested in 1994, and in early 1995 serious steps were taken by the government to block further real appreciation: the forint was devalued by 9%; the switch to a crawling peg system was announced with monthly 1.9% (and later 1.3%) devaluations until the end of the year; a temporary 8% import surcharge was introduced for most imports; plans were made to control wage increases; and social expenditures in the budget were slashed. As indicated above, the impact of the measures on exports was not unambiguously beneficial.

As a recent survey disclosed, Hungarian exporting companies are not completely enthusiastic about substantial devaluations. The earlier real appreciation of the forint drove many products from the market and consequently their capacities were dispensed with; this cannot be corrected now. Given their weak position on foreign markets, most firms cannot pass on the increased import costs that accrue due to the devaluation: as a rule, following a substantial devaluation in Hungary, foreign buyers immediately initiate a reduction of foreign-currency-denominated export prices. Especially hard hit by the devaluation are projects where fixed investments are already being carried out with long-term loans denominated in a foreign currency. Exporters whose production technology can only be obtained from foreign markets, or whose sales go mostly to the domestic market also consider massive devaluations detrimental.[15]

In the Czech Republic, despite substantial real appreciation, export performance in 1993 and 1994 was sufficient and there was no need to question the use of the exchange rate as a nominal anchor. However, 1995 brought alarming growth in the trade deficit. As indicated in Section 9.2, leading politicians disagreed about the cause of this development: the prime minister attributed it to the highly justified rapid growth of imports, especially those of investment goods, whereas the minister of trade and industry blamed it on the dwindling competitiveness of Czech exports. In any case, almost no experts advised a devaluation to remedy the situation, especially because the massive inflow of foreign capital (mostly in the form of foreign credits to enterprises and portfolio investment) brought strong pressure to revalue the long-fixed rate of the koruna. Finally, at the end of February 1996, the Czech National Bank introduced greater flexibility of the koruna when it announced that it was widening the bidirectional band in which the koruna can fluctuate from 0.5% to 7.5%. Analysts predicted greater volatility of the koruna rate but did not predict clear nominal appreciation or depreciation.

Slovakia was not as prudent in avoiding devaluations as the Czech Republic: the Slovak koruna was devalued by 10% in 1993 and was devalued several times against the accounting unit used in trade with the Czech Republic (the XCU). The developments of trade between the Czech and Slovak Republics are not easy to analyze because of accounting problems. However, it should be noted that according to Czech interpretations, the exceptionally favorable net export performance of the Slovak Republic in trade between the two republics in 1994 (about a US$400–600 million surplus) was mostly attributable to the excessive devaluation of the Slovak koruna. Either this was the case or Czech accusations and pressures were effective, because in May 1995 the National Bank of Slovakia implemented a 4% revaluation of the Slovak koruna against the accounting unit. With respect to the rest of the world, the favorable export performance in 1994 took the issue of further general devaluations off the agenda. Largely due to their comparatively low wages, Slovak exporters find their products highly competitive in comparison with those of other East Central European suppliers.

9.3.2 Tariff and nontariff measures impacting exports

Trade liberalization in Eastern Europe has also meant the deregulation of exports. There has been a reduction in obligatory licensing of exports and in the use of quota regulations, which now apply to only a small number of goods. In addition to obvious cases such as trade of arms, explosives, drugs, and dangerous materials, control currently is applied either to induce domestic exporters to stay below import quotas in other countries, or to implement "voluntary" restraints the respective government has promised to keep. The fear of antidumping procedures in export markets might also have induced governments to check individual export deals: in this way they attempt to prevent any single exporter from damaging an entire industry in their own country.[16]

When quotas, whether "voluntary" or not, or suggested prices are to be adhered to, questions arise as to which bodies should be entitled to enforce them and how the impartiality of these bodies should be ensured. In Hungary, so-called Commodity Councils and different trade associations are frequently used for this purpose. It is widely suspected that these bodies favor incumbent producers and exporters. For instance, after a rapid expansion in goose liver exports from Hungary in 1994, which effectively ruined the export price, the government gave the respective producers' association the right to allocate newly introduced quotas for 1995. New producers, mostly with foreign participation, subsequently complained that they were given almost no quotas because the rules used for quota allocation favored large, established exporters.[17] In Hungary, other kinds of quotas (such as those covered by textile agreements) are allocated through competition.

The extent of the remaining nontariff measures can be gauged by recalling that in the Czech and Slovak Republics in 1992 20% of exports required licensing (such as livestock, plants, some natural resources, textiles, and steel). In recent years about 25% of Hungarian exports have been subject to licensing (fuels, wheat, and industrial raw materials) (EBRD, 1994).

In Eastern Europe export duties are used only infrequently. However, they have been applied in Slovenia (with rates of 15% and 25%), especially on raw materials such as wood and certain metal waste. These taxes were considered a temporary measure to avoid supply disturbances in the domestic market.[18]

Import duties protect domestic producers but hinder exports. According to a well-known theorem of international economics (Lerner's symmetry theorem), in a general equilibrium framework import duties correspond to similar taxes on exports. To exempt exports from the burden of tariff protection, General Agreement on Tariffs and Trade (GATT) rules permit drawback on those parts of exports that physically originate from imports. Because the accounting and checking of duty drawback is not easy (see Nash, 1994), in many countries exporters prefer special duty-free arrangements such as free trade zones, in-bond manufacturing arrangements, and inward processing transactions.

Duty drawback systems are in place in most East European countries, but the actual working of these systems usually leaves much to be desired. In Hungary, a recent enterprise survey showed that about 56% of exporters experienced difficulties with the working of the drawback system. Of these respondents, 68% found the procedure too bureaucratic and 87% found it too long. It usually takes 50 to 120 days for reimbursement of the duties paid, which, when combined with the import surcharge, the valued-added tax (VAT), and turnover tax, could more than double the original price of the imported product. In a country with high inflation and lending rates [in Hungary in 1995 the producer price index was 30.2% and the lending rate was 32.2%], tying up funds for several months may significantly burden and discourage exporters. Moreover, the average may conceal extremes, such as cases where companies waited 1.5 or 2 years after exporting for reimbursement of the customs duties (Nagy, 1996).

As can be seen from the country studies in this book and the case studies of the accompanying volume, as well as from other sources (for example Sorsa, 1994), these complaints by Hungarian exporters are also characteristic of the experiences of exporters in the other countries of Central and Eastern Europe. Moreover, problems also occur with VAT payments on imports (usually with higher rates than average customs duties in most countries) that are due to be reimbursed on exports, as well as with import surcharges where they are used.

From our picture of tariff and tax regulations in this region (which is probably incomplete), the duty drawback regulation used by Slovenia seems to operate most smoothly for exporters. In this system, importers receive advance conditional relief from payment of import tariffs on raw materials and production materials if these goods are to be used in exports within one year (in the general case) and if the value of the exports is at least 30% higher than the total value of the imported inputs. However, if they do not use the imported inputs for exports, the duty must later be repaid with interest.

In the near future, those countries that have concluded Association Agreements with the EU may have to give up their systems of drawbacks with respect to exports to the EU, regardless of whether or not these systems work smoothly. This demand by the EU was recently presented to the countries concerned, and its implementation would require the modification of the original Association Agreements. If this requirement materializes, those exporters will suffer most who base their exports to EU countries on large-scale imports of raw materials or components from non-EU, usually East Asian, countries.

9.3.3 Export subsidies

Recent analyses of government subsidies to enterprises in Eastern Europe (Bod, 1994; IMF, 1994; Chu and Schwartz, 1995; and Schaffer, 1995) report a general reduction of subsidies in the state budgets of countries in this region. In 1986 subsidies in the state budget (whatever they meant in the different countries) made up 25.4% of the GDP in Czechoslovakia, 25.4% in Hungary, and 16.3% in Poland. In 1993 these shares were 4.4% in the Czech Republic, 4.8% in Slovakia, 4.8% in Hungary, and 2.5% in Poland (Schaffer, 1995).

From the plethora of transfers, taxes, and subsidies of the former system, it is impossible to identify those items that were associated with exports. As for the more transparent system in use in 1993 or 1994, it would be considerably easier to make this selection if all the necessary data were available. However, given the low level of total subsidies, even without the detailed data we can surely state that only extremely small amounts of subsidies support exporters. Schaffer (1995) emphasizes that most remaining budgetary subsidies in the Visegrád countries are related to extant price controls, such as subsidized prices in transport or housing.

From Hungary's example, one can see the limited and decreasing role outright export subsidies play in transition economies.[19]

In Hungary by 1992 trade denominated in transferable rubles was completely eliminated. Accordingly in 1991 the entire complicated system of taxes and subsidies related to ruble trade was phased out.

In the late 1980s short-term encouragement of non-ruble exporters (such as bonuses to the managers of the best-performing exporting firms) was gradually abolished and replaced by a system that was considered more progressive. Under this system companies competed for those government funds serving the development of export capacities. In this framework, agreements were concluded between the government and enterprises that planned to expand their exports. The enterprises offered to develop exports and in exchange the government offered different kinds of benefits such as subsidies, credits with preferential interest rates, liberalized imports, and to some extent liberalized wages. In the early 1990s, however, as the liberalization of the entire economy progressed, many benefits lost their importance or could not be sustained. The real targets of the system, the large state exporting firms, were also transformed: those that were not approaching liquidation were split into several small firms and/or were privatized. Whereas in 1986, 44% of total exports originated from firms that had export agreements with the government, by 1992 this figure had declined to 31%, with the potential for a further plunge. Many foreign investors who became producers in Hungary were less interested in expanding their exports (and receiving some benefits from that expansion) than in capturing the domestic market and collecting the substantial benefits offered for foreign direct investors (Oroszki and Hanzmann, 1994).

At the same time the system of export development contracted, all export subsidies became indirect and minimal in size; they have gradually been attached to financing, insuring, or guaranteeing exports, to cofinancing of marketing studies, and to participation at trade fairs, among other things.[20] The source of most of this support was a government fund which, to confuse the enterprises, changed names three times between 1991 and 1995. The budget of this fund in 1987 was 1.3% of the state budget; in 1991 it was 0.6%; and in 1994, 0.2% (see Bod, 1994; and Csaba, 1995). With such a low starting level, the decision to more than double the amount of this fund from 1995 to 1996 is not likely to have a significant effect (Molnár, 1995).

An example of indirect support is the Hungarian government's recent program to support progressive large enterprises. Here the support of exports is only a complementary target. In this program, 18 large companies were granted a 100% corporate tax exemption for five years. To be eligible to compete for this benefit companies had to have at least 500 million forints (over US$5 million) of equity capital and plans for at least 200 million forints (over US$2 million) of investment. Other criteria also had to be fulfilled, of which only one was export expansion. Of the 18 winning companies, 13 had substantial or full foreign participation.[21]

The recent emphasis of Slovenian's economic policy on the development of economic competitiveness also implies the use of some indirect (and direct) export subsidies. Special assistance, either outright subsidies or subsidies in the form of preferential loans, is provided to enterprises that have suffered financial losses due to the too-strong position of the domestic currency, the tolar. A large number of these firms were exporters of labor-intensive products. Because the Slovenian government's revenues originate mainly from taxes levied on wages and salaries, this category of enterprises is considered to be especially deserving of support. In 1995 and 1996 the Slovenian government also subsidized the social security contribution of net exporters, again with the aim of mitigating the effect of the too-strong currency on exporters of labor-intensive products (Cesen, 1995; and Institute of Macroeconomic Analysis and Development, 1995).

9.3.4 Economic diplomacy

When the CMEA dissolved in 1991, the governments of small East European economies were only able to carry out damage control, and even this was done without much success. Obviously, once the decision had been made in early 1990 to abandon the old system of trade, there was little the former CMEA countries could do to maintain export demand and their buyers' abilities to pay for their deliveries in the Soviet Union, their largest market. Bulgaria and Czechoslovakia attempted to keep certain parts of their exports in the framework of bilateral clearing arrangements, but the other countries shifted almost totally to convertible currency payments. In addition to the abolishment of clearing arrangements, the Soviet government introduced a general ban on barter agreements; only some oil and gas deliveries were exempted. These fuels were exchanged for certain products as determined by the Soviet government or by Soviet republican and local governments (see UN ECE, 1991). Over the course of 1991, after the effects of the dramatic drop of post-CMEA trade were felt, a plethora of bilateral deals were signed between Poland, Czechoslovakia, and Bulgaria, on one side, and the Soviet Union and republican authorities, on the other. These agreements aimed at realizing some kind of countertrade. The arrangements, however, could not stop the decline of trade with the Soviet Union, a consequence of the disappearance of former political and economic institutions such as the Warsaw Pact and the CMEA, and of the accelerated disintegration of the Soviet Union.

Moreover, the governments of the Central and East European countries were not in the position to mitigate the emerging shortage of foreign exchange in the Soviet Union (and to a lesser extent in Bulgaria and Romania) that thwarted payments for supplies from former CMEA partners. Discussions about an East European payments union, an institution aimed at easing foreign exchange shortages, was more on the agenda of scholars than that of policy makers. However, even in scientific discussions this arrangement was found to be infeasible and unpromising for political and economic reasons.

Nonetheless, efforts could have been made to counteract the dramatic decline of trade among small East European economies, especially through the maintenance of tariff-free trading in the short run [i.e., until a more sophisticated agreement like the Central European Free Trade Agreement (CEFTA) could be set up]. However, for the first democratically elected new governments of Eastern Europe, this task did not seem attractive enough to merit a place at the top of their policy agenda.

Although these first governments were somewhat reluctant to show a willingness to regain old "socialist" markets, their successors, especially those who had close ties to the old communist party, were ready to elaborate new forms of cooperation to revive trade with former partners, especially with republics of the former Soviet Union (FSU). For instance, in 1995 and 1996 the governments of Slovakia and Hungary emphasized increases in exports to Russia, Ukraine, Kazakstan, and the other FSU republics as their major trade policy targets. Among the signs of a strong commitment to these goals are the frequent visits by top-level politicians as well as lower-level government delegations, the creation of intergovernmental committees, and initiatives for foreign direct investments (FDI) and industry-level cooperation. However, these efforts have not brought much success.

Another attempt to regain old markets was the recent establishment of a free trade area between Slovenia and Macedonia with asymmetric conditions (in favor of Macedonia). Given the small volume of trade between the two countries, this act had mostly symbolic value.

The free trade agreements negotiated, signed, and ratified since 1991 with EU and EFTA countries and with the countries of the Visegrád group represented major achievements in the economic diplomacy of East European governments. The mainly politically determined access to the large markets of the former CMEA, especially those of the FSU, was replaced by easy access to the markets of Europe based more on economic principles and legal foundations than on political commitment. It is justifiable to say that, because of the wide-ranging relations of the new free trade agreements, East European governments have been left with few methods of intervention in exports.

Although each country had its own agreement with the EU and EFTA, the differences between these agreements are not substantial and tend to reflect the established structure of trade between a given country and the regional organization (i.e., the EU, EFTA, or CEFTA) rather than differences in negotiating tactics, commitments, or power among the individual governments. In addition, West European integrations often treat East European countries as a homogeneous bloc, as was reflected in several political and economic events between 1990 and 1995. Among these events were the antidumping procedures or embargoes of 1992 and 1993, which the EU and EFTA countries automatically extended from "guilty" to "innocent" countries in Eastern Europe. The general provision of additional market access benefits at the Copenhagen summit of the EU in 1993 and the recent approach to negotiations concerning the enlargement of the EU also support this bloc view.

As for initiatives from the East European side, our impression (one that is not easy to prove) is that in East and Central Europe economic diplomacy differs by country more with respect to the protection efforts used against imports than the attempts to obtain concessions for exports.[22]

9.3.5 Institution building for export financing

Following the abandonment of most forms of direct subsidies to exports, the governments of East and Central European countries realized that their primary disadvantage was the poor financing infrastructure available for exports. The export financing infrastructure entails, among other elements, pre-financing of production for export, financing of payment on the seller's or the buyer's side, long-term financing of exports of large equipment and complete plants, and insurance and guarantees against political and commercial risks. The financing issue is crucial because firms inherited substantially undercapitalized operations, payment discipline deteriorated in both the domestic and East European markets, and pressure to export to the West pushed East European exporters to accept long payment periods (60 to 90 days) and unfavorable payment conditions for their exports.

It is clear that many promising export deals fall through because East European suppliers cannot compete with the generous payment conditions that Western or Far Eastern suppliers offer, or because they cannot pre-finance the purchase of inputs necessary for processing.

The recent growth of inward processing in Eastern Europe (outward processing from the West European side) is one response to the lack of available financing: according to the UN Economic Commission for Europe (UN ECE, 1995), in 1994 50% of textiles and clothing exports from the Czech Republic to the EU were carried out in the form of inward processing; these shares were 51% for Slovakia, 70% for Hungary, 50% for Bulgaria, and 70% for Romania.[23]

In trade with other East European countries, one of the main stumbling blocks is unreliability of payments. In the absence of professional export insurance agencies, the primary way to cope with this difficulty has been the use of Western intermediaries. The extent of this kind of intermediation can be demonstrated using Hungarian exports and imports as an example. According to our calculations, in 1993 9% of Hungary's exports to the FSU went through mediators, and 31% of Hungary's exports to the Czech and Slovak Republics and 19% of the exports to Poland were arranged by (mostly Austrian and Swiss) intermediaries that usually enjoyed strong banking support. In the other direction, 53% of Poland's exports to Hungary and 22% of Czech and Slovak exports to Hungary were carried out by intermediaries. According to Törzsök (1995), in 1994 the share of Hungarian trade carried out by mediators was the highest in exports to Slovenia (52%), followed by Bulgaria (45%), Croatia (29%), and the Czech Republic (27%). In the case of imports, the largest share of trade handled by mediators was in imports from Russia (46%), followed by Lithuania (42%), Bulgaria (42%), and Poland (36%). There is no reason not to assume that intermediation is similarly intense in trade among transition economies where Hungary is not a trade partner. This unusual pattern of high intermediation in trade between countries with traditional trade links, many of which share common borders, is clear evidence of either the lack of trust in implementing payment obligations (which is well-founded in most cases) or the poor state of market research activities in the region.

By 1994 most East European governments had realized that only a few acceptable instruments for enhancing exports were at their disposal. However, in one critical field, the financing of exports, problems could not be solved without governmental activity. Since 1993 almost every East European government has established its own export-import bank and export insurance agency or corporation. These institutions are not yet strong in any of these countries. In fact, in some countries they hardly function at all.[24]

The operation of the existing organizations shows that merely establishing these institutions does not mean they will function effectively. Preparing policies, recruiting experts, setting up information channels, and gathering funds all require time and additional budgetary sources. Other tasks include properly defining the role of the new institutions vis-à-vis the old ones (like the commercial banks and other government agencies) and using company information that commercial banks possess to further the goal of smooth and moderately subsidized export financing.

The Hungarian Export–Import Bank and the Hungarian Export Insurance Corporation (MEHIB) can be considered "old" in the Central East European environment, but even as late as 1995 they were planning to serve only a paltry 5%

of Hungarian exports.[25] A comparison of this share with the ratio of official credit authorizations related to exports of manufactured goods in developed market economies, which varies between 10% and 45% (Hufbauer and Erb, 1984), makes it clear that much has to be done to improve the financial backing of exports. Klauber (1995) reports that between 1993 and 1995 about 10–14% of Hungarian exports were covered by export-related financing provided by the Hungarian banking sector; two-thirds of this, however, was export pre-financing, which basically had no subsidy or preference elements.

In addition to its infant export-import bank and export insurance corporation, the Slovenian government also uses a nontraditional method to help enterprises, especially exporters, to receive cheaper credits. Those banks that have government bonds in their portfolio are informally pressured to "voluntarily" charge interest rates below the market rate on loans granted to exporting enterprises.

9.3.6 Management of enterprise restructuring

Once most forms of direct government support were abolished, individualized support for exporters was available only if the exporters were involved in general and broader assistance programs. Most of these programs targeted enterprises that were in trouble and were rarely aimed at exports or export deals. However, several factors imply that these programs must have had a considerable impact on export potential: first, all the small East European countries in our sample are largely open to world markets, therefore almost all activities are connected with exports; second, most enterprises experienced trouble because of losses incurred due to the collapse of their former export markets; and third, these programs triggered significant budgetary allocations.

Between 1992 and 1994 Hungary's debtor consolidation program centered its efforts on financial restructuring of the enterprises associated with enterprise strategies, which had to be prepared for real restructuring. Bad loans, which enterprises were unable to service let alone pay back, were canceled, rescheduled, or swapped for equity. Additional programs were organized to consolidate banks burdened with bad loans. The primary method of this relief was that the bad loans of the banks were swapped for long-maturity government bonds. Simultaneously, restructuring strategies had to be elaborated by the enterprises and accepted by supervising agencies or banks in exchange for financial assistance. Occasionally the State Property Agency provided special reorganization subsidies. Banks or specialized institutions were entrusted with managing the turnaround of selected companies. We will not go into detail here as to the efficiency of the different forms of these assistance programs. It is sufficient to indicate that large shares of the government budget or extrabudgetary funds were used to restructure the companies eventually, if not directly, to maintain or improve their export potential.

Similar measures were carried out in 1993 in the Czech Republic. These arrangements included a one-shot clearing of enterprise obligations; capitalization of claims in favor of creditors; the launching of a special bank, Konsolidacni Banka, which buys the claims of main creditors and arranges revitalization programs in large companies; and attempts at solving the bad loan problem of banks.

In Slovenia in 1992 the government had to tackle the problems of several hundred companies that were on the verge of bankruptcy. Special development funds were created to negotiate with companies in order to restructure their claims, to change debts for equity, to inject fresh capital, to find new managers, to initiate the elaboration of new restructuring programs, and to initiate foreign partnerships. Later, the European Bank for Reconstruction and Development (EBRD) extended ECU 30 million to establish a special joint company with special funds to support the above-mentioned efforts.

The international principles used to evaluate how domestic subsidies damage other trading partners are not as well defined as those used to evaluate the distorting impact of outright export subsidies or other kinds of indirect subsidies to exports. The main criterion is whether an adverse trade impact can be attributed to the indirect subsidization of exports stemming from assistance to production (Hufbauer and Erb, 1984). Because in East and Central Europe most assistance in the category of enterprise restructuring aims at saving ailing firms, it would be hard to show that it leads to aggressive export expansion on foreign markets. Still, if the efforts manage to improve the competitive potential of the enterprises rather than conserve old enterprise structures, they might be the governments' most significant contributions to the enhancement of exports.

9.4 Summary and Conclusions

In the early 1990s the first and most important direct contribution the governments of Central and Eastern Europe made to support export activities was the liberalization of trade, including the elimination of state intervention in trade. This policy aimed at establishing market conditions and incentives in this field, and through them, at improving the efficiency of trade. It did not directly assist trade volumes or balances, however: the volume of trade did not show an unambiguous growth in the region following liberalization and, with some lag, disturbing trade balances also emerged.

Trade liberalization vitalized the enterprises' general trading activity. At the same time, contrary to theoretical predictions, opening up to the world market did not simply provide more incentives for exporting activities at the expense of import substituting activities. The multiplicity of shocks completely rearranged the positions of enterprises, products, and markets. In many cases, industries and enterprises struggled merely to survive. During this period, the fates of exports and import substitution were closely interrelated.

Even if the move away from the former system cannot be easily characterized using traditional concepts, the end result is easy to identify: by 1996 each country had a trading system with relatively few distortions and little governmental intervention. The international commitments that these countries have recently made (free trade agreements, World Trade Organization membership, and aspirations to EU membership) are also binding in this respect. This distortion-free structure is attractive for most economists, because experience has shown the virtues of governments' taking a hands-off approach to trade. In addition, for historical reasons there is a general perception that in this region a little government intervention would soon lead to a plethora of interventions.

The problem with this distortion-free trade system is that in most East European countries it is coupled with a fragile production base for exports and a poorly developed infrastructure. Exporters from the region are at a disadvantage with competitors in both Western and Eastern (that is, former CMEA) markets, especially when they want to sell more processed, differentiated manufactured products. Unless these exporters completely abandon plans to market goods of this nature, they need support. The support can come either from strong Western partners through different kinds of cooperation and FDI, or from the exporter's own government. The government here has a role in helping to place its exporters on an equal footing with competitors. However, the methods of this assistance are limited and, due to interventionist traditions, must be used with caution.

Most forms of government support that have recently been used are horizontal. Economic diplomacy has played a crucial role in providing market access for domestic companies. However, distributing information about these new market possibilities and possible external impediments is a task that not all the governments have performed well. In the early years the devalued currencies were of help, but once the initial phase of transition is over exchange rate policies seem to have limited potential for support. Augmenting the infrastructure of exports is a slow, sophisticated process that involves, among other activities, setting up export-import banks and export insurance agencies, distributing information, and supporting marketing studies and participation at trade fairs. The East European governments seem to have given far less support for their exports than the international commitments allow. The reasons for this have included the lack of budgetary and intellectual resources and probably an overemphasis on conforming with the etiquette of the developed economies.[26]

Government assistance for salvaging or reorganizing enterprises has become widespread and has helped to strengthen the base of exports. However, it has been characterized more by "fire fighting" than by foresight or clever planning. Governments are too cautious about outlining selection criteria, although even their improvised "rescues" represent a kind of selection. The fear of increased government involvement in business and the uncertainty concerning these countries' comparative advantages have prevented the administrations from drawing up and accepting even indicative industrial policies. Unlike the earlier policies of some of the successful East Asian exporting countries, current export policies of East European countries are not centered on a vision for future development of exports.

As this chapter evidences, it was not accidental that the basically soft and hesitating export promotion policies went along similar lines in all four countries discussed (the Czech Republic, Hungary, Slovakia, and Slovenia). However, based on our knowledge of recent developments, it seems safe to conclude that in the future export assistance will play a larger role than in the recent past, and given the divergence in the countries' trade developments, this assistance will not necessarily be identical in all countries.

Notes

[1] For more details, see *Table I.1* in the Introduction to this book.

[2] The author is grateful to Franjo Štiblar and Jan Fidrmuc, who generously helped to organize study trips to Slovenia and Slovakia, respectively. The discussions with ministry officials, scholars, policy makers, and other experts there were extremely valuable. Special thanks should go to Petr Zahradnik, who helped to collect information for the Czech Republic. Comments by participants of an IIASA workshop in 1995, especially suggestions by Richard Cooper, were also utilized. All errors remain the responsibility of the author.

[3] The authors of a recent World Bank project that covered many developing countries agree that the usual framework for the analysis of trade liberalizations is not directly applicable for former centrally planned economies (Michaely *et al.*, 1991).

[4] In fact, it turned out that under the conditions of these extreme shocks, treating the two activities separately was not fully justified: the shock in the domestic market, coupled with bad management by the government, had the potential to destroy exporting activities, while the external shocks could lead to the collapse of the institutional base of many import substituting activities. For example, in Hungary, ". . . the bankruptcy and liquidation procedures in process in 1992 have affected about one fourth of the industrial exports and half of food exports. . . . Bankruptcy procedures as a rule . . . decrease exporting activities, while liquidation in most cases phases out exports." (Lányi and Csermely, 1994, p. 34).

[5] See Chapter 6 for more information.

[6] Since December 1992 there has been a 6% additional turnover tax for all products imported into Poland; since March 1994 there has been a 10% import surcharge on consumer goods in Slovakia.

[7] Some East European suppliers and brand names were well known in the successor states of the USSR, but due to lack of marketing efforts this advantage seems to be fading. For evidence see Chapter 10.

[8] For information on the program in Slovakia, see SRGO, 1994. In Hungary, a September 1993 decision by the government addressed the implementation of the economic policy in 1994, the core of which dealt with export promotion.

[9] The priorities of business managers were somewhat different. For instance, a recent survey of enterprise managers in Hungary disclosed that 25% of the managers think that exports would be best promoted by devaluation; 13%, through the improvement of credit conditions; and 15%, through a reduction of taxes and social security contributions. (What do the enterprises expect? *Figyelő*, 1995, no. 14.)

[10] *Mlada Fronta Dnes*, 19 May 1995.

[11] We had better years earlier – interview with State Secretary Imre Dunai, *Figyelő*, 1995, no. 1; Interview with the minister of industry, *Figyelő*, 1995, no. 22; Crisis in granting loans to enterprises, *Figyelő*, 1995, no. 9.

[12] For more information, see the Introduction to this book.

[13] Step-wise devaluations were carried out in 1990 in Czechoslovakia. In Slovenia devaluation preceded the creation of the tolar in 1991, and in the successive months the tolar further depreciated.

[14] However, exporters are more concerned: "... [real appreciation] ... caused complaints from active exporters, mainly in the industrial sectors and demands for reconsideration of economic policy in this field" (Chamber of Economy Slovenia, 1995).

[15] Exporters on the devaluation, *Figyelő*, 1995, no. 11.

[16] In Romania export quotas were also used extensively for domestic purposes, i.e., to protect natural resources and to prevent the outflow of underpriced manufactures, such as drugs (see Messerlin, 1995).

[17] Quota dispute, *Figyelő*, 1995, no. 20.

[18] In Latvia in mid-1992 export quotas were replaced by export taxes. Higher taxes were levied on exports to areas with nonconvertible currencies, with the aim of encouraging exports to the West. The coverage, level, and dispersion of export taxes were later reduced. Most export taxes are applied to raw materials such as timber and wood products, metal and metal products, and leather and furs to encourage domestic manufacturing as opposed to direct exports (Sorsa, 1994; EBRD, 1994; and UN ECE, 1994). In 1994 and 1995 in Bulgaria, export taxes were applied on wood and wood products and on copper products (see EBRD, 1994; and Chapter 1 in this book).

[19] As for the other countries, it is worth mentioning that over the course of our consultations and collection of information we did not come across any sign of a system of export subsidies used by any of the governments of the four countries (except for subsidies to agricultural and food products).

[20] Export promotion and liberalization, *Figyelő*, 1994, no. 14.

[21] See *Figyelő*, 1995, no. 2. In fact, this program replaces one that provided hefty tax exemptions only for new joint ventures.

[22] This view is difficult to prove because there are many other countries outside Europe with which each country has prepared and will prepare new bilateral agreements on trade, freight, protection of investments, and avoidance of double taxation, among other things.

[23] Naturally, inward processing also has other advantages and disadvantages not related to financing.

[24] The Czech Export Bank was expected to start its real operation in July 1995, and the Slovak Export-Import Bank has not yet been established.

[25] Recent reports do not seem to confirm that even this moderate plan was implemented.

[26] For instance, the countries concerned take it for granted that they must conform to OECD guidelines on officially supported export credits, despite the fact that as of late-1995 none of them was yet a signatory to the OECD. In their relations with the EU they did not even contemplate applying for a status similar to those of the developing countries, which would have given them more room to provide export subsidies.

References

Balassa, B., 1982, Reforming the system of incentives in developing economies, in B. Balassa *et al.*, eds., *Development Strategies in Semi-Industrial Economies*, Johns Hopkins University Press, Baltimore, MD, USA.

Bod, P.A., 1994, Subsidies, transfers and the prospects for sustainable growth – The case of Hungary, *West-Ost Journal*, 5–6:20–22.

Cesen, T., 1995, The Industrial Policy in Slovenia, Institute of Macroeconomic Analysis and Development, Ljubljana, Slovenia [mimeograph].

Chamber of Economy of Slovenia, 1995, Slovenia Current Economic Trends, Ljubljana, Slovenia, February.

Chu, K., and Schwartz, G., 1995, Output decline and government expenditures in European transition economies, in R. Holzmann, J. Gács, and G. Winckler, eds., *Output Decline in Eastern Europe – Unavoidable, External Influence or Homemade?* Kluwer Academic Publishers, Dordrecht, Netherlands.

Csaba, L., 1995, The political economy of trade regimes in Central Europe, in A. Winters, ed., *Foundations of an Open Economy*, Centre for Economic Policy Research, London, UK.

Dietz, R., 1995, Währungsdisparitäten und Preisrelationen in Ost und West am Beispiel von Löhnen und Energieträgern, The Vienna Institute for Comparative Economic Studies (WIIW), Vienna, Austria [mimeograph].

EBRD, 1994, Transition Report: Economic Transition in Eastern Europe and the Former Soviet Union, European Bank for Reconstruction and Development, London, UK.

Fidrmuc, J. *et al.*, 1994, The Slovak Republic: After One Year of Independence, Bank Austria, Vienna, Austria.

Foreign Trade Research Institute, 1993, *Polish Foreign Trade in 1992: Annual Report*, Foreign Trade Research Institute, Warsaw, Poland.

Gács, J., 1994, Trade liberalization in the CSFR, Hungary and Poland: Rush and reconsideration, in J. Gács and G. Winckler, eds., *International Trade and Restructuring in Eastern Europe*, Physica Verlag, Heidelberg, Germany.

Havlik, P. *et al.*, 1995, Growth in Central and Eastern Europe Contrasts with Recession in the CIS, The Vienna Institute for Comparative Economic Studies (WIIW), Vienna, Austria.

Hufbauer, G.C., and Erb, J.S., 1984, Subsidies in International Trade, Institute for International Economics, Washington, DC, USA.

Hughes, G., and Hare, P., 1991, Competitiveness and industrial restructuring in Czechoslovakia, Hungary and Poland, *European Economy*, Special Edition No. 2.

IMF, 1994, World Economic Outlook, International Monetary Fund, Washington, DC, USA, October.

Institute of Macroeconomic Analysis and Development, 1995, Budget Memorandum for 1996, Ministry of Economic Relations and Development of Republic of Slovenia, Institute of Macroeconomic Analysis and Development, Ljubljana, Slovenia.

Klauber, M., 1995, Export Promotion Experiences in the West, in the Visegrád countries and Hungary, KOPINT-DATORG, Budapest, Hungary [in Hungarian].

Lányi, K., and Csermely, Á., 1994, On the Main Causes of the Decline of Hungarian Exports – Can the Decline Be Stopped? KOPINT-DATORG, Budapest, Hungary [in Hungarian].

McKinnon, R.I., 1991, *The Order of Economic Liberalization – Financial Control in the Transition to a Market Economy*, Johns Hopkins University Press, Baltimore, MD, USA.

Messerlin, P.A., 1995, Central and East European countries' trade laws in the light of international experience, in A.L. Winters, ed., *Foundations of an Open Economy*, Centre for Economic and Policy Research, London, UK.

Michaely, M., Papageorgiou, D., and Choksi, A.M., eds., 1991, *Liberalizing Foreign Trade – Lessons of Experience in the Developing World*, vol. 1–7, Blackwell, Cambridge, MA, USA.

Molnár, L., 1995, On the Foreign Economic Strategy in "Nut-shell", *Ipari Szemle* (*Industry Review*), **XV**(6):24–25 [in Hungarian].

Nagy, Á., 1996, Claiming Back Duties, VAT, and Surcharge Paid on Imports by Exporters in Hungary, KOPINT-DATORG, Budapest, Hungary [in Hungarian].

Nash, J., 1994, Institutional policies for export development, in C. Michalopoulos, and D. Tarr, eds., *Trade in the New Independent States, Studies of Economies in Transition*, no. 13, The World Bank and UNDP, Washington, DC, USA.

Oroszki, S., and Hanzmann, J., 1994, The state of export development and export promotion, *Ipari Szemle* (*Industry Review*), **XIV**(1):8–12 [in Hungarian].

Potocnik, J., Senjur, M., and Stiblar, F., 1995, *The Strategy for Economic Development of Slovenia: Approaching Europe – Growth, Competitiveness and Integration*, Institute of Macroeconomic Analysis and Development, Ljubljana, Slovenia.

Sass, M., 1995, Export Promotion in the Transition Economies – The Case of Czech Republic, Poland and Slovakia, Institute of World Economy, Hungarian Academy of Sciences, Budapest, Hungary [in Hungarian].

Schaffer, M.E., 1995, Government Subsidies to Enterprises in Central and Eastern Europe: Budgetary Subsidies and Tax Arrears, Discussion Paper No. 1144, Centre for Economic Policy Research, London, UK.

Sorsa, P., 1994, Latvia: Trade issues in transition, in C. Michalopoulos, and D. Tarr, eds., *Trade in the New Independent States, Studies of Economies in Transition*, no. 13, The World Bank and UNDP, Washington DC, USA.

SRGO (Slovak Republic Government Office), 1994, Programme of support to Slovak Republic's exports, in *Concept of Slovak Republic's Foreign Trade*, SRGO, Bratislava, Slovakia.

Törzsök, É., 1995, The foreign transit trade and the Hungarian trade balance, *Külgazdaság*, vol. XXXIX, no. 10, pp. 37–53 [in Hungarian].

UN ECE, 1991, Economic Bulletin for Europe, vol. 43, UN Economic Commission for Europe, Geneva, Switzerland.

UN ECE, 1994, Economic Bulletin for Europe, vol. 46, UN Economic Commission for Europe, Geneva, Switzerland.

UN ECE, 1995, Economic Bulletin for Europe, vol. 47, UN Economic Commission for Europe, Geneva, Switzerland.

WIIW, 1995, WIIW Handbook of Statistics: Countries in Transition, The Vienna Institute for Comparative Economic Studies (WIIW), Vienna, Austria.

Chapter 10

Foreign Direct Investment, Exports, and East–West Integration: Theory and Practice

Richard E. Stern

The economic transformation of Central and East European countries (CEECs) is largely dependent on their integration with the West. The most obvious channels through which economic integration occurs are trade and foreign direct investment (FDI). Through imports of goods and capital, a country can potentially accelerate its economic growth. Through exports, a country can expand markets (allowing firms and industries to exploit economies of scale) as well as earn necessary foreign currency.

Although the impact and importance of trade and FDI on economic development and growth have been studied separately, their intersection has not been sufficiently explored. Trade and FDI can be integrally related. If trade is obstructed through formal or informal barriers, if foreign currency reserves are severely constrained, or if exports or imports are not easily accessible due to market failures, then FDI can be a substitute for trade by facilitating imports of both physical and human capital. In this situation FDI can be vital for the host country's ability to grow. Alternatively, FDI can facilitate trade directly if it is used to develop

This project was generously funded by IIASA's Economic Transition and Integration Project. Special thanks go to János Gács, who supervised, directed, and provided expert guidance for this project. The author also gratefully acknowledges Pál Gáspár, László Halpern, Judit Hamar, Matija Rojec, Manfred Schekulin, Miklós Szanyi, Petr Zahradnik, the Česky Statisticky Urad, and especially Shari Jandl. All errors remain the responsibility of the author.

export sectors, or indirectly if it is used to develop sectors that producc for the local market and eventually contribute to sales abroad. In this case, trade and FDI are complementary, which can be of great benefit for both the host and home countries. Of course, FDI can act as both a complement to and substitute for trade simultaneously.

The experience of trade and FDI from the West to Eastern Europe is an example of the coexistence of complementarity and substitutability. FDI works as a substitute for trade mainly on the import side. During the initial phase of economic transformation (which, arguably, is still occurring in some of the countries), the CEECs attempted to reorient trade away from former Council for Mutual Economic Assistance (CMEA) countries toward European Union (EU) economies to establish new markets for domestically produced goods and to obtain necessary imports to satisfy consumer demand and facilitate growth. Though trade between CEECs and EU countries grew dramatically from 1989 to the present [at a rate of 23% per year according to Faini and Portes (1995)], it became clear that FDI was an effective means of acquiring goods and services from the West where direct importation was not possible or practical (due to high costs or lack of local skills to organize production, for example). In sectors such as consumer goods, financial and other services, and technology-intensive industries, FDI can substitute for the importation of goods and services and provide for the know-how and expertise to organize these activities at home. Thus, during the early stages of transformation, FDI as a substitute for trade was an extremely important part of the marketization process because it allowed for quick absorption and implementation of goods and services to fill gaps in the transition economy.

FDI works as a complement to trade in both imports and exports. On the import side, FDI can augment existing import capabilities through the transfer of technology and human capital. On the export side, FDI can enhance the external demand for goods because the foreign investor can gear production and distribution of goods to be competitive in the home or target country market. Thus with FDI exports can be enhanced because goods can be produced for specific export markets and investor networks (for distribution and marketing, for example) can be used to gain market access for the domestic country's goods.

Given the uncertainty about the path and duration of economic and political transition, the lack of transparency in the legal framework, the lack of working financial markets, the uncertainty of macroeconomic stability, and the varying levels of exchange rate convertibility, all set within the backdrop of the 1991–1993 recession in Europe and the USA, the initial levels of FDI were disappointingly low relative to *ex ante* predictions and the capital requirements of each CEEC. Low levels of FDI capitalization combined with short-term investment are a manifestation of investor uncertainty and are consistent with the theory of irreversible investment (see Borensztein and Montiel, 1991). The majority of investments were characterized by projects that sought to meet the immediate needs of CEEC domestic markets or by extremely short-term investments with high payoffs.[1] These projects targeted consumer goods and services, financial services, and tourism. Levels of capitalization were low and tended to decline from 1991 to 1994, which reduced exposure risk. FDI during this stage was limited to local markets.

Although this initial FDI phase continues in many CEECs, a second stage has begun in some countries where FDI complements international trade. Foreign investors, especially from crucial border countries such as Austria, have begun to develop new FDI ties that take advantage of both the CEECs' labor cost differential and their strategic locations on the edge of the European Economic Space (EES) as places to relocate production.[2] The change in investment behavior is a result of changing conditions within the host countries that have made their domestic environments more attractive to foreign investors. First, the CEECs that border the EES (Poland, the Czech Republic, Slovakia, and Hungary; known as the Visegrád Four) have rapidly transformed their economies to the point where the transparency of the legal structures, the relatively easy access to CEEC resources and markets, and the prospects for medium- and long-term stability and growth have convinced many investors that the risk premium associated with FDI has fallen. Additionally, the reduction of trade barriers due to the EU Association Agreements with the individual CEECs (the "Europe Agreements"), as well as the agreement in principle that the CEECs will eventually accede to the EU, which was made during the December 1994 European Summit in Essen, reflects a commitment by the West to integrate Eastern economies into the Western economic community. This commitment has had an extremely powerful influence on investors' decisions.

In theory, this stage of FDI should be characterized by investments flowing first into manufacturing sectors (taking advantage of the wage differentials) and then into more highly industrialized sectors that involve higher capitalization, longer time horizons, higher payoffs for the investor, and greater risks. During this phase, one would expect FDI into the tradable sector to increase as well. Further, locational decisions should also play an increasingly important role. Firms located at or near borders with EU countries are in better positions to service both the Western and Eastern markets because of easy accessibility from the home country and lower transportation costs. The focus of foreign investments on these specific benefits is known as the *maquiladora* effect, a characteristic of FDI into Mexico by US firms in the late 1980s.

This study is the first in a series that will analyze the effects of FDI from West to East. In this study an analytical framework is proposed to assess the process and impact of FDI; the preliminary evidence from the region is also considered. In the following section, a theory of FDI cycles is developed and its applicability to the CEEC case is shown. In particular, the theory highlights the role of FDI into the trade sector. In the second section, empirical evidence is looked at to test the theoretical hypotheses set out in the first section. Conclusions are presented in the third section.

10.1 Toward a Theoretical Framework for Understanding FDI in CEECs

10.1.1 The roles of trade and FDI, and their intersection

Two of the most important links between an individual country's economy and the world economy are trade and FDI. Most analysts look at the roles of trade and FDI as two distinct entities. In this chapter it is argued that they can and should be integrally related: depending on the stage of development of the host country, FDI can be either a substitute for or a complement to trade. In countries that do not have a developed export sector or that cannot generate sufficient export revenues to pay for imports, FDI might provide a channel for obtaining necessary imports of physical goods and physical and human capital that are necessary for economic development.[3] In this situation, which is most common among developing countries and economies in transition, FDI is a *substitute* for trade.

When FDI is a substitute for trade, it is usually undertaken to fill existing holes (or market failures) in the host country's market. Foreign investments of this nature are typically found in the consumer market, in the low-tech (labor-intensive) manufactured goods sector, and in the financial system, especially when the financial system is still in its fledgling stage. These investments tend to be characterized by low levels of capitalization and high levels of return. The motives for investment on the part of home country firms include taking advantage of holes in the host country's market, especially where there is no competition from domestic sources, and securing a foothold in the host country's domestic market. This foothold could result in strategic market power for the investor, created either by the lack of viable alternatives or by government intervention protecting/creating a monopolistic or oligopolistic market structure.[4] This behavior is consistent with Dunning's (1988a) description of FDI's capturing the advantages of market internalization.

FDI can also be a *complement* to trade or can augment trade, especially if it is aimed directly at the export sector. That is, a foreign investor might have a better sense of what products will sell in foreign countries, how to market those products, and how to raise quality standards to conform to foreign demand. Thus, in addition to bringing in new technology, physical capital, and know-how, FDI could change the composition of a country's exports, significantly altering the country's comparative advantage, direction, and terms of trade. FDI into the foreign trade sector could also facilitate the internalization of foreign marketing strategies, ease the entrance into foreign markets (for example, via brand-name recognition), and give access to foreign distribution channels. These effects are extremely important as entry into foreign markets, especially those in developed countries, is difficult even in the absence of formal trade restrictions.[5]

In addition to the primary complementary effect of FDI and exports, which facilitates trade directly through the production and distribution of goods for export, there can also be secondary effects such as the enhancement of the host country's credibility and subsequent trade creation. By exporting goods a firm, and eventually a country, builds a reputation for being a reliable exporter of goods demanded in world markets. As a minimum, the establishment of credibility in foreign markets via FDI-induced trade will accelerate the process of opening those markets and is likely to result in the creation of new trade flows that might not have been possible without market penetration via FDI. That is, after a firm or set of firms gains credibility in developed markets in particular, they might be able to establish a foothold for new products produced either with or without foreign capital. As this process continues, and as more firms engage in foreign trade, demand for goods from the exporting country grows, which generates export revenues and growth in the export and corresponding support sectors. If the growth of the exporting sectors is sufficiently large, there can be measurable positive effects on the trade balance and on economic growth at the macroeconomic level. As is argued below, this credibility through FDI-augmented trade should have an important impact on the CEECs given their location on the border of EU countries.

Whether FDI is a substitute for or a complement to trade depends on the motivations of the home firm and the recipient, the sector receiving the investment, the explicit and implicit barriers to trade, the level and direction of existing trade flows, and the receptivity of the targeted export market. Although it seems more likely that FDI will substitute for trade than serve as a complement to it during the earlier stages of domestic development, it is entirely possible for some FDI to substitute for imports and for some to complement and enhance trade.

10.1.2 The FDI cycle in transition economies

This paper treats FDI as a dynamic, evolutionary process and thus breaks the development of FDI down into sequential phases. This section presents a descriptive model of an FDI cycle in countries in transition.[6] Section 10.2 uses this theory in the context of preliminary experiences in the CEECs.

Viewing FDI as a developmental process is a shift from past characterizations of FDI. In particular, it is argued here that the scope, scale, and distribution of FDI change as the macroeconomic and microeconomic conditions within the host country develop. The following characteristic phases in the FDI cycle in transition economies are identified:

- The initialization stage
- The internationalization stage
- The mature investment stage

The Initialization Stage. This first phase of FDI is characterized in the host country by a period of economic and political uncertainty, the existence of a mixture of market- and nonmarket-driven sectors, a strong state presence in the investment sector, a financially shallow capital market, pervasive market gaps and failures, and uncertainty about the extent and timing of economic reform. Perhaps the most important aspect of this phase is that the crucial legal infrastructure is either not in place, is not conducive to FDI, or is in flux. This problem was especially important in CEECs because legal and tax codes were from the communist (or in some cases, pre–World War II) era and needed to be completely overhauled. Without transparency of the tax and legal codes, a foreign investor could not have any guarantees about the security of the investment from nationalization, about the possibility of repatriating earnings and assets, or about projected profit levels (net of taxes).[7] It is clear that the lack of an institutional framework or the lack of transparency of the existing framework has scared off many would-be investors.[8]

Market gaps and failures provide strong incentives for foreign investment, especially where entire sectors can be captured with little investment.[9] At this stage in the FDI cycle investors see areas that are clearly backward or absent in the host country as the most natural sectors for investment: consumer goods, light manufactured goods, and perhaps most important, infrastructure and financial services. Thus the primary goal of an outward investor during this stage is gaining a foothold in the domestic market in order to use that market as a platform for future expansion.

These sectors require high levels of human capital and some technology but little start-up capital. Because these sectors (especially telecommunications) are so important to the basic development of the economy and to consumer welfare (with consequent political benefits), and because there is an absence of domestic competition due to the lack of physical or human capital, in these sectors a foreign investor can secure strategic market power at this stage unless the government or legal systems prevent it. In most cases the legal system cannot prevent the monopolization of markets because of the inadequacy of the code itself. For this reason, foreign firms can accrue substantial economic rents either by exploiting market failures or by exploiting holes in the legal and tax systems.

Another important aspect of FDI in this period is that it takes place alongside the privatization process; therefore, the majority of FDI is likely be in the form of joint ventures (including establishing 100% foreign ownership of existing companies), rather than greenfield investments. FDI in the context of privatization has been an extremely controversial issue for most CEECs. On the one hand, FDI during privatization accelerates the transformation and restructuring process through the transfer of physical and human capital. At the market level, it forces wholly domestically owned competitors to adopt cost-saving and/or quality-improving production techniques in order to be competitive. Thus, from an efficiency point of view, FDI and privatization should generate positive results. On the other hand, this use of FDI could be detrimental to the creation of competitive markets either directly (through the purchase and subsequent elimination of competitors) or indirectly (through the introduction of new products, which eliminates competition through loss of demand for the products of wholly domestically owned firms). The issue is extremely difficult to address. In an attempt to rectify the situation, many countries implemented so-called competition laws to at least lessen the likelihood of foreign or domestic oligopolization or monopolization of fledgling markets.[10]

Given the level of uncertainty about the depth, breadth, and speed of economic transformation during this period, investors are likely to question the security of their investment from an economic point of view. At the same time, the advantage of timing (that is, being first to invest) provides some counterweight to the economic uncertainty. Added to the economic uncertainty is political instability. Whereas political instability might be a feature of the initial period of economic transition, most investors feel that other, more direct obstacles to FDI are more discouraging, for example, legal protection of investments and transparency of the tax codes. When these microlevel problems are solved, political instability heads the list of deterrents to investment.[11]

FDI in this period is expected to be limited, with low levels of capitalization. In fact, the longer the period of legal, economic, and political instability, the lower the level of capitalization.[12] The technology component of these investments is also expected to be low in physical terms (in most cases this is because the sectors invested in do not require high levels of technology transfer), but may include considerable human capital such as new production techniques, new managerial systems, and new marketing skills.

The Internationalization Period. The character of FDI changes dramatically when the environment of the host country becomes more conducive to longer-term, larger-scale investments. Investors are more likely to try to take advantage of the specific assets of the host country once market fundamentals (commercial codes governing transactions, legal safeguards against nationalization, transparency of the tax structure, and the distribution and repatriation of profits) are in place, and once markets have been liberalized, privatization is either moving forward or is complete, financial markets are deepening and widening, and infrastructure is becoming more developed. In particular, the strategies of the investor firms go beyond gaining a foothold in the domestic market. During this stage, firms begin to act strategically to use host country locations, factor market endowments, and cost differentials as means for market penetration in foreign markets as well as in the host country's domestic markets.

The main motives for investment at this stage are to continue capturing domestic market share and to exploit the comparative advantages of the target country in international markets. Thus, FDI should be drawn into the export sector along with FDI into nontradables; therefore, the location of FDI becomes crucial. FDI into the export sector is expected to be strategically located near the countries targeted for trade and where infrastructure (transportation and storage) is the most developed. Where factor costs are relatively low (particularly labor costs), strong incentives are present for foreign investors who envision the product of FDI being sold both on domestic and international (Western) markets. In fact, the prospect of exporting back into home country markets (or in the case of EU countries, into EU markets) is one of the greatest gains to the foreign investor during this stage. Exploitation of factor cost differentials can be a strong incentive to engage in FDI, especially for firms that have had difficulty competing in home country markets.

FDI during the internationalization phase is likely to be characterized by higher levels of capitalization than those in the previous phase, by large and small projects operating simultaneously, and by investments with longer time horizons in non-financial services.[13] The degree to which levels of capitalization rise and time commitments lengthen is a function of the potential investor's perception of legal, economic, and political stability. Investments during this stage tend to embody higher levels of technological and human capital than in the first stage of development, again raising the risk that a failed investment will be even more costly to the home firm. FDI in this period shifts to the production of goods that can be traded internationally; the manufacturing sector is a likely target, including goods produced in Standard International Trade Classification (SITC) categories 6, 7, and 8. As a result, the structure of FDI should also begin to shift from "interindustry" FDI to "intra-industry" FDI as home firms begin to take advantage of host firms' comparative advantages.[14]

CEEC access to Western markets has been hampered by the legacy of low-quality products and products that do not meet Western safety standards, and by the perception that goods continue to be low quality. Establishing a good reputation via a joint venture could facilitate the creation of future trade flows from East to West.

As mentioned above, with a Western partner, presumably with some credibility in Western markets, a joint venture can provide access to Western distribution channels, and efficient and targeted marketing strategies can be adopted using the home firm's expertise. Moreover, an implicit quality guarantee is given to each product because of the Western firm's name. Over time it is likely that the CEEC partner's credibility would also be enhanced as consumers become accustomed to the CEEC firm's output.

This establishment of CEEC credibility in the West through FDI and trade should have a secondary effect, that of *augmenting or creating trade*. As a minimum, the establishment of credibility in Western markets via FDI-induced trade will accelerate the process of opening Western markets and is likely to result in the creation of new trade flows that might not have been possible without market entry via FDI. That is, after a firm or set of firms gains credibility in Western markets, it might be able to establish a foothold for new products produced either with or without foreign capital.

Finally, for CEECs the host country's location, growing market stability, and increasing potential for growth play a significant role in attracting FDI during this phase. Thus the host country can withdraw external FDI incentives (tax holidays, for example) and accord foreign investors national treatment. This is an important step because it forces foreign investors to compete with domestic investors. In theory this competition should increase efficiency, which provides a net gain for the host country's government (in terms of tax revenues) and for the economy as a whole.

The Mature Investment Phase. This final period, which has yet to be realized by any CEEC thus far, is a post-transition phase. In particular, this phase occurs when markets in the host country function as markets do in the West, where privatization is complete, financial markets are sufficiently wide and deep to be able to absorb monetary shocks (positive and negative), and macrostabilization has been achieved (that is, stabilization that was necessary due to the micro- and macroeconomic shocks of transition, but not necessarily due to the effects of the business cycle).[15] It is also assumed that the legal and tax structures are sufficiently stable and transparent and do not form part of a potential investor's risk premium calculation.[16] Again, political instability plays an important role in an investor's decision during this phase, because when the economic situation is stable, political considerations carry more weight.

Although FDI is expected in all sectors during this phase, a heavy emphasis will again be placed on FDI into tradables. Although the factor price equalization process between the EU and the CEECs (or CEEC factor price convergence to world market levels) is currently under way, it is unlikely to be completed during this phase. Thus the labor cost advantage of the East will still be a significant incentive for Western investors even in the long run.[17] The factor price advantage will attract FDI into the tradables sector during this period, especially as barriers to trade between CEECs and the EU continue to fall. Again, the CEECs' locational advantage will continue to provide EU investors with a low transaction cost base from which to export. In addition, as economic transition accelerates in CEECs, intra-CEEC trade should also grow, further augmenting the incentive to invest in CEECs for locational reasons. Thus, home countries will continue to gain from the locational advantages of FDI into CEECs and the exploitation of economies of scale and scope.

For host countries, the gains from FDI during the mature investment period will continue to have a strong impact on sectoral and macroeconomic growth. Rojec *et al.* (1995) argue that the higher the stage of development of the host country, the stronger the positive effects of FDI. Technology transfer, in particular, will have an even stronger impact during this period than during previous phases. The diffusion of technology during this phase is expected to have strong spillover effects both within and between sectors when it is deployed in sectors with high technological content (see Lowell and Stern, 1995). As in the internationalization period, the transfer of human capital might become relatively less important than physical capital transfers. During this stage, as the spillovers affect more sectors, there can be a strong, aggregate macroeconomic effect; in other words, FDI should affect economic growth during this phase. FDI into the trade sector will also be extremely effective in expanding access to foreign markets. The difference between FDI into the export sector during this phase and the internalization phase is that during this phase, "intra-industry" FDI resulting in export expansion (especially if the goods have a high technological content) will improve the terms of trade, which should generate substantial gains from trade and eventually lead to economic growth.

10.2 Preliminary Country Studies

The framework for studying FDI in the CEECs was developed to better understand the current and future state and importance of FDI in the transition process. The use of the following country studies is meant to illustrate the emerging pattern of FDI. Given the shortness of the time period and the difficulty of obtaining detailed and comparable data, the results should be considered preliminary. The data presented below suggest that at least the Visegrád Four (Poland, Hungary, the Czech Republic, and Slovakia) and Slovenia have entered a new phase in their economic development that corresponds to a new stage in the inward FDI they receive. Furthermore, it is argued here that in the current phase FDI into the export sector is a crucial aspect of the overall economy from the standpoints of both the home and host countries.

The Visegrád Four and Slovenia border on the EU countries that are the largest trading and investing partners with CEECs, namely, Germany and Austria. Their locations give these countries a significant advantage over the other countries in transition. In many cases, production centers in the Visegrád Four and Slovenia are closer to some EU markets than domestic production centers within the home country. Thus it is logical for investors from Germany, Austria, and Italy to use their locational advantage to exploit labor cost differentials and low transportation costs. Firms located at or near borders with EU countries are better poised to service both the Western and Eastern markets.

In terms of the framework presented above, given the institutional and economic characteristics of the Visegrád Four and Slovenia, one should expect that although the initialization phase of FDI continues to operate, the internationalization phase has also begun. We should expect a shift in the behavior of foreign direct investors toward exports oriented at crucial border countries such as Austria. The change in investment behavior results from many interrelated factors. First, several of the countries on the borders of EU countries have rapidly transformed their economies to the point where transparency of the legal structure, easier access to CEEC resources and markets, and continuing stability and growth have convinced many investors that the long-term prospects for investment look good. In addition, the reduction of trade barriers due to EU Association Agreements with individual CEECs and the plans that the CEECs will eventually accede to the EU reflect a commitment by the West to integrate Eastern economies into the Western economic community. This commitment has had an extremely powerful influence on investors' decisions.

10.2.1 Country characteristics

The three countries studied in this chapter, Hungary, the Czech Republic, and Slovenia, are at relatively similar levels of both macroeconomic and microeconomic (as reflected in the legal and institutional frameworks) development. Each country, for example, has reversed its economic decline and has begun to grow in terms of GDP. Unemployment has stabilized, at least temporarily, and stabilization following the initial macrolevel shocks has occurred. In each of the countries, exports to the EU per GDP ratio is rising, showing the growing importance of EU markets to the CEECs. Regarding the microeconomic situations of these countries, *Table 10A.1* in the Appendix to Chapter 10 summarizes the various legal and institutional foundations that either stimulate FDI or at least remove legislative barriers to FDI in Hungary, the Czech Republic, and Slovenia.[18]

Table 10.1. FDI stock in Hungary, the Czech Republic, and Slovenia, 1991–1994.

	FDI stock (mln. US dollars)[a]				Rate of growth of flow (previous year = 100)	
Country	12/91	12/92	12/93	7/94	1992	1993
Hungary	3,137	5,502	8,119	8,401	175	148
Czech Republic	595	1,556	2,053	2,543	1,161	132
Slovenia	808	959	1,097	1,130	119	114

[a]Figures are cumulative as of the end of the month given.
Sources: UN ECE, 1994b; Ministry of Economic Relations and Development of Slovenia, 1994a.

10.2.2 Indicators of FDI

The basic FDI trends in Hungary, the Czech Republic, and Slovenia are summarized in *Table 10.1*.

Hungary remains the regional leader of inward FDI, but due to the decline of FDI in 1994 and the fact that the record investments of 1993 and 1995 were mostly related to one-time privatizations of infrastructural networks, there is a probability that Hungary will not maintain its regional leadership in the medium term. It is likely that FDI will continue to grow rapidly in Slovenia and the Czech Republic, while it will grow more slowly in Hungary.

In general, in the three countries the manufacturing sector will continue to attract the highest share of inward FDI, constituting over 50% of the total on average in all of the CEECs combined. Not surprisingly, the higher the level of FDI into the manufacturing sector, the higher the level of trade with EU countries.

Finally, FDI in the export sector appears to be highest in the countries that share borders with EU countries. In the past three years firms that receive FDI (foreign investment absorbing enterprises, FIEs) have become more oriented toward foreign trade than the average domestic enterprise. The share of FIEs in foreign trade is extremely high relative to their number and size in each economy as a whole. In Hungary FIEs account for more than 50% of exports, in the Czech Republic, about 30%, and in Slovenia, 16%.[19]

10.2.3 Hungary

Hungary emerged in 1990 as the region's leading recipient of FDI, primarily due to its close ties with the West dating from the 1970s and from its stepwise liberalization during the 1980s. Basic statistics are presented in *Table 10.2*. In addition to having a more developed business infrastructure, a longer history of FDI, and closer contacts with the West than the other CEECs, Hungary also had a reputation for being the most "outward oriented" of the CEECs. Moreover, Hungary's privatization policy

Table 10.2. Basic FDI statistics for Hungary, 1990–1994.

	1990	1991	1992	1993	1994
Number of joint ventures (cumulative)	5,693	9,117	17,182	15,205	17,278
Stock (in mln. US$)	–	3,137	5,502	8,119	8,281
Average capitalization of new firms (in US$1,000)	–	320	340	534	117

Source: UN ECE, 1994b.

was more open to foreign participation than that of any other CEEC. Taken in combination, these phenomena have made Hungary a logical target for FDI.

Despite Hungary's relatively advanced initial conditions for economic transition, it has sustained lower-than-expected growth in FDI. Analysts such as Szanyi (1994) attribute the declines in growth of FDI and degree of capitalization to the sluggishness of the privatization program, which was only resolved in 1994, and speculate that the rise of political uncertainty may also have played a part.

The direction of FDI has not changed perceptibly since 1991. Germany is still the largest home country, constituting about 23% of all inward FDI. The next two largest investors, the USA and Austria, contribute 18.3% and 17% of the total share, respectively (HCSO, 1995, Table XI). These statistics are somewhat deceptive in that the number of FDI projects initiated by the USA is very small but each project has high capitalization.[20] It is important to note that by value the highest portion of FDI from the USA was in telecommunications; these investments are likely to be one-time occurrences. The high *number* of German and Austrian investments reflects that these countries tend to invest in the manufacturing sector, whose products are mostly tradable. It is argued below that the motivation for such investments is a desire to re-export the goods produced back into EU markets.

The sectoral structure of FDI also has not changed dramatically in aggregate terms from 1991 to 1994. It is clear from *Table 10.3* that manufacturing remains by far the largest recipient of inward FDI, especially from the EU. As expected, the other sectors (financial services and domestic trade, for example) reflect FDI aimed at the domestic market. All but the manufactured goods sector were part of the initialization phase of FDI, where FDI was directed at filling gaps in the market or taking advantage of market imperfections. The motivations behind investments in the manufacturing sector are more difficult to discern from the data than those behind investment in other sectors.

Although the share of FDI in the manufactured sector decreased slightly from 1990 to 1994, the level of FDI increased fourfold during the same period (author's own calculations). Some of that investment went into manufactured goods for the

Table 10.3. Sectoral structure of FDI in Hungary, all enterprises (in percent).

Sector	1991	1994
Manufacturing	55.9	49.6
Financial services	11.4	15.9
Domestic trade	12.5	13.5
Transport, post, telephone, telecommunications	2.0	9.0
Construction	4.3	4.0
Hotels and restaurants	3.3	3.9
Mining	1.0	1.4
Other	9.6	2.8
Total	100.0	100.0

Sources: HCSO, 1995; UN ECE, 1994b.

Table 10.4. Commodity composition of Hungarian exports by SITC category (in percent).

SITC category	1990	1994
0 Food, live animals	19.8	16.6
1 Beverages, tobacco	1.3	2.0
2 Crude materials except fuels	4.7	5.2
3 Mineral fuels and related goods	3.1	3.9
4 Animal and vegetable oils	1.2	0.8
5 Chemicals	12.4	11.2
6 Manufactured goods (by material)	18.5	18.1
7 Machinery, transport equip.	25.6	25.5
8 Miscellaneous manufactures	10.7	16.5
9 Other	2.7	0.2
Total	100.0	100.0

Sources: IKM Információ, 1991, 1995; author's own calculations.

domestic market, but at the same time there was a structural shift into exports from the manufactured goods sector. FDI into manufactured goods grew from 28% of all tradables in 1991 to over 61% in 1994 (HCSO, 1995; UN ECE, 1994a). FDI in most countries of the world is concentrated in the manufactured goods sector; thus the concentration of FDI in this sector in Hungary is not surprising. However, a close examination of the structural shift in exports (see *Table 10.4*) suggests a link between FDI and trade, and provides a plausible explanation for the shift in investor motivation from merely seeking the domestic market share to using FDI for re-exporting products. *Table 10.4* shows the absolute increase in exports of miscellaneous manufactured articles and machinery and transport. These sectors are also the top recipients of FDI. Growth in these sectors increased substantially in 1993, which can be explained by the fact that FDI began to increase in these sectors

Table 10.5. Percentage exported by FIEs to EU and EFTA countries out of total exports of that sector in Hungary.

Sector	1992	1993	1994
Agriculture	12.2	23.2	30
Food industry	40.7	51.9	54
Minerals	25.0	21.1	20
Chemicals	33.0	37.5	35
Wood and paper	42.8	53.3	26
Light manufactured goods	40.8	52.2	61
Textiles, apparel	46.6	54.0	45
Building materials	33.2	34.2	58
Metals	14.3	36.7	28
Machinery	60.1	66.4	67
Retail trade	48.9	50.8	n.a.
Financial services	93.1	94.1	95

Sources: Data from KOPINT-DATORG, Budapest, Hungary; data from the Hungarian Central Statistical Office; author's own calculations.

earlier, and after a lag of one or two years, started to influence the composition of exports.

From 1990 to 1993 exports of FIEs increased fourfold, primarily to EU and European Free Trade Association (EFTA) countries; the export sector as a whole increased by 27% in terms of value during the same period. Not surprisingly, the share of FIEs in the export sector increased from 16.5% in 1990 to 50% in 1993, and to 65% in 1994 (UN ECE, 1994a; author's calculations based on data from KOPINT-DATORG, Budapest, Hungary). The United Nations Economic Commission for Europe (UN ECE, 1994a) estimates that at least 27% of exports in 1993 were from firms that received FDI and then re-exported the products back into the home country.

Table 10.5 shows share of FIEs in sectoral exports from Hungary into Western Europe. It is important to note that FIEs have significantly increased their share of exports in Hungary's important export sectors. These numbers, combined with the overall structural change of exports, show the impact of FDI in the trading sector. These results also show that FDI has had a significant impact on the export sector.

As far as intangible results go, the UN ECE (1994a) survey concluded that FIEs were more successful at export promotion abroad than comparable firms that export but do not receive FDI. Although they do not give concrete reasons for this phenomenon, perhaps the FDI cycle theory can shed some light on the issue. Specifically, when a Western firm invests in a CEEC export sector, it is assumed that the home firm will help the FIE in the target market. Western firms also have the advantage of having marketing and distribution systems in place in their normal target markets; therefore, incorporating the joint venture's product into these systems should not prove difficult. Thus, the joint venture can bypass traditional informal market barriers to entry using the credibility gained by the Western firm's name as means for introducing the Eastern good into Western markets.[21]

Although it is too early to measure the spillover effects, Western consumers are becoming used to consuming goods originating from CEECs. Clearly, as the reputation for good quality grows over time demand for goods from CEECs will rise. Hungary, which has the longest experience of exports to the EU, is likely to feel this ripple effect first. Because the time series (1990–1994) is too short to measure the impact both domestically and internationally (in terms of productivity, output, spillover effects, and economic growth), we can only make conjectures concerning the primary and secondary impacts.

Halpern and Kőrösi (1995) conducted an empirical study of changes in the behavior of approximately 950 Hungarian exporting firms between 1989 and 1993. One important result of this study was that initially the profitability of exporting FIEs was much higher than that of wholly owned domestic firms (WODs), suggesting that productivity levels were also much higher. However, this gap between FIEs and WODs diminished as time went on. Two interpretations of this result can be offered. The first is that WODs were forced to learn new production techniques, update their capital stock, and become more efficient in order to compete. This behavior would support the hypothesis that FDI generates spillover effects within the sector first. The other interpretation is that FIEs were able to hide their profitability through transfer pricing. Multinational businesses are notorious for their use of transfer pricing; therefore, this hypothesis must explain some of Halpern and Kőrösi's results. Although transfer pricing must be taking place, it is clear that if WODs are also to become competitive, they must adapt their behavior to rise to the challenge posed by FIEs.[22]

Finally, if FDI into the export sector is growing rapidly in Hungary, it is likely that a *maquiladora* effect is also beginning to occur. The Hungarian Central Statistical Office (HCSO, 1995) reports that in 1990 about 95% of inward FDI was located in the Budapest region. In 1993 that figure dropped to about 65%, with FDI in the regions bordering Austria, Slovenia, and Slovakia rising to about 25% in 1993 and an estimated 33% in 1994.[23] Based on these preliminary figures, it seems clear that that investments' location near export markets of the EU (i.e., Austria) has gradually become important. The growth in the number of FIEs, especially along the Austrian border (about 50% above 1990 levels in 1994), may also explain the explosion of Hungarian exports to Austria.

To sum up, FDI into the export sector in Hungary appears to have facilitated the growth and sectoral change of Hungarian trade. Thus, Hungary must be experiencing the internationalization of FDI to some degree. The internal and external impacts of this stage in the FDI cycle can only be conjectured at this point in time and should be the subject of further research.

10.2.4 The Czech Republic

Unlike Hungary, Czechoslovakia had few ties with Western Europe before 1989.[24] After 1989 the Czechoslovak and subsequently the Czech government was committed to rapid integration into the world economy and EU economies in particular. During the period between 1989 and 1994 FDI was a problematic issue for the Czech Republic. Ironically the problem was not attracting FDI; rather, the unresolved issue was how much FDI was desirable. The ambivalence toward inward FDI was evident during the first two stages of mass privatization (1991 to 1993), when foreign investors were not allowed to participate directly in the initial rounds. Yet, controlling interests in key industries such as Skoda (a car manufacturer), CSA (the national airline), and the telecommunication system were bought up quickly and early (by 1992) by foreign firms and sequestered from the privatization process.

Although the Czech government has not yet resolved its position on FDI, it has accorded national treatment to all investors (foreign and indigenous) and has done little to restrain investment. The Czech Republic meets the economic, legal, and political stability criteria for entering the internationalization phase of FDI; the following analysis looks at the effects of foreign investment on the structure, size, and target markets of the export sector.

The enormous growth of FDI from 1991 to 1994 can be seen in *Table 10.6*. The number of new investments from 1993 to 1994 is an important statistic when considered together with average capitalization. According to the FDI cycle theory, low levels of capitalization are characteristic of the first stage of FDI; high levels of capitalization suggest that investors are willing to take greater risks, which occurs during the second phase. The large number of new ventures from 1993 to mid-1994, each with higher average capitalization than ventures set up earlier (an increase from US$4.77 million to US$19.38 million), represents a substantial change in the character of FDI. The number of new investments suggests that investors are willing to make greater commitments than they previously were, thus increasing the risk. These results are significant, especially as the Czech government eliminated many tax incentives at the end of 1993. The fact that both capitalization and the number of projects increased also implies that the Czech Republic's attractiveness as a recipient country for FDI has grown. By 1993 the rate of growth of FDI in the Czech Republic had surpassed that in Hungary, which is possibly a reflection of the fact that the Czech Republic's political and economic

Table 10.6. Basic FDI statistics for the Czech Republic.

	1991	1992	1993	1994[a]
Number of joint ventures (cumulative)	–	3,100	5,500	15,000
Stock (mln. US dollars)	595	1,556	2,053	2,490
Average capitalization of new firms (mln. US dollars)	–	1.99	4.77	19.38

[a]Figures given are for the first half of 1994.
Sources: UN ECE, 1994b; author's own calculations.

Table 10.7. Sources of inward FDI in the Czech Republic (in percent of total FDI).

	Cumulative stock		New investments,
Country	1991	Mid-1994	January–June 1994
Germany	74.5	29.9	24.1
Austria	6.3	6.7	9.6
France	2.6	13.3	15.3
Belgium	5.6	6.2	2.1
United States	9.1	25.9	12.8
Other	1.9	18.0	36.1
Total	100.0	100.0	100.0

Sources: UN ECE, 1994b; author's own calculations.

systems were quite stable compared with those of Hungary, or is possibly due to a more advanced state of privatization. The sectoral distribution (which will be discussed below) combined with larger capitalization suggests that FDI has entered the internationalization stage in the Czech Republic.

Table 10.7 shows that the source of FDI has shifted dramatically: in 1991 FDI came predominantly from Germany; by 1994 about 75% came from the EU and 25% from the USA. The 1991 figure for Germany represents the single Volkswagen-Skoda deal, which skewed the figures. The rise of Austria's share in new investments in 1994 is an important statistic because it could be an indication of Austria's interest in the Czech Republic as a platform for re-exports back into the EU and EFTA.

The sectoral structure of FDI into the Czech Republic is similar to that in Hungary (*Table 10.8*). During the first few years of economic transition, FDI flowed into sectors that were oriented toward the domestic market, such as the food industry, financial services, construction, and low-technology manufacturing. The principal exception to this trend was the large investment in the automotive industry (the Volkswagen-Skoda deal), which, as a one-time, high-capitalization investment, distorted the sectoral distribution. The data in *Table 10.8* reveal that

Table 10.8. Sectoral structure of FDI in the Czech Republic (in percent).

Sector	1991	1994
Food industry	17.0	8.3
Financial services	10.1	15.3
Domestic trade	4.9	4.7
Automotive[a]	70.7	17.4
Construction	21.0	12.5
Services	3.1	5.1
Chemicals	6.9	5.1
Electrotechnical	0.0	10.0
Engineering	4.0	12.0
Other	1.4	7.2

[a]The automotive figure is distorted by the large Volkswagen/Skoda deal; it also contains derivative investment in other sectors such as engineering, services, and construction, which is why total percentage is greater than 100.
Source: CzechoInvest, 1995.

from 1991 to 1994 the greatest growth of FDI was in high-technology sectors such as engineering and electro-technical goods. As with Hungary, we conjecture that these goods are more likely to be traded, especially on the European market, than to be produced for the home market.

Although it is clear that FDI has moved away from primary goods and services toward more highly industrialized goods, it is necessary to look at the pattern of trade to see whether FDI has moved into the export sector. *Table 10.9* shows that exports have decreased in the primary commodity sectors and increased relatively and absolutely in SITC category 8 industries. Not surprisingly, manufactured exports to EU countries as a whole have boomed, more than doubling in the past four years. It is highly likely that the growth in high-skill, medium-to-high technology manufactured goods is impacted by the increased levels of FDI in the sectors that produce these products.

The size and direction of exports is also revealing. Czech exports in general have grown 112% (in constant Czech koruny) from 1990 to 1994, whereas exports to EU and EFTA countries have grown 246% over the same period (Česky Statisticky Urad, 1994). With the Czech Republic's reorientation of trade away from the former Soviet Union and CMEA countries toward the West, Germany has become the largest recipient of Czech goods (35% of exports in 1994) and Austria's share of Czech exports has also grown markedly, from 5% in 1990 to 9% in 1994.

CzechoInvest estimates that 85% of FDI takes place in a relatively concentrated area from Prague southward, with the two most concentrated regions being the Prague area and Southern Bohemia (CzechoInvest, 1995). The location of

Table 10.9. Structure of exports to the EU from the Czech Republic by SITC classification, all enterprises (in percent of total exports).

SITC classification	1990	1994
0 Food, live animals	6.0	4.6
1 Beverages, tobacco	0.1	0.5
2 Crude materials except fuels	15.8	9.0
3 Mineral fuels and related goods	3.1	4.9
4 Animal and vegetable oils	0.2	0.2
5 Chemicals	9.5	9.0
6 Manufactured goods (by material)	15.2	29.4
7 Machinery, transport equip.	37.7	25.8
8 Miscelleneous manufactures	10.5	16.7
9 Other	1.9	0.0
Total	100.0	100.0

Sources: Česky Statisticky Urad, 1994, 1995; and author's own calculations.

investments in combination with the principal sources of investment (Germany and to a lesser extent Austria) and the primary export destinations (Germany and Austria) suggest that a significant proportion of FDI from the West is going to the export sector with the aim of targeting both EU and local markets. A firm-level study is needed to confirm this hypothesis.

Thus, given the characteristics of the domestic political, economic, and legal infrastructure, it is clear that the Czech Republic has moved into the internationalization phase of FDI. It is also evident that FDI is concentrated in the export sector as well as in industries aimed at the domestic market. The impact on both the Czech Republic and the home countries of the FDI has yet to be determined, but given the structural change in both the character of FDI and in Czech exports it is likely to be strong and positive.

10.2.5 Slovenia

Slovenia was the most developed republic of Yugoslavia, which of all the CEECs had the strongest FDI and the closest trade ties with the West at the beginning of transition. Therefore, Slovenia started with a relatively strong FDI position: its economic, legal, and financial structures were more "marketized" than those of other CEECs; it had close economic relations with Germany, Austria, and Italy; and it began its transition with a strong, new convertible currency. Yet despite these advantages, FDI in Slovenia has not grown as quickly as was envisaged by policy makers and economists. Slovenia has a population of approximately 2 million; its small size suggests that foreign investment is not made chiefly to

Table 10.10. Basic FDI statistics for Slovenia, 1991–1994.

	1991	1992	1993	1994[a]
Number of joint ventures (cumulative)	1,285	2,755	3,169	–
Stock (mln. US dollars)	808	959	1,097	1,130
Average capitalization of new firms (mln. US dollars)	0.67	0.10	0.42	–

[a]Figures given are for the first half of 1994.
Sources: Ministry of Economic Relations and Development, 1994a; and author's own calculations.

capture the domestic market. Rojec *et al.* (1993) suggest that initially the keys to Slovenia's success as a target for FDI were its geographical location on the edge of Western Europe and, more importantly, its position as the gateway to the former Yugoslav market. Since the war in the Balkans began in 1991, the former Yugoslav market has collapsed; thus for the time being Slovenia has lost part of its locational advantage (see Rojec *et al.*, 1995, Chapter 4). Those who had investments that were already in place were forced to reorient their output to foreign (mainly EU) countries in order to find markets, because FDI for the small domestic market was not necessarily profitable.

Despite the fact that Slovenia lost the markets of former Yugoslavia, FDI continued to rise slowly but steadily. It seems clear that in the first stage of FDI Slovenia lost some of its appeal as a target country. This observation is confirmed by the sharp drop in the level of capitalization between 1991 and 1992, accompanied by a sharp increase in the number of new joint ventures (see *Table 10.10*). During these two years, FDI went into small enterprises that were able to operate in the domestic market as a primary source of sales. The drop in capitalization could also be a reflection of the political and economic uncertainty caused by Slovenian independence, the introduction of its own currency, and the beginning of a formal economic transition program. Similarly, the rise in capitalization in 1993 could also be a reflection of investor perceptions that the economic and political situations had both stabilized. In addition, as Rojec *et al.* (1993) point out, investors were forced to reorient production toward West European markets as alternatives to the markets of former Yugoslavia. Thus in some sense the Slovenian movement from the initialization to the internationalization phase of FDI might have been forced by the political realities of the crisis in the Balkans.

Unlike in Hungary and the Czech Republic, the composition of foreign investors in Slovenia has not changed dramatically in the past 10 years. In this period, the top three investors were West European countries (see *Table 10.11*). Again, Germany has played a dominant role in FDI into Slovenia, with Austria and Italy (Slovenia's immediate neighbors) in the second and third positions by value,

Table 10.11. Sources of FDI in Slovenia, 1985 to 1993.[a]

Home country	Number of joint ventures	Percentage of total	Invested capital (mln. DM)	Percentage of total
Germany	580	20	721	45
Austria	670	23	332	21
Italy	663	23	257	16
France	20	1	115	7
Croatia	461	16	33	2
Others	510	18	146	9

[a]Figures given are cumulative.
Sources: Ministry of Economic Relations and Development, 1994b; author's own calculations.

respectively. It is important to note that German investments tend to be larger in terms of capitalization (DM 1.2 million) than those of Austria or Italy (DM 0.5 and 0.4 million, respectively). Of Slovenia's top 100 enterprises by gross income (including all enterprises, not only those with FDI), German investors control 10, Austrian firms account for 3, and Italian investors for 1.[25] Germany's strong commitment to investment in Slovenia is based on long-standing trade and investment ties going back 30 years or more. Austria and Italy's interest in Slovenia is likely to be in keeping with the FDI cycle theory, which suggests that border countries have a higher incentive to invest in the foreign sector to take advantage of market (and in this case labor market) differentials. France's position as a top investor is based on one investment by Renault, which is the largest investment in Slovenia. Finally, it is interesting to see that Croatia has been and continues to be a foreign investor in Slovenia. Capitalization remains low in investments from Croatia, which suggests that the aim of Croatian investors is limited to break into the Slovenian market.

The sectoral structure of FDI (see *Table 10.12*) confirms that in Slovenia, as in Hungary and the Czech Republic, the trend is for investment to move first into domestic-market-based goods and services (food industry, financial services, transportation, and construction). Investment shifts to higher-technology, export-oriented goods and services (manufacturing, electro-technical, and engineering) when the goal of investment includes capturing domestic as well as foreign markets. As mentioned above, the realities of the political situation in the Balkans partially explain why FDI went into more export-oriented goods in Slovenia. Additionally, the success of the Slovenian reform program, especially in the macroeconomic sphere (stabilization and currency stability), has provided incentives for investment.

Although it is difficult to make any claims about the long-term impact of FDI on the export sector given the limited time series on exports from Slovenia to EU countries (see *Table 10.13*), it is clear that the bulk of exports is in SITC categories

Table 10.12. Sectoral structure of FDI in Slovenia (in percent).

Sector	1991	1994 (first half)
Food industry	10.3	5.3
Financial services	5.5	2.3
Domestic trade	8.0	7.2
Transport/infrastructure	13.4	16.6
Construction	9.7	0.5
Services	n.a.	4.1
Chemicals	14.0	7.7
Electrotechnical	11.0	23.8
Engineering	n.a.	8.2
Other manufacturing	19.6	24.3
Total	100.0	100.0

Abbreviation: n.a. = Not available.
Sources: Ministry of Economic Affairs and Development, 1994a; UN ECE, 1994b; author's own calculations.

Table 10.13. Structure of exports to the EU from Slovenia by SITC category (in percent).

SITC category	1992	1994
0 Food, live animals	5.1	4.0
1 Beverages, tobacco	1.3	0.7
2 Crude materials except fuels	1.9	1.7
3 Mineral fuels and related goods	2.6	1.0
4 Animal and vegetable oils	0.1	0.1
5 Chemicals	9.1	10.3
6 Manufactured goods (by material)	27.1	27.5
7 Machinery, transport equip.	29.4	30.0
8 Miscellaneous manufactures	23.2	24.0
9 Other	0.1	0.2
Total	100.0	100.0

Sources: Ministry of Economic Relations and Development, 1994b; author's own calculations.
Note: Discrepancies due to rounding may exist.

6 to 8, corresponding to the sectors in which FDI is the most concentrated. In particular, FDI into engineering, electro-technical, and other manufacturing sectors corresponds to Slovenia's largest export industries. The UN ECE estimates that 90% of FIE exports were in mining, manufacturing, and electro industries (UN ECE, 1994a). These results are not too surprising, as the FIEs' targeted export market is the EU; thus, foreign investors are attempting to use Slovenia's cost differentials to the greatest extent.

Finally, the direction of Slovene exports closely follows the pattern of inward FDI into Slovenia. Exports in Slovenia have more than doubled since 1991 (Ministry of Economic Relations and Development of Slovenia, 1994b), and thus Germany's growing share in exports (from 27% in 1991 to 31% in 1994) represents an absolute as well as relative increase. Austria's rank as the fourth largest recipient of Slovenian exports (following Germany, Italy, and Croatia) understates the tremendous growth in that export market, because Austria's increase in relative share is also a substantial increase, about double, in absolute terms (Ministry of Economic Relations and Development, 1994b; author's own calculations). Thus the data suggest a strong correlation between the volume of FDI from a home country to Slovenia and the volume of Slovenian exports to the home country, which implies that one motivation for FDI is re-exports. Anecdotal evidence from the Austrian Ministry of Economic Affairs suggests that a large number of Austrian firms have begun working in the northern part of Slovenia (either near the Austrian border or close to Ljubljana, where transport networks are centered) as part of a *maquiladora* situation in which goods to be used in the Austrian market are either produced or assembled in Slovenia.

10.3 Conclusions

FDI's most obvious contribution to economic growth occurs directly through the transfer of physical, financial, and human capital. Perhaps equally important are FDI's indirect effects. In addition to providing the transfer of capital, FDI also facilitates the transfer of skills and knowledge, which can be adapted to local production structures or generalized for use in other production situations. For the host country (especially a CEEC), this spillover effect is extremely important as it is one of the links between FDI and economic growth.

An even more subtle but crucial benefit is generated by FDI into the trade sector, where in addition to expanding exports, a firm, sector, or country can penetrate markets for the first time with the help of a joint venture. Once credibility is established, the firm can expand its trade (with or without the help of its foreign partner) to foreign countries. Thus, FDI into the export sector complements and augments trade, which has positive effects on the industry and on the country's trade balance. Aggregated to the macrolevel, expansion of trade and the spillover effects felt by the firm, the immediate industry, and associated industries, both domestically and internationally oriented, can all contribute to economic growth.

The FDI cycle theory suggests that a country can only experience this type of FDI if the domestic conditions (economic, legal, and political) are stable enough to encourage longer-term, more highly capitalized investments; if the location of the host country is such that low transportation costs increase the benefits of the host country's existing cost advantage; and if the indigenous population and infrastructure can support the production of goods in demand in the target market.

The CEECs studied in this chapter appear to meet all three criteria. It is likely that Hungary, the Czech Republic, and Slovenia are now starting to see the initial export enhancement effects of FDI. However, it is argued here that they are only at the beginning of the internationalization phase and that the real growth effects are yet to come. For the host countries, exploitation of the re-export advantages has begun to appear in the *maquiladora* phenomenon that is becoming more prevalent, especially around the Austrian and German borders. If these countries have entered the internationalization period of FDI, then they are now competing for the roughly US$60 billion currently available to emerging markets.[26]

Future research should include a quantification of spillover effects in the host country. This quantification is especially important if a measurement of the impact of FDI on growth is to be made. Another important study would be an assessment of FDI's impact on competition in the export sector in the host country and in the export-receiving country. That is, are exports from CEECs changing the competitive nature of home country markets? Are they causing fundamental shifts in the structure of employment and production, as occurred in the USA as a result of increased trade with and FDI into Mexico? In order to get a true picture of FDI from West to East, these questions should be answered based on empirical evidence.

Notes

[1] Many CEEC analysts believe that these "get rich quick" investments were an attempt to make quick profits by taking advantage of the fledgling legal and tax systems. In most cases these investments into the "Wild East" were of no substantial benefit to the host country. Examples include foreign exchange dealerships and certain consumer goods outlets. These types of investments required minimal sunk costs and gave maximal return on investments, especially while the legal and tax frameworks were not in place. Many of these investments lasted less than one year.

[2] For the purposes of this paper, the European Economic Space comprises EU and European Free Trade Association (EFTA) countries. In January 1995 three EFTA countries, Austria, Finland, and Sweden, joined the EU.

[3] A country's difficulties in generating export revenues might be due to a lack of quality, a lack of price competitiveness due to high production or transportation costs, a lack of demand, or an inability to penetrate markets.

[4] For example, the Austrian bank Creditanstalt has been successful in setting up operations in most CEEC capitals, and thus establishing itself as the leader in international banking in the region. Because of its speed of entry into each domestic market, it has now become the most popular bank for international transactions.

[5] It is clear from the CEECs' experience that a reduction in formal trade restrictions (tariffs and quotas) does not necessarily guarantee market access. In fact, intangible barriers such as lack of access to distribution agents, lack of appropriate marketing skills, and difficulty introducing a new product make market entry a formidable task.

[6] The term "cycle" is used in the same sense as in the life-cycle theory of product development.

[7] For a comprehensive treatment of the early period of FDI, see Rojec *et al.* (1995), pp. 88–93.

[8] It should be noted that some investors used the lack of laws or ambiguity of laws to engage in speculative FDI. Such ventures were high risk, short term, and very lucrative. The gains from this behavior were accrued solely to the investor, and most CEECs tried to protect their domestic markets against these investments through commercial and tax codes. This behavior, common during the first few years of transition in the CEECs, has fallen off drastically in the past few years.

[9] In the consumer sector in particular, where CEEC markets were weak at the beginning of transition, a foreign firm could invest in one small firm that had a large market share and either close it down (eliminating competition) or introduce its own products (effectively superseding the domestically produced product), thus creating a monopoly.

[10] Hungary, in particular, was sensitive to this issue and enacted a competition law after privatization was started; however, its effect has been minimal.

[11] See Szanyi (1994), and Rojec *et al.* (1995) for further discussion of the obstacles to investment.

[12] That is, during the initialization phase the level of capitalization might decrease over the period if investors do not see significant progress in the legal framework, in economic transition, and in political stabilization.

[13] As the level of capitalization and the commitment to longer time horizons rise, the degree of reversibility drops, making the investment more risky than those undertaken in the first stage of FDI.

[14] Intra-industry FDI is analogous to to intra-industry trade, that is, trade between firms in like industries; for example, Japanese cars traded for US cars. Inter-industry trade refers to trade between sectors; for example, US computers for Czech glass.

[15] It is important to note that in areas such as privatization there is no set percentage of output that should be in private hands. On the contrary, among EU countries the level of privatization varies considerably. The condition that privatization is complete is taken to mean that the *ex ante* plans for privatization have been realized.

[16] Thus, risk premiums are calculated by using standard economic rates of return and political risk.

[17] Studies such as those by Éltető *et al.* (1995) and Gual and Martin (1995) have shown that factor price convergence to EU levels happens only slowly, even after EU accession. Éltető *et al.* in particular analyze the growth and impact of FDI in Spain and Portugal from the EU before, during, and after the countries' accession to the EU as a basis for comparison with the similar situation in the Visegrád Four countries' accession to the EU. They found that FDI increased dramatically after the timetable for EU accession was set. Stern (1995) found that although the aftermath of

joining the EU was a period of rapid and sustained growth, it did not result in absolute convergence of basic economic statistics such as per capita GDP. These arguments suggest that despite high levels of trade and FDI between the CEECs and the EU, the CEECs will retain their cost advantages in the medium to long runs.

[18] That is, the more transparent and consistent these institutional structures are, the lower the risk premium, because investors know the extent of their legal rights.

[19] Data in this section are from the UN ECE (1994b), pp. 3–5. The percentage of exports listed for Slovenia is deceptively low, which will be discussed in greater detail below.

[20] The disproportionate share of US-based FDI is from four investments (Ameritech, General Electric, General Motors, and US West) in infrastructure building and car assembly. It is not likely that the share of investment from the USA will be maintained.

[21] Anecdotal evidence from the Austrian Ministry of Economic Affairs confirms this statement. Apparently, many Western consumers do not realize that numerous manufactured goods originally produced in EU countries are now produced in the CEECs through joint ventures and are re-exported back to the EU, sometimes under Western labels and trademarks. Evidently, almost one-third of all "Italian" suits are actually produced in Romania.

[22] A possible future research program could include an attempt to measure the spillover effects (via output and productivity measurements) in related industries. Also, looking at longer time series of comparative profitability rates might shed some light on this question.

[23] Based on Hungarian Central Statistical Office, 1995, Table 10, page 38; and author's own calculations based on an interview with Dr. Judit Hamar of KOPINT-DATORG, Budapest, Hungary.

[24] All data before 1993 reflect Czechoslovak statistics; from 1993 on the statistics are solely for the Czech Republic.

[25] Data from Social Accounting Service Head Office, Ljubljana, Slovenia.

[26] This estimate is from staff members of the International Monetary Fund; it will appear in the forthcoming 1995 Balance-of-Payments Statistics.

References

Borensztein, E., and Montiel, P.J., 1991, *Savings, Investment, and Growth in Eastern Europe*, June, International Monetary Fund, Washington, DC, USA.

Česky Statisticky Urad, 1994, Ukazatele: Socialniho a Hospodarskeho Vyvoje Ceske Republiky, no. 4.

Česky Statisticky Urad, 1995, Zahranicni Obhod, Foreign Trade, no. 18, March.

CzechoInvest, 1995, Foreign Investment into the Czech Republic, data sheets, March 13.

Dunning, J., 1988a, *Explaining International Production*, Unwin Hyman, London, UK.

Dunning, J., 1988b, The eclectic paradigm of international production: A restatement and possible extensions, *Journal of International Business Studies* **1**(19):1–31.

EBRD (European Bank for Reconstruction and Development), 1993, *Economic Outlook 1993*, EBRD, London, UK.

EBRD (European Bank for Reconstruction and Development), 1994, *Transition Report*, EBRD, London, UK.

Éltető, A., Gáspár, P., and Sass, M., 1995, Foreign Direct Investment in East-Central Europe in Comparative Analysis with Spain and Portugal, February, Budapest, Hungary.

Faini, R., and Portes, R., 1995, *European Union Trade With Eastern Europe*, Centre for Economic Policy Research, London, UK.

Gual, J., and Martin, C., 1995, Trade and foreign direct investment with Central and Eastern Europe: Its impact on Spain, in R. Faini and R. Portes (eds.), *European Union Trade With Eastern Europe*, Centre for Economic Policy Research, London, UK.

Halpern, L., and Kőrösi, G., 1995, Market Power and Firm Size Effects in Transition: Econometric Analysis of Hungarian Exporting Firms, 1985–1993, April, Budapest, Hungary.

HCSO (Hungarian Central Statistical Office), 1995, *Foreign Direct Investment in Hungary*, HCSO, Budapest, Hungary.

IKM Információ, 1991, Külkereskedelmi Termékforgalom 1. Kötet, Budapest, Hungary.

IKM Információ, 1995, Külkereskedelmi Termékforgalom 1. Kötet, Budapest, Hungary.

Lowell, J.F., and Stern, R.E., 1995, Foreign Direct Investment into the United States: The Issues Both Resolved and Unresolved, RAND Corporation, May, Santa Monica, CA, USA.

Ministry of Economic Relations and Development of Slovenia, 1994a, Foreign Direct Investment in Slovenia: Some Aspects of Foreign Investor Considerations, April, Ljubljana, Slovenia.

Ministry of Economic Relations and Development of Slovenia, 1994b, Foreign Trade Regime of the Republic of Slovenia, April, Ljubljana, Slovenia.

Rojec, M., Artisien, P., Galli, A., and Svetlicic, M., 1993, *The Role of Inward Foreign Direct Investment in Transformation of Socialist Into Market Economy*, ACE Project ERB4012PL910044, Ljubljana, Slovenia.

Rojec, M., Artisien, P., Dunning, J.H., Illes, M., Jermakowicz, W., Svetlicic, M., and Zemplinerova, A., 1995, *Foreign Direct Investment and Privatization in Central and Eastern Europe*, ACE Project 92-0108-R, February, Ljubljana, Slovenia.

Stern, R.E., 1995, *European Union, Southern Europe, and the Mediterranean: Integration or Disintegration*, RAND Project Paper, May, Santa Monica, CA, USA.

Szanyi, M., 1994, *Experiences with Foreign Direct Investment in Hungary*, Blue Ribbon Commission project, Investment-worthiness of Hungary, Budapest, Hungary.

UN ECE (United Nations Economic Commission for Europe), 1994a, *The Impact of Foreign Direct Investment on the Trade of Countries in Transition: Results of a Preliminary Survey*, Trade/R.617, UN ECE, Geneva, Switzerland.

UN ECE (United Nations Economic Commission for Europe), 1994b, *Statistical Survey of Recent Trends in Foreign Investment in Eastern European Countries*, GE.93-33267, UN ECE, Geneva, Switzerland.

Appendix to Chapter 10

Table 10A.1. Institutional environment for FDI in Hungary, the Czech Republic, and Slovenia as of September 1994.

Law/instit. framework	Hungary	Czech Republic	Slovenia
FDI-specific laws	Act XXIV of 1988 on FDI (amended 1990, 1991,1994); Corporate Tax (amended 1992, 1993).	Commercial Code (1991), supplants law on FDI transactions (1988).	FDI Law (1967; amended in 1988); Law on Trade.
Restrictions	Approval in banking sector needed, otherwise national treatment of foreign firms.	Prohibited in some infrastructure, large privatization, financial sector, defense industry and some trade sectors.	100% ownership prohibited in military, rail & air transport, mass media, and insurance sectors; min. investment is $950 for limited liability, $9500 for joint stock.
Profit and capital repatriation	No restrictions; 50% of expatriated salaries may be remitted outside the country.	No restrictions on profit. Capital repatriated at cessation of business; restrictions on salary repatriation of businesses.	No restrictions on profit or capital repatriation in currency of original investment; capital may be repatriated at cessation; 15% tax on paid-out dividends.
Property ownership	Restrictions on acquisition by foreigners; no restrictions for Hungarian companies with foreign participation.	Property ownership protected by law; all companies must be registered.	Foreign companies or joint ventures may own real estate, but no foreign legal or natural persons may
Tax and incentives	Corporate tax rate 36%. Tax holidays eliminated in 1994, with grandfathering until 2003. Priority investments get preferences (as do domestically owned firms).	Corp. tax rate 42%; most exemptions eliminated in 1993, but negotiable priority sectors; some special treatment remains.	Corp. tax rate 30%, but reduced to 20% in first year; reinvested profits taxable at 10% for 4 years.
Participation in privatization	Permitted with agreement from State Property Agency and State Holding Company.	Requires permission from MOP.	Requires permission from MOP; decision also made by management and employees.
Other	Free economic zones. Export licenses required for certain goods. High technology and infrastructure projects may receive grants from IPF.	Free economic zones. For ownership >30%, one-year exemption from customs duties.	Six free economic zones. Discounts on customs duties.

Abbreviations: MOP = Ministry of Privatization; IPF = Investment Promotion Fund.
Source: EBRD, 1994, Table 9.3, pp. 126–127.

Index